UNAPOLOGETIC EXPRESSION

André Marmot is an agent at Earth Agency in London, specialising in the common ground between African, jazz and global electronic music. Active professionally in music since 2007 as agent, musician, promoter and label owner, André believes passionately in the power of music to connect people across cultural and social boundaries. *Unapologetic Expression* is his debut book.

Further praise for *Unapologetic Expression*:

'Marmot is well placed to speak on this s[...] for the nine-piece jazz and afrobeat group ......yan Twist and many other notable acts, he has watched this story unfold from the inside. Rather than employing just his own perspective, however, Marmot has assembled many voices in this book, building an oral history from interviews with musicians, promoters, label bosses and DJs, and creating something which is closer to folklore than academia . . . The informal, conversational style gives the book a credibility unlike anything else I've read on the subject.' Deb Grant, *Big Issue*

'Marmot has been able to engage in a more than superficial way with the key artists he covers . . . [the artists] are given a chance to speak on a wide range of issues, above all on the self-sufficiency of their generation that has built an audience from the ground up . . . the prevailing theme of the text is the power of the grass-roots initiative . . . [the book has] a brisk, lively energy.' Kevin Le Gendre, *Jazzwise*

'One of the main threads of Marmot's well researched and highly readable narrative is the socio-cultural parallel between this generation of London jazz artists and the historical roots of the music. The forces of imperialism, colonialism and globalisation that brought jazz into existence over a century ago, he argues, continue to shape the music's evolution in the UK today, with London at its epicentre. This is a story not just of jazz, but of post-colonial Britain . . . Marmot is well placed to tell this complex and muti-layered story . . . *Unapologetic Expression* will no doubt stand as an essential reference to anyone seeking to make sense of the London/UK jazz scene.' Ian Patterson, *All About Jazz*

André Marmot

UNAPOLOGETIC EXPRESSION

The Inside Story of the UK
Jazz Explosion

faber

First published in 2024
by Faber & Faber Ltd
The Bindery, 51 Hatton Garden
London EC1N 8HN

First published in the USA in 2024

This paperback edition published in 2025

Typeset by Sam Matthews
Printed and bound by CPI Group (UK) Ltd, Croydon, CR0 4YY

A CIP record for this book
is available from the British Library

ISBN 978–0–571–37449–6

Printed and bound in the UK on FSC® certified paper in line with our continuing
commitment to ethical business practices, sustainability and the environment.
For further information see faber.co.uk/environmental-policy

Our authorised representative in the EU for product safety is
Easy Access System Europe, Mustamäe tee 50, 10621 Tallinn, Estonia
gpsr.requests@easproject.com

2 4 6 8 10 9 7 5 3 1

To Effra,
whose arrival gave me the courage and motivation to do this.

And Holly,
who supported me every step of the way.

Contents

Introduction
The 12-inch Promo

Sunday, 28 May 2023. Early evening sunshine is glinting off the grey concrete high-rises, turning the windows of Brixton's 1960s estates into myriad tiny solar systems. Inside Brockwell Park, ten thousand young people of all races and genders are losing their shit to Alfa Mist. I'm watching the big screen, the bottom section of which is devoted to the signer at side of stage interpreting a hyper-noodly piano swirl, arms caressing the air, broad smile. How the fuck do you do BSL to instrumental music? He's managing it in some kind of beautiful fusion of sign language and dance, and a whole lot of people are appreciating it.

This is just the beginning. An hour and a half and two craft beers later and the crowd is twice as deep for Ezra Collective, shacking out to a high-energy, muscular fusion of Lagos Afrobeat and the syncopated echoes of the music's more screw-faced London cousins, garage and grime.

Friday it was drum and bass, hip-hop, dubstep and grime with Project 6; Saturday it was indie and electronica at Wide Awake; tomorrow it will be reggae, dancehall and Afrobeats at City Splash – but today the flagship park of London's most famously Afro-Caribbean area is hosting Cross the Tracks, 'London's #1 Jazz, Funk & Soul Festival . . . a day festival that's about more than just music. It's about community, culture, family, flavour, history and creating a space for all of our passengers to feel at home.'[1] No one thinks this is weird. A new generation of diverse, media-savvy musicians have helped reclaim jazz as just one urban music among many,

1

unapologetically taking its place both in the rich seam of London's postcolonial music and the long lineage of jazz itself.

This book is a tribute to that energy, and the energy behind it.

* * *

'The new UK jazz scene' has already enjoyed several years of sustained media coverage, with countless newspaper articles breathlessly hailing the musicians who 'are reinventing the genre for a young, politicised generation, mixing it with Afrobeat, grime, house and R&B'.[2] Schooled in jazz's history, first through music education charities like Tomorrow's Warriors and later through degree-level courses at the country's top conservatoires, but plugged into the sounds of the streets, celebrating their (primarily) African and Caribbean heritages while very much a product of the UK, they have created their own scene. Having built their communities and polished their chops with ram-jammed, sweat-dripping-from-the ceiling, self-promoted nights in grassroots spaces in Lewisham, Deptford, Hackney and Peckham, they are selling out major concert venues and appearing on festival line-ups all over the world alongside pop and electronic artists well outside of the jazz circuit.

Yet even ten years ago, it would have been unthinkable that prime-time Saturday main-stage slots on one of the biggest festival weekends of the summer in one of the most diverse areas of the UK's most diverse city would be taken in this way. I've been working on this book for over three years and closely involved with this scene for more than ten, but it still amazes me to see this ongoing level of support and acceptance for musicians playing music not a million miles away from the type of jazz fusion that, when I was growing up, was anathema to all but a handful of extreme enthusiasts.

Oscar Jerome

Everyone's like, 'Oh, this thing has happened, where did it come from? But for the people that have been involved in it, it feels like we've just slowly grown. From doing loads of pub gigs, then doing slightly bigger, then starting doing some international stuff and then obviously now everyone's like, 'All of these people, it's this scene!' and you're just like, 'Oh, I suppose it is, yeah.'

Bradley Zero

A lot of the music that I was playing on the radio and playing in the club, started to get to a point where they were not just selling out the club, it's selling out huge concert venues. I mean, if you would have said even five years ago that a drummer could sell out Brixton Electric or a tuba player could sell out Village Underground, they would laugh! Five years ago, it was a risky thing to play a tuba-led song in a club, and now these guys are borderline superstars. It's mad! And the people who were playing the music, your Nubyas and your Theons and your Poppy Ajudhas, your Oscar Jeromes, they're at the club too! They're not just academic jazz heads who sit down practising rudiments all day. They're into garage. They're into house. They're into techno. And they're there when you're playing your set and you drop one of their tunes. This sense of togetherness is the key thing. It's not like you've got the jazz guys doing the jazz thing, you've got the club guys doing the club thing. It's all kind of mixed up.

Zara McFarlane

I don't think that I was aware of the movement. I think it is hard to see when you are in the middle of it. You're just busy doing what you're doing. What was fun was seeing my friends creating their own projects, hearing their style and seeing them progress as artists. When people started asking that question I didn't really see it. I was thinking what movement? Everyone is just out there doing their thing.

By 2019, the new wave of jazz had had so much coverage and was now so self-evidently cool that Shoreditch hipster magazine *Vice* ran a wry profile of 'the Nu Jazz Lad'[3] who pretends to be into jazz in order to

3

impress girls, holding 'long, coked-up conversations about how jazz is the new punk'. For all its mockery and swagger, the piece actually defines the new scene and its appeal quite well, noting that this 'isn't the jazz your parents put on when they're trying to reignite their waning sex lives . . . there is a youthful jazz resurgence happening in south-east London'. It highlights a dynamic energy originating in new venues and unusual spaces; a different audience from fans of 'Actual Jazz' who 'wear porkpie hats and a general air of condescension and involuntary celibacy'; a collaborative atmosphere among young players; support from tastemaker DJs; and crossover with some of the DIY aesthetic of punk and grime.

Femi Koleoso

I wanted to be associated with Max Roach and I dressed like him and I thought he was cool as hell. But I also wanted to be associated with Skepta and I still dress like him and think he's cool as hell. The difference is I never saw jazz as a compromise for wanting to be like Skepta. I think that way of thinking is unique to the jazz that my generation is producing, where we were looking at grime MCs and garage, dub, reggae, drum and bass, and we weren't looking at jazz as this different, separate world. We made jazz sound like London. You know what I'm saying, fam?

Gilles Peterson

There's a swagger and self-confidence about this movement. There's a respect for the elders, but not too much respect for the elders. There's an understanding that by being young and not being just promoted by the institutions, creating their own spots, whether it's Steez or TRC, they're creating a movement and an audience that wants to be part of it. And once you've got that, then that just expands and becomes word of mouth and then everybody wants to be part of it. That's why it's so, so good at the moment. I mean, when people see a bunch of young people on stage playing fucking great music they've never heard live before, they're gonna go mad for it. It's super exciting.

As someone who had loved jazz since my teens alongside drum and bass, garage, reggae and hip-hop, then UK funky, grime, house, techno and a range of African music, the energy around this new wave was refreshing and in sharp contrast with the moribund way that jazz had been presented and perceived for much of the past twenty-five years. Like many people who grew up in the 1990s, I remember a time when being into jazz was accompanied by a distinct social stigma; now *Vice* was mocking people who *pretend* to like it because it's cool.

One of the major nodes perpetuating the negative jazz stereotype was cult mid-nineties sketch show *The Fast Show*, in which actor John Thomson plays 'Jazz Club' presenter Louis Balfour. A middle-aged white man with a slight pot belly, clad in a burgundy polo neck, a cheap shiny suit with wide lapels and a gold medallion, he looks at the camera, fag in hand, and says: 'Hello . . . And welcome to Jazz Club, bringing you all that's best in the world of jazz . . . *niiiiice*.' This sketch branded jazz as deeply uncool for an entire generation.

The catchphrase, devastating in its simplicity, stuck around for a very long time. Just as it was impossible to run around a park without some joker shouting, 'Run, Forrest, run!' for years after the 1994 release of *Forrest Gump*, for the rest of the nineties and well beyond, it was hard to mention jazz outside of enthusiast circles without some Green Day, Blur or Coldplay fan pointing their finger at you and saying, '*Niiiiice*'. While astute observers and jazz aficionados may have seen in Balfour a specific mockery of BBC music programmes of the 1960s and 1970s like *Jazz 625* and *The Old Grey Whistle Test*, most casual viewers didn't differentiate between the types of jazz being mocked, nor did they knowingly chuckle along with the creators at the niche cultural references. For the average viewer in their teens and twenties with no external co-relative to tell them different, this was simply what jazz was: a self-evidently laughable form of music, loved by out-of-touch, out-of-shape white men with deeply questionable taste.

For many musicians who came up in this sketch's long shadow there is still some anger, often accompanied by a reluctant acceptance that there was more than a grain of truth behind the joke.

Seb Rochford

I just found it disrespectful. It's like he was ignoring the social context of jazz, it wasn't coming from a place of knowledge of what that music is about.

Binker Golding

That did more damage for jazz in this country than a lot of things. I do think it's pretty accurate. But that was the thing, it was actually too effective, too honest and it stuck. It completely stuck. That show hasn't been on the airwaves in almost thirty years and still to this day, we're using memes from that show. People still put images of that up on the internet, 'Niiiiice'. And you think, my God, what do we have to do to shake off this image and get it in the past?

Shabaka Hutchings

I think jazz WAS very uncool. It wasn't summarily uncool but there was just a lot of uncool things about it. That's the hard pill to swallow, that if you went to your average jazz night fifteen years ago, ten years ago, it was just a lot of old men. Sitting around listening to the music. It was guys in suits being very stiff playing it. Not everybody, of course. And not the kind of big-name players that you might see written in history books. But if you were just to go to any unknown jazz gig, there was a lot of not very cool stuff being done, especially in relation to how musicians were interacting with the audience. So many gigs I've been to where you just had a bunch of guys looking really miserable onstage, trying to play really difficult tunes. Looking like they are trying to solve the puzzle onstage.

introduction

The Fast Show, of course, did not invent the idea of jazz as the exclusive pursuit of outmoded middle-aged white men. It drew on and amplified a stereotype that was already lurking in the corners of popular culture: a stereotype which spoke to many people's lived experience.

Ciro Romano

Jazz for a long, long time, you go to these shows, people dress as if they were your dad or your grandma. There wasn't a lot of sexiness about it. And there wasn't a lot of modernity or any feeling of being contemporary. And I think that put a lot of people off.

Nick Lewis

It had gotten all a bit pretentious and navel-gazing in the nineties, and very white, very middle-aged. Maybe it had just gotten stale. The only audience left as a result of that was, you know, your dad and my dad. Who had grown up with it. Because no new audience was being cultivated. There was no new spokesman of their generation.

And while *The Fast Show* mocked the self-importance of jazz enthusiasts, the launch of Yves Saint Laurent's Live Jazz aftershave in 1998 and the use of jazz on countless car and jewellery advertisements reinforced a perception of jazz as American, safe, white, elitist; music to sell luxury watches and create an atmosphere at expensive restaurants. I will always remember the ad that ran repeatedly on Jazz FM at that time, with an alluring American female movie-star voice advertising Sunday champagne jazz brunch at 'Smollensky's on the Strand' amid a background of smooth piano jazz. Tastemaker DJ Gilles Peterson had been on the original Jazz FM roster in 1990 but was kicked off for inviting listeners to join a demonstration against British involvement in the first Gulf War. American? Yes. High-class? Of course. Political? Absolutely not!

unapologetic expression

Courtney Pine

I found it funny that jazz was used as a kind of posh music. And the reality of the thing was you're dealing with music that is really from the community for the community.

Emma-Jean Thackray

My first degree was at the Royal Welsh College of Music doing jazz trumpet. And they had this club there called Jazz Cafe. When I was there in 2007–11, it was bullshit, the stage faced the wall. It didn't actually face any people. And as soon as you finished playing they would kick you out. They were trying to be this Ronnie Scott's kind of vibe: people are just here to have a nice glass of wine and there's some furniture music going on. And then I started getting the Megabus to London to go see gigs, trying to pop into Ronnie's and thinking, 'What is this bullshit, I can't even afford to get into Ronnie's' – that's when I really started noticing this kind of white-washed, clean, fake image of jazz that was going on rather than the stuff that I had been listening to and seeking out.

Dave Okumu

It just felt like a misrepresentation. It didn't really relate to what I was experiencing. I think there was this kind of myth constructed, it's like what happened with classical music, there's a sense that it's intellectual or it's cerebral or it's smooth or it's ridiculous in some way.

While I cultivated a love of jazz through learning jazz guitar at school, discovering standards in the ubiquitous *Real Book** and getting hold of some of the original artists on CD, I couldn't reconcile this portrayal with the wild energy I could hear in the music. I remember reading this account of Benzedrine-addled beat poets freaking out to

---

* A book of sheet music of popular jazz tunes (the name is a reference to the 'fake books' of unofficial sheet music which many musicians used).

the solo in Jack Kerouac's 1957 novel *On The Road* and thinking, what happened? How did it go from that to this?

> Out we jumped in the warm, mad night, hearing a wild tenorman's bawling horns across the way going, ee-yah(ph), ee-ya, and hands clapping to the beat and folks yelling go, go, go. And far from escorting the girls into the place, Dean Moriarty was already racing across the street with his huge bandit's thumb in the air yelling, blow, man, blow.

I wanted to yell, 'Blow, man, blow!' But nothing I could see or hear would provide that context. As I got more interested in the music and began to read autobiographies like Miles Davis's *Miles* and Charles Mingus's *Beneath the Underdog*, I was struck by the contrast between the clean way jazz was presented in the 1990s and the gritty depictions of the bohemian lives of the pioneers of the 1940s and 1950s. Miles, himself no prude, gives a shocked description of the behaviour of legendary alto player and innovator Charlie Parker that could have come straight off the pages of a Kerouac novel:

> That's the way Bird was; he was a great and genius musician, man, but he was also one of the slimiest and greediest motherfuckers who ever lived in this world, at least that I ever met . . . I remember one time we was coming down to The Street to play from uptown and Bird had this white bitch in the back of the taxi with us. He done already shot up a lot of heroin and now the mother-fucker's eating chicken – his favorite food – and drinking whisky and telling the bitch to get down and suck his dick . . .*

Mingus goes still further, with an autobiography devoted far more to graphic and misogynistic anecdotes about women and his 'cousin' Billy Bones – 'the only black pimp that's made over five million dollars

---

* Reading this again in 2021, it is hard not to wonder what the taxi driver might have been thinking, and be relieved, for Bird's sake, that Uber was some sixty-five years in the distance. One can only wonder what his rating would have been.

a year in hustling alone' – than anything to do with his relationship to the music. Not generally held to be strictest fact, this sensationalism can likely be attributed to a combination of commercial motivation and Mingus's famous contrariness, revelling in a book that would both shock and thrill white middle-American audiences.* Whether or not it is precisely accurate is far less significant than the fact that a musician of Mingus's stature would even *choose* to fill his autobiography with anecdotes that paint a picture of the jazz underworld of his era as being far closer to nineties gangsta rap's self-conscious glorification of the hustler's lifestyle than the shiny image cultivated by that decade's jazz musicians.

This parallel between the culture around early bebop and nineties gangsta rap is significant: both are musics originated by marginalised young black males that suddenly found extreme popularity among white audiences. While its defenders saw gangsta rap as a means of highlighting the social problems faced by young urban blacks dealing with racism, poverty and limited opportunities, many of its consumers, especially white teenagers, saw exoticised glamour rather than any call to action.[4] The music industry, of course, capitalised on this emerging market, supporting a shift away from the subversive political hip-hop of acts like Public Enemy and KRS-One to what many perceived as a glorification of misogyny, criminality and conspicuous consumption in the work of Snoop Doggy Dogg, 2Pac and the Notorious B.I.G.

Similarly, jazz was a music originated by the children and grandchildren of slaves in New Orleans, cultivated in the black ghettos of 1920s and 1930s Chicago, St Louis and Kansas City, reinvigorated in the 1940s and 1950s in the densely packed clubs of New York; but here it was, in late-twentieth-century London, being used to sell

* Iceberg Slim's *Pimp*, published in 1967, had been a huge commercial success, and this may well have contributed to publisher Alfred Knopf's decision to retain the pimping section while cutting two-thirds of Mingus' 1,500-page manuscript, dramatically increasing its proportional weight in the book.

cars, watches and premium fragrances, or derided as a deeply uncool minority interest.

The stereotyping of jazz and its followers continued well into the new millennium. Building on a trope established in *The Simpsons* with Bart's brilliant but awkward jazz-loving sister Lisa, cult 2002–4 series *The Mighty Boosh* further dented jazz's reputation with the character of jazzercise-practicing, jazz fusion enthusiast Howard Moon. His pompous self-obsession and ambitions of being 'the greatest jazz player in Yorkshire' are contrasted with the charismatic easiness of proto-hipster Vince Noir, addicted to the eighties synth-pop of Gary Numan. As well as a reappearance of the polo neck and medallion trope from *The Fast Show*, *The Mighty Boosh* even indulges in blackface as Noel Fielding embodies 'the Spirit of Jazz', signing a contract for Howard's soul in an echoing of the famous legend about proto-bluesman Robert Johnson.

As late as 2012, jazz was being openly mocked on mainstream media, not only by comedians but by professional music critics.

Dave Okumu

I was invited to be a talking head on the Mercury Awards after the second *Invisible* record. I remember sitting on a sofa with a bunch of music journalists, earnestly talking about the nominations, and then they were like, 'Yeah, and the jazz nomination,' and they all started giggling. It stands as one of the most grating experiences in relation to this whole thing of how jazz is perceived, because they were basically belittling this music. It was like jazz is a joke, and this is a token nomination, and let's all make *Fast Show* jokes. It was unbelievably reductive. I remember just being so alarmed that these adults who work in music and write about music and criticise music and have actually an immense amount of power have not evolved sufficiently to basically understand what music is. I was in shock! It was really, really distasteful and really, really disappointing. And I just try to imagine if we were doing that about punk or about electronic music. It's just, why is this happening?

And yet that very same year, the year London reannounced itself to the world as an international, global city with the spectacular post-colonial fanfare of the 2012 Summer Olympics (bulldozing much of East London in the process), the seeds of the new generation were already quietly beginning to germinate.

How did UK jazz change from the 'dry and unsexy' music of 'your dad', 'my dad' and 'your grandma' to the vital, politically charged, inclusive sound of modern London? This book is a homage to the remarkable generation that made jazz cool again, putting their achievement in the context of wider social, cultural and political issues. You'll hear about Britain as the centre of empire, the Caribbean and African migrations that powered this wave of jazz, and the other London musics with which jazz intersected to give this wave its unique identity. I'll tell the story of the Jazz Warriors generation whose support, examples and horror stories helped the new cohort avoid many of the same mistakes, and examine the changes in the music industry and the growth of social media that allowed them to claim their independence. I'll look at the new narratives around race and gender which spoke to an increasingly politicised generation in a background of savagely right-wing domestic politics and a growth of extremism worldwide, rejuvenating jazz's original purpose as a music of spiritual freedom, the unapologetic expression of an oppressed people. And I'll explore the forty-year career of DJ Gilles Peterson to tell the story of the UK's unique lineage of jazz for the dancefloor.

But the first question immediately invites a follow-up: how did jazz ever come to be seen as uncool, stale, white, elitist, 'classical' in the first place? This is a story that is impossible to tell without telling a wider story of capitalism, slavery, migration, racism and tension between (mostly black) jazz innovators and a (mostly white) industry that has accompanied the music at every stage in its development.

Even the apparently harmless mockery of jazz in *The Fast Show* was seen by some as just another sinister iteration of the long history of racist stereotyping of black culture and black people.

introduction

Cleveland Watkiss

I thought it was a bag of bollocks, man. I thought it was insulting. I didn't find anything funny about it at all. I thought it was disrespect to our culture, total disrespect to our music and our culture. By white people just making fun of our music, what they do all the time. I don't find that kind of thing funny because I got a lot of respect for the art form and the music and the people that died for this music, the Charlie Parkers and the Duke Ellingtons and Thelonious Monks, man. And I'm gonna go and look at some bullshit like that? That's not funny to me. Like Ali G's not funny for me. And he's getting fat on that. To me, there's no difference between him and that guy that used to paint himself black and go and do the Chitlin' Circuit. The black-and-white minstrel guy, 'Mammy, Mammy, how I love ya Mammy.' What are you doing, man? It's that same shit.

Seen from this angle, it is easy to draw a line between *The Fast Show's* mockery of jazz and – in Channel 4's 2002–4 *Bo' Selecta!* – an even more brutal assassination of another art form that had started as a black urban subculture: UK garage, as personified by vocalist Craig David. Having become an instant star in November 1999 with the lead vocal on Artful Dodger's 'Re-Rewind', David had rapidly become one of the biggest artists in the UK, with solo singles 'Fill Me In' (April 2000) and '7 Days' (July 2000) going straight in at #1 in the UK singles chart. Parent album *Born to Do It* (August 2000) *still* holds the record for fastest-selling UK album of all time by a solo male artist, going on to sell over eight million copies worldwide and going platinum in the UK a staggering six times.

The gravy train ground to an excruciating halt when white comedian Leigh Francis appeared in a grotesque latex mask caricaturing David's trademark beard and pronounced chin, in a visual nod to 1980s political satire *Spitting Image.* Not content with accentuating David's real-life attributes, and apparently totally comfortable with

blackface, Francis furnished him with the fictional gifts of inconti-
nence, a Yorkshire accent and a pet peregrine falcon called Kes.[*] The
series saw David through a string of embarrassing misadventures,
watching porn, pissing himself on his tour bus, endlessly repeating his
own name and the catchphrase, 'It's proper bo', I tell thee!'

Unsurprisingly, the show had a devastating effect both on David's
career and mental health, and with record sales plummeting, the
singer eventually decided to move to Miami to avoid the daily abuse
in the UK. Leigh Francis and the *Bo' Selecta!* team, by contrast, were
thriving. Capitalising on the success of the TV programme, Christmas
singles were released in both 2003 and 2004, charting at No. 3 and
No. 4 respectively. Love or hate Craig David's music,[†] it is hard not
to feel sympathy for a young man in his early twenties looking on in
bewilderment as a comedian launches an utterly unprovoked attack
on his career and reputation, proceeding to cannibalise the success
that had been his just a short while earlier.

By 2019, after a comeback as spectacular as it was unexpected, David
was referring to *Bo' Selecta* as 'a blessing in disguise', and it is testament
to his immense resilience, integrity and a very particular set of circumstances that things worked out as they did.[5] But he could easily not have
made it. Echoing Cleveland Watkiss' reading of *The Fast Show* as a white
comedian's racist dismissal of a black art form, the parallels with *Bo'
Selecta* are obvious: both shows are on the dark road that leads right back
to the ugly traditions of blackface and minstrelsy,[‡] a road strewn with

[*] The accent and falcon are a nod to Ken Loach's 1969 kitchen sink drama *Kes*. Francis
also personified Michael Jackson and Trisha Goddard in the same series. Blackface
was bizarrely common in this period; David Baddiel famously blacked up to portray
footballer Jason Lee with a pineapple on his head in nineties football TV programme
Fantasy Football League, not attracting serious condemnation until much further down
the line.

[†] I was never much of a fan and always inwardly blamed him for the
commercialisation of garage, so didn't feel much sympathy at the time; now the whole
thing just seems bitterly cruel and unfair.

[‡] This is especially true in *Bo' Selecta*'s portrayal of Michael Jackson, who is recast as a
sex-crazed misogynist speaking an extreme parody of 1970s blaxploitation 'jive talk'.

the corpses of black performers and art forms, with white comedians exploiting stereotypes around black culture for their own personal gain. A similar process had unfolded in Baddiel and Skinner's jokes about footballer Jason Lee's braided topknot in *Fantasy Football League* and Nick Hancock's obsession with the size of sprinter Linford Christie's penis on *They Think It's All Over*, where the hard work and astounding achievements of black stars were obscured by white comedians' obsession with their physical attributes, causing lasting emotional damage.

Perhaps the most horrific landmark on this road is the 'Disco Demolition' event of 12 July 1979, in which radio DJ Steve Dahl, dressed in a combat helmet and military fatigues, literally blew up an estimated seventy thousand disco records as interval entertainment at the White Sox vs Detroit Tigers double-header* in Chicago's Comiskey Park.[6] This constitutes one of the largest singular deliberate acts of cultural destruction of all time, terrifyingly reminiscent of the mass Nazi book burnings of 1933.

Disco, like both jazz and garage, had begun as a primarily black but racially inclusive subculture, exploding into the mainstream in 1977 with the quadruple Grammy-winning film *Saturday Night Fever*.[7] Responding to disco's sudden popularity among white audiences, Dahl's station had told him he would have to play disco or quit. Embittered, he joined another station in March 1979 and began 'blowing up' disco records live on air, dropping the sound of an explosion after dragging the needle across the record. Disco was, he claimed, 'an intimidating lifestyle, an intimidating culture being forced down our throats'.[8] Some might hear in his choice of words an oblique reference to disco's origins in New York's gay scene; the 'Disco Sucks' slogan he adopted for his campaign, with accompanying T-shirts, made the point rather

---

* Mystical readers may see a cosmic resonance in the fact that it was these two places that became synonymous with house and techno respectively; cynical readers may see the choice of this match as deliberately provocative, Detroit and Chicago being two of the US cities with the largest black populations and hence presumably the largest chance of black people watching their culture publicly destroyed.

less subtly. Mike Veeck, son of the Chicago White Sox's owner, loved the show: the result was an offer of discounted entry to the stadium for anyone showing up with a disco record. Seventy thousand people poured in clutching, as future house music pioneer Vince Lawrence noted, not only disco records but 'mostly just black records'.[*]

Whether or not the protagonists were conscious of their own roles (and on the whole I dismiss their claims of innocence as either disingenuous or naïve to the point of blameworthiness), it is no great leap of the imagination to see Disco Demolition, *The Fast Show* and *Bo' Selecta!* as an attack on black culture as represented by disco, jazz and garage, and by implication as an attack on the legitimacy of black people in general as active members of US and UK society.

But, paradoxically, just as Disco Demolition made way for house and techno and *Bo' Selecta* for grime, *The Fast Show* and subsequent mockeries did not kill jazz. Rather, the general lack of interest in the music provided cover for a new generation to hone their craft and develop organically, away from commercial pressure and media attention. Cultivating their own community, developing their own scenes, they recombined diverse elements of jazz's history, both musical and cultural, to create the unapologetic expression that is the subject of this book. And when they finally put their head above the parapet, the scene was already fully developed, providing a perfect story for the media to amplify, allowing its rapid growth both nationally and worldwide.

* * *

This is not a story I would have wanted or felt empowered to tell without the active participation of so many of the amazing characters who made it happen. While the Covid-19 pandemic of 2020 onwards wreaked death and destruction globally and the resulting lockdowns and travel restrictions froze the live music industry in its tracks, severely

---

[*] In an amusing subversion of Dahl's intentions, he admits to reading the titles of the records and stashing away any he recognised in his locker at the stadium.

threatening the livelihoods of all those who make their living from it, it provided an unprecedented opportunity to conduct in-depth interviews with the architects of this and previous waves of UK jazz. As well as providing practical opportunities for long-form Zoom interviews without the pressure of relentless touring schedules (and normalising the remote conferencing technology itself), the strange stillness bookended years of intense and organic growth for the scene and its major players, presenting a perfect moment for reflection. And while the horrifying murder of George Floyd in May 2020 and the global outpouring that followed it provided a stark reminder of just how present a force racism remains, the event and its aftermath provided a framework for me to ask interviewees direct and difficult questions about racism and identity, for which I believe the book is much richer.

I have tried to let interviewees speak for themselves as much as possible. Two of the books that affected me most deeply in my research for this project were Nat Shapiro and Nat Hentoff's *Hear Me Talkin' to Ya* and Arthur Taylor's *Notes and Tones*, both of which privilege direct speech from the artists.[9] I was deeply moved by the intimacy and immediacy of these long-dead artists' voices, defying those stuffy old uncles Space and Time and sounding oddly familiar. In that sense, this book represents an attempt to record this generation's voices for posterity and I hope that, at whatever date in the future you read this, they speak to you as clearly as those long-dead musicians did to me. In order to avoid cluttering the text, I have included a brief biographical description of each interviewee in an appendix. I should also acknowledge a subconscious debt to South American novelist Roberto Bolaño's *The Savage Detectives*, which I read just before starting work on this book, and in which multiple characters give their subjective opinions and rambling recollections of the book's central characters and events, which the reader assimilates to form their own picture. In the same way, I've chosen to let verbatim quotes stand alone, generally without introduction or comment; they can be interpreted as solos or accents that respond to and colour the main narrative.

Cleveland Watkiss

The idea of free form is the natural condition of the human being: being able to flow in the moment and let that moment be what it is. Let it be what it is and then let it go: 'That's what it was. But this is what it is now.' And in that spirit is how we play, how we sing or how we make music or how we do anything, how we walk, how we talk. More or less you call me up and you press play. And here we are, you didn't give me any sort of questions beforehand. I like that because then it's more real. In the moment, it's raw, I feel like I can be more succinct and honest, I'll speak from the gut and from the heart. Let the soul be what it wants to be. Don't try and abort it, which happens a lot – we abort our ideas because of fear, loads of reasons. I think that's why music, and especially improvised music, jazz, is so special, because it's a real reflection of the human condition in that moment. And when we are able to flow like that, oh, man, there's nothing like it.

As the interview process went on, I came to regard the interviews as something like an old-fashioned 'recording date'. In the modern days of multi-tracking, overdubs and home studios, this term has almost disappeared from the lexicon, but it's all over the biographies of Miles, Mingus, Duke Ellington and Horace Silver: you turned up for the date and you played. And if someone was drunk or hungover or couldn't get heroin or having trouble with their partner, that's what the record sounds like; sometimes it was magic and sometimes it was sludge.

I'm pleased to say that while I experienced many of the interviews as magic, none felt quite like sludge. But some interviewees may have felt that they didn't deliver their best work on that date. While I prepared questions ahead of time for my own reference, in what might loosely be compared with 'the head' of a bebop tune – the basic melody and chord changes which form the structure around which musicians can improvise – I almost never shared these with the interviewees in advance.[10] This was not about creating an unequal balance of power but simply about hearing my collocutor's true thoughts in the immediacy of that conversation, unmediated by their ideas about what they ought to say and how they ought to be perceived.

This generated, at times, some brilliantly awkward and controversial results, and though many of these comments would have made great reading, I am not a journalist striving to sell papers through sensationalism and exploitation. This book is intended as a homage to this cultural moment and the cultural moments which led to it, not to create divisions. For this reason I've avoided some of the more provocative comments, and offered all interviewees the chance to read transcripts of their interviews and redact any comments.[11]

The depth of the scene is such that there will inevitably be key voices that are not included: to those artists and their fans I say only sorry. I think particularly of Blue Lab Beats, Alfa Mist, Kaidi Tatham, IG Culture, Ego Ella May, Mark Kavuma, Chelsea Carmichael, Ashley Henry, Floating Points, Daniel Casimir, Alabaster DePlume, Kamaal Williams, Tenderlonious, Soweto Kinch, Eska, Pete Wareham, Four Tet, Errol and Alex Rita from Touching Bass, Pete from On the Corner . . . but there are so many others I would have loved to speak to. With over eighty interviews, it was essential to draw a line somewhere.

This book is different also from the oral histories mentioned above in that I spoke to promoters, venue owners, agents, managers, label bosses, broadcasters and writers as well as artists. This reflects my belief that there are many ways to contribute to music without playing an instrument. I've tried to represent a broad spread of those whose contributions made this scene happen. The one group not represented here is audience members, the silent majority whose presence and support made this entire movement meaningful. I can only say, to everyone who came through to shows, bought records, supported and continue to support this scene: big respect. You truly are the ones who make it what it is.

* * *

Three caveats:

Firstly, I've generally avoided detailed description of the music, both because I think music works better as music than words and because there is so much music in this wave that will speak to people in different ways. But each of this book's chapters takes its title from a piece of music which highlights its theme, and I've combined all these and other relevant music in a series of Spotify playlists, accessible at bit.ly/unapologeticexpression. I warmly invite you to listen to these, and the work of all of the artists mentioned, whilst reading.

Secondly, while this book's cover proudly references 'the UK jazz explosion', the vast majority of the scenes and artists described here are from London. Partly this reflects my own bias as a lifetime Londoner, and it needs to be acknowledged that London is not the only UK city with a thriving jazz scene: there are powerful grassroots scenes in Leeds and Manchester, Liverpool and Bristol, Glasgow and Edinburgh and Birmingham.

But this is not only Londoncentrism at play. London is by far the biggest city in the UK and the third most populous metropolitan area in the whole of Europe.[12] It has more musicians, more clubs, more festivals, more conservatoires, and a far, far larger audience. Artists and agents have found out the hard way that many acts that can sell over five hundred tickets in London will struggle to get to one hundred in most places outside it. London is the centre of the UK's media and politics, and the best-known British city internationally, so it is perhaps inevitable that the London scene has been written about more than others and attracted more attention, both in the UK and abroad.

It is also London's vital role as the centre of the British Empire that has given the city its immense cultural richness. Of course, the capital is not the only city with a large diaspora population and accordingly diverse music scene: the chest-melting bass of Leeds's Iration Steppas sound system; the hybrid electronic hip-hop of Manchester's Levelz; the heavy sound system culture of the West Midlands, from the Specials right through to the drill/Afrobeats of Coventry's Pa Salieu; the powerful reggae heritage and warehouse party scene that fed Bristol's post-punk, trip-hop and drum and bass scenes; and Luton's vibrant late-nineties UK garage scene. All these are stories worth telling, but they are different stories.

And lastly, while I've allowed space for other voices to speak to you directly, I've tried to pick a path through the forest of material, experiences and ideas, telling the story in my own way and highlighting the things I believe are important. I claim no absolute authority: mine is a partial, subjective tale, reflecting my own politics and priorities. I've drawn on my own lived experience where relevant: first and foremost, on twenty-five years of deep love for jazz and the many musics of London, the city in which I was born in 1982, grew up in the 1990s and still live now, but also on nearly twenty years of work as artist, promoter, agent and record label owner. I promoted over five hundred shows at venues and festivals around the UK between 2007–18 under the Wormfood brand, set up a booking agency in 2012 and a record label in 2015, representing and releasing music by many of the artists mentioned in this book, including United Vibrations, The Comet Is Coming, Nubiyan Twist, Tony Allen, Nubya Garcia, Zara McFarlane, Maisha and Vels Trio. I've played over two hundred shows as percussionist with my own band Afriquoi, and countless more DJ sets, and so hope to be able to offer an artist's perspective as well as a writer's. I have continued to work as an agent at Earth Agency throughout my work on this book, representing a combination of jazz, African and global electronic artists. I've been closely watching the scene since its inception, personally attended most of the events and venues described in this book, and already had long relationships with many of the interviewees; conversely, there were many I was meeting for the first time, and I am not so embedded in the scene as not to be able to see the wood for the trees. While most of those interviewed would probably consider themselves 'insiders', in so far as any jazz musician is willing to accept that notion, I would consider myself both inside and outside the scene I am describing, and I hope that this semi-amphibious perspective is a useful one.

* * *

These caveats aside, my hope for this book is to put one of the millennium's most exciting musical moments into a broader context: musically, culturally and politically. This is a tribute to the independence and energy of a new generation of musicians, and those who paved the way for them, both directly and indirectly. It is a loving paean to the vital role music can play in the life of individuals, communities and the city itself, as a tool for identity creation, community cohesion, political expression. And it is a meditation on modern, post-colonial Britain – in all its diversity, hypocrisy, division and flawed, self-destructive brilliance.

THE ALBUM

1
'Rye Lane Shuffle'
The New UK Jazz

Moses Boyd

I can talk about the history of how we met and all of this, but I've always felt there was something bigger than us that I can't explain that was just happening in the universe. I've always felt there's been this thing that's going on beyond all of our control, that we've kind of come at the right time.

There is no clear beginning to this wave of jazz, nor will there be a clear end, for the most beautiful of reasons: because jazz is a lineage. An unbroken tradition of community music stretching back a hundred and twenty years, looking both ahead and behind, straddling multiple generations and styles. Even in 2023, the current crop of UK jazz musicians reaches directly back to the very birth of jazz in just a few steps. Nubya Garcia was taught by Jean Toussaint who played with Art Blakey, who played with Charlie Parker, who played with Earl Hines, who played with Louis Armstrong, who learnt from Joe Oliver, who played with Buddy Bolden.

Courtney Pine

The important thing to know is that it's a chain. And everybody in that link chain is imperative to keeping this freedom of expression called jazz alive.

Nevertheless, our story must start somewhere, and in this chapter I want to pay homage to the excitement and energy around 'the new

UK jazz scene', highlighting some of its key artists, releases, venues and promoters.

'They are the template'
(United Vibrations)

For me, the story began with United Vibrations. I first heard them at a OneTaste event at the Bedford in Balham in November 2009: the three Dayes brothers, Ahmad (trombone), Kareem (bass) and Yussef (drums), and 'brother from another mother', Anglo-Caribbean saxophonist Wayne Francis.[*] Wayne would later co-found the raucous Steam Down nights in Deptford, and Steam Down Orchestra, as well as producing and performing under moniker Ahnansé; Yussef would go on to be one half of the brightly burning but short-lived flame that was Yussef Kamaal, subsequently achieving success simply as Yussef Dayes, and through his collaborations with Tom Misch.

Heavily influenced by the 1970s free jazz and Afrofuturism of Sun Ra, the syncopated grooves of West Africa, a DIY punk aesthetic and the grime, drum and bass and UK hip-hop of urban London, United Vibrations were way ahead of their time. Using Afrofuturist imagery long before Kamasi Washington brought it back into fashion (and the film *Black Panther* brought it to a wider public), they described their music as 'cosmodelic Afro jazz punk', a definition largely lost on both promoters and audiences. People just didn't know what to do with them.

Aly Gillani

United Vibrations created space for a lot of other people that have come since.

---

[*] Wayne's heritage includes Barbados, Grenada and St Lucia, hence the catch-all term here.

26

'rye lane shuffle'

Wozzy Brewster

The first terminology that I gave it as a band manager for United Vibrations was cosmodelic Afro punk, because you couldn't just call it jazz. It really wasn't just jazz. It was something else. And I think when you've got three brothers and the brother from another mother creating such tight pieces. Whoa! Blow your mind. They are the template. If you look at that history, they are the template for the new jazz movement.

Wayne Francis

I think with United Vibrations, there were a lot of people that liked the energy of the music. However, I don't think the music had the ability to travel as much because we were kind of the only ones doing what we were doing at the time. We were just this band that is doing something that nobody knows quite where to place. We were like the misfits of the scene.

Emma Warren

They were just before their time because they were the evolutionary bridge that got to this time. You need those people.

I fell in love seeing them busking at Glastonbury in 2010, setting themselves up in the no man's land between the Other Stage and the Dance Village,* rinsing out their independence anthem, 'My Way', with the English mantra sung insistently over a powerful 6/8 groove to make it sound like a West African chant.

I started to work with them, initially as a promoter, putting them on at many Wormfood nights and festival stages. I became their agent in 2011, the first band I signed to my new agency, epitomising the intersection between jazz, African and electronic music that has been the central focus for my own career as musician, promoter, agent,

---

* This area of Glastonbury had been simply 'the Dance Tent' and was later renamed 'Silver Hayes', its current name.

label owner, festival organiser and educator. But from an agent's point of view, I found most promoters baffled as to where to pitch them. Some wanted to put them in peak-time party-band slots, where the political content of the music confused and alienated some audiences; others would try to put them in classic 'jazz' slots, where the percussive energy of the music would demand seated audiences to rise.

Ahmad Dayes

So we start this thing, we go out and we gig, and we know the music's good. We know we've got something special, we're hyped on what we're doing. Sometimes I remember standing up on a stage and looking out at the crowd and they look baffled! Like, 'What the fuck is this? I don't know what to do – do I dance, do I jump, do I focus on what they're saying?' Sometimes you come off stage thinking, 'How the fuck did that go? Was that a good gig? Was it bad?' You wouldn't know! And then people would come up to you and be like, 'That was like, yeah!'… I don't know, them early days, it did feel like we were feeding something to the masses that they weren't ready for.

Lubi Jovanovic

They were so ahead of the curve, what they were doing. That's how it happens. Sometimes those people don't get the respect they should. They were going up the M1, coming to the HiFi Club on a Sunday night, and driving back down, doing their gigs and that. But as the Charlie Parker song goes, now is the time. The young musicians now, I don't begrudge them. 'Cos there's going to come a time when jazz is going to just disappear down that rabbit hole of niche music again. And then you'll be back playing your fifty-quid-a-man gigs in a local pub. So why not?

This was a moment when political content in music, at least in the UK's popular music, was rare. After thirteen years of Labour rule, a generation accustomed to reasonably progressive social policies (while national assets were sold off in the background) and disaffected by the

Blair administration's support for the Second Iraq War of 2003, had largely turned its back on politics altogether, with voter turnouts in 2001, 2005 and 2010 at their lowest since 1918.[1]

This all changed after the 2010 general election, when David Cameron's Conservatives formed a coalition with Nick Clegg's Liberal Democrats – spikily referred to as the ConDem coalition – ushering in ten years of 'austerity'. Public spending cuts off the back of the Northern Rock crisis of 2008, especially to social services for the most in-need communities, created the exact 'double-dip recession' prophesied by Gordon Brown, the outgoing Labour prime minister and long-standing Chancellor of the Exchequer under Tony Blair. By summer 2011, the mood of tension, anger and resentment erupted into rioting in protest at the suspected police murder of Mark Duggan in the same traditionally black areas that had rioted against police brutality and racism in 1981 and 1985: London's Brixton and Tottenham, Digbeth in Birmingham, Moss Side in Manchester and Toxteth in Liverpool.

Seeking to avoid blame by severing any connection between the rioting and their social policies, the Tory government and right-wing media launched a powerful campaign to brand the rioters as 'opportunistic thugs', motivated not by flagrant corruption, inequality and the mass closure of community centres and libraries but lured by the chance to acquire the newest trainers and electrical goods without paying. This was backed up by draconian sentencing for those found guilty, sending a clear message to disaffected urban youth of exactly who was in charge.

Driving back home through Brixton on the Monday of the August 2011 riots, having missed most of the carnage on a hedonistic weekend performing at the last ever Big Chill Festival in Warwickshire, I saw United Vibrations playing in Windrush Square, expressing solidarity with the rioters while appealing for calm amongst the mayhem. I was struck at the time by this connection between the music and the politics: aware as I was of the rich history of jazz as a political music, this was the first time in my lifetime I'd witnessed jazz used in such a way as a direct part of local community politics. By this time, protest and live music had become increasingly separated, with live music rarely performed at marches beyond the obligatory samba band.

While the band's presence in Brixton on that night linked them with jazz's history as a political music and the long tradition of live music in political demonstration, it was also a natural continuation of the community politics in which the Dayes brothers had been raised. They had grown up in a house on Walters Way in Hither Green, South-East London, an entire street of houses self-built by residents on a template designed by architect Walter Segal. The project was a council-funded response to the housing crisis of the late 1970s, giving those on the council's waiting list the chance to take matters into their own hands.

Kareem Dayes

The message was born out of the politics of land ownership, but linked to climate change and how that links to wider issues. The underlying thing around poverty or inequality, is essentially those who own land and those who don't. And that's how it's always been. All the inequality is augmented from that split. The unique thing of growing up in London on essentially what was a council estate but done differently: you can move as a reaction to the negative or as an affirmation to the positive and I think both avenues are needed. And the land thing is where a lot of things meet: inequality, climate change. And often when the music and message come together it's about painting that picture of a destination we can all move towards, which is better than where we're at now. You can say, 'Yeah, the world's shit and fucked up, let's burn it down.' But at the same time, where we moving to? When we burn this one down, what's going to be left? We tried to put those two things together, looking up to our heroes, but doing our version, relative to where we are now, and where we're from.

The band amassed a cult fan base around South London, with *Galaxies not Ghettos*, released on their own 12 Tone label in 2011 with distribution support from Peckham-based label First Word Records, showcasing their raw, percussive, Afro-inflected and politically charged sound. This was followed in February 2016 with *The Myth of the Golden Ratio* on American label Ubiquity.

The most popular song of this era was 'Grow', with Kareem's menacing bassline and Yussef's tight grooves providing a powerful bed for the provocative central lyric:

> We are the 99 per cent.
> Why are we ruled by 1 per cent?
> We are the 99 per cent.
> We can no longer blame the 1 per cent.

Borrowed from a 2011 *Vanity Fair* article[2] by left-wing economist Joseph Stiglitz, the phrase had become the rousing slogan of the international Occupy movement. Originating in September 2011 with Occupy Wall Street in New York City, by October of that year the movement had staged protests in hundreds of cities across the world. This included a five-month occupation of St Paul's Cathedral in London.

Wayne Francis

That was United Vibrations referencing the Occupy movement, but there was a general socio-political stance in the band in terms of how it thought about things. But I would take it away from viewing it as just politics and social commentary, I'd say maybe more an ideological stance which the band always had. You can attach it to politics or to social commentary. But it was more personal, like these are things that we are frustrated with or things that we think we need to speak about, for ourselves but also for the audiences that we're speaking to. It was really more about a message of coming together, because that's what music does. It was the most natural conversation for some of us to have so it was quite natural for us to write about it.

The band started to get increasing international opportunities after a successful 2016 appearance at international music conference

Womex, and were booked to play Texan music conference South by Southwest (SXSW) in March 2017 and Glastonbury's coveted West Holts stage in June of the same year.

Neither of these shows took place. The band were unable to play their SXSW show after being refused entry to the USA by the nascent Trump administration, quite possibly on account of the Muslim names of the three Dayes brothers. They cancelled their West Holts appearance, and other summer engagements, in order to take time out after the death of their mother. Although their manager Wozzy Brewster has always maintained it was a 'pause' rather than a break-up, United Vibrations have not resurfaced as an active band and remain legendary to those who remember.

Ahmad Dayes

I look at that period of time when we really pushed the band: we were positive and open-minded and we had a belief that we could change the world. We meant it. We were genuine, and most importantly, we felt what we were doing. We figured, if we can convince ourselves, then there's going to be a handful of people out there who are going to get it, and that's enough, you know?

Kareem Dayes

Naivety is not necessarily negative. Some of the greatest things have been done because a certain amount of naivety allows you to even try. If you knew too much about the subject, you would never try, because of the complexities: you'd think it's too difficult to even start.

'Such a strong foundation'
(Steez, Brainchild, Total Refreshment Centre)

United Vibrations maintain a legendary reputation among attendees of Steez, a grassroots South-East London event series founded by Luke Newman, a schoolfriend of United Vibrations' drummer Yussef.

Starting life as a vehicle for Newman's band Southpaw, Steez grew a huge following, and is justly credited as one of the main forces galvanising a community of musicians, poets, dancers and activists across South-East London, with an audience drawing musicians from the Trinity Laban Conservatoire in Greenwich, Goldsmiths, University of London, in New Cross, Camberwell College of Art and from a wider cross-section of young people of all backgrounds.

Poppy Ajudha

Steez was my place. That was where all my friends were. I think I would have gone in a completely different direction had I not joined that Steez crowd. I have so many memories there. I don't even know where to start. I was learning how to bare my soul. I think we took for granted how special and how unique it was. We all have a lot we that we owe to Luke for putting that together and bringing us all together before we knew how to organise or knew what we wanted to do. It was such a special place.

Shirley Tetteh

I was hearing, 'Young people don't listen to jazz.' And then I'd be going down to Steez and be like, 'That's not true.' Steez was a massive eye-opener because you had people who played jazz going there to perform, they'd start the whole event with spoken word and poetry and then kind of segue into music and then there'd be a jam session. But the music could be anything from King Krule to just a saxophone and drum duo. It just felt like basically everything that wasn't mainstream bundled into this one night. It was accessible. You did also have people who were really geeky about jazz going there. But the love of jazz was accepted as a love of music in general as opposed to a snobbishness.

Marina Blake

It was such a strong foundation, to have a thousand people turn up to a pub. That's how big Steez got at the end, at the Fox and Firkin.

It would run every month. It would be packed to the rafters full of the most valuable audience you can get for musicians, which is die-hard young people in their twenties, who are just like, 'This is the most important thing ever.' Steez was the place where you were playing to your peers, with your peers, organised by your peers. Everyone was like twenty, really! I remember Nubya [Garcia] talking about it and saying that was the moment she realised that the audiences that she needed to play for were people like her. That people like her friends would be into what she's doing, instead of playing these lofty jazz bars to people twice her age. And the other thing that Steez and Brainchild have brought is an interdisciplinary approach: collecting together people of a really similar age with similar ideals, similar values and similar energy, visual artists or poets or dancers or musicians or DJs and creating a space for all of those people to get together and improvise and mix. The Steez events were just so, so powerful. Like the beginning.

A thousand ethnically diverse kids in their late teens and early twenties cramming into a ramshackle venue in Lewisham to dance to jazz and poetry? Really? For a generation raised on *The Fast Show* and *The Mighty Boosh*, the idea of jazz claiming its position as a vital part of youth culture was as refreshing as it was unlikely.

Steez burned brightly for the first few years of the 2010s before losing momentum, in no small part due to the withdrawal of prime mover Luke Newman. He is an elusive figure; I was not able to track him down for an interview, with the phone number I had for him long out of use, his Facebook account deactivated and email address bouncing. Steez leaves behind very little digital footprint, but its grassroots, youth-led energy is embedded in the DNA of the current scene and lives on in the hearts and memories of those who were part of it.

The energy of Steez was harnessed by the organisers of Brainchild, a new boutique festival founded in 2012 by UCL student Marina

Blake and friends. After a chance meeting with Newman in a night-club smoking area, he was invited to co-programme the festival, providing first festival appearances to many of the leading artists of this generation. Running from 2012 and still active now, Brainchild was vital in fostering a community of young musicians away from the commercialisation of the mainstream festival industry, while at the same time providing a media-friendly story to help give the scene wider publicity.

Marina Blake

I'm just glad that Brainchild still exists. It's rare that something lasts eight years when it has the origins that we do. And I'm glad that we still carry the torch. We're still holding the connections between the same people and more. And I think because of Steez's absence, that became an even greater priority for us. It's been the space where people always know they can do what they like. They can bring any project, no matter where it's at and how fledgling it is. It's the festival that gave a lot of these bands their first festival gigs and has always felt like a bit of a homecoming for them in that regard. Like Ezra Collective playing in 2013. Seven years ago, when T.J. was too young to be on site. Or Moses playing in 2015 or Nubya, or SumoChief, which was Oscar Jerome and Joe. United Vibrations. We also had Myriad Forest after David died.* So it was a Myriad Forest made of Nubya, Shabaka, Yussef, Jamie Benzies. It was an amazing gig. But also never happened again. It was very emotional.

Brainchild was also responsible for the first foray of 'the South-East London scene' across the river, when Marina and friends used the Total Refreshment Centre (known generally as TRC) in Hackney as the venue for a launch event for that summer's Brainchild Festival on the third day of 2015.

* David Turay had come up through Tomorrow's Warriors and was a close friend of many of the musicians of this wave until his tragic death at the age of just nineteen.

TRC had started life as a sweets factory, turning raw materials from the Caribbean into treats for white English people, a psychogeographical point made brilliantly by Emma Warren in her book *Make Some Space*. After the demise of its previous incarnation, reggae venue and radio station Mellow Mix, the building had lain derelict until being taken over by French DJ/promoter Lex Blondin in 2012. As well as two separate performance spaces, TRC contained a warren-like maze of music studios, rented by producers and artists including Dan Leavers (The Comet Is Coming, Soccer 96), Capitol K, Snapped Ankles, Henry Wu and Alabaster DePlume.

Situated in the Ocakbasi badlands just off the Kingsland Road on the fringes of Dalston and Stoke Newington, TRC was deeply DIY in both feel and attitude. Once much-loved community venue Passing Clouds, just down the road in Haggerston, finally lost its protracted battle against gentrification in 2016,[3] much of the grassroots energy (as well as many of the staff) immediately shifted a mile north to TRC, cementing its position as one of London's most important underground venues and a homemade bastion in the battle against commercialisation. Shoreditch had transformed in ten years from vital creative hub to crassly commercial wilderness; Dalston was well on the way to the same culturally tragic destination.[*]

While Lex had always been a jazz lover, he had come to London at a time when very few of the people he met were interested in jazz. Open-minded and ever the pragmatist, he had simply immersed himself in other forms of music. Since the formation of TRC, the music had taken on a distinctly psychedelic tone, in no small part due to the

---

[*] In December 2021, Cargo, on Rivington Street in Shoreditch, had its licence revoked due to a spate of thefts and violence. It had become one of London's most important live music venues in the early 2000s under the programming aegis of Bar Rumba founder Chris Greenwood and assistant Claudio Lillo (future agent for Moses Boyd, Poppy Ajudha and Jordan Rakei). This all changed after it was bought by Shoreditch Bar Group in 2009 and completely stopped live music, running commercial DJ nights for a mainstream crowd: a classic case of what can happen to culture once commercial interests predominate over musical ones.

presence of producers Dan Leavers and Capitol K and drummer Max Hallett, who would go on to form The Comet Is Coming and produce Snapped Ankles. But the Brainchild event was Lex's startling first encounter with the new generation of jazz musicians, and he made a point of welcoming them into TRC.

Lex Blondin

Marina did the launch of her festival at TRC and brought Nubya [Garcia], Theon [Cross], Joe Armon-Jones and I was just like, 'What? Are you serious? Young people playing this shit?' I was just over the moon. Joe Armon-Jones was beginning SumoChief with Oscar Jerome and all these cats, they were not formed. No one knew them really, beyond their South London circles. No one in our circle knew them. But from that point on, I kept them in the back of my mind and I kept on booking Nubya as part of other line-ups, and there would be all of the other people coming through.

Marina Blake

TRC was just the most amazing venue. I'd never seen anything like it. It felt like the most natural home we could ever have had. I mean obviously Brainchild and the artistic community we work with is very South London focused. But man, that place! Even if it hadn't been for our show, which definitely put it on Lex's radar, it would have found its way to TRC. A space like TRC cannot exist in a city like this without things finding their way.

Music is nothing without context, which is in part provided by the physical spaces in which it is performed. From bars to theatres, warehouses to arenas, venues have been intrinsic to the growth of every musical scene, affecting the political and emotional development of the music as well as the sonics of how it is made. This was true of the square mile of bars, venues and 'sporting-houses' in New Orleans' Storyville in the early years of the twentieth century; it was true of

Minton's Playhouse in Harlem, where bebop's pioneers first began to incubate their new sound in the 1940s, and the plethora of clubs on 'The Street' (52nd Street in Midtown) where it was exposed to a wider (whiter) audience. It was true of the disused industrial spaces which facilitated the growth of techno in both Detroit and Berlin, and of Shoreditch's Plastic People, whose weekly FWD night was a definitive session in the development of dubstep ten to fifteen years earlier.

It was true in Dalston immediately before TRC, as the international community around Passing Clouds supported the formation and growth of African, Latin, Balkan and Middle Eastern fusion bands including Electric Jalaba, Wara, The Turbans, London Afrobeat Collective, Seeds of Creation, Awalé, Gipsydelica and my own band Afriquoi. Regular nights at the venue and sister venue the (New) Empowering Church* like Cal Jader's Movimientos (Latin), Dele Sosimi and Koichi Sakai's Afrobeat Vibration (Afrobeat), Planetman's Little Blue Ball (Reggae) and my own Wormfood series had provided a meeting space for musicians from diverse backgrounds and a context for them to play their music before an appreciative audience and get paid for it.

In the same way, TRC provided a vital space for musicians to meet, hang out, and trial new ideas with the support of a young, open-minded, politically engaged and dance-ready community. It was also here that the scene began to reach a wider audience, in no small part through the proximity to Gilles Peterson's Brownswood Studios HQ on Brownswood Road and the Stoke Newington studio of his nascent Worldwide FM. A central figure in this and multiple previous incarnations of UK jazz, Peterson connected quickly with the DIY spirit of the venue, hosting his own events and bringing influential friends to see

---

* Initially referred to as 'Passing Clouds 2', the Empowering Church was opened above an African church (hence the name) just 50 metres up Richmond Road, as the venue's founders, Eleanor Wilson and Khwaja Page, sought to offer space to more people than the 350 Passing Clouds could safely accommodate. After the couple broke up and the second site faced some licensing difficulties, Page relocated the Empowering Church to a ground-floor section of Netil House, deeper into Hackney just off Broadway Market – hence the New Empowering Church.

artists including Shabaka Hutchings, Nubya Garcia and Joe Armon-Jones: a vital development for the scene's international reputation.

This interest crystallised in the *We Out Here* compilation on Peterson's Brownswood Recordings in 2018, a paean to the scene that featured original material from Nubya Garcia, Ezra Collective, Kokoroko, Maisha, Shabaka Hutchings, Moses Boyd and Theon Cross. Accompanied by a documentary film by photographer and filmmaker Fabrice Bourgelle, this compilation helped define the new sound, using Peterson's reputation and Brownswood's distribution channels to carry the sound globally.

The importance of TRC as a permanent, dedicated space run by people sympathetic to the music and its culture cannot be overstated.

Quinton Scott

Total Refreshment Centre was the first time in a long while that a specific music scene had built up around a venue in London, from my memory. Because of the internet and streaming, primarily, dance music, soulful music and jazz had become more fragmented. DJs like Gilles Peterson were still a vital magnet for new directions in jazz and Dingwalls were still running their nights to bring together original jazz heads to revive their Sunday afternoon sessions. But I think for a younger generation to get so heavily into one hub like Church of Sound and TRC was unusual, and it was really exciting. Lex's approach to jazz and music in general was very open and progressive and not tied too tightly to tradition. He curated the space in his own unique way and naturally built a community of musicians and enthusiasts who really bought into his approach.

TRC's live music licence was revoked in 2018 after multiple complaints from local residents, despite extensive soundproofing and impassioned pleas at the venue's deliberately nondescript entrance to leave and arrive quietly. Lex is still in charge, and TRC remains active as a studio complex and live-stream location, but no longer as a venue. It will go down as yet another casualty in the ancient war between creative and commercial interests. But not before making a vital contribution to the development of London's music and the international story of jazz.

'The energy of it was so hip-hop'
(Jazz Re:freshed)

Over in West London, hip-hop DJs and promoters Adam Moses and Justin McKenzie were unimpressed with the way they saw jazz events being presented.

Like so many of my generation and those slightly older, they had been led to jazz through reverse-tracing the samples in hip-hop – with love for the new form leading them back to the source – and through the Street Soul parties of their youth in the late 1980s and early 1990s, where jazz was played as one black music among many, including soul, funk and rare groove. Frustrated by the presentation of jazz in the media and the blatantly racist door policies of many London clubs, they took the grassroots community energy of the warehouse parties they had grown up with in Harlesden, fused with a hip-hop swagger, and began marketing their new Jazz Re:freshed nights to the black community in exactly the same way they had promoted their hip-hop nights.

Adam Moses

People don't necessarily understand the nuance of promoting to a black audience. When we started Jazz Re:freshed . . . we'd print flyers, go and stand outside jazz venues. And in honesty, we were greeted with total and utter apathy. People coming out of events assumed that we were flyering for other things. They'd see a bunch of black guys outside and ignore our fliers. The organizations at the time – same thing. We were contacting them saying, 'Hey, look, we're doing this jazz thing, we're trying to bring in a younger audience. We're trying to make it a more diverse audience' – no one's interested. So we went, 'Actually, let's just do what we've always done.' There's this whole community of people that weren't going to jazz events and we don't feel like it's because of the music, it's because of the way it was presented. So we pushed to our audience who used to come to our hip-hop parties. But I tell you this, we got more response from being outside a reggae dance and promoting a jazz event than we did at any jazz event. For the black community coming into any jazz event, there was an element of how things are presented to you. Mainstream media, at that point, anything that was to do with jazz was black-and-white bow ties, tuxedos, the crooners, that kind of image. Black-and-white shoes and a sharp suit. A lot of people were turned off because, especially in the black community, 'it's very white' or 'it's not for us' kind of thing. I've had those conversations countless times with people and then we were like, 'Nah, come down check our thing.'

Starting in 2003 as a Sunday board-games session, with jazz played on vinyl in the background, Jazz Re:freshed morphed into a weekly live jazz night at the tiny Mau Mau Bar on Portobello Road. The consistent energy attracted a dedicated following, week in week out, and provided a vital opportunity for emerging musicians to reach a very different crowd from the one they might meet at Ronnie Scott's.

Adam Moses

We had all kinds of bands. And you can speak to those guys who played in the early days who will tell you they played to an audience that they never played to in their life. I mean, the early days of Jazz Re:freshed, the energy of it was so hip-hop. We had bands come in and we've got our guys on the side like, 'Ra, blap blap blap blap,' when someone's playing, you had Rastaman next to them, like, 'Yo yo yo yo!' And they'd never experienced those kind of things. So it was a bit of a shock to the system for a lot of people. But it was amazing.

Adam, Justin and their crew built the night slowly, with patience, dedication, positivity and an enormous amount of hard work, for very little financial reward. They eventually attracted the attention of Huey Walker, a local resident, Arts Council officer and former venue owner.

Huey Walker

I was living just off Ladbroke Grove and cycling along Portobello Road and going past Mau Mau and seeing these massive tour buses outside, massive bands who had other gigs with Serious or whoever it might have been, and then just doing a little impromptu thing and piles of black people piling out of this small venue. I was like, what the hell is going on here?

The son of Trinidadian Wilf Walker, a prolific promoter of African music, jazz and reggae, Walker Junior had grown up with his father's stories of being forced out of the business by the disloyalty of artists and the scepticism of the Arts Council's new diversocracy in the 1980s. Having run his own Flyover venue off Ladbroke Grove for several years in the early 2010s, Huey had his own experiences of disloyalty, corruption and opportunistic landlords happy to profit from the added value created via the cultural capital of grassroots music scenes while making no investment in the culture itself.

He would also no doubt have absorbed his father's analysis of the racism in the music industry and the limited way in which jazz had been marketed, making Jazz Re:freshed's attitude and methodology even more refreshing.

Wilf Walker

There's never been a substantial black audience for jazz in England. Until the advent of the Jazz Warriors and those people, jazz was very white here: audience and musicians. And in fact, the white people, they didn't really encourage blacks too much. All the promoters all around the country were white. It's like the beginnings of that world audience. They were into jazz first and then into world music. The shows weren't really sold to black people – you'd never hear a jazz concert being advertised on one of the black radio stations or see it in a black newspaper.

Always keen to support grassroots creativity, Huey Walker invited the Jazz Re:freshed organisers into the Arts Council for a meeting, an invitation which was vital in the organisation's growth, eventually leading to them gaining the coveted National Portfolio Organisation status within the Arts Council, guaranteeing modest annual funding.

As well as continuing their weekly nights, Jazz Re:freshed went on to host three editions of their Jazz Re:Fest festival on London's South Bank and seven in Brighton. They launched the Jazz Re:freshed label with a compilation in 2008, launching the *5ive* series to spotlight artists including Richard Spaven, Kaidi Tatham, TriForce, Rosie Turton and Nubya Garcia, as well as releasing full albums by Maisha, Daniel Casimir, SEED Ensemble and others.[4] The weekly Jazz Re:freshed session at Mau Mau ran solidly, with very few interruptions, for a monolithic sixteen years until the bar's new owners decided to change things up in 2019. But it left an indelible mark on London's nightlife, and built a solid foundation for the scene's current success.

'My mind was exploding'
(South By Southwest)

An extremely significant part of Jazz Re:freshed's impact was a partnership with British Underground, an NGO founded by musician and journalist Crispin Parry, whose mandate is to promote contemporary British culture internationally, supporting British delegates at Womex and running showcases for UK artists at SXSW in Austin, Texas, and SiM in São Paulo, Brazil.* Having enjoyed massive success

---

* Like the Great Escape in Brighton, Eurosonic in Groningen, Trans Musicales in Rennes, Amsterdam Dance Event and the peripatetic Womex, SXSW and SiM are both conferences whose primary purpose is for music industry professionals to connect with each other and see new artists, as well as the artists gaining fans through performing for a

with their 'Grime 2.0' showcase at SXSW 2016, British Underground were on the lookout for the next hot thing, and the nascent 'new UK jazz scene' fit the bill perfectly.

Crispin Parry

We have a number of levers we can pull, one of which is the very important South by Southwest, which can elevate pretty much anything really, really quickly into a thing of interest that people haven't seen before if we get it at the right time. So it reflects back in the UK and ultimately reflects it around the world as well. 2016 was probably when I first came across this new pack of jazz. It served the purpose of being the next thing on from that new wave Grime 2.0, which Stormzy came out of. We'd created a really good narrative around that particular genre at South By, so I was ready for the next story. I was looking for something with that energy. I'd been down to Jazz Re:freshed. It was Moses, Theon and Nubya. They played as a trio. And honestly, it blew me away. I thought, 'What is this? This energy, this crowd, this is so exciting.' And then Moses came to the office to do his interview. And I thought, 'He's telling me about all of these people making all of this music and all of these venues. There's obviously something going on here that we should be locked into.' For me, it doesn't need to have any commercial merit, because that will come once you get it right. It's actually, can we tell a great story about British music here that isn't being told yet?

It is a surprising twist in the tale that the events I am about to describe may not have taken place at all if not for the presence of an act whom *no one* would describe in the same breath as Moses Boyd, Ezra Collective or Nubya Garcia: Manchester-based trio GoGo Penguin.

Signed initially to Matthew Halsall's Gondwana Records, GoGo Penguin had emerged from an earlier era of atmospheric,

new public. Good showcase slots at such events can be vital in opening new opportunities, and SXSW in particular is an established entry route to the American market.

44

orchestral-influenced sample-based jazz, that includes The Cinematic Orchestra, Submotion Orchestra, Hidden Orchestra and can perhaps trace its genesis to DJ Shadow's seminal 1996 *Endtroducing.....* album on James Lavelle's Mo' Wax, via the crate-digging, genre-defying compilations, parties and DJ sets of Mr. Scruff, Manchester's answer to Gilles Peterson.

After a 2014 Mercury Prize nomination for their album *Version 2*, the band begged Halsall to release them from their contract with Gondwana in order to sign to Blue Note, the legendary American label founded in 1939 by the 'animal brothers',[*] Francis Wolff and Alfred Lion, Jewish escapees from Nazi-ruled Germany. Immediately recognisable for Lion's striking photography of each artist on the cover of their albums, Blue Note was responsible for so many of the greatest jazz recordings of the 1950s and 1960s, releasing music by artists including Herbie Hancock, Lee Morgan, Art Blakey, Freddie Hubbard, Thelonious Monk, John Coltrane, Horace Silver and Donald Byrd. After a period of dormancy, the label was relaunched in 1985 under EMI's Bruce Lundvall, who presided for a quarter of a century, signing new artists including Norah Jones and St Germain and opening the vaults to remixes in 1996 with *The New Groove: The Blue Note Remix Project* after seeing the success of Us3's bootlegged remix of Herbie Hancock's 'Cantaloupe Island'. This was followed by Madlib's *Shades of Blue* (2003) and *Blue Note Revisited* (2004), where the producer was given carte blanche to make new music from the entire Blue Note back catalogue.[†]

---

[*] Because their surnames are Lion and Wolff, rather than anything to do with their savagery in business or poor table manners. The appellation comes from the 2016 film *I Called Him Morgan*.

[†] It is interesting that this happened again in 2020, with a special *Blue Note Re:Imagined* dedicated to the UK jazz scene, featuring remixes and versions by artists including Emma-Jean Thackray, Alfa Mist, Ezra Collective, Nubya Garcia, Poppy Ajudha and Shabaka Hutchings, as well as a version of St Germain's hit 'Rose Rouge' by soul/pop/R & B star Jorja Smith. The 2022 sequel, *Blue Note Re:Imagined II* featured Nubiyan Twist, Ego Ella May, Oscar Jerome, Daniel Casimir and Binker Golding.

The Blue Note seal of approval lent GoGo Penguin enough credibility for Crispin to convince the SXSW organisers that a showcase
of new UK jazz was a feasible prospect. The showcase was confirmed
only after they were added to the bill. That the band are rarely associated with most of the other acts described in this book, and virtually
unknown to younger fans of 'the new UK jazz', reaffirms both the
importance of lineage and the mysterious and complex workings of
the international music industry.

A few months prior to SXSW 2017, Shabaka Hutchings was already
in talks with Universal after an electrifying showcase with his South
African project Shabaka and the Ancestors at New York's Winterjazz
conference.

Kerstan Mackness

It's difficult to explain how big the hype machine was in New York,
how hard Shabaka walked into that town with the Ancestors. The town
went MAD, there was a full-page *New York Times* story. He played
with the Ancestors, but in the same run, he also did a gig with Pharoah
[Sanders]. And they lost their shit. Shabaka walks in, this six foot
something, incredibly cool black guy who's incredibly articulate, got all
this shit to say, towers over everybody. He gets his horn out and he just
fucking blows the roof off the city.

SXSW 2017 not only sealed the deal for Shabaka but announced
the whole scene as a major international musical force, with extensive
coverage on national radio stations KCRW and NPR. Filling the gap
left by United Vibrations, an impromptu trio of Moses Boyd, Shabaka
Hutchings and Theon Cross electrified audiences with shows which
were by many accounts the highlights of SXSW. Shortly afterwards,
Shabaka signed a three-album deal with Impulse, the label that had
been the home for jazz greats including John Coltrane, Charles Mingus, Archie Shepp and Sonny Stitt. This opened the door for a spate
of signings to American labels, including Nubya Garcia (Concord),

'rye lane shuffle'

Steam Down (Universal), Melt Yourself Down (Universal), Yussef Dayes/Tom Misch (Blue Note), Blue Lab Beats (Blue Note) and Ashley Henry (Sony).

Dahlia Ambach Caplin

We were all like, 'What the fuck is going on right now? This is the greatest!' Because Moses Boyd: incredible. And Theon is incredible. Yussef Kamaal were supposed to come in the country, they couldn't come in. So Shabaka came. He wasn't supposed to be there. Insane! That video, to this day I have it on my iPhone. Incredible. With him there's just always more layers. Every time I see him perform, every time I read anything he says. I feel very, very blessed to have met him. He's one of the best people that I've ever come across. Not just as a talent, but as a human being. Being around Wayne [Shorter] showed me that these people who have this incredibly special soul and bring out the music, I feel Shabaka is blessed with a similar quality. He's one of the greats, period. He's a teacher, he's a mentor. He's a force of nature. And I couldn't feel more fortunate to be able to work with him. I feel very grateful that he agreed to join us on Impulse and we relaunched Impulse around him because he fits the spirit of Impulse so perfectly, I couldn't have thought of a better way.

The impact of this international recognition was not limited to the USA: it significantly changed the game in the UK and Europe as well, confirming the age-old trueism that people in your own community are the hardest to please, and it can be difficult to get their respect until you have gone out into the world and proved yourself.

Huey Walker

You can be doing things in this country and it's great and it's building, but to then take it abroad and have the people from here seeing it's in *New York Times* and all that kind of stuff, it puts a real spotlight back on what's happening here.

Gordon Wedderburn

Let me tell you, anybody who talk to you about the new London jazz scene was never following it before. They've only just discovered it. The reason why suddenly everybody is jumping on this bandwagon is because suddenly it went to the States. The States started to talk about it because the journalists here weren't talking about it. The DJs here weren't playing the music. If you go back seven, eight years ago to some of the known DJs who held sway, they weren't playing this music at all.

'A spontaneous aspect of African diasporic culture' (Steam Down)

Back in South-East London, United Vibrations' sax player Wayne Francis held the torch for the inclusive, community-based intentions of that band with Steam Down, a weekly jam session which exploded into Deptford's Buster Mantis, a bar and restaurant in an unassuming railway arch named after the first prime minister of Jamaica, Alexander Bustamante. Choosing Buster Mantis as its home was a clear nod to the Caribbean heritage of Francis himself and many of the regular musicians, a point reinforced by the name of the event itself: Wayne's take on a Grenadian dish called 'Boil Down'. Combining the multi-disciplinary, boundary-pushing, youth-driven creativity of Steez and the sweaty, carnivalesque energy of Jazz Re:freshed, the night ran every Monday from May 2017 until December 2018. This regularity galvanised a dedicated community for whom the weekly session was almost a religious experience.

Bradley Zero

It doesn't really make sense unless you've been to Steam Down. You see the way that the instruments are played, they have more of a debt

'rye lane shuffle'

to Wiley than they do to Max Roach. The rhythms and the kind of staccato high energy. It's a London thing. It's just blended with the way that people would get down in a club rather than a real style of dance that you'd practise at home.

Wayne Francis

I don't think there's necessarily a reclamation of jazz. What there is is a reclaiming of improvised music culture within Black British youth. And I think now there is a large enough group of musicians that are not afraid to tap into their traditions and heritages and let that influence their current time, and they're not afraid to let contemporary black British music of our time influence what they are doing. There's a kind of unapologetic nature of expression that's happening at this point in time. And I think this unapologetic expression through improvised music, which is called UK jazz, is taking ownership of a wider narrative around black improvised music as a core aspect of African diasporic culture. I think for the first time, a lot of musicians are really fearless in representing the cultures they come from, and bringing that into what they create.

Whatever it was conceptually, it was very, very sweaty. I only went a handful of times but remember being super impressed not just by the driving music but by the energy of the crowd: the 'blap blap blap' that Adam recollects of Jazz Re:freshed; the interpretive dance and performance art that were such a feature of Steez; the spontaneous guest poets, singers and MCs; and the whole thing wrapped in an infectious, utterly unapologetic energy.

It was also deeply, celebratorily uncommercial. Crammed into the back room of a tiny bar when the night's popularity could have easily accommodated twice as many people, cameras prohibited, no online advertising. Wayne's main method of creating a community was to sing out his mobile number and get the entire audience to repeat it. Send him a WhatsApp message and you could be added to the Steam

Down WhatsApp group to be reminded about next week. Not that there was much need: you'd do all you could to be back next week anyway.

Steam Down also came at the perfect moment in the music's evolution. Whereas earlier antecedents like Steez and the Good Evening Arts sessions in Oval's Cable Cafe provided a vital space for the music to cohere away from the eyes of the media, by the time Steam Down launched, the scene was already beginning to attract intense media attention. Steam Down provided an opportunity for journalists and interested parties to soak up the hype.

And yet it maintained its community spirit, in no small part due to the fact that it took place on a Monday night in an out-of-the-way corner of London that you would be unlikely to go to regularly unless you lived nearby. Most of Steam Down's multi-disciplinary set of core members – which included drummer Edward Wakili-Hick (Sons of Kemet, Cleo Sol), poet Brother Portrait, DJ/illustrator Alex Rita (Touching Bass), keyboardist Dominic Canning (aka DoomCannon) and singer/poet And Is Phi – were South London-based and coming primarily for the love, but it also regularly hosted guest musicians including Kamasi Washington and Nigerian trumpeter Etuk Ubong.

Steam Down also provided a launchpad for the Steam Down Orchestra, for whom the weekly Steam Down session provided such a strong support base that they sold out the 470-capacity Jazz Cafe for their first ticketed live show in 2018, being offered festival bookings all over the world before even releasing any music. Along with Melt Yourself Down, they were swiftly signed to Universal Music, in a domino effect eerily reminiscent of the Jazz Warriors era of the late 1980s and early 1990s.

It is no coincidence that Steez, Steam Down and Total Refreshment Centre all were based in areas – New Cross, Lewisham, Deptford and Hackney – that had traditionally enjoyed less than salubrious reputations. Whereas the seedy basement clubs of Soho had provided the backdrop for modern jazz, skiffle and blues in the 1950s and early

1960s, Kings Road had been the home of punk in the 1970s, Camden of jazz dance in the 1980s, and Shoreditch of Blue Note in the 1990s and Plastic People in the 2000s, by the late 2010s, the corporatisation of inner London was becoming so total that youth culture was being shunted to ever more distant locations. The intense gentrification that spread like a cancer up Hackney's Kingsland Road from the late 1990s, changing the face first of Shoreditch, then Haggerston, Hoxton, Dalston and Clapton, continually threatened to choke the vital creative organs of the areas that hosted it. Artists, musicians and other young creatives were increasingly replaced by young professionals and families as grassroots venues, workshops and studios morphed into microbreweries, sourdough bakeries, natural wine shops and specialist coffee houses.

South-East London, with its strong student population, long-established African and Caribbean communities, and still relatively cheap rental accommodation, was the natural place for the next iteration of grassroots creativity.

And yet, like Jazz Re:freshed at Mau Mau, like Steez as a night and TRC as a venue, Steam Down at Buster Mantis is no more. While the Steam Down Orchestra has begun to cultivate an international reputation and a bright future, Steam Down, as it was, will remain a happy, sweaty memory for those who were there.

'I think the passion showed'
(Church of Sound)

If Steam Down was the rowdy younger brother, Church of Sound was the slick, still-hip young uncle: money in his pocket but still down for adventure. Held in the round at Saint James the Great, an active church just south of the Clapton Roundabout in Hackney, the series was born out of necessity in 2016 when TRC had to pause activities while appealing the first loss of their music licence – a successful appeal, though ultimately only a temporary stay of execution.

Programmed and promoted by TRC founder Lex Blondin, with vital logistical support from collaborator Spencer Martin, Church of Sound provided some magisterial, intimate performances while shining a spotlight on some of the scene's deeper musical roots. The initial concept was to invite named artists to play 'songbooks': a tribute to one of their key influences, showing a side of themselves their fans may not have seen before, and introducing them to some great music in the process. The first show was Yussef Dayes and Kamaal Williams (aka Henry Wu) – the project that became Yussef Kamaal – playing the music of Idris Muhammad, with a line-up that included saxophonists Nubya Garcia and Nick Walters and percussionist Crispin 'Spry' Robinson as well as future Yussef Kamaal members Mansur Brown and Rocco Palladino (son of legendary bassist Pino, who had collaborated with J Dilla and D'Angelo, among many others including The Who, Gary Numan and Jeff Beck).

Lex Blondin

I was working with Spencer from the band Lunch Money Life and he basically vocalised the idea of doing a gig in a church. It took about a year to put it all together. And at the time, Yussef Dayes and Henry were working on the Yussef Kamaal stuff, way before it was even called Yussef Kamaal. They had a studio at TRC, so I got to hang out a lot with them and bond over ping-pong games. And it always made me trip out how much Yussef reminded me of Idris Muhammad. I started chatting to him about that and he said, 'Oh yeah, that's one of my big influences. My dad used to play that shit when I was younger in the house.' So I started pitching the idea of doing a songbook. That was the very first one. And somehow, the combination of the line-up with the songbook was a match made in heaven; it just all fell into place. I had this concept for the artwork where we'd do a take on the cover of *Power of Soul* by Idris Muhammad, and instead of having him obviously we took pictures of Henry and Yussef in the studio, and

instead of New York City in the background, we had the Barbican.
So it was like, 'Yeah, we're playing this music, but we're also very
London.' Obviously the band was also very exciting to everyone. So
the combination of a brand-new band playing some really cool shit in
this brand-new place we've never heard about meant we sold out the
first gig, just working with people that we knew. Everyone came with
the best of themselves.

Further songbooks included Moses Boyd Exodus playing the music
of Art Blakey, Kokoroko paying tribute to Ebo Taylor, Nubya Garcia
honouring Joe Henderson and Maisha channelling Alice Coltrane.
Although centred around this wave of London-based musicians,
there was space for older musicians and those from further afield:
Jazz Warriors alumnus Orphy Robinson paid homage to vibraphon-
ist Bobby Hutcherson with a band that included 'middle generation'
Jazz Warriors alumni Byron Wallen, Tony Kofi and Robert Mitchell
alongside Nubya Garcia and Moses Boyd; South African group The
Brother Moves On – led by Siyabonga Mthembu of Shabaka and the
Ancestors – performed the music of legendary South African folk/
jazz groups Malombo and Batsumi. Iconic posters by TRC in-house
designer Raimund Wong (who also designed this book's beautiful
cover) helped provide a clear visual identity, often echoing the style of
original CTI and Blue Note records.

Although centred on the songbook concepts, Church of Sound
expanded to host album launches and nights of original music
as well. Performers in this format included Yazz Ahmed, Matters
Unknown, Collocutor, Jaimie Branch, Neue Grafik and Greg Foat,
Louis Moholo-Moholo, Dave Okumu, Tom Skinner and IG Culture. Church of Sound even hosted Billy Harper's super-group The
Cookers as well as Afrobeat co-founder Tony Allen, who launched
his album with the late Hugh Masekela, *Rejoice* (World Circuit,
2020), with two concerts at the church in March 2020. Taking place
immediately before the first national lockdown put in place for the

Covid-19 pandemic,* these proved to be the last Church of Sound gatherings with a live audience for nearly two years, and were the last ever shows for Tony Allen, who himself joined Masekela and Fela Kuti in the realm of the ancestors on 30 April 2020.

Lex Blondin

We try and keep it fresh. Creating collaborations, or workshopping different ways of people playing their tunes. What we stay away from always is, 'Oh, we're the last date of the tour and we're going to play the same show that we've done in every fucking venue'; that's kind of boring to me. It's cool, I'll go to Ronnie Scott's to see that. But with us, it's like, 'No, we're not having that. Sorry! You're going to have to make it a bit different than everything else.' It can be a songbook, or changing the line-up, or adding guests or instrumentation. And people play differently in Church of Sound just because of the set-up and the audience.

The religious overtones were not lost on people. Many have described the communal, religious intensity of so many of the new London jazz events; holding this event series in an actual church reinforced the point.

Lex Blondin

When we started, I was a bit freaked out about selling booze in a church; sometimes people forgot about where they were and acted like you would in a nightclub, making out in a corner, etc. I was like, 'Oh my God, this is weird.' But what it brought at the start was a real sense of, 'Yeah, we're in a spiritual place.' There is a focus that you get in a space like this, people tune into what you're doing a bit more than other places, and it's good to use that space in a different way, but

---

* The album had been recorded ten years earlier but not finished, and was finally finished in 2019 with contributions from many of the new UK musicians including Mutale Chashi (Kokoroko, bass) and Joe Armon-Jones (Ezra Collective, keys).

also make the most of what it makes you feel. I don't want to take the religious analogy too far, but there's definitely a ritual in the sense that things happen always the same, you come in, you get some food, it's slightly different from a normal gig in the sense that there's definitely like a good hour and a half where you meet and greet and you see people. And that's a real communal thing, for sure. There's definitely loads of people that meet during those moments.

While the setting and accordingly early finish provided an environment in which older fans and journalists could feel comfortable, the intimacy of the performances and simple clarity of the brand helped nurture a dedicated following and growing international reputation. By 2019, Church of Sound were running additional events in Paris and hosted the centrepiece of the final Saturday of the London Jazz Festival at the Royal Festival Hall, further establishing themselves as figureheads for the scene.

'The venue was smashing it' (Jazz Cafe)

While the scene I describe is mostly closely associated with the DIY, underground energy of Steez, TRC and Steam Down and the long-running community of Jazz Re:freshed, credit must be given to the London institution that is Camden's Jazz Cafe. Though it is dismissed by many as commercial, particularly since the 2016 takeover by the Columbo Group,* such a verdict unfairly diminishes its role not only in supporting the present generation but in providing a dedicated home for multiple generations of jazz and adjacent musics since 1990.

* Starting in 2006 with the Old Queen's Head in Islington and Paradise By Way Of Kensal Green, Columbo expanded rapidly to operate a portfolio of venues including the Jazz Cafe, Blues Kitchens in Camden, Shoreditch and Manchester and Brixton's Phonox (formerly Plan B) as well as owning a share in the Maiden Voyage and (now defunct) Sunfall festivals.

This dismissal also underestimates the immense achievement of keeping a music venue going for over thirty years in a central part of a city like London, and the importance of permanent spaces, open every day of the year, in opening the music to a wider audience while paying decent fees for performers.

Situated in a former Barclays Bank branch at the bottom of Parkway, under a minute from Camden Town Tube station, its roots were anything but commercial. The original Jazz Cafe was founded in 1987 in Stoke Newington by Jean Marshall and her life partner Jonathan Dabner, an ex-teacher, community activist and jazz lover with strong left-wing sensibilities.

Jonathan Dabner

It was a tiny little place, a hundred capacity. We used to have people standing outside watching through the window. People said to me, 'I'm surprised, you get a lot of black people in here, don't you?' It was a very mixed audience. Age wise. Race wise. Sex wise, gender wise. It was anything goes as long as it's tolerant, open-minded. It was a great place. It was only open for three years, '87 to '90. But it did have a big impact.

Packed every night, the first iteration became a key meeting point for the upcoming Jazz Warriors generation (Courtney Pine, Orphy Robinson, Cleveland Watkiss) as well as older heads like jazz/blues saxophonist Dick Heckstall-Smith (Colosseum, The Graham Bond Organisation, Blues Incorporated), who was involved in booking musicians.

Seeking a larger, more central venue to accommodate bigger audiences and provide an opportunity to book international stars was a natural move.

Jonathan Dabner

We were always looking for a bigger premises. And we tried all kinds of different things, none of which came off. One day, I'd been to meet a guy in Camden Town who ran the World's End pub and I looked across the street and I saw for sale the old Barclays Bank on Parkway, which was to become the Jazz Cafe. Cut a long story short, I got a loan to buy the lease, and we started work on it. And then things started going drastically wrong because of the nineties recession, financial crash, suddenly our main contractor went bust. I got that place open and running – well, Jean and I did – by the skin of our teeth. But I was crippled by debt before we even started somehow.

Oliver Weindling

It was like Roadrunner running off a cliff. There was a massive recession when he moved in '89 to Camden, blop. He overextended himself. He thought he could run the same sort of venue he'd run in Stoke Newington and just put an extra nought on to every price and it would be fine. But it's not really like that. He was out of his depth.

Jonathan Dabner

Most of my time was taken up booking great American acts. I was like a little boy in a sweet shop, being able to book people like Pharoah Sanders and Jimmy Smith and Don Cherry. Ahmad Jamal. Amazing artists, but I didn't keep my eye on the ball financially. The place always traded successfully, but there was this huge debt. Whitbread had loaned us £350,000. I couldn't service that debt and they put us into administration and that's when Vince Power took over. I have to admit, I'm not a great businessman. I just love music. And would do crazy things and book expensive acts just because I wanted to hear them play in the venue. Where other people would be saying no, you can't afford them, you're going to bankrupt yourself, I was thinking, whatever. I'm an adventurer! And come a cropper.

After going into receivership, the venue was bought by Vince Power's Mean Fiddler Group, which grew to become one of the biggest venue, concert and festival operators in Europe.*

Adrian Gibson programmed the venue from 1992 until part-ing ways with new owners MAMA Group in 2007. A serious music head with an enormous record collection, he had to tread a fine line between artistic and commercial concerns. This often involved open-ing the doors to a far wider definition of jazz than under Dabner.

Adrian Gibson

The mid-nineties, when the first wave of the Acid Jazz thing finished, probably '96, that was about as bleak as it got for real jazz. '95, '96 was the boom of the whole neo-soul thing. So we would be filling up the diary with D'Angelo and Erykah Badu and Angie Stone and Maxwell and all that stuff, which was great, because it was packing it out and it was a golden time for all of that. Okay . . . but where's the jazz? So I had to start really trying to put on more styles of music intentionally because I didn't want to lose the identity of what we were. I didn't want it to be the No Jazz Cafe.

Things didn't get any easier through the mid-2000s to mid-2010s for jazz and related genres, either.

Dom Servini

It was acid jazz, then it became the nu jazz thing, then there was broken beat. And then there was what I would call the wilderness years, which were probably the time when I was playing jazz the most, sort of 2003 to 2010, 2012, years where it was utterly unfashionable.

* Named after the original Mean Fiddler venue in Harlesden, the company grew to operate multiple iconic London venues including the Forum in Kentish Town, the Garage in Highbury, the Astoria in Charing Cross Road, Subterania off Ladbroke Grove and the Borderline in Soho, as well as founding the Reading, Leeds and Latitude Festivals and operating Glastonbury from 2002 to 2012. The group was renamed Festival Republic in 2007 after being acquired by Hamsard Ltd (a joint venture between international megacorporation Live Nation and Irish promoter MCD) and selling off its venues to MAMA Group.

'rye lane shuffle'

There wasn't a lot of that kind of music coming out. Broken Beat had happened, been and gone. The nu-jazz thing had been and gone. That was the real hard time, because people just weren't interested in black music. It's only really in the last seven or eight years that it's become fashionable – not just jazz but black music in general. Because people are much more open. But that period in between was fucking horrible.

Like the music itself, the venue had some difficult years between 2007 and 2016, falling victim to a commercialisation that was unacceptable even for a pragmatist like Gibson.

Adrian Gibson

The MAMA Group came on board and I just didn't see eye to eye with them. They had no interest in music at all. They started the 'I love the eighties' night on the Saturday and went, 'Yeah, your Saturday doesn't make enough money. So we're going to put this eighties night on.' And obviously, that was like fingers down the chalkboard to me. Don't get me wrong, they knew what they were doing. They were packing it out. But there was probably more fights in those three hours on a Saturday night than the last twenty years in the venue, people vomiting everywhere. It was properly horrible.

After being bought out by concert giant Live Nation in 2016, MAMA Group began selling off their venues. Columbo stepped up, acquiring the venue in early 2016 and relaunching in June of that year after a massive re-fit. Gibson's story of a fifteen-year dance between artistic credibility and commercial success was echoed by music programmer Lev Harris.

Lev Harris

We were open every single day of the year. I'd like to challenge another person to try and put on a show every day of the year without there being the occasional tribute show to balance the books. If you go on to the website of any other venue that programmes in-house, you'll see that they'll have one, maybe two cool shows a week and the rest of it will be tribute nights of some sort. But we got to a stage where we were so prominent, all the bands were coming to play there, it did feel like all eyes were on us. So I felt like if we did do anything that was a bit commercially minded, it would be scrutinised times ten. But people didn't understand how expensive it was to run that place. I think we did actually get to a point around the end of 2018 where I'd look at the diary and think, 'Well. Every single show I've got on sale at the moment is high quality. Maybe not all to my taste, but all very credible.'

The venue's relaunch coincided perfectly with the emerging scene. Nubya Garcia, Ezra Collective, Shabaka and the Ancestors, Maisha, Steam Down Orchestra and Nubiyan Twist all played there between 2016 and 2019, some of them multiple times. Having found their feet and refined their live shows amongst their peers, the new Jazz Cafe gave the new wave of artists a chance to play to a wider public. The venue's central location and established history provided a natural place for journalists to come and write about the music.

Lev Harris

The venue was smashing it at that point. I was just gifted this seemingly endless supply of bands to come and sell the venue out, it was great. We had Harvey Sutherland do the first Rhythm Section* at Jazz Cafe, which sold out. And then we made it a quarterly session from there. We did a series with NTS. We had Boiler Room film Makaya McCraven. We did stuff with [The] Wire magazine, gal-dem, we actually did stuff with TRC as well – it helped make it feel like a scene. And the fact that we were connecting the dots in that way – cherry-picking a band and putting them on a Rhythm Section line-up, doing a TRC songbook with

* The long-running night curated by DJ Bradley Zero, and affiliated to the label Rhythm Section International.

another one, doing a *gal-dem* show for International Women's Day with another one and putting them in all these different contexts. I think it kind of made it bigger. I don't want to overstate Jazz Cafe's importance in this, I'm sure all of those bands would have got to where they are regardless of if I was involved or not.

'I had no idea who Floating Points was' ('Rye Lane Shuffle')

While I've generally avoided discussing specific releases, it would seem wrong to conclude this chapter on key moments of the music's development without detailed discussion of two releases which stand out as major game-changers, not just musically but as focal points for the development of the entire scene: Moses Boyd's track 'Rye Lane Shuffle' and Yussef Kamaal's album *Black Focus*.

Active professionally since 2010, Moses had already achieved media recognition through his album with saxophonist Binker Golding, *Dem Ones* (Gearbox, 2015). Moses and Binker had met through the Tomorrow's Warriors youth programme and bonded through playing together in the band of Zara McFarlane, signed to Gilles Peterson's Brownswood Records.

Dem Ones was a major milestone for UK jazz, not only for its refreshing prioritisation of raw, improvised music, but also for its presentation: two young guys, posed against a very London wall, looking away from the camera, faint smoke drifting up from Binker's mouth; this was a world away from the dressed-up-for-the-wedding, jazz cliché look of their immediate musical forebears Empirical.

Even the patois title of the album* seemed to announce a more streetwise approach to London jazz, steeped in Caribbean heritage. But *Dem Ones* was very much still jazz, and while it may have been refreshing within the jazz world, it did not travel far outside it.

---

* *Dem Ones* as in 'one of them ones', i.e. 'one of those things that is hard to explain'.

'Rye Lane Shuffle' was something different altogether, combining Theon Cross's menacing tuba bassline with Moses's urgent, grime- and Afrobeat-inflected drumming. The tune's aggressive sonics and bumping 135 bpm tempo meant it could be played in a club as part of an electronic set – the key to helping the tune (and ultimately the entire cohort) reach a wider audience.*

Moses had been encouraged by Tomorrow's Warriors mentor Peter Edwards to seek support from the recently formed Steve Reid Foundation. Created in tribute to the American drummer who died of throat cancer in 2010, unable to pay for the medical treatment that might have saved his life, the Foundation was set up 'to help people working in music who are in crisis, especially those suffering from illness' and 'to support emerging new talent through education and information initiatives'.[5] It boasted illustrious trustees including taste-making electronic producers Floating Points (Sam Shepherd) and Four Tet (Kieran Hebden); its founder was the ubiquitous DJ, broadcaster and label boss Gilles Peterson.

Moses Boyd

I'd written 'Rye Lane Shuffle' round about the time I met Gary and Warriors, about seventeen, just as a song we'd played with Theon. It was called 'C Tune' because it was in C minor. That's how much I didn't care! And then Peter Edwards told me to apply for the Steve Reid grant, that had just started. I had no idea about it. I had no idea who Floating Points was, I had no idea who Four Tet was. Obviously I love that world of music, but I think retrospectively, people may take for granted our worlds have now collided, but they weren't, d'you know what I mean? DJs like that, it was only a few that were spinning music relatively close to us. Festival line-ups weren't like they are now; I didn't know them, they didn't know me.

---

* Most grime, dubstep and kuduro is at 140 bpm, with garage, UK funky and the faster styles of house generally between 125 bpm and 135 bpm. Despite not being recorded to click, the tempo is consistent enough to be mixed with any of those genres.

'rye lane shuffle'

So, cut a long story short, I get the grant. They give me some money. And I was like, 'I'm going to record some tunes.' They were like, 'What are you going to record?' And I was like, 'Well, I've got these songs that I've written since I was seventeen. Why not go and do that?' I literally recorded it in two days and sent them all the rough mixes and they both came back to me like, 'What's C Tune'? In my head, I'm like, that's not even my favourite song! And then Kieran was like, 'Oh, can you send me the stems? If you don't mind, I'd love to do a mix for you.' So I sent him the stems and he did a mix, and then I was seeing a lot more of Floating Points as a sort of mentor. I recorded 'Drum Dance' at his Studio. He just oversaw a lot of stuff at the time, gave me advice, helped me set up my label. Anyway, Kieran had mixed it, and Sam had cut a dubplate. And then they were DJing a lot. Kieran put it on his Instagram, and that was the beginning. Everybody in my DMs: 'Oh my gosh, what's this song'? I'm like, 'What, THIS song, really?' Then literally it just went mad from there. I took it back to Sam, Sam did a proper mix with the stems that Kieran gave me. And then we pressed the vinyl. And the rest is kind of history . . . they both wanted to put the song out. It was that thing of two friends: we're not going to argue over this song, they were like, 'Actually, Moses, do it yourself.' And Floating Points put me in touch with his distributor, his accountant, he helped me set up a lot of stuff, we pressed it and then . . . that was kind of the beginning of this. I guess Yussef Kamaal happened at the same time. But, you know, not just bigging myself up, it was one of those songs that really changed a lot of things, just hearing DJs play it out, it kind of kick-started that bubble.

While the energy and vigour of the music itself would surely have inspired growing fan bases, the intersection with the electronic music world and the support of key figures like Four Tet, Floating Points, Bradley Zero and Gilles Peterson were vital for the growth of the scene as a whole. And for all its power as a track, it is doubtful if it would have had the wider cultural resonance it did were it not for its brilliantly evocative new name, magically linking the music with Peckham's emerging sub-cultural credibility and that of South London more generally.*

Peckham, the famously working-class area of 1980s TV wide boys Rodney and Del Boy in *Only Fools and Horses,* had been home to a large Nigerian population since the 1990s.† Traditionally poorly served by public transport, with a network of buses and old National Rail lines running sporadically and mostly terminating at London Bridge or Victoria, this historically deprived corner of South-East London had always felt very far away to anyone who didn't grow up nearby. Like Hackney and Camberwell, the lack of a Tube station and easy transport links to other parts of London is the exact thing that can help an area develop a strong community spirit. The London Overground – aka 'ginger line' – changed all that in 2012, creatively remixing the tracks from the old South and East London Lines to create a new route from Clapham Junction to Dalston via Camberwell, Peckham, Whitechapel, Shoreditch, Hoxton and Haggerston. In the words of my brother, 'finally linking the hipsters of Hackney with the hipsters of Peckham'.‡

This large-scale infrastructural project combined with the general post-millennium London housing boom meant that South-East London became the next focus after Hackney peaked. Combine that with the large student population of Goldsmiths, Trinity Laban and Camberwell College of Art, and the availability of warehouse and railway arch space, and for a short time Peckham, like Dalston before it, felt like the centre of the universe.

---

* Though it is fair to point out Floating Points and Four Tet were excited about 'Rye Lane Shuffle' when it was still called 'C Tune' – in their minds, the tune's appeal had nothing to do with Peckham.
† Apparently you can see 'I LOVE PECKHAM' T-shirts on sale in Lagos. Afrobeat innovator Tony Allen reported enjoying the best *moi moi* he had had in thirty years after he sent me to buy him some before his Ghost Notes show with Amp Fiddler in 2018.
‡ The first phase of this project had been completed in 2010, when the East London Line was reopened, linking New Cross (and hence Goldsmiths, an important creative hub within the University of London) with Dalston Junction.

A key node was the vast Victorian industrial estate of Copeland Park and the adjoining Bussey Building. Built in the late nineteenth century by sporting goods manufacturer George Gibson Bussey, it specialised in cricket bats but was requisitioned during the Second World War to make weapons designed to project considerably further than the boundary of the village cricket field. Having lain derelict for several years, it was acquired by DJ, promoter and cultural entrepreneur Mickey 'Jazzheadchronic' Smith and Peckham Vision in 2007. Initially struggling with attendance and dry-hiring the venue to anyone willing to pay, by the mid-2010s it was rammed every Friday and Saturday, mostly with young, South London-based students. As the building expanded in popularity, it grew to include three floors of nightclub space as well as a co-working space, yoga studio, rooftop cinema and much-loved basement record shop, bar and nightclub Rye Wax. One of the main engines powering the development of the Bussey Building and ultimately Peckham more widely was South London Soul Train, the night Smith started at the Bussey in 2011.

Dom Servini

You look at what's happened with South London Soul Train. Mickey's bringing a thousand eighteen- to twenty-five-year-olds into a venue to listen to black music . . . there's also people upstairs playing rare funk records, people playing Northern Soul Records, and us in the basement playing edits and electronic stuff and forward-thinking black music. That's an amazing achievement. And that's only been possible in the last few years.

Mickey Smith

My approach has always been, I love jazz and I love funk and I love soul, and I don't give a fuck what's popular. I don't book according to how famous somebody is or you've got a big fucking name or they're going to sell tickets. Couldn't give a shit. For us, especially South London Soul Train, people just didn't care. I could put anybody on stage, people would just trust our judgement and come. All the DJs come ready to destroy it, and if you play one or two bad tunes for the whole night, you'll go home thinking about those one or two bad tunes. Seriously, it's that philosophy of every tune must kill. And I think that's why South London Soul Train worked so well.

The rest of Copeland Park continued to develop, hosting bars, a venue, a sake distillery and independent traders of all kinds. It even plays host to an annual Christmas makers' market, appropriately called Pexmas. Just a few metres up the road, Peckham's multi-storey car park began hosting the summertime rooftop pop-up Frank's Cafe, which for many was emblematic of gentrification due to the close association with Practice Architecture (co-founded by Paloma Gormley, daughter of sculptor Anthony) and the demographic contrast with Rye Lane below. More and more of the area was colonised, reflecting Peckham's new residents' preferences for duck fat chips, IPA, yoga studios and screen-printing shops over car parking spaces. Holdrons Arcade, initially a 1930s department store, played host to a range of micro-businesses including Yam Records and the Balamii radio station. Somehow, 'Rye Lane Shuffle' perfectly captured the spirit of an area in transition.

Moses Boyd

It was renamed because . . . well, I'm not gonna put it out as 'C Tune'! But I just thought about when I was writing and it was around the time I used to go to this workshop in Camden. So I used to have to get the 171, which would always get to Rye Lane and then change driver on a Sunday. And I just always vividly remember sitting on the top deck, watching Rye Lane. It's such an interesting place on Sunday because you've got the market, you've got people going and coming to church, people coming out of clubs, people just doing shopping. It's such an interesting mix of just life. And when I was thinking about titles, I was like, 'Well, I remember writing it around that period and getting the 171' and I was like, 'Okay, thinking of it musically, it's kind of like Afrobeat with a grime bassline, so there's no other place that would define it better than Rye Lane.' And the Shuffle is obviously just people shuffling about. It's funny. Looking at it now, I'm like, man, did I help gentrify Peckham? That whole South-East London scene wasn't a thing back then. I'm not even from Peckham! I've got cousins like, 'Why didn't you call it "Lewisham Shuffle"?' It doesn't make sense, but it served a higher purpose, and creatively, what was happening around that time in Peckham, it was a springboard, really, Balamii, a lot of the Bussey building nights, Bradley's Rhythm Section night. Again: greater forces. That's all beyond my control. I just named the thing what I felt made sense, you know what I mean? And then the rest happened.

'That album blew my mind'
(Black Focus)

Equally important in bringing this new wave of jazz to the attention of young, non-traditional jazz audiences was Yussef Kamaal's *Black Focus* album, released on Gilles Peterson's Brownswood label in November 2016.

The project began as a collaboration between United Vibrations drummer Yussef, the youngest of the Dayes brothers, and keyboard player and producer, Henry Williams (aka Henry Wu, aka Kamaal Williams, the Muslim name he adopted in 2011).

Having started playing gigs around South London in live future garage band Stepsons and later playing keys for Brixton-based pop star Katy B, Williams first made a name for himself as Henry Wu. Releasing dark house, garage and dubstep-influenced London jazz, or jazz-inflected electronic music, depending on your perspective, he developed a strong following with limited-edition vinyl releases on Floating Points/Alex Nut's Eglo Records and Tenderlonious' South London-based 22a.

These releases had attracted the attention of Gilles Peterson, who invited Williams to perform a guest slot at his 2016 Worldwide Awards at Koko, Camden's grand fourteen-hundred-capacity art deco theatre. Henry took this opportunity to showcase the new Yussef Kamaal project, with himself and Yussef supported by a live band that included Tenderlonious, Cuban trumpeter Yelfris Valdés, bassist Tom Driessler and guitarist Mansur Brown.

The show was so powerful that Peterson immediately offered them a record deal and, although they had started negotiations with Aly Gillani's (DJ Gilla)'s First Word Records, who had invested in the recording,* this was obviously too good a deal to pass up. They signed with Brownswood, with the *Black Focus* album selling over thirty thousand vinyl units and putting UK jazz on the map for a new generation of fans who had grown up on dubstep, future garage, techno, house and disco.

Emily Moxon

Gilles tried to sign them, like, on stage practically. They weren't playing live that much. They'd done a Boiler Room. They didn't have massive social media numbers; I remember talking to our distributor and we were like, 'This record's going to be quite big.' But it didn't get any press, really. They didn't want to do anything. It's weird because as soon as we announced the record, it just starts selling like crazy. It just felt like everything came together. I don't know if people had watched the Boiler Room or knew about them. But I remember we did the release party at Jazz Re:freshed and they were gassed to sell out Jazz Re:freshed at Mau Mau! It just built really fast. And I think that music very quickly engaged with people across Europe and around the world, the way that instrumental music does really well.

Naomi Palmer

Their cultural impact as an entity, I felt, was established way before there was any record. There was so much buzz coming at me from

---

* To Williams' credit, he paid First Word back the money they had invested.

all types of music aficionados and promoters – 'Have you heard this band?' They had gained a lot of traction before I ever even met them. It seemed like a very organic development, and they struck upon something unique. That was a real instinctive and primal chemistry, what happened between those two as musicians. And they were embraced as the flagship act of this new movement of new London jazz.

Femi Koleoso

Yussef Kamaal, *Black Focus*: that album sounded like London to me. It was jazz but it was London. You can't hear 'Strings of Light' and not hear Peckham High Road, you know what I'm saying fam?

Recklessly disregarding my own strictures about the tedium of attempting to describe music in words rather than simply listening to it, I will take a moment to highlight a few key musical elements which are important in understanding the significance and popularity of the record.

One is the presence throughout the album, and especially on 'O.G.', of vocal samples by DJ and radio presenter Gordon Wedderburn.* His dubbed-out vocals reminded me immediately of the kung fu and mafia movie samples that featured heavily in nineties gangsta rap, especially Wu-Tang Clan, as well as the UK jungle and drum and bass that Wu, like me, grew up with. Using spoken-word samples in this way referenced the traditions of hip-hop, jungle and drum and bass, while Wedderburn's heavy Jamaican accent spoke to the demographics of contemporary South London, nodding to Yussef's Jamaican heritage. The specific choice of Gordon – a

* I got to know Gordon in 2015 as compère for the main stage of Camberwell Fair, a free festival I started in that year on Camberwell Green, near my house, as a vehicle to bring the whole community together and celebrate the area's cultural diversity. Hearing *Black Focus* for the first time, I remember thinking 1) 'Wow this record is amazing,' and 2) 'That's Gordon!'

long-standing jazz champion – linked the record with jazz as well as Jamaican sound system culture.

Gordon Wedderburn

I got a call from Yussef to say, 'Look, we want you on the album.' I had to laugh. I say, 'You serious?' Say, 'Yeh, man.' And I ask dem why, dem say, 'Beca ya bring the energy.' And they came and pick me up one evening outside the house. We went to a number of places and then we ended up on a side street by Streatham Common. And we parked up in the car, myself, Kamaal and one of their artist friends. We siddown and I just said, 'Let me hear the music.' And I started responding to the music, just talking, trust me, it was a ten-minute uninterrupted stream coming from me. Lot of colourful language I should say. But at that time, that album blew my mind. Then and even now. Yeah, man. And they took the little bits from the ten minutes. And that's what made it into the album.

Another element is the unapologetic disco beat of the track 'Lowrider'. Disco had had (yet another) resurgence in popularity in the early years of the decade, culminating in French duo Daft Punk's unashamedly disco-influenced *Random Access Memories* (Columbia, 2013). This provided many people's song of the summer in 2013 with 'Get Lucky', featuring N.E.R.D.'s Pharrell Williams and legendary producer Nile Rodgers (Chic), who performed the song live as part of Chic's closing set on the West Holts stage at that year's Glastonbury. This was followed by Todd Terje's* heavily disco-inflected *It's Album Time* (Olsen Records, 2014), which features the 2012 nu-disco anthem 'Inspector Norse'. Getting in on the action, British band Coldplay even featured a remix by Italian disco pioneer Giorgio Moroder on their 2014 single 'Midnight' (Parlophone).

At a more underground level, DJs like Floating Points had begun

* The name Todd Terje is itself a tribute to seminal black American house producer Todd Terry.

lacing their club sets with heavy doses of disco, with DJs from other genres like Bristol's DJ Die (drum and bass) and Addison Groove (UK footwork) suddenly starting to play back-to-back three-hour disco sets. Reissues of vintage African disco like *Lagos Disco Inferno* (Soul Jazz Records, 2010) and Kiki Gyan's *24 Hours in a Disco 1978–82* (Soundway, 2012) provided further dance floor ammunition, with long-running nights like Horse Meat Disco and DJs like Greg Wilson consistently championing the music around the UK. The disco groove of 'Lowrider' provided an easy access point for younger audiences coming of age in the midst of this revival.

Finally, the starkly Afrocentric title *Black Focus* combined with the Islamic artist name – reinforced by the Arabic script in thick black calligraphy on the album sleeve – immediately linked it with the 1970s tradition of political instrumental jazz for anyone with those reference points at their disposal.

Lex Blondin

Yussef Kamaal to me is very directly referencing CTI, 1970s records, including Idris Muhammad and Ahmad Jamal. This whole mystique behind it and even the sound, it's basically repackaging it for today and it's really well made, really well produced. That shit was dope then. It's still dope now. People who weren't familiar with the music would be totally hyped and others who've rinsed the stuff are chuffed to hear it live in front of them with musicians they love!

While Henry, born in Peckham to British and Taiwanese architect parents,[6] had adopted the Muslim name 'Kamaal' in 2011, Yussef was given his at birth: a product of the Black Power/Nation of Islam movement of the 1960s and 1970s that had caused many in America's black communities to convert to Islam, adopting Muslim names for themselves and their children: Ahmad Jamal, Idris Muhammad, Muhammad Ali, Umar Bin Hassan (of the Last Poets), Amiri Baraka (LeRoi Jones) and Abdullah Ibn Buhaina (Art Blakey). Although not practicing Muslims, all four Dayes brothers received Muslim names as a direct continuation of this tradition, a result of their Jamaican father's time in New York in the 1970s.

Ahmad Dayes

Dad left London when he was nineteen, was like, 'Fuck this country.' Obviously, civil rights have just happened in the States. Being a teenager in the sixties here in London would have been shit if you were black, the racism would have been vile. There were signs on pubs – 'no blacks, no Irish, no dogs'. That was the environment. So going to the States where it was perceived things were more progressive, at least within the black community: the civil rights, the music, the arts; the things that were happening in the States were what people here were looking to for guidance, for inspiration. So he was like, 'Yeah, fuck this gaff, let's go and see what we can do over there.' The very fact that we've all got Islamic names is part of that legacy. Even now, if you look at people of our age in the states, 'nuff of them have Muslim names. They're not Muslim! There's a lot of Kareems, a lot of Ahmads, a lot of Yussefs, Jamals, that's part of our parents' heritage. Or at least thinking anyway, so definitely that shaped him and shaped the way we've been brought up. Certainly shaped the tunes we were fed from day dot.

The popularity of *Black Focus* was such that it crossed over to electronic music fans, introducing a whole new public to jazz. As *Vice's* 'Nu Jazz Lad' knowingly stated, these were mostly people who had not been listening to 'Actual Jazz'. But if this record and 'Rye Lane Shuffle' turned a young audience back on to jazz, what true jazz fan would knock it?

Yussef Kamaal split in May 2017, just six months after the record's release, amid the chaos of the fallout from their cancelled show at SXSW, the passing of Yussef's mother, and personal issues between Yussef and Henry. Most of the confirmed engagements that summer were split between the new Yussef Dayes Trio and Kamaal Williams.

Both continue to make music, with Dayes reaching No. 4 in the UK album chart in 2020 with his collaboration with Dulwich-born singer and producer Tom Misch, *What Kinda Music* (Blue Note, 2020). Williams made sure to capitalise on the huge popularity of *Black Focus* by setting up his own Black Focus record label. Williams' continuing presence on diverse festival line-ups, including live appearances at tastemaker electronic festivals like Dekmantel in the Netherlands in 2018, and 2022 appearances at mainstream pop festivals including Primavera in Spain, Melt in Germany and Oya in Norway, provides clear evidence of the extent to which UK jazz has been accepted as part of mainstream pop and electronic culture.

'A dream come true'
(Sunfall/Field Day/Cross the Tracks/We Out Here)

One consequence of the increasing popularity of live jazz and jazz-influenced genres among electronic music fans was the possibility of sneaking jazz artists on to electronic line-ups. This was hugely welcome to promoter Noah Ball, who had cut his teeth promoting jazz and hip-hop shows while at university in Leeds in the late 1990s and early 2000s, in collaboration with First Word Records founder Aly Gillani.

Moving to London in the mid-2000s, he had become increasingly involved with the lower end of the frequency spectrum, co-founding Outlook festival in Croatia to celebrate the heavier side of UK music: dubstep, grime, bassline, garage, jungle, drum and bass, hip-hop, reggae and dancehall. Having achieved huge popularity with Outlook, and waded through the logistical and legal challenges of running a festival in a remote part of Croatia, its creators inaugurated the smaller Dimensions festival in 2011, also in Croatia, to showcase the slightly less rowdy side of electronic music, with a focus on house, techno and disco.

As the borders between electronic music and jazz became increasingly porous, Ball was thrilled to be able to programme an increasingly diverse array of music that reconnected him to his original love of jazz. This was evident at the 2016 Sunfall festival in Brixton's Brockwell Park, a joint venture with Columbo Group, the owners of the recently reopened Jazz Cafe. Though the event received bad press for poor toilet facilities and an unpopular, complicated, European-style token system for food and drink, it proved without question that it was possible and popular to mix jazz and electronic music.

Noah Ball

Kamasi Washington's first big London show was at Sunfall in 2016. We had Yussef Kamaal, Moodymann. Yussef Kamaal came and played for us out in Croatia in the amphitheatre. Sunfall for London was very much a Dimensions line-up. We had Ben Klock, Benji B, D-Bridge, Digital Mystikz, Joy Orbison, Jeremy Underground, Hunee, Jamie xx.

That you could put jazz acts on an electronic line-up and not have any backlash whatsoever was made abundantly clear in the 2018 edition of tastemaker music festival Field Day. Having moved from Victoria Park in Hackney to Brixton's Brockwell Park for the first time, one of the conditions of the licence was that the organisers would have to run an extra day, and Ball was approached to programme the Friday, initially under another brand.

He programmed high priestess of hip-hop/R & B, Erykah Badu, supported by Moses Boyd, Ezra Collective, Nubya Garcia, Jordan Rakei and both of Shabaka Hutchings' UK-based projects (Sons of Kemet and The Comet Is Coming), as well as, of course, Gilles Peterson. Fearing that the headliner for the extra Friday was stronger than the main event, the Field Day organisers incorporated Ball's line-up. Although this decision had its origins in technical, financial and marketing rather than aesthetic reasons (and Ball did eventually launch his originally envisaged stand-alone event, Cross the Tracks, in 2019), to those unaware of the machinations behind it, the message was clear:

UK jazz is back on the map, regaining its rightful place in the canon of the UK's popular music.

The success of the programme on that day was also the moment that convinced Gilles Peterson it was the right time to launch a dedicated festival for this music. Displaying the talent for cross-branding that had seen Worldwide evolve from a BBC radio show in the 1990s to a compilation series, festival and radio station, Peterson used the We Out Here name – originally the title of the 2018 Brownswood sampler album – to launch the We Out Here Festival in 2019, with programming and production support from Ball and his company NVS Promotions.

Noah Ball

It was a dream come true, to be honest. It was actually the Field Day Erykah event where Gilles was playing – I'd been booking him for fifteen years, and contacting him every few years going, 'Shall we do our own festival, let's do our own thing. Let's do a UK thing.' And he'd been like, 'Now's not necessarily the time.' But it was at Field Day on the Friday, he was like: 'Noah. Yep. Now's the time, let's do it.'

The first We Out Here Festival took place in 2019 in Abbots Ripton in Cambridgeshire, on the same site that had hosted the infamous Secret Garden Party festival 2004–17.* That had been a notoriously Dionysian affair:† glitter, skin-tight Lycra onesies, sock-wrestling,‡ animal costumes, the 'Suicide Olympics',§ unbridled libidinous energy,

---

* Secret Garden Party was in fact resurrected on the same site in 2022 after a five-year hiatus.
† I co-programmed a stage there from 2007 to 2012 with my close friend Nikhil Shah, co-founder of influential content platform Mixcloud. We were blessed to host early shows by artists including Ghostpoet, Kae Tempest, Portico Quartet, Jamie Woon, Gentleman's Dub Club, United Vibrations, Nick Mulvey, Julio Bashmore, Mosca, Hessle Audio founder Ben UFO and Boiler Room co-founder Blaise Bellville.
‡ A contact sport in which two participants aim to deprive each other of both socks by any means necessary. Biting, scratching, spitting, gouging all encouraged.
§ Run by arch-pranksters Bearded Kitten, the concept was to ride customised, homemade wheeled vehicles down a hill, at pace, and see what happened.

pills, powders and tinctures of all colours and properties all watched over by majestic trees, lit from below in an eerie green.

Returning to We Out Here 2021 on the Sunday after going back to London to collect my two-year-old daughter, I remember encouraging her to shout 'OY!' as we both bounced up and down to the hectic energy of Sons of Kemet's closing set on the Main Stage, and thinking, There is absolutely no way this would have happened ten years ago.

I remember observing to my friend Nikhil: 'There's nothing to make you feel the passage of time quite as starkly as coming back to the scene of the most hedonistic moments of your twenties, at thirty-eight, with a two-year-old, only to find it's been transformed into a jazz festival!'

Had we got older or had jazz got younger?

The truth, of course, was both.

2

'You Can't Steal My Joy'
Jazz, Ownership and Appropriation

So here they stand: a new generation building their own scene, confidently embracing jazz in a celebratory atmosphere in new spaces alongside the diverse sounds of contemporary London. But if jazz is only one part of the musical and cultural mix, why call it jazz at all? Certainly, not everyone from this generation loves the definition. But where UK musicians of the 2000s like the F-ire Collective and Dave Okumu's The Invisible often strove to avoid it entirely, wanting to dissociate themselves from the weight of history and contemporaneous prejudice, this generation is generally happy to have the word used in connection with them, and equally happy if it isn't.

Some say it's an honour to be spoken of in the same terms as their musical heroes, while stressing the need to keep things looking fresh.

Femi Koleoso

Jazz musicians are the deepest thinkers of all time. I'm honoured that someone could listen to my thing and would use this word that could describe John Coltrane. If you look at John Coltrane and say 'jazz musician' and say 'Femi Koleoso, jazz musician', I feel honoured by that!

Moses Boyd

I had no problem with the word because the word and the history gave me so much. My problem was more the perception. And that's what I was fighting via my music to change. I was like, 'Hey, man, when I go and see Roy Haynes, this is just as wild as going to see D Double E!'

But I'd rather see Roy Haynes somewhere like Steez than in Ronnie Scott's. I'd rather see Roy Haynes dressed in Nicholas Daley than in a zoot suit and a flat cap! I was like, it just needs a bit of a rebrand and just looking at it from a different angle.

For others, it's more of a grudging acceptance.

Shabaka Hutchings

The word is problematic, and what musicians have said about it from Ellington to Mingus to Miles, is that the word has never been a good word in the way that musicians have wanted it to be used, but people just define themselves as jazz musicians. As time goes on, we can then deconstruct what it means to play jazz music, and if you should be even calling it jazz music. But at that time it was just like, they all played jazz music. The word is problematic, but that was just the description that we'd been handed. We definitely weren't calling it anything else.

Some feel the word insufficient to describe the range of different styles in their music, while recognising its usefulness as a marketing term.

Oscar Jerome

I don't really like my music being called jazz, to be honest. I mean, I love jazz, and I know it's a big influence on me. But I feel like it's become a slightly lazy term for people to just talk about any music with some sort of musical depth or with live instruments in it. I get a bit frustrated with that. But at the same time, it's really been beneficial to a lot of us as well that it's become more of a cool thing, we've profited from that and we're able to also make music that we're passionate about. And if people want to call it that, that's cool. And if they don't, that's cool as well. I don't know, I kind of just said very opposing things just then.

'you can't steal my joy'

For others, it's more of a thematic pointer.

Poppy Ajudha

I'm going to sound like such an anthropologist. But when we talk about jazz, what is jazz? Is it not just an entry into a space? And maybe for a lot of black people or people of colour, maybe that is an entry to understanding music in a way that relates to them, because isn't any genre of black music just an entry into understanding who you are or how to express yourself?

Some just want to focus on the music and leave descriptions to journalists and marketers.

Joe Armon-Jones

I don't really identify, as an action, so I don't have any problem with other people identifying it towards me, you can identify whatever kind of music you want, I don't really mind. But I'm not putting my music categorised as anything because: what's the point?

Emma-Jean Thackray

I've been trying not to label what I do and just leave that to journalists. I'm very happy to be called a jazz musician, that's what I studied, and what I do is definitely jazz. Not all of it is, though. But no matter what I do, it's still gonna have some language from jazz, because it's just so ingrained in me, the vocabulary that I use and the stuff I'm listening to, there's so much jazz in there that if you want to call it that, great. If you don't, I don't mind.

Yet in accepting the label, no matter how begrudgingly, this generation are implicitly acknowledging a connection with the entire history of jazz, taking their place in one of music's most important lineages. For as long as the term has existed, jazz has danced through an uneasy tension between mostly black innovators and a mostly

79

white industry. From Acker Bilk to *The Fast Show*, Paul Whiteman to *La La Land*, the appropriation, adulteration, commodification and mockery of jazz are indivisible from the unequal power dynamics, life opportunities and straightforward racism which brought about its original creation. Exploring the history of the term and its development over the course of more than a hundred years can shed vital light on the present generation, seeing their emphasis on independence and authentic self-expression as the latest skirmishes in a war that is as old as jazz itself.

Jizz on a summer's day

The origins of the term 'jazz' remain hotly disputed, so much so that the American Dialect Society named it the 'Word of the Twentieth Century' in 2000.[1] It has been variously claimed to have African origin; to have derived from the jasmine-scented perfume worn by prostitutes in New Orleans' red light district; from the biblical 'jezebel' (giving the term jazzbelle – also a prostitute); and from the semi-mythical figure of itinerant blues musician Jazbo Brown, who appears in Gershwin's *Porgy and Bess*.

The above etymologies have been largely denounced as false, with most scholars agreeing that the word derives from 'jasm', a variant of 'jism' (spirit/energy/spunk): a slang term for semen still in use today.

To appreciate the meandering distance of jazz's journey from its condemnation as a 'gully-low' music, played and listened to by the seediest sorts of people in the brothels and barrel-houses of New Orleans, to 'black classical music',[2] appreciated in the velvet seats of acoustically treated concert halls all over the world, I invite you to consider: how would you feel sitting down with your aunt to watch the seminal film about the 1961 Newport Jizz Festival, *Jizz on a Summer's Day*?

How about taking her to Wynton Marsalis' long-running 'Jizz at Lincoln Center' series, made possible only after a hard-fought campaign to have jizz appreciated as an all-American art form? Or inviting a new date to see 'the cream of the new London jizz scene' at Camden's Jizz Cafe?

These somewhat facetious examples illustrate just what an astounding distance jazz has travelled from the defiant music of an oppressed people to the anaemic way it was portrayed and understood by many in the mid-1990s. Thelonious Monk was so under-appreciated in his own time that even Alfred Lion of Blue Note (one of the few label heads who actually liked his music and had been willing to sign him) dropped him in 1952 after five years of losing money on his releases. By the early 2000s his version of Ellington's 'It Don't Mean A Thing (If It Ain't Got That Swing)' was the background tune for Marketplace, American public radio station NPR's morning stock market report.[3]

While notions that 'jazz' has an African etymological origin have not been proven, the term was certainly popular among African American communities in New Orleans in the late nineteenth century. In this regard, jazz as a musical genre named after a lascivious word popular in the black community is in extremely good company: boogie-woogie (syphilis), rock 'n' roll (sex), funk (the smell of sex), reggae (from 'streggae', meaning prostitute). Even jazz's self-proclaimed originator, Jelly Roll Morton, is named after a . . . never mind.

The process of vocabulary and even syntax (man is listening now) originating in marginalised communities and spilling into the mainstream is a very old one, with black communities having a disproportional influence on the language of every country in which they dwell in significant numbers, and many in which they don't. This is attributable largely to the cultural capital acquired through music, from jazz, R & B, funk and disco right through to hip-hop, grime and trap. Words like 'cool', 'hip' and even 'bro' as a term of address have become so much a part of the fabric of the English language that most people are not even aware that their roots lie in African American communities.

Every language expands and changes as its users absorb their favourite parts of the speech of those with whom they interact. But this process is rarely neutral: language is a living archaeological excavation site that bears witness to successive colonisations, wars, trade routes and allegiances. The English language itself owes its West Germanic elements to the Anglo-Saxon 'settlers' (read 'invaders') of the fifth century, its Norse to the Viking invasions of the eighth and ninth centuries, and its Latin and French to the Norman Conquest of the eleventh century. It has continued to be shaped by its interaction with other cultures, absorbing vocabulary from every territory in the British Empire even as that empire's dominance dictated that its colonies should speak English. The fact that black Americans speak English at all is a product of this exact process.

Words like 'cool' and 'hipster' originated in the 'jive talk' of black communities in the Harlem renaissance, a deliberately secret language whose function was not only an opportunity to display verbal dexterity but also a protection from being understood by 'squares' i.e. mainstream white society.[4] This type of speech has long held a fascination for people outside the community. Way back in 1938, black bandleader Cab Calloway capitalised on this interest with the publication of *Cab Calloway's Cat-ologue: A Hepster's Dictionary*, helping transmit Harlem slang into the linguistic bloodstream of white America. The book's success was followed the next year with *Professor Cab Calloway's Swingformation Bureau*, which instructed readers on the correct way to use words from his dictionary. The 1946 autobiography of Jewish clarinettist and proto-'white negro'[5] Mezz Mezzrow (who claimed to be the first person to bring Mexican 'gauge' into Harlem) recounts a series of conversations held with 'vipers' coming to dig his 'hard-cuttin' mezz', helpfully providing a translation of the entire nine pages of jive in his book's appendix. Jive is, to him, 'not only a strange linguistic mixture of dream and deed; it's a whole new attitude towards life'.[6] Francis Newton (the jazz-loving alter ego of revered Marxist historian Eric Hobsbawm) sees parallels between jive talk's quickfire extemporisation and that of jazz itself, calling jive 'a continuous, ever-renewed virtuoso collective improvisation which depends on talent, on speed, on imagination, and a sort of primitive verbal bravura . . . a set of variations on themes and rhythms unstated, because assumed'.[7]

The appropriation of Ebonics has often been met with disgust within the black community. A friend told me recently that she has been added to the local 'Cool parents' WhatsApp group. Like the 'cool jazz' of the 1950s, this is a world away from the term's original meaning, as LeRoi Jones (later Amiri Baraka) explained incredulously in 1963:

> To be *cool* was, in its most accessible meaning, to be calm, even unimpressed, by what horror the world might daily propose. As a term used by Negroes, the horror, etc., might be simply the deadeningly predictable mind of white America . . . The term was never meant to connote the tepid new popular music of the white middle-brow middle class. On the contrary, it was exactly this America that one was supposed to 'be cool' in the face of.[8]

If entire ways of speaking can be appropriated by mainstream culture, it is no surprise that maintaining ownership over an art form has been even more difficult in a society that is rigged against the very group that created it, with virtually every means of disseminating the music owned outside of the community. This is not an unfortunate historical accident: this inequality is a central part of the context from which jazz emerged.

Shabaka Hutchings

We're talking about America. So it's only shocking if you don't really appreciate what America is. That's literally what it is: it's the land where naked white supremacy has been there since the founding of it. At the point where jazz was started, black people weren't even equal in the law, couldn't sit in the same places on the bus. So of course, the music is set up with one party thinking the people that are making the music isn't equal to them. So all the structure of the industry is made with that basic assumption. That though these people can entertain us, they're not our equals and we can take their money. Or rather, we can take their ideas and make money from it.

The Original Dixieland Jizz Band

The first recordings bearing the name 'jazz' (or 'jass' as it was then spelt) were not by Buddy Bolden or Freddie Keppard, Kid Ory or King Oliver, but by a white group who called themselves The Original Dixieland Jass Band, recording 'Livery Stable Blues' and 'Dixieland Jass Band One-Step' for the Victor Talking Machine Company in 1917. Just as General Levy aroused the fierce hatred of the jungle community with the pop success of 'Incredible' in 1994, in which he claimed to be the 'original dancehall junglist', so the Original Dixieland Jass Band's claim to be 'original' laid the template for countless acts of appropriation over the next hundred years.[9] The band were immediately sued by black ragtime pianist Joe Jordan, whose claim that the 'One-Step' contained portions of his 1909 composition 'Tiger Rag' was upheld in court, belying the band's claim to originality. When 'Livery Stable Blues' was challenged in a similar way, the judge declared that it was based on a pre-existing melody and therefore in the public domain. Many musicians, both white and black, condemned this bastardisation; Mezzrow dismissed the band as 'really a corny outfit, and if they ever had a touch of New Orleans it was frail as a nail and twice as pale, strictly a white man's version'.[10] The Original Dixieland Jass Band's leader Nick La Rocca doubled down on his position in 1932:

> Our music is strictly a white man's music. We patterned our earlier efforts after military marches, which we heard at park concerts in New Orleans in our youth. Many writers have attributed this rhythm that we introduced as something coming from the African jungles, and crediting the Negro race with it. My contention is that the Negroes learned to play this rhythm and music from the whites.[11]

This re-writing of history is as inaccurate as it is brazen. The music had been emerging organically for over twenty years from New Orleans' particular mixture of African, French, Spanish and Irish elements, but there is no question that black and Creole musicians like Bolden, Ory, Oliver, Keppard, Jelly Roll Morton and Sidney Bechet had been developing the music long before 'the white kids who later became world-famous as the Original Dixieland Jass Band, hanging around and listening open-mouthed to the music'[12] of black jazz bands won the hearts of white listeners across the country.

Indeed, to many of its pioneers, jazz was 'an old, old story by 1917'.[13] New Orleans bands had performed on steamboats up and down the Mississippi river since the turn of the century, bringing the music to Baton Rouge, Memphis, Tennessee and St Louis, with every stopping-point developing its own regional style. Freddie Keppard's Original Creole Jazz Band had been touring the vaudeville circuit since 1911, even playing the Winter Garden in New York. Yet they never recorded; whether due to a fear of their music being stolen[14] or because Keppard 'played too "hot and dirty" for the family trade',[15] we may never know.

Whatever the truth around Keppard's failure to record, the Original Dixieland Jass Band's recordings initiated a pattern that has persisted up to the present day, with the first white artist to record a black style winning enormous popularity and achieving infinitely more financial success than the black originators on whose creativity their work is based. From Elvis Presley to The Rolling Stones, Eric Clapton to Eminem, black creativity has fuelled white commercial success at almost every stage. As Stearns expressed succinctly as far back as 1954, 'The Negro has always been the chief innovator throughout the history of jazz . . . [He] creates the latest jazz products while the white man packages them.'[16]

There is a special irony in the fact that the Original Dixieland Jass Band's first recordings were released in 1917, the very same year that Storyville, New Orleans' fabled red-light district in which so much of the music was incubated, was disbanded by order of the US Navy. In other words, jazz was introduced to mainstream white America at the very same moment at which the original context from which it grew disappeared.

King of Jazz, Kings of Swing, Prince of Cool, King of the Swingers

The pattern cut by the Original Dixieland Jass Band – a white band unashamedly bastardising a black style, winning money and fame in the process – was followed in every successive decade and with every new innovation in jazz, with commercial forces initially ignoring or resisting, eventually assimilating and repackaging, often in diluted form and with significant adjustment to the spice:syrup ratio. It is a pattern which every jazz musician, including the present generation of UK musicians, stands in relation to and has to address.

In the 1920s, this was nowhere more evident than in the 'symphonic jazz' of the unambiguously named Paul Whiteman. Delivering a polished, orchestral version of jazz for an exclusively white audience, by 1922 Whiteman controlled twenty-eight bands playing on the East Coast and grossed over a million dollars annually. This was a vast sum at that time and far more than that earned by Fletcher Henderson, leader of the most successful black band, from whom Whiteman purchased many of Don Redman's arrangements. The Whiteman project culminated in a concert at Aeolian Hall on 12 February 1924, the stronghold of academic music, with the explicit aim of gaining recognition for jazz as a respectable music worthy of serious attention.

By the late 1920s, the concert-going and record-buying audience for jazz was mostly white, with record companies operating separate lists of 'race records' which were sold only in black neighbourhoods: primarily the blues of artists like Bessie Smith and Ma Rainey. This category was rebranded 'rhythm and blues' in the 1940s and 'urban' in the 1970s, but the belief in the need for a euphemistic term to refer to a separate part of the industry aimed specifically at black consumers has persisted until today. Equally persistent has been the pattern of black audiences turning to other forms once a black style has been diluted.

Adam Moses

When something is culturally appropriated, you have two things you can do as a black creator or black audience: you go, 'No, I'm going to fight for it and come back,' or you just go, 'All right. Well, that's done. Let's move on to the next thing now,' and that becomes the new pop thing to be into.

As the 1920s gave way to the 1930s, the 'swing era' began, with the large white orchestras run by Benny Goodman and Glenn Miller enjoying far greater financial success than black counterparts Count Basie and Fletcher Henderson, from whom they often bought arrangements. Very few black musicians reaped the benefits of the music's success, with lucrative studio work going almost entirely to white musicians.

It was in direct opposition to this commercialisation that Charlie Parker, Dizzy Gillespie, Kenny 'Klook' Clarke, Charlie Christian and Thelonious Monk began to develop bebop in the mid-1940s. Fast, fiendishly complicated, angular and obtuse, it was an attempt to reclaim jazz not only from the concert halls of white musicians but also from the crowd-pleasing antics of Louis Armstrong, who Miles Davis repeatedly dismissed as an 'Uncle Tom'.[17] Bebop's innovators reclaimed jazz as an improvised, expressive music played for majority black audiences in small, sweaty clubs like Minton's Playhouse in Harlem. Yet it was not long before the music travelled downtown to 52nd Street, where it could more easily be seen by white audiences, including journalists and other musicians.

Within just a few years, the music changed again, with the term 'cool jazz' coined to refer to music with slower tempos and lighter tone showcased on Miles Davis's 1948–50 recordings for Capitol, initially released as 78 rpm singles but eventually compiled as *Birth of the Cool*. Despite the powerful influence of Lester Young's laid-back tenor and Davis himself in defining this style, the term became most closely associated with the 'West Coast jazz' of Chet Baker, Stan Getz, Gerry Mulligan, Jimmy Giuffre and Art Pepper, with Baker dubbed 'Prince of Cool'.[18] It was partly to distance the music from this perceived softening, sweetening and whitening that the term 'hard bop' was coined[19] to refer to the funkier, R & B-inflected second wave bebop of Horace Silver, Art Blakey, Clifford Brown, Lee Morgan, Jackie McLean, Sonny Rollins and early John Coltrane. Yet this, too, rapidly became the dominant sound of American jazz, with its African American origins becoming increasingly obscure the further it passed into the mainstream. It was in response to this new wave of commercialisation that the 'free jazz' or 'new thing' of Albert Ayler, Cecil Taylor, Ornette Coleman, Sun Ra and John Coltrane began in the late 1950s, reclaiming a freedom which Val Wilmer sees as an integral facet of black music: 'The music of Black Americans has always been free. It is the white critics and the media, it seems to me, who want to chain it.'[20]

Nor were these trends confined to music: the film industry cemented the whitewashing of jazz in the popular imagination. Notorious examples were *The Jazz Singer* (1927), in which Jewish vaudeville performer Al Jolson performs in blackface; *Birth of the Blues* (1941), where Jeff Lambert (Bing Crosby) eventually wins the crowd and gets the girl after initial resistance to his all-white jazz band; and *Some Like It Hot* (1959), in which Joe/Josephine (Tony Curtis) and Jerry/Daphne (Jack Lemmon) disguise themselves as women in order to escape the wrath of the bootleggers they have crossed, joining Marilyn Monroe's all-female and, of course, all-white band. All these films glamourise jazz while normalising it as a white style.* Even as late as 1967 – the peak

* The 2016 film *La La Land* was a significant contribution to this questionable subgenre.

of the civil rights movement – it was the Italian American Louis Prima rather than Louis Armstrong employed to voice King Louie ('King of the Swingers') in Disney's *Jungle Book*, even though the character was clearly based on him.

Strangers on the shore

While the pattern of black innovations eventually entering the mainstream after a period of initial resistance can be seen throughout jazz's history, it is worth noting also the way that jazz as a whole has disappeared from the conversation around many of the genres it has helped to birth. Like the words 'cool' and 'bro', jazz's assimilation has been so complete that most people are unaware of its foundational role in a vast swathe of Western popular music.

To illustrate this point, I want to tell the story of the links between jazz and the best-selling band in the world. John Lennon's famous dismissal of jazz as 'just a lot of old blokes drinking beer at the bar, smoking pipes and not listening to the music' contains no hint of how much the Beatles themselves owed to jazz.

The 'New Orleans Revival' had begun in America in the late 1930s when white collectors begun seeking authenticity, not as Bird, Diz, Klook and Monk had, in sweaty basement clubs, but on the dusty grooves of old records sequestered in the corners of the nation's thrift stores. Like John and Alan Lomax – the father-and-son team who travelled the length of the Deep South in the 1920s and 1930s, recording black singers in penitentiaries and work camps – they fetishised the music of New Orleans and its surrounds as a repository of creativity, seeing in the black music of twenty and thirty years earlier an antidote not only to the monetaristic swagger of big band swing but to the commercialism of mainstream American society as a whole.

The movement rapidly spread to the UK. In 1941, workers at the Vickers machine-gun factory in Crayford began giving weekly concerts in the back room of the Red Barn pub, Barnehurst, as George

Webb's Dixielanders. This kicked off the UK's 'trad jazz' movement, with Chris Barber, Ken Colyer, Humphrey Lyttelton, Kenny Ball, George Melly and Monty Sunshine causing huge excitement across the country. The apogee of this unexpected arc was the 1962 release of Acker Bilk's 'Stranger on the Shore', which spent fifty weeks in the UK charts and became the first ever British recording to top America's Billboard Hot 100, breaking the seal for future British acts including The Beatles, The Rolling Stones, Elton John, Rod Stewart, Pink Floyd and Queen. The irony of a bowler hat-wearing, striped waistcoat-toting, cider-sipping clarinettist from Somerset summitting the American charts with a slow, saccharine-heavy take on the black music of New Orleans laid the template for the compound set of ironies that would change American music over the rest of the decade. Bilk's popularity was such that 'Stranger on the Shore' was one of a handful of recordings that the crew of the Apollo 10 spaceship took with them on their mission to the moon in 1969. Not only is Whitey on the moon – he's listening to trad.

As far back as 1950, the Crane River Jazz Band had been notable for its 'breakout sessions', where Ken Colyer's brother Bill would play 78 rpm blues records between sets, giving mini-lectures to accompany them. This had morphed into Ken and Bill playing the songs of blues pioneer (and one-time driver and butler for the Lomaxes) Huddie Ledbetter, aka Lead Belly, on guitar and washboard. By 1953, the blues breakout sessions had eclipsed the popularity of the main band. To differentiate it from the band's main New Orleans jazz output, the music needed a name, and where else but black America to provide it? The music was named 'skiffle', a term referring to 1930s 'rent parties' in Chicago, where 'guitar-pickers' had traditionally played a more traditional, 'down-home' blues style in contrast to the urban jazz played in the clubs.

Skiffle's seminal moment was the release, in November 1955, of Lonnie Donegan's 'Rock Island Line'. Born Tony Donegan in Glasgow, but raised in the East End, he had taken the name Lonnie in order to sound like an American bluesman.* Having cut his teeth playing skiffle songs as a member of Colyer's Jazzmen, Donegan's version of Lead Belly's 'Rock Island Line' slammed into the UK top ten in January 1956, 'the year that the nation discovered the teenager'.[21] The tune had originally been written in the late 1920s by engine-wiper Clarence Wilson as a promotional jingle to advertise the 'Rock Island Line', an obscure stretch of Southern railway near Little Rock, Arkansas. It was a version by prisoner Kelly Pace, collected by the Lomaxes, which had been recorded by Lead Belly and re-released.[†]

Donegan's raucous version, complete with spoken intro in faux American accent, was a massive hit. Guttural and raw, it was a complete antithesis to the smooth, manufactured British pop stars of the time, with names like 'Dickie Valentine'. Among those inspired were thirteen-year-old George Harrison and fourteen-year-old Paul McCartney who, along with thousands of other teenagers, went to see his show at Liverpool's Empire Theatre in November 1956. Sixteen-year-old John Lennon started playing guitar the very next month, forming the 'Quarrymen Skiffle Group', named after his secondary school, Quarry Bank. McCartney joined them in 1957, George Harrison in 1958, and the group mutated first into 'Long John Silver and the Beetles', then 'the Silver Beatles' and eventually just 'the Beatles'. They had their first US Billboard No. 1 in February 1964: the beginning of the British Invasion which would see British acts topping the US charts for fifty-two weeks out of 104.[22] That the best-selling band of all time and the group most closely associated with the sixties should have been inspired to form by watching an escapee from the UK's New Orleans revival play bastardised versions of backwater blues songs from the

* His official line was that he adopted it after supporting American bluesman Lonnie Johnson at the Royal Festival Hall in 1952, when the announcer mistakenly announced him as 'Lonnie Donegan', but this claim was undermined by the fact that he had already been using the name for several months before that concert. Clearly, though, it made a better story than 'I wanted to sound more American'.
† The Lomaxes, naturally, took the lion's share of the intellectual copyright (and hence the publishing royalties), with little for Leadbetter and nothing for Pace or Wilson.

1920s and 1930s is yet another of the strange ironies of the history of jazz. And in a further twist of the knife, it was this same British Invasion – and white American groups that followed like the Grateful Dead, Jefferson Airplane and The Doors – that kicked jazz further and further away from youth culture and mainstream popular music.

Nor were the Beatles the only group of the British Invasion to have started playing music as part of the skiffle craze. Nine of the ten British groups to top the US charts in the 1960s – including The Rolling Stones, The Animals and Manfred Mann – owed their formation to the skiffle craze of the mid-1950s. This was equally true of later artists including Led Zeppelin, Cream, Rod Stewart, David Bowie, Small Faces and Elton John. Even the Bee Gees – the band most associated with the whitening of disco – began life in 1955 as a Manchester skiffle group called the Rattlesnakes.[23]

In brief: it took a series of white British groups to sell a version of black American blues back to white America. As with the innovations within jazz itself, black Americans received little credit and virtually none of the financial renumeration. Just as jazz had been divorced from its black roots with Whiteman's 'symphonic jazz' orchestras of the 1920s and Goodman and Miller's swing orchestras of the 1930s, the white rhythm and blues groups of the 1960s became millionaires with scant acknowledgement of where the music had come from.

In some cases, indeed, like La Rocca's comment above, this appropriation was accompanied by outright racism. The lowest point of this trajectory was perhaps the disgraceful spectacle of Cream guitarist Eric Clapton, drunk on stage at Birmingham's Odeon Theatre in 1976, expressing support for Enoch Powell's infamous 1968 'Rivers of Blood' speech:

> Stop Britain from becoming a black colony. Get the foreigners out. Get the wogs out. Get the coons out. Keep Britain white . . . Britain is becoming overcrowded, and Enoch will stop it and send them all back. The black wogs and coons and Arabs and fucking

Jamaicans and fucking . . . don't belong here, we don't want them here. This is England, this is a white country, we don't want any black wogs and coons living here. We need to make clear to them they are not welcome.[24]

While such opinions may have been terrifyingly widespread in the UK in 1976, the tirade is made especially repellent by the fact that Clapton owes his entire livelihood to his (admittedly skilful) appropriation of black musical styles. Not only was his music utterly steeped in the blues tradition, but he had just had his first No. 1 in 1974 with a cover of Bob Marley's 'I Shot the Sheriff'.[25]

Perhaps even scarier is how little public condemnation of Clapton there was and how quickly his reputation recovered. Clapton's rant lit the fire for the Rock Against Racism movement, where a central office supported grassroots activists across the UK to organise anti-racism concerts featuring artists including The Clash, Dennis Bovell's Matumbi, X-Ray Spex, Steel Pulse, Sham 69 and Misty in Roots, accompanied by the *Temporary Hoarding* fanzine. But by the time I was growing up in the 1990s, the incident's stain had all but disappeared and Clapton was once again a major figure in pop, reaching No. 2 on America's Billboard Hot 100 and No. 5 in the UK charts with 'Tears in Heaven' in 1991, his tribute to his deceased four-year-old son Conor. The ensuing 1992 album *Eric Clapton Unplugged*, a live recording of his acoustic session for the *MTV Unplugged* television series, became the best-selling live album of all time, shifting 26 million units. Clapton attempted to affirm his non-racist credentials through a collaborative album with blues legend B. B. King in 2000 and continued to receive accolades even in the last decade, ranking second in *Rolling Stone*'s '100 Greatest Guitarists of all Time' in 2012. He even joined arch jazz classicist Wynton Marsalis for the 2011 concert and live album *Play the Blues: Live from Jazz at Lincoln Center*. And yet Clapton, given the chance to apologise on numerous occasions, repeatedly blamed it on his alcoholism or maintained that he thought it was 'funny'.* Even David Bowie – who has a large mural dedicated to him in London's famously black area of Brixton – expressed support for fascism in the same period, describing Adolf Hitler as 'one of the first rock stars'.[26] Bowie did at least apologise for these comments later in his career – but I still find it amazing how these incidents have disappeared from view.

'We don't own nothing, man'

The process of white artists appropriating black musical styles and making infinitely more money than the black originators is, of course, not unique to jazz. Similar patterns can be seen in almost every style of black music, with the first white artists to bottle the latest variety of black creativity in a form that is palatable enough for white audiences to swallow achieving fantastic levels of success.

It needs to be stated that black musicians are not the only ones with tales of exploitation by the music industry: it has been non-discriminatory in that regard, equally happy to exploit musicians of all races. But whereas white musicians have been able at least to see themselves in the label hierarchy, black people have always been woefully under-represented inside label offices. The vast majority of record labels, including those that specialise in black music, have always been white-owned and run. This is still the case, both in the USA and UK.

Cleveland Watkiss

Listen man, we're three per cent in this country; how can it get any whiter? Because we don't own nothing, man. We don't run our own festivals and clubs. We don't have that power. We could, but we don't.

There have been a few notable exceptions, like Berry Gordy's Stax/Motown empire, which grew from a jazz record store in Detroit to the

* He did finally say he was ashamed of these comments in the 2017 documentary *Life in 12 Bars*, but this was very, very late in the day.

most successful black-owned label of all time. Achieving no fewer than seventy-nine top ten hits in the 1960s, Gordy recorded and released artists including The Supremes, Stevie Wonder, Diana Ross and Marvin Gaye.[27] Chicago's Vee-Jay Records, founded by husband-and-wife team Vivian Carter and James C. Bracken, broke artists including John Lee Hooker, Memphis Slim, Lee Morgan and Wayne Shorter. They were also the first American label to release The Beatles after signing a licensing deal with their British label EMI, whose US affiliate Capitol declined to release them. And as far back as 1921, Harry Pace founded Black Swan Records in Harlem, the first black-owned label, with the support of luminaries including James Weldon Johnson (chair of the NAACP) and writer W. E. B. Du Bois. Featuring legendary arranger Fletcher Henderson as the recording manager, the label launched the careers of Bessie Smith and Ethel Waters.

But this is a handful of outliers. Black-owned labels have always been as rare as Pace's evocatively titled Black Swan. It was not until the advent of hip-hop that the concept of independence became widespread, with black-owned labels like Sugarhill Records, Eazy E's Ruthless, Sean Combs's Bad Boy, Dr Dre's Aftermath, Jay-Z's Roc-A-Fella and Anthony Tiffith's Top Dawg Entertainment. Yet even within this area, it rarely took long for any label showing success to be partly or wholly bought by white-owned major labels. Similarly, in the UK, neither of the most important and influential labels for jazz and related music, Emil Shalit's Melodisc and Denis Preston's Lansdowne, were run by black people. This changed a bit from the 1990s onwards with the advent of independent electronic labels like Bryan Gee and Jumpin Jack Frost's V Recordings (drum and bass/jungle, 1993) and Mala, Coki, Loefah and SGT Pokes's DMZ (dubstep, 2004). Black-owned labels like Jazz Re:freshed and Gearbox have made significant contributions to the current jazz scene, as have artist-led imprints like Moses Boyd's Exodus and Shabaka Hutchings' Native Rebel. Nevertheless, these labels are very much still the exception rather than the rule.

unapologetic expression

The lack of representation within the labels is not only a question of artists being forced into unfair and illegal contracts, but also of not having control over how the music is presented and promoted. And in many cases, not being free to develop their artistry in the way they want to, because of a label's limited and highly commercial outlook. The pattern of major labels cottoning on quite late to a powerful grass-roots energy, watering it down and destroying it has been repeated over and over again.

Emily Moxon

I've been in the jungle scene in the nineties. And then the broken beat scene. So I've been in those scenes where you can see it's exploding. And typically what happens is major record companies come in and sign stuff and water the music down.

Kerstan Mackness

It reminds me of the Young Lions scene that came up after Wynton Marsalis. You had Wynton and you had Mulgrew Miller and some big musicians who were bringing jazz back to being jazz because it had been fusion for so long. And then after that every major jazz record label signed a Young Lion, to the point where there was a lot of that around and then everybody lost interest. That's the thing that we need to watch out for here. Record labels have a terrible tendency to sign things that sound like other hit things.

'I make black music, essentially'

I do not wish to set up a simple 'black good, white bad' binary or dismiss all white musicians as imitative and insincere. Lest I be called a snowflake, keyboard warrior or armchair activist, or be said to form part of Stan Getz biographer Dave Gelly's fear of 'some doomed attempt to write white people out of jazz history altogether',[28] let me state unequivocally: I have no problem whatsoever with white people playing jazz or any other black music form, in America, France, Germany, Sweden, Poland, the UK or anywhere else. Nor do I think it's true that white people have made no meaningful contributions to the art form. From Bix Beiderbecke to Stan Getz, Dave Brubeck to Tubby Hayes, John Surman to Bugge Wesseltoft, white musicians have made spiritually meaningful contributions to jazz, as well as technically clever ones.

But it is precisely through the recognition of jazz's origins as a black music of rebellion that its potential as a universal music of freedom can be unlocked. In foregrounding the role of black creativity within jazz innovation (and that of most other popular music genres also), I am not seeking to question the sincerity, skill or creativity of white musicians in general but to point out that in almost all cases, white musicians have reached a level of public success and approbation vastly different from their black contemporaries, who in most cases were the true originators of the style.

This legacy of appropriation and unequal life outcomes between black and white musicians is inseparable from the wider history of slavery, colonialism and racism out of which jazz first grew and which it is obliged to continue navigating. I believe that a clear-eyed acceptance of this fact is the first step towards jazz truly fulfilling the claims that have been repeatedly made on its behalf as a vehicle of universal expression and togetherness. For the white musicians of this generation, openly acknowledging the music's black roots and chequered racial history is the best route through the complexity.

Oscar Jerome

I was definitely always very aware of being a white musician playing African music and how that can be a complex thing. If you're just profiting from that and the people that have created and influenced the music are not getting the rewards that they deserve then obviously that is a problem.

unapologetic expression

Emma-Jean Thackray

I make black music, essentially. And I know that what I do is part of a black movement of liberation music that has evolved and become all these different genres throughout time, that has landed at this point where we are now. I know how complex it is to be part of that.

3

'Movementt'

Jazz, Colonialism, Slavery and Migration

Claude Deppa

I think of jazz as a migratory music. It was the harmonies and rhythms that went with the slave trade to the Americas across the Atlantic. There they came across Western instruments, trumpets. We had lots of drums, we had the kora. And then when they are introduced to military music, military instruments, they incorporated that.

Emma-Jean Thackray

The Movementt* mantra is 'move the body, move the mind, move the soul'. So stuff that has this visceral connection to groove, but also has the connection to the cerebral: is the actual musical content forward-thinking and interesting? And move the soul: stuff that's about real issues that need to be spoken about. The term Movementt is about these things, but it's also about recognising the movement of people. And the music I make is only possible because of the movement of people.

'Only the best will do'
(jazz as 'intercultural music')

One of the claims that has repeatedly been made about jazz is that it is 'intercultural music', born from the organic merging of African and European musical traditions. Celebrated British saxophonist John

---

* 'Movementt' is the name of Emma-Jean Thackray's label.

Dankworth explained in his 1998 autobiography (just a few years after *The Fast Show*):

> French military marches, English hymns, Irish dance tunes and African drum rhythms all made their mark, and out came a fresh, vital, compelling new musical language to match a new way of life . . . Jazz has since its beginnings been an instrument of goodwill and peaceful and gradual change rather than anything really revolutionary. An amalgam of origins, of styles, of methods, its attitude to race and ethnic background has always been all-embracing, and its view of society classless. Only its musical standards have remained from the outset unswervingly devoid of compromise – only the best will do.[1]

This passage's characterisation of jazz might to certain people, even on the book's initial publication in 1998, have seemed like the self-satisfied ramblings of a successful musician who had bought a large mansion in Buckinghamshire and become very much an establishment figure. Dankworth makes no mention of the history of slavery and colonialism that allowed the 'African drum rhythms' to 'make their mark', and seems, even by a moderate 2023 reading, to be wilfully ignoring both the racial and political context of the music. Whereas in the 1990s to say 'I don't see colour' was supposed to be understood as a sign of non-racism, by the early 2020s it had become widely understood that 'colour-blindness' is exactly that: blindness to the truth of the situation that, whatever the attitude of jazz itself to 'race and ethnic background', the attitude of those who disseminate it and buy it has often been a long way from 'all-embracing'.

Rather, jazz has been the site of multiple appropriations, elisions and sleights of hand, so much so that Dankworth renders its very origin story as a natural, gradual and peaceful evolution as opposed to the desperate struggle for survival and identity of multiple generations of brutalised people in a background of the most naked avarice and racism. The reconnection with these aspects of jazz's origins

– jazz as the unapologetic expression of an oppressed people, and jazz as the incidental by-product of wider geopolitical forces – are two of the major factors that have imbued the present wave of UK jazz with such power.

The Dankworth passage is very much of its time: Tony Blair's New Labour government had won a triumphant majority the previous year, promoting an optimistic vision of 'multiculturalism' that has since been characterised mockingly as 'saris, samosas and steel drums'; a multiculturalism that promotes the most visible cultural manifestations of diversity without acknowledging or addressing British society's structural racism, the legacy of its colonial past and the direct relationship between the two. This is the same multiculturalism whose 'failure' has been held responsible for the rise of the far right, the resurgence of xenophobic, anti-immigration narratives on both sides of the political spectrum, and the colossal economic and political own-goal that was the Brexit vote of 2016, when 52 per cent of those who voted decided to leave the European Union, many of them apparently attracted by a nostalgic mirage of imperial glory.

Falling in love with jazz in the late 1990s, I pretty much swallowed the Dankworth line that jazz was a vehicle for interracial and cross-cultural collaboration. I knew that Miles Davis had mixed bands, and a long and deep friendship with white arranger Gil Evans; I loved *Time Out* by the Dave Brubeck Quartet, but also *Mingus Ah Um*; I learnt to play 'Corcovado' and 'The Girl from Ipanema' from *Getz/Gilberto*,* which I interpreted simply as an open-minded fusion of jazz and Brazilian music. Any discussion of 'cultural appropriation' was a long way in the future, at least for me. This was the era of Alex Garland's cult 1996 backpacker novel *The Beach,* Manu Chao's *Clandestino*, the Western discovery of *feng shui*; there was a feeling that you could pick and choose the best elements of global cultures in the creation of an open-minded, globalised identity. Global travel was not a privilege but

* This was also a favourite of my infant daughter, who heard it more than any other record before the age of six months.

a right, not only a right but a good deed: it would make you broader in your outlook, a 'citizen of the world'. Young people like myself from middle-class, affluent families enjoyed unprecedented access to the world's culture, from Accra to Addis Ababa, Bali to Mumbai. Widespread awareness of the one-sidedness of this kind of travel, the unequal power relations which facilitate it, and the environmental and cultural devastation it leaves in its wake, would come later.

Dankworth, of course, is not totally wrong. Jazz has consistently been a vehicle of cross-cultural collaboration, for both musicians and audiences, and still is; indeed, the diversity of its musicians and the musical traditions it draws on has been one of the most celebrated elements of the current UK jazz scene. Yet his promotion of a 'compelling new musical language to match a new way of life' – conjuring images of the American dream, mass production, a grinning white dad driving a brand new Buick on a wide American highway in a toothpaste advert – ignores so many of the important aspects of jazz's history which give the music meaning.

The story of jazz's birth in New Orleans and subsequent spread to the rest of America and worldwide suggests that jazz has always been the unapologetic expression of people battered by forces that have nothing to do with music, people who are struggling to make sense of life in a brutally unjust world. This understanding of its central meaning and purpose is coded deep inside the music itself and continues to bear relevance.

Theon Cross

The history of jazz is documented in New Orleans and in Congo Square and the story of that is very powerful. You had these people that were enslaved that came from various parts of Africa and some that even migrated from various parts of the Caribbean and Haiti, which were all in this one place where they had to work forcibly against their will. And then were permitted on Sundays to actually perform and be resilient and express themselves away from having to be labourers.

And the joy comes from having that freedom to express themselves away from being in bondage. That energy is powerful and has radiated so much different sounds and feelings, entwined with gospel and entwined with blues. It's a very powerful root, and something we need to bear in mind every time we play. These are people that were embarrassed and shamed and brutalised, but out of that brutality they were able to have the resilience and strength to create music that still has longevity today. So I think with that mindset, with us that have so much less against us – I'm not saying things are perfect but we have much less against us – we must also use our music as spiritual freedom.

'What were those soldiers doing there in the first place?' (A brief history of New Orleans)

It is no accident that the music that came to be known as jazz originated in New Orleans, with its unique combination of ethnic elements. Marshall Stearns, founder in 1952 of the Institute of Jazz Studies[2] and author of *The Story of Jazz* (1956), identifies many of jazz's musical elements as distinctly West African: rhythmic complexity (affectionately rendered as the 'rhythmic spark'), blue tonality (especially the famous flattened fifth), call and response, the falsetto break, and the tradition of insult songs, which also gave rise to calypso.

Stearns suggests the Spanish preference for Yoruba slaves, the French for Dahomean and the British for Ashanti was responsible for the diverse musical traditions across colonial territories. Further, he identifies New Orleans as unique for having both a genteel community of prosperous 'Creoles of colour', many of whom would be sent to study in Paris and could play classical music, and the surrounding plantations as a repository of African musical traditions, with many plantation slaves having little or no contact with European musical styles. He notes the persistence in New Orleans of an underground culture of *vodun* (voodoo/hoodoo), identifying striking similarities with the ceremonies practiced in Haiti and Togo, and showing how these rituals fed into the energetic 'escape valve' represented by the weekly performances in Congo Square from 1817 to 1885. And he sees in the fusion of the European marching band tradition and West African funeral parade one of jazz's most important breeding grounds.

Yet while it is satisfying on an ethnomusicological level to recognise these elements in jazz's development, they shed very little light on the music's actual meaning and purpose as regards the individual lives of those who played and heard it. Okay, so jazz originated in New Orleans through a combination of African and European elements, but how and why did those elements get there in the first place? Everyone knows that military bands were an important element in the creation of jazz, but how many people ask the follow-up questions: who do military bands work for and what was the objective of these armies? If jazz is 'a peaceful instrument of goodwill', it is ironic that it owes its existence, in part, to warfare.

New Orleans was founded in 1718 by the French Mississippi Company in the homeland of the Chitimacha, a tribe whom archaeological evidence shows had occupied the region for six thousand years. They were decimated, as per the usual colonial pattern in the Americas, by a combination of disease and warfare: first through infections of measles, smallpox and typhoid, contracted through trade dealings with French colonists, and later through outright warfare as they fought to maintain a hold over their ancestral territories.

Like the British East India Company (standing army: three hundred thousand), the Dutch East India Company (forty warships, ten thousand private soldiers) and the Hudson's Bay Company (at one point the largest landowner in the world, exercising control over 15 per cent of the North American land mass), the French Mississippi Company was one of a few hundred chartered companies that were integral to colonialism.

I mention this detail to reinforce the point that the ethnic history of New Orleans – and America in general – is not simply a historical accident of various groups organically blending together to create the hybridised 'new way of life' which Dankworth evokes. Rather, the city owes its very formation to the exploratory avarice of French colonists who came there to make money, and had no qualms about exterminating the local population in order to repossess their fertile land. To support the cultivation of this land, they brought slaves from Africa in such large numbers that, by 1810, slaves and free people of colour made up 63 per cent of the city's population.[3]

It is this French presence that puts the 'dix' in Dixieland, referring to the 'dix' on the ten-dollar bills printed in the city, with the wider state of Louisiana named after Louis XIV. The city itself was named after Philippe II, Duke of Orléans. It was under French rule that the *Code Noir* – Black Code[*] – was formalised in 1724, forbidding all religions except Catholicism, effectively forcing the *vodun* traditions of many of the slaves underground. As the practice of *vodun* is a question not only of private faith but of group ritual involving singing, drumming and dancing, it is possible to see here the beginnings of jazz as a form of underground community-building and rebellion, bringing its practitioners together in joyful, defiant self-expression. These roots have persisted throughout jazz's history, right through to the present UK wave.

New Orleans was ceded to Spain in 1763 as part of a complicated three-way treaty to resolve the Seven Years War. Spain controlled the city until the French reclaimed it in November 1801, only for Napoleon to sell it to the British in 1803 as part of the Louisiana Purchase, in which Britain bought from France the right to exploit the entire Louisiana territory.[†] This marked an era of rapid expansion as New

[*] This is the same Black Code that gives its name to Wynton Marsalis' 1985 album *Black Codes (from the Underground)*, very deliberately reinforcing Marsalis' position as the custodian of the New Orleans tradition.
[†] Far larger than modern-day Louisiana state, this was at that time a vast territory of 828,000 square miles covering the whole length of the Mississippi river, stretching right up to Canada and including land that now forms part of no fewer than fifteen modern US states and two Canadian provinces.

Orleans became the main access point for settlers in the new southern territories and the main port for sending raw materials back up north, as well as one of the most important interfaces between the United States and the rest of the world. The city's population doubled between 1803 and 1810, in part also because of the immigration between 1791 and 1810 of a large number of French planters and their slaves from Haiti, who fled the island after Toussaint L'Overture's successful revolution of 1791, in which a community of slaves overthrew their French colonial masters.[4] This was followed by a secondary immigration in 1809 of French planters who had fled Haiti for Cuba but were expelled by the Spanish in 1809, adding Yoruba influences into New Orleans' cultural mix.

Not even in the top ten in 1800, by 1840 the city had grown to become the third most populous in the United States and by far the biggest in the South, a position it maintained until it was overtaken by Houston in the 1950 census.[5] Then, as now, home to a population of majority African descent,[6] it was notable for a sizeable population of *gens de couleur libres* – 'free people of colour' – descended both from black slaves and white slave owners. Enjoying an elevated status according to a colour hierarchy not unlike that which still obtains in modern Jamaica, this group was often prosperous and highly educated and considered themselves very different from 'Negroes', even after slavery was formally abolished in 1864. Universal (male) suffrage gave blacks the right to vote when the Fifteenth Amendment was ratified in 1870, and so in 1872 Louisiana elected its first governor of African descent, P. B. S. Pinchback; no American state would elect another black governor until Virginia selected Douglas Wilder in 1989, nearly 120 years later.

Yet these political gains were short-lived, with the violent white supremacist White League and Red Shirts active from 1874 suppressing the black vote and supporting the Redeemers (white Democrats[*])

---

[*] Unlike now, where Democrats are usually seen as left-wing and Republicans on the right, in the nineteenth century it was the Republicans who abolished slavery and the southern Democrats who wanted to maintain it.

to gain political power. The situation in the city worsened with the introduction of Jim Crow laws from 1889, effectively disenfranchising the majority of the city's black and Creole citizens and initiating an era of racial segregation which did not formally end until the civil rights era of the mid-1960s. Where the city's Creoles had previously enjoyed a separate status and social life, they were, from this period, 'forced to join their darker brothers'.[7] This was an extremely significant moment in jazz's development, as Creoles of colour like Kid Ory, Sidney Bechet, Alphonse Picou and Jelly Roll Morton – schooled in the European classical, written tradition – began to interact with musicians more steeped in African traditions.

The story of jazz is intimately connected with military conquest, slavery, oppression and segregation. This is the real context that gave rise to jazz, and its meaning as an art form is intrinsically linked to the wider forces which created it. I believe that to see these contexts as responsible for the technical and stylistic development of jazz but not also to see jazz as a spiritual and political reaction to them is in large part responsible for the mainstream sense of jazz by the 1990s as stuffy, pompous, self-indulgent and pointless; in other words, as a music that had lost touch with its fundamental purpose. It is in reaction to this apolitical, colour-blind stance that the present wave of UK jazz is so vital.

The Great Migration
(the jazz diaspora)

While the birth of jazz in New Orleans was an inadvertent by-product of colonialism and slavery, the second phase of its development was directly related to modern warfare and consumer capitalism, as over a million black people migrated from the rural South to the cities of Kansas, Chicago, St Louis and New York during the 1910s and 1920s, changing the urban culture of those cities and creating new contexts for the music.

unapologetic expression

This was the first phase of a migration which saw 6 million African Americans move from the South to other parts of the United States between 1916 and 1970, changing the black population from mostly rural to mostly urban. Proactively recruited by Northern factories as the supply of cheap European migrant labour dried up due to the First World War, many blacks rushed at the chance to escape a lack of social and economic opportunities in the segregated South, exacerbated by the spread of racist ideology and the infamous Jim Crow laws.

Once jazz had penetrated America's major cities, it was rapidly disseminated worldwide, a story intimately linked to America's political and economic dominance in the twentieth century. As early as 1916, dance bandleader James Reese Europe was recruited to create a permanent regimental band for the 15th Heavy Foot Infantry Regiment (Colored) in order to recruit more black soldiers to America's war effort. By 1918, the band was in France, performing in twenty-five French cities in February and March to boost morale both amongst soldiers and the French civilian population,[8] giving many people in Europe their first encounter with a music broadly recognisable as jazz.

This technique was repeated in the Second World War, when dance bandleader Glenn Miller was recruited in 1942 to set up his American Dance Band for the Allied Expeditionary Force. Originally a tool of recruitment and morale-boosting, this became a vital instrument of American soft power throughout the Second World War (despite Miller's disappearance in 1944),[9] performing and broadcasting across Europe.

The American consumer capitalist boom of the 1920s, still referred to as 'the Jazz Age', had established a powerful link between jazz, prosperity and consumer products, with jazz helping to position America as the land of freedom and plenty, idealised by many in a still industrialising Europe. This image became even more pronounced after America's intervention in the Second World War, and the tactic was formalised in 1955 with the official adoption of jazz as a tool of cultural diplomacy. This was the height of the Cold War, and between 1955 and 1963 the US State Department sponsored no fewer than four-teen 'Jazz Ambassadors' tours, sending artists including Dizzy Gilles-pie, Louis Armstrong, Dave Brubeck and Jack Teagarden beyond the Iron Curtain to the USSR and Communist Eastern Europe, as well as South America, Africa, Asia and the Middle East. These tours were vital in inspiring a love of jazz in these territories, many of which still have vibrant jazz scenes.

The irony that the black jazz artists being co-opted into promoting Brand America were not even allowed to sit on the same buses as their white colleagues back home was not lost on the musicians themselves. Even the famously diplomatic Louis Armstrong was so incensed at President Dwight D. Eisenhower's failure to censure the segregationist stance of Arkansas governor Orval Faubus* that he cancelled an inter-national goodwill tour in 1957, denouncing Faubus as an 'uneducated ploughboy' and Eisenhower as 'two-faced'.[10] Nevertheless, jazz contin-ued to be used to promote an idealised vision of America well into the current century.

'Once the sound gets out there' (the Black Atlantic)

In the Soho jazz scene of the 1940s and 1950s, being told you 'sounded American . . . was the highest compliment you could ever receive'.[11] It was to this end that John Dankworth, Ronnie Scott and friends joined 'Geraldo's Navy',† a dance band playing on the transatlantic cruise ship *The Queen Mary*, in order to hear their American idols live on New York's famous 52nd Street. To that generation, jazz was an American art form which English musicians could only hope to imi-tate. Stuart Nicholson has observed that 'the halo effect of American

* This is the same Faubus lampooned in the Mingus composition 'Fables of Faubus', where the awkward, loping groove of the music mocks the ungainly physicality of Faubus himself.
† So named for its leader, Gerald Bright.

culture as the home of modernity, futurity and the always new often creates a "cultural cringe" factor in certain contexts; that is, a feeling of inferiority causing people to dismiss their own (jazz) culture or aspects of their (jazz) culture as inferior to the American model'.[12]

This view relies on the idea of America as the birthplace of jazz and American musicians as the ultimate authority. Where many in Dankworth's generation strove to 'sound American', later British musicians like Django Bates, founder member of 1980s big band Loose Tubes, consciously rejected the American tradition.

Django Bates

Although we didn't talk about it that much, there was just this tacit understanding that we would play no swing in Loose Tubes. It was important for us to play at Ronnie Scott's club and not play one bar of American jazz. It was quite funny and quite a statement. We didn't have to explain or defend our position. In the environment of Ronnie's, the thing one was most aware of and wary of was American jazz, so we played everything else.

In both cases of imitation and rejection, though, America remains the central star around which all others must orbit. But the most interesting and 'authentic' local jazz scenes, in my view, are those which assimilate local elements, be they the highly jazz-influenced Ghanaian highlife scene around E. T. Mensah, the township jazz of Abdullah Ibrahim (Dollar Brand) or the clean, Scandinavian sound of Esbjörn Svensson, Nils Petter Molvær and Bugge Wesseltoft.

Shabaka Hutchings

Americans might like to think that they can own everything. But once the sound gets out there, someone can listen to it and decide: I want to take it as a starting point. That's just the way music has been for ever. That's what it means to play and enjoy music. You hear something you like and it stays with you. And you add to that.

The present crop of UK jazz musicians have undoubtedly achieved this, consolidating a powerful local identity outside the shadow of American dominance through drawing on their own cultural heritages and London's extreme musical richness. Indeed, it is this distinctive and unique local identity that has caused America to take note, with many of the UK jazz musicians in this wave being signed to American labels. In this sense, they fit into a wider history of UK musicians reshaping black American music, whether the Beatles, the Rolling Stones, The Yardbirds and Cream taking black American blues and selling it back to white America as pop, or jungle's pioneers adding speed and MDMA to black American soul and gospel and shoving it through the mad grinder of the UK's rave scene. Even EDM (short for electronic dance music), the term that emerged in the late 2000s when the white American music industry suddenly 'discovered' electronic music (despite black America being the birthplace of house and techno), drew much of its sonics from UK dubstep, with the bass wobble of pioneers like Skream, Mala and Benga rendered as the harsher, more aggressive 'brostep' of acts like Skrillex and sold to a new generation of white ravers across the USA who may not even have known the music's black origins.

Bradley Zero

Americans respect it more when we do it in our way. Like with rap and grime. So much early hip-hop was just people putting on American accents. They never took it seriously. But now, the whole wave of grime, they're like, 'Okay. You've got something different going on here.' Stormzy or Kano or whoever it is coming through, they're actually listening now. 'Cos the guys are not just parroting them. And there seems to be a whole lot of communication back and forth between the US and the UK now in terms of the new wave of jazz coming through.

I would go further and say that assessing jazz simply as an American or not-American art form is a reductive and myopic view. Rather, jazz and its myriad associated forms should be seen as part of a wider collection of hybrid musics born from the colonial and postcolonial experience. In this view I am indebted to Paul Gilroy's concept of the 'Black Atlantic', densely but wonderfully articulated in his 1993 book of that name. Referring to the triangular trade between Europe, Africa and the Americas, Gilroy posits a unity of Afro-diasporic cultures that transcends national borders. Black musical styles in Europe, the Americas and the Caribbean are linked by 'Black Atlantic' commonalities that place jazz as part of a continuum that includes American blues, funk, disco, hip-hop, house, techno, Jamaican reggae and ska, UK lovers' rock, jungle, garage and grime, Brazilian samba, Colombian reggaeton, Cuban rumba, Congolese soukous, Nigerian Afrobeat, Afrobeats and every other style of black syncretic music that has been created before and since.

Oscar Jerome

Jazz is just *a* form of music that is continuously evolving with popular culture and youth culture. That's what jazz has always been. Think about Dizzy Gillespie, when a lot of Puerto Rican and Cuban people started coming to New York, he got really involved in mixing that into his music. Or if you think of the seventies: funk; eighties: people were using a lot more electronics and synths and stuff and then nineties: hip-hop. What people are doing in the UK seems like it's an obvious continuation of that. You're just mixing up the sounds that are going on around you with your love for jazz and the heritage of that music.

Kehinde Andrews, Professor of Black Studies at the University of Birmingham, points out the analogous relationship between the Great Migration from the Deep South to the Northern industrial power-houses of the United States and that from the Caribbean to the United Kingdom during the Windrush era of 1948–62.[13] Although separated from the seat of imperial power by the Atlantic Ocean and nearly 5,000 miles, Jamaica was technically British soil until 1962. Its citizens were British citizens.* In both the Caribbean and the American South, Africans had been transported as slaves in order to work the land after the indigenous population had been annihilated. In both cases, former slaves migrated to the industrial centres when beckoned by job opportunities.

Seen from this angle, it is possible to see parallels between the development of British Caribbean communities in the UK, following the migrations of the Windrush era, and the communities of black people from the Deep South formed in Chicago, Detroit, St Louis, Kansas City and New York out of the mass migrations of the early twentieth century, and those formed in Los Angeles and Oakland in the mid-twentieth century. It was from exactly these communities that disco sprang in New York in the 1970s, and house and hip-hop in the 1980s; Motown, p-funk and techno from Detroit from the sixties through to the nineties; and West Coast funk and gangsta rap from LA from the seventies through to the nineties.

In brief: somewhere between twenty and thirty years after a mass migration, second generations began to create their own original culture, influenced by but distinctly different from the culture of their parents and grandparents. Is it not logical that, from the 1980s onwards, the Black British children of the Windrush generation – the generation of jazz musicians Courtney Pine, Orphy Robinson, Cleveland Watkiss, but also Omar, Fabio, Grooverider, Goldie, Jazzie B, Norman Jay, Trevor Nelson, Daddy G, Roni Size – should have begun to develop their own unique UK styles, powered by the interaction between the music they

---

* Technically they were 'citizens of the United Kingdom and colonies'. This was part of the post-war rebranding of the British Empire in which the occupants of her many dominions suddenly became 'citizens' rather than 'subjects' – a branding exercise not unlike many supermarkets' elevation of 'staff' to 'store colleagues'. Mass immigration to the UK was an inevitable but apparently largely unintended consequence of Britain's refusal to give up her self-image as global superpower and centre of the empire. This became extremely problematic at different points, such as the Kenyan Asian Crisis of 1967, when Britain flouted international laws by refusing entry to her own citizens (South Asians living in Kenya but holding British citizenship). See Ian Sanjay Patel's excellent *We're Here Because You Were There* for more about this.

heard at home and the music they heard at school, in clubs and on the radio, giving rise not only to the Jazz Warriors but Good Times, Metal-headz, The Wild Bunch, Shake 'n' Fingerpop, Soul II Soul?

Similarly, the 1990s and 2000s saw unprecedented African immi-gration to the UK, with nearly half a million African-born black people in the UK by 2008, many fleeing persecution and poverty. They came primarily from former British colonies – Nigeria, Ghana, Somalia, Zimbabwe, Uganda and Kenya – with Nigerians by far the largest group.[14] This demographic and their descendants have con-tributed enormously to the sound of UK jazz: the brothers Femi and T. J. Koleoso (Nigeria) of Ezra Collective, Sheila Maurice-Grey (Sierra Leone), Onome Edgeworth (Nigeria), Mutale Chashi (Zambia) and Cassie Kinoshi (Nigeria/Jamaica) of Kokoroko, Camilla George (Nigeria), Blue Lab Beats (Ghana) and Mark Kavuma (Uganda) among many more, along with those of Caribbean heritage like Sha-baka Hutchings (Barbados), Wayne Francis (Grenada/Barbados/St Lucia), Yussef Dayes (Jamaica), Zara McFarlane (Jamaica), Theon and Nathaniel Cross (Jamaica/Guyana), Moses Boyd (Jamaica/Domi-nica), Nubya Garcia (Guyana/Trinidad) and Poppy Ajudha (Guyana).

Many if not all of these musicians were influenced from an early age by Afro-diasporic musical styles via their parents' record and CD collections. Rather than thinking of jazz in the UK as simply an Amer-ican art form given a specific regional flavour, I believe that the process of cultural fusion that has occurred as a result of the Caribbean migra-tion of the Windrush era and the African migration of the 1990s and 2000s is akin to factors that occurred at some of the most significant moments of jazz's development, specifically its birth in New Orleans and its growth through the Great Migration. Whereas many Ameri-cans have a generalised 'black American' identity, meaning that Amer-ican jazz has continued to draw on the blues, soul, R & B and hip-hop for cultural inspiration, it is the closer connection of UK musicians to cultural and ethnic influences outside of the American jazz tradition which has given this wave its vitality.

Shabaka Hutchings

If you acknowledge that you are in the industry of the spectacle, how do you keep yourself new and innovative? And that's maybe a question that a lot of American jazz musicians haven't needed to ask because they've been so wrapped up in the self-righteousness of their own culture. Whereas in England, there's not that preciousness about what it has to be.

Sheila Maurice-Grey

What's happening in America and what's happening here are two different things. In so many ways we are trying to be as hip and cool as Americans. And then in so many ways, the Americans are actually now looking to the UK and being like, 'Oh, okay, hold on. You guys are playing Afrobeat and you guys are doing all of this and all of that, calypso.' I feel like we've got a bit more of a direct connection to our Afro-Caribbean heritage than Americans might do. So actually, we play Afrobeat way better than Americans do.

Tapping into their own heritages while intersecting with the freshest developments in youth culture have helped this generation reclaim jazz as a vital and meaningful form of self-expression.

Gordon Wedderburn

They play what they live, listen and grow around, so whether it is in Brixton, where you have that multicultural community, where you hear reggae, you hearing Fela, you hearing Indian music, whether it is in Catford, Dalston or Hackney. They're playing what they're hearing and they're playing from their origin. So Nubya is a blend of Trinidad and Guyana. Moses is a blend of Dominica and Jamaica. Ezra between them, Barbados, Nigeria, and they're playing what is there, what they're seeing.

Poppy Ajudha

My dad owned a nightclub in Deptford, he was from sound system culture; my nan came over on the *Windrush*. The reason that I'm making music in South London is because my dad was there and decided to open a club there, and was part of the sound system culture before that. Artists like Yussef or Theon, Moses Boyd, who bring culture back into it: that's natural. You can't create that just from inspiration, I think that comes naturally from your cultural background. That's mixing where you're from with what you've learnt, which is always the way that something new and innovative is created.

Aly Gillani

One part of the British Empire to another. And then to the heart of it. Here we all are.

'How do you know Ghanaian music?'

There is a deep circularity underpinning so much of the UK's black music. UK jazz is not simply an imitation of an American art form; both American jazz and the current wave of UK jazz are expressions of a wider Black Atlantic culture. It is true that the vitality of this wave of UK jazz is the direct result of movements of people that are analogous to conditions that gave rise to earlier key phases in the music's development, but it is also important to clarify that these developments do not always happen in a linear way. The development of jazz is as complicated and multifaceted as the movements of the people who created it. Though it can be helpful to describe a broad pattern of African and European elements fusing to create jazz in New Orleans via blues, spirituals, gospel and military marches, the reality is a complicated circle of cross-penetrations and shifts that defy simple explanation.

This has always been the case, but has become even more pronounced in the internet age, when developments in a regional scene are instantly disseminated worldwide.* While untangling the web of musical influences informing the present wave of UK jazz is both impossible and unnecessary – it is this very complexity which gives the music its richness – there are two complications worth observing.

The first is the fact that there are multiple generations co-existing simultaneously. According to my theory above, the music produced by second-generation immigrants is marked by a particular vitality born from the intersection of their cultural heritage with the local influences they have absorbed: this is the case with the children of the Windrush generation (like the Jazz Warriors) and the children of African immigrants (like the Koleosos). But there are also third- and fourth-generation descendants of Windrush immigrants (like Poppy Ajudha) as well as the British-born children of immigrants who spent formative years in their parents' homelands (like Shabaka Hutchings and Wayne Francis).

Second is the total lack of purity of these 'ethnic' influences. Even the origin story of jazz, which posits the idea of pure 'African' tribal music as its source, involves a reduction of complexity that negates, for example, the hundreds of years of Islamic influence on West African music, long before slaves were taken to the Americas. This problem is even more pronounced when discussing African and Caribbean influences on the current wave of UK jazz, as the 'source' materials in these cases are already hybridised forms: reggae, calypso, Afrobeat, highlife; as well as US- and UK-created hybrids like grime, hip-hop, house, drum and bass, broken beat, disco and techno. What is being discussed is, in fact, a hybrid of a hybrid of a hybrid. Wayne Francis has strong memories of listening to a particular kind of US hip-hop while growing up in the Caribbean: is that an American influence, or a Caribbean one?

---

* Paradoxically, although this has resulted in a broadening of many people's musical horizons, it has in some ways resulted in a flattening of localised sounds; this is one of the reasons for the strong similarities between the sound of some UK Afrobeats artists and Nigerian counterparts like Burna Boy and Davido: musical developments influence each other so fast that it can become difficult to tell them apart.

It has been noted that the Caribbean heritage and experience of sound system culture of US hip-hop pioneers like Kool Herc, KRS-One and Notorious B.I.G. was integral to the creation of hip-hop, just as it was to the birth of jungle, garage, dubstep and grime in the UK. But there is a deep circularity in this: reggae grew from ska, ska from Jamaican versions of American R & B. Where did R & B come from? Like the Indian father in the late nineties sketch show *Goodness Gracious Me*, who constantly claims central figures from Western culture and religion as Indian,* we have no choice but to shout, 'R & B? Jazz! Ska? Jazz! Reggae? Jazz!'

Examples abound of the cross-fertilisation of Black Atlantic cultures. The Afrobeat style of Fela Kuti and Tony Allen has been noted as a major rhythmic force for UK bands like Kokoroko and Ezra Collective. But to regard this as a purely African influence would be to misunderstand the music's complex history. Now seen as a definitively Nigerian style, Afrobeat was always a hybrid, derived from the intersection of jazz, funk and Yoruba musical styles. Kuti trained at Trinity in London – the same college as Moses Boyd, Femi Koleoso, Nubya Garcia and Oscar Jerome – and was inspired by Soho's jazz scene of the 1950s, and by the 1960s and 1970s godfather of funk, James Brown. The patriarch of Afrobeat drumming, Tony Allen, was heavily influenced by the 1950s jazz drumming of Art Blakey, before he himself came to influence the new generation of UK drummers in the 2010s.

Further, just as new musical styles in New York and Chicago affected what was played in New Orleans, there was a constant interface between music created in the UK and its Caribbean and African sources. People in Jamaica did not stop following Joe Harriott simply because he had left for the UK; quite the opposite: success in the UK could often lead to even greater support in Africa and the Caribbean. Nor was it limited to the country of origin; support could travel all across the Commonwealth. The Trinidad-born, UK-based calypso star Young Tiger was so

---

* e.g. Superman ('Runs faster than a train: must be an Indian train!'); Jesus Christ ('Works for his father . . . Indian!') and so on.

popular in Nigeria that he was invited to compose the new country's national anthem in 1960 (he declined); reggae and dancehall have long been huge in West Africa. Even Mulatu Astatke's haunting Ethio-jazz sound was honed during his time as a student in London in the 1960s.

The UK's free jazz scene as espoused by John Stevens, Derek Bailey and Evan Parker was heavily influenced by the South African Blue Notes and Brotherhood of Breath – musicians who had themselves, like Abdullah Ibrahim, created a unique fusion of American jazz through mixing it with South African styles like kwela and mbaqanga. Even jungle, one of the UK's proudest and most distinct musical genres, is based on sped-up samples of Gregory Coleman's 'Amen break', performed on the black American soul group The Winstons' B-side 'Amen, Brother'.[*]

My favourite example of this deep circularity and cross-pollination between African diasporic musical styles was when I was DJing at a festival in Ghana in 2018, and the (Ghanaian) DJ before me, Gafacci, played 'Man's Not Hot'. Mocking an insistence on keeping on one's coat in the most inappropriate settings, it's a spoof grime track by Big Shaq, the comedy alter ego of London-based actor and rapper Michael Dappah, Croydon-born child of Ghanaian immigrants. I noticed two German girls singing along with gusto to some of the most memorable parts ('The ting goes grrrrrrrrrrrrrrrrrap! Bup bup kak ka kak!! Skidiking bak bak! Ana Whoop boop beerap boom!') and then witnessed their surprise as they saw another European girl doing the same and asked her – with a hint of the competitive nativism I've often observed in Europeans who live in Africa for more than a few weeks towards those whom they consider simply tourists – 'How do you know Ghanaian music?'

---

[*] A seven-second drum break, the 'Amen break' is the most sampled passage in the history of recorded music. In 2021 it had been sampled over five thousand times by signed artists including Salt-N-Pepa, N.W.A and Oasis, as well as electronic artists of all flavours but especially hardcore, drum and bass and jungle; it even made an appearance in the *Futurama* theme tune. Coleman died homeless and destitute in 2006, having never received a cent in royalties.

4

'London Town'

Jazz and Postcolonial London

Femi Koleoso

I can only talk for me and TJ, really. But we are so London, we can't dress it up any other way. Listen to my accent, bruv! You can't really hide that. And I think previously, in some ways, [London] jazz lacked a localised identity. That was something that was very, very strong in jazz in the early days, you can hear a New Orleans trumpet player from a New York one in seconds. You can hear that beat, you can hear that Chicago swing. And hip-hop has always had that so strong, you listen to drill, I'll be like, 'That brother is from Brixton, I can hear it.' I can hear the difference between a North London grime sound and a Manchester hip-hop sound. You can hear LA in Kendrick . . . Hip-hop's always had that, and jazz used to have that, but it lost it for a bit – there's a bunch of records that I can't tell where they're from. You know like ECM – it was a label sound, it wasn't a city sound; I couldn't hear it. Maybe an expert would be able to hear it. But bands like the Ezra Collective, we made jazz sound like London again for a bit, d'you know what I'm saying? And I think that is something that people find attractive. People are proud of where they're from and they love to discover where they're not from. It's important to stamp where you're from in a vivid way and I think it's been done well with the London jazz sound.

It is no accident that the UK in general and London in particular served as the central focus for the blending of musical styles from Africa, the Caribbean, Europe and the Americas. As the symbolic and administrative centre of the British Empire, London was the natural meeting place for its global subjects, and it is this fact more than any other that can take credit for its unique position in the world's cultural landscape. Successive generations of immigrants – Huguenots, Jews, Irish and, especially after the Second World War, Caribbeans, Asians and Africans – have shaped the city's musical culture. Paris can tell a similar story, with musical styles from Mali, Senegal, Côte d'Ivoire, Algeria, Tunisia, Morocco, Réunion, Madagascar and Martinique informing the city's music. Same thing in Lisbon, with Angolan *kizomba* and *kuduro,* Cape Verdean *morna, funaná* and *batuque* and Mozambiquan *marrabenta* exerting a powerful influence.

Pioneering Trinidadian steel pan player Russ Henderson, a central figure in the founding of Notting Hill Carnival, once remarked that he did not meet Caribbeans from other islands until coming to the UK. Prince Buster became good friends with Ambrose Campbell, the Nigerian guitarist and percussionist based in London at the same time, who was a major influence on the UK's jazz musicians of the 1950s and 1960s and lauded by Fela Kuti as 'the father of modern Nigerian music'. Even the Beatles' major pop hit 'Ob-la-di Ob-la-da' is inspired by a Yoruba phrase (meaning 'life goes on') 'borrowed' from Nigerian conga player Jimmy Scott-Emuakpor.[*1]

The effect of London's diverse postcolonial population on the city's music has been amplified by the lack of ghettoisation facilitated by London's post-war reconstruction. Whereas the Parisian *banlieues* dramatised in films like *La Haine* (1995) and *Gagarine* (2020) are almost different cities from Paris,[†] and the picturesque, crumbling grandeur of the digital nomads' central Lisbon is belied by the vast social housing projects and quasi-legal favelas on the surrounding hills, London is famous for having million-pound houses within

* Interestingly, Scott-Emuakpor asked for a publishing share of the song, but was refused, with Paul McCartney insisting it was 'a common phrase'. Not in Liverpool, though, mate!

† This is literally true: the city of Paris has an official population of only 2 million while Greater Paris (i.e. outside the Peripherique) is far larger. The *banlieues* are technically different cities.

metres of council estates, and this mixture is reflected in the music.

Nor is it simply a question of pouring ingredients into London's famous 'melting pot' and serving the mixture that comes out at the end. A more apt metaphor would be multiple pots constantly boiling, burning, growing cold and overflowing, with steaming mixture being poured between the pots in vague and haphazard quantities and periodically served out after repeated imprecations by stressed, underpaid waiters.

Around the turn of the millennium, I first encountered the term 'psychogeography' in Iain Sinclair's accounts of walks around the metropolis, haunted by ghosts of its past. It became fashionable to talk about the city as a palimpsest: literally a reference to a sheet of parchment which, given the preciousness of paper as a resource, would be multiply inscribed by successive generations of monks in a kind of medieval upcycling. In literary terms, this meant having your own experience of the living city encroached on by that of Blake, T. S. Eliot, Rimbaud and, in the case of Sinclair's East London, jazz-loving gangster twins the Krays and Alan Moore's *Watchmen*.

This is true in architectural terms also. London has none of Haussmann's grand, Napoleon-sponsored nineteenth-century reconstructions of Paris that spelt the end of its arcades, the 'human aquariums'[2] beloved of the city's *flâneurs;* instead it remains a higgledy-piggledy mess of architectural generations superimposed on top of each other, with 'a mind of its own, organic and anarchic, at its best when it grows from the gutter up'.[3]

Musically, also, it is a palimpsest. It is not only that London's astounding cultural diversity has been the breeding ground for some of the world's most creative hybrid music. It is also that *the hybrid forms and the ingredients which made the hybrid forms are all still existing at the same time*. Yes, you can trace a linear route from reggae to dub to jungle to dubstep. But you can also still find every one of these genres played in some corner of one of London's thousands of venues, not to mention the uncountable house parties and after-hours sessions that take place in the city every single night. Jazz can mix with grime

– which itself evolved from garage and jungle, which evolved from reggae, dub and funk, soul, house and hardcore. But each of these forms still exists; jazz can also mix with any and every one of these genres individually, creating a layering of hybrid music upon hybrid music, intertwined with successive migrations and constant circular connection with Africa, the Caribbean and the Americas.

In genealogical terms this would be something like conceiving a child by a man, then conceiving subsequent children by his father, his grandfather, and multiple half-brothers and distant cousins. Scientifically fascinating but messy, dangerous and likely to result in some scary mutations and almost certainly multiple levels of intergenerational familial strife.

Marshall Stearns described each Caribbean island as 'a sort of musical test-tube in which West African and European music have been mixed in more or less known quantities, thus furnishing possible clues to what must have happened in the United States'.[4] London is the opposite, destined to frustrate any scientific experiment, with the ingredients in the tube mixed so many times that it is impossible to separate the components. Like the clean and separate colours of my daughter's Play-Doh, they are destined to arrive at a composite mush, frustrating all attempts to separate them, but it is worth identifying and paying tribute to some of the musical shades that have contributed to London's unique mix.

Moses Boyd

You look at the UK music industry, there is this big shift of like, we're not pandering to America. We're looking at what's happening here, which wasn't a thing when I was growing up. You look at your Stormzys or your Skeps or your AJ Tracey, these man are superstars here. Back in the day, it was just So Solid Crew or Dizzee. The fact we've got an ecosystem of all of these things – there is definitely something bigger that I can't explain what it is and why it's kicked off.

unapologetic expression

'I'm a badman from Nigeria'
(grime and Afrobeats)

First hitting the mainstream in 2003 with Dizzee Rascal's Mercury-winning *Boy In Da Corner* album, grime had evolved as a faster, harder, more MC-driven form of UK garage. Garage artists like Oxide and Neutrino, So Solid Crew, Heartless Crew and Wiley's Pay As U Go Cartel had begun alienating older, slicker, champagne-swilling garage ravers with rapid vocals accompanied by hyped-up, bass-heavy 140 bpm beats,[*] and by the first few years of the millennium this off-shoot of garage had carved out its own unique identity.

Grime holds a special significance for this wave of UK jazz for three reasons: musical, organisational and representational. Grime had been *the* major musical influence for many of the musicians of this wave as teenagers. This affection audibly resonates within the music: the skippy, stuttery, staccato rhythms of Moses Boyd's drumming; the heavy, threatening basslines of Theon Cross's tuba; the urgent, driving offbeat skank of Ezra Collective.

The unapologetic swagger of grime's pioneers affirmed an attitude of independence, both in terms of aesthetics and career choices, signifying independence from traditional music industry power structures and a distinctive London identity. Rather than trying to fit in with earlier clichés about how jazz musicians should dress, speak and carry themselves, the success of grime stars like Skepta and Dizzee showed that you could wear a tracksuit and still win the Mercury Prize.

Femi Koleoso

I used to dress like what I thought jazz musicians would dress like – I used to wear hats and I used to wear suits. Very earliest Ezra gigs, man

---

[*] The default tempo on FruityLoops, the grime producers' weapon of choice (along with the PlayStation) and apparently the reason for almost all grime (and kaduro and dubstep) being at this tempo. The same logic probably accounts for the popularity of 120 bpm for house music made on Ableton Live.

would've worn a suit. Yeh bruv! That's what we thought we were meant to do! We looked at Empirical as our heroes. Then one day we were like, we're playing loads of Afrobeat, let's wear African clothes, we did some gigs wearing some of Dad's African tops and stuff. And then it came to the point where it was like, you know what bruv, I'm from *Enfield*, man, let me just wear the uniform like everyone else and I would put on a tracksuit, play the gig and the rest is history, know what I'm saying?

Despite the excitement around *Boy in Da Corner*, the first wave of grime was hamstrung almost at its inception by a demonisation of young black males that was manifested in ASBOs – the notorious antisocial behaviour orders that could be used to issue curfews and bans on appearing in certain places for even some of the most basic infractions – and the hated Form 696 that nightclub owners and promoters were required to fill out, detailing the type of music that would be played and offering demographic expectations about their clientele. Introduced in 2005, this was essentially a racist requirement of the Metropolitan Police, labelled as 'risk assessment', designed to crush black music under the guise of protecting against an explosion of gun and knife crime. Garage and grime were disproportionately targeted, with events in these genres regularly refused permission to go ahead. This and a crackdown on pirate radio stations meant that many of grime's pioneers simply gave up, finding themselves unable to earn a living. Music industry prejudice and fear, public demonisation and licensing crackdowns made it difficult for grime to expand its following to the larger white market that would have sustained its creators, as it had for hip-hop in the USA.

Dizzee Rascal and Wiley had both followed up their initial success with deliberately commercial releases like Dizzee's 'Dance wiv Me' (with Calvin Harris, 2008) and 'Bonkers' (with Armand van Helden, 2009) and Wiley's 'Wearing My Rolex' (2008). This initiated a brief period of utterly disposable pop/grime/dance crossover tracks like Tinchy Stryder's 'Number 1' (ft. N Dubz, 2009) and Tinie Tempah's

'Pass Out' (2010), but apart from a handful of pop outliers, most of grime's original pioneers stopped working altogether or moved on to other genres like then-popular 'UK funky'.*

This began to change around 2014, when what came to be known as 'Grime 2.0'[5] picked up steam, with Skepta winning the coveted Mercury Prize in 2016. By 2019, Stormzy was headlining the entire Glastonbury Festival. Backed by international stars like Kanye West[†] and white singer-songwriter Ed Sheeran, Grime 2.0 was truer to the spirit of grime than many of the pop-dance emissions of the previous years. Early grime instrumentals were upcycled, like Ruff Sqwad's 2004 'Functions on da Low', which forms the instrumental for Stormzy's No. 8 chart hit 'Shut Up'. Grime 2.0 managed to repackage itself as responsible, mature, adult and serious, in a way that could be reliably loved and consumed by a white audience, with far less of the danger that put them off the first time.

'Act like a wasteman? That's not me!': Skepta's 2016 'That's Not Me' (with brother Jme) distances himself from the kind of promiscuous, materialistic behaviour glorified by other grime artists like the unreconstructed weed-smoking chauvinism of one of grime's founding fathers, D Double E. In contrast to the notorious unreliability and often bizarre Twitter outpourings of grime godfather Wiley,[‡] Skepta and Stormzy positioned themselves as the leaders of a new generation of grime artists: decent, reliable, humble, intelligent, together.

This was nowhere more evident than Skepta's 2016 Mercury Prize acceptance speech where, clearly moved, he brought his mother and father, in full Nigerian dress, on to the stage with him, thanking them

* A fusion of grime, funky house and soca, with upbeat, syncopated club rhythms often accompanied by vocals about sex and partying, like Funky Dee's 'Are You Gonna Bang Doe', Donae'o's 'Party Hard' and LJ ft. C. Los's '079 Me'.
† Kanye invited many of grime's stars to come on stage with him at the 2015 Brit Awards, an event referred to through kissed teeth in Stormzy's 2015 single 'Shut Up' where he voices his displeasure at being referred to as a 'back-up dancer'.
‡ This reached its apogee in the anti-Semitic outpourings of July 2020, which resulted in him being shunned by much of the music industry.

and his whole community of supporters and collaborators. I was at that ceremony as the agent for nominees The Comet Is Coming and remember Pulp's Jarvis Cocker explaining that while Bowie's post-humous *Blackstar* album was a serious contender, the committee of judges finally chose Skepta because Bowie would have wanted Skepta to win. The symbolic power of a legend of Britpop projecting the blessing of a legend of art-pop on to a new legend of grime was huge: a powerful affirmation of Black British culture not seen since Dizzee Rascal's 2003 Mercury win for *Boy In Da Corner*, the album that kick-started the original grime wave.

Not only was this a great result for grime, it was a celebration of DIY culture in general, a common ethos linking grime with both punk and UK jazz. Skepta had achieved his success with minimal industry backing but vast support from within his own community, with the *Konnichiwa* album released on Boy Better Know, the label run by himself and Jme.* In this sense, Grime 2.0 served as a shining example of what could be achieved independently without dampening down your sound or selling out to major labels. Though Boy Better Know and others struck distribution deals to make use of major label infrastructure and resources, they maintained ownership and brand control: a hybrid model which would be adopted by Ezra Collective, Moses Boyd, Poppy Ajudha and others.

Kerstan Mackness

What jazz does at its best and the way that it grew up in London, is it's community music. And that's where the parallel with early hip-hop is. Or grime. You're talking about community music made by people in the community for people in the community. That's the nub of this thing.

* An amazing figure who, after demonstrating his ability to solve a Rubik's Cube in under a minute while extolling the virtues of 'mud hump jumping' on a BMX in the 2006 *Run the Road 2* bonus DVD, went on to popularise veganism to a new generation and encourage black people to vote in the 2018 and 2019 UK elections as the poster boy for the 'Grime 4 Corbyn' campaign.

Skepta's success was another powerful boost for British Africans, fore-grounding the specific contribution to UK culture made by African rather than Caribbean immigrants. Whereas in the 1980s and 1990s it was sometimes thought to be cool to be Jamaican but not African, with many teenagers of African descent adopting Caribbean mannerisms and speech, a new generation grew up taking confidence from grime stars expressing pride in their African heritage, including Skepta (Joshua Joseph Adenuga, Nigeria) Stormzy (Michael Ebenazer Kwadjo Omari Owuo, Jr, Ghana) and Dizzee Rascal (Dylan Kwabena Mills, Ghana).

This new confidence was epitomised by the slick, tech-savvy lead characters of Michaela Coel's enormously popular 2020 BBC series *I May Destroy You*, code-switching between hypermodern London patter and the African accents of their elders.

Femi Koleoso

Nigerians have started becoming superstars. When you think of Wizkid, Burna Boy, Skepta, Jme – especially Skepta and Jme: I remember one bar when I was in year six, Skepta says, 'I'm a badman African bwoy, in school used to hit man with the ruler, English teacher try and make me hoover, but I'm a badman from Nigeria':[6] I heard that when I was about ten years old. And that put pride in me: 'I'M a badman from Nigeria', do you know what I'm saying?'

And the moment you see something that you look like and it's successful, that's powerful. And that's why young black kids don't get particularly inspired by cricket or horse racing or classical music because we can't see ourselves in it, because there is no representation. But then you see yourself in grime and you see yourself in hip-hop and then I found jazz and now I'm seeing myself everywhere.

Even fiction began to reflect the change; the third series of *Top Boy* (Netflix, 2019), the gritty drama telling the story of Hackney's street gangs, showed Dushane and Sully (played respectively by Ashley Walters of garage crew So Solid and grime/hip-hop star Kano), the

Anglo-Jamaican kingpins who 'ran the roads' in the original 2011 series, finding their territory controlled by Jamie, new 'top boy' on the estate. The show made absolutely clear Jamie was of African descent, stressing his strong commitment to family and patriarchal role in looking after his two younger brothers after the death of their parents, supporting his middle brother's university studies and tenderly making sure his youngest brother has done his homework before going out to murder Turkish gangsters in cold blood. Looking out-of-shape and washed up after his exile in Jamaica, Dushane is forced to confront London's new diaspora power dynamics.

'Just jazz music from an African' (world music)

Grime was not the only factor generating pride in African heritage: the 2010s saw a generally increased pride in heritage of all kinds in opposition to Americanised mass culture, and the explosion in popularity of the new global African pop genres Afrobeats and Afro-swing also had an influence, especially on UK artists of African heritage like Not3s, J Hus, Yxng Bane, Tion Wayne, NSG and Kojo Funds.

Anyone who has ever played Scrabble knows the value of an 's' in adding to an existing word and scoring all the points of that word before even starting your new word. I have no idea if DJ Abrantee – the Anglo-Ghanaian DJ reportedly responsible for coining the term 'Afrobeats' in 2011 – is a Scrabble player but I would like to believe he is, so perfectly does it encapsulate what happened. Like 'swing', where the swaggering big band jazz of the 1930s and 1940s was re-appropriated in the 1990s to refer to the sleazy bedroom slow-jams of R. Kelly and Jodeci, or R & B, where the rhythm and blues of the 1960s was reclaimed by nineties female harmony groups like Destiny's Child, the addition of an 's' to 'Afrobeat' brilliantly ingested that music's symbolic power while creating an entirely new and much more commercial genre.

The original 'Afrobeat' referred to the political fusion of jazz, funk and Yoruba rhythms created in Lagos in the 1960s and 1970s by vocalist/trumpeter/activist/womaniser Fela Kuti and drummer Tony Allen. 'Afrobeats' refers to the range of musical styles created in the 2000s and 2010s in Nigeria, Ghana and London from a fusion of funky house, UK funky, R & B, dancehall, hip-hop and West African rhythms and melodies, especially the ubiquitous kpanlogo bell pattern.[*] While artists like Wizkid, Davido and Burna Boy became huge stars both locally and internationally, the close postcolonial connection between Nigeria, Ghana and the UK rapidly resulted in UK versions, as well as direct collaborations across the Atlantic (e.g. between UK funky pioneer Donae'o and Ghanaian hip-hop artist Sarkodie, and later larger collaborations between Skepta, Burna Boy and others). This was the Black Atlantic on steroids, with the ubiquity of the internet and smartphones and the increased prosperity of West Africa creating an accelerated feedback loop with the UK.

The visibility and financial success of Afrobeats was in stark contrast with the Western portrayal of Africa and its music in the 1980s, where African pop stars had tended to be ignored entirely or seen through the lens of world-music exoticism. The former was epitomised by the 1985 Live Aid benefit concerts in London and New York arranged by Bob Geldof (Boomtown Rats) and Bono (U2). Although organised to provide support for the relief of the 1983–5 Ethiopian famine, these concerts disregarded not only the vibrant and unique music of Ethiopia itself, but of the entire continent: not a single black African artist appeared among a who's who of British, Irish and American pop acts including Queen, Madonna, Sting, David Bowie, Mick Jagger, Bryan Adams and even Eric 'the UK will become a black colony' Clapton.[17] This omission, despite the availability of African artists – including Fela Kuti, Miriam Makeba,

---

[*] Also known in Cuba as the son clave, this is a cornerstone of much African music: *_ _ *_ _ *_ _ _ *_ *_ _ _ (*=hit; _=ghost note).

[†] African pop stars Mory Kanté and Manu Dibango did in fact launch their own Pan-African single, 'Tam-Tam pour l'Éthiopie', to raise money for Médecins sans Frontières, but that hardly excuses the omission.

King Sunny Adé, Manu Dibango, Hugh Masekela, The Bhundu Boys, Thomas Mapfumo, Salif Keita, Ladysmith Black Mambazo, Mory Kanté and Oumou Sangaré, and Ethiopian masters like Mulatu Astatke, Mahmoud Ahmed and Tlahoun Gèssèssè – helped create a stereotype of Africa as backward and desperately in need of help whilst totally ignoring its cultural richness.* This reinforced the implication of the Band Aid single 'Do They Know It's Christmas?', written by Geldof and Midge Ure, which went to No. 1 in the UK charts in December 1984 and went on to sell 3.8 million copies, making it the best-selling UK single ever until displaced by 'Candle in the Wind 1997', Elton John's tribute to Princess Diana. Painting a picture of Africans so poor they do not even know it's Christmas, the song, for all its good intentions, remains a monument to the arrogance, ignorance and cultural insensitivity of the West. Does Geldof even know that not all Africans are Christian?

By contrast, the first edition in 1982 of ex-Genesis member Peter Gabriel's WOMAD festival sought to shine a light on global talent. UK artists like Echo and the Bunnymen, The Beat, Simple Minds and Gabriel himself performed alongside an international line-up including the Drummers of Burundi, Shankar, Prince Nico Mbarga, Tian Jin Music and Dance Ensemble, Ekomé and Ustad Amjad Ali Khan, many of whom came up to join Gabriel for the closing set.† WOMAD – 'World of Music and Dance' – has become a successful global brand, celebrating forty years in 2022, attracting over forty thousand people each year to its flagship UK edition and running regular festivals in

* I remember as a small child in the late 1980s being told by my nanny, 'Think of the starving children in Africa,' any time I didn't want to finish all my fish fingers. These images can be hard to shake. Despite knowing that the Ethiopian famine had much more to do with politics than actual scarcity, I am ashamed to say I was still surprised on my first trip to Africa (Ghana, 2003) by the sense of abundance, generosity and well-fed people eating hearty meals of *kenke*, *banku* and *fufu*.
† A video of their performance of 'Biko' – Gabriel's song in support of South African anti-apartheid activist Steve Biko – can be seen on Gabriel's website (petergabriel.com/news/biko-at-womad-1982). It confirms many people's worst stereotypes of 'world music', with master musicians from multiple traditions blended into a dull slurry, subordinated to the predictably insistent rhythms of early 1980s drum kit.

Australia, New Zealand, Singapore and Spain. Gabriel and his team would also go on to found Real World Records in 1989, part of a clutch of 1980s UK labels including Stern's Africa (1983), World Circuit (1985) and Riverboat Records (1989). Yet while WOMAD and similar festivals sought to spotlight global talent rather than ignore it, it is possible to see WOMAD and Live Aid as two sides of the same hierarchical, neo-colonial coin. Just as development organisations from the IMF and World Bank down position the West as global philanthropists while exerting a powerful hold on exactly what that development should look like, ignoring the history that caused such global inequality in the first place, so the positioning of Western organisations as arbiters of the world's culture is deeply problematic.

Paula Henderson

What we can't escape from is the fact that WOMAD is a UK-based events organisation that is mainly run by white men and women. We are cherry-picking the best that we can. But that's so that we're giving that opportunity to as many musicians as possible. Someone like the Malawi Mouse Boys wouldn't ever have received the kind of fee that we're prepared to pay in order for them to come and play the festivals and do a tour, and have successfully carried on working because actually they're worth an investment in order to see them and support them to carry on. And that's always felt like a good thing, because if an event like WOMAD doesn't put out a reasonable fee in order for them to be able to play, they're never going to leave that roadside selling mice on sticks. That's just a fact. Artists need us as much as we need them. And it does feel like a partnership that's letting us do this, I'm not sat there thinking, 'I've bestowed this on to you in order to play our marvellous festival.' We have a huge appreciation for all the artists that come. That's why we respect them and we wouldn't ever have an artist feel like they haven't been treated properly or paid appropriately in order to be able to come to the event.

These festivals and labels were part of a broader movement of 'world music'. Coined in the 1960s by ethnomusicologist Robert E. Brown, 'world music' gained currency in the 1980s as a marketing term to cater for the growing interest in music outside Western pop, rock, jazz and classical traditions. Essentially, it was used as a catch-all for any other music, lumping together everything from Celtic folk music, Rajasthani classical music, Mongolian throat-singing, Scandinavian hurdy-gurdy and the diverse musical traditions of Latin America, Africa and the Caribbean.

Tom Excell

I don't think it takes a genius to realise that the term 'world music' is just stupid and doesn't make any sense. We don't live in any other world than this one, so that's all music essentially, which is a bit of a mad term if you break it down.

As far back as 1978, Edward Said's *Orientalism* noted the fascination of British writers with the East and their unfortunate habit of blinding themselves to the realities of lived experience through the super-imposition of exotic stereotypes. This fascination with a stereotypical idea of a primitive Other has been manifested in the way 'world music' has often been presented: the prevalence in programme notes and press releases of adjectives like 'pure', 'traditional', 'unbroken', 'tribal', an obsession with 'authenticity', traditional dress, customs and languages, and a focus on the personal histories of the performers.* This captivation with the spectacularly exotic links world music as a movement with the stereotypical depictions

---

* I remember going to WOMAD in Reading in 2006 and seeing Emmanuel Jal, who the programme was at pains to point out had been a child soldier in Sudan and Ethiopia. I remember watching the crowd of well-meaning middle-aged people in tie-dye and African prints and thinking, 'They all love the fact that he had been a child soldier, and wish him well. But am I the only person in this entire field who can see that the guy can hardly rap?' It is only fair to note that Jal's rapping did improve, and his career had a second bump at a time when African music had become more fashionable among electronic audiences after German house master Henrik Schwarz's remix of 'Kuar' became an international club anthem.

of otherness at the World's Fairs of the Victorian era that followed the Great Exhibition of 1851, and the shameful story of Sarah Baartman, the 'Hottentot Venus', who was exhibited semi-naked for nineteenth-century Europeans to gawp at her 'vulgar' proportions.

That a catch-all like 'world music' can have existed in the first place is not so surprising. Like most genre terms, its primary function was to allow music to be categorised for display in record shops and label catalogues, and in this regard it was reasonably successful. More surprising is that so self-evidently absurd a term should have continued to be used up until now by sensitive, intelligent individuals who have dedicated their whole lives to working in this field.

Part of the problem is the term itself, which carries the full weight of Anglocentric entitlement. Some people now prefer the term 'global music', which conveys a similar meaning without the same painful images of silver-haired white couples in tie-dye dancing awkwardly to Baaba Maal in a Wiltshire field.* But the issue is not only linguistic – it is to do with the innate absurdity of lumping the musical output of the entire world into one term. As well as the uneven global power dynamics that this reinforces, it also leaves little space for the intense circularity of the world's musical cultures. Much of the 'world music' that occupied stages in the 1990s was deeply influenced by other musical forms, especially – dare I say it – jazz. This was true not only of 'world fusion' projects but of much music that was presented simply as African: Fela Kuti, Manu Dibango, Mulatu Astatke, etc.

Adam Moses

We were putting Dele Sosimi on as African jazz in the early 2000s, before Afrobeat became cool again, and that's another part of how things are presented by press and media, because they'll tell you, 'This

* The alleviation of some of the historical burden through the use of a linguistically equivalent term without the same complications has parallels with 'coloured' – a common term in the UK in the 1970s, which by the 1990s was considered offensive; it re-emerged in 'people of colour' in the 2010s.

is world music and this is Afrobeat.' When I hear Afrobeat, I'm like, 'Yeah, but that's just jazz music from an African.' It's purely jazz music. It sounds like jazz music, it's jazz funk and it's just got an African accent to it. It's just part of the spectrum.

That a lot of the music to have graced WOMAD and other festivals over the years was clearly jazz-related but considered to be 'world music' rather than jazz may have to do with musical tribalism: music needed to be put into categories and people would self-identify as jazz fans or world music fans, but not both.

Paula Henderson

If you go back twenty-five years ago, there was a jazz scene that was almost unreachable unless you were involved in it. There was the world scene and indie and pop. We were all put into little boxes.

This sectarianism was not only a facet of the world music scene: David Jones, the 'world guy' at Serious, recalls the anger and hostility he and partners had to face when putting on African acts at the London Jazz Festival in the 1980s and 1990s.

David Jones

So many things in the eighties were quite stifling compared to what they are now. There were opportunities, there was money to do some things, but there were so many assumptions that have just been blown aside by change and by people who quite naturally will relate to any kind of music. You wouldn't believe the shit John* and I got for the first five years of setting up the London Jazz Festival until about the year 2000 – that was the watershed. But until then, people were going, 'You're booking all these African artists, what do you think African music's got to do with a jazz festival?' It's like, where do you think jazz came from?

* The late John Cumming, co-founder of Serious and the London Jazz Festival.

Glastonbury's West Holts stage was known in the 1990s and 2000s as the 'Jazz World' stage. This should perhaps be taken not as evidence of a perceived synergy between those two 'genres' but as part of the same attitude that created the term 'world music' in the first place: *we'll stick everything that is not rock, pop or indie over there.*

Also at work may well have been some of punk's hostility to jazz. The world music scene has been said to have been founded 'once punks grew up and had kids', and the fact that many of the people who were instrumental in the creation of 'world music' as a category tended to have backgrounds in punk and post-punk may have meant that any jazz links were overlooked or suppressed rather than encouraged.

Paula Henderson

A number of the founders that were working with Peter [Gabriel], their focus was far more on that kind of indie-punk side of things. And it shows in a lot of the programming, Siouxsie and the Banshees played in '84/'85 kind of time. I mean, if you turned around now and said, 'Would you put on Siouxsie and the Banshees at WOMAD?', you'd say, 'Really? can't quite see it myself.' But that was what was going on then. Jazz was kind of seen as pretentious, people with their trendy little goatee beards, drinking Martinis. At that point you wanted something very raw, which is what that punk and indie scene felt like at that time. It was basically two fingers up at prog rock and all that kind of nicety that had been going on for so long. And I think jazz also got put into that, which is, 'That's for nice middle-class people who sit around in groups and chat over cocktails,' and so on.

For all the problems with world music as a term, WOMAD, Real World and associated festivals and labels played an important role in diversifying the musical tastes of the UK public and offering musicians a chance to see non-Western performers live. While the early days of the world music industry put a strong emphasis on showcasing 'traditional' cultures or on very obvious fusions like Transglobal Underground or Afro Celt Sound System, by the 2000s new generations had grown up attending WOMAD and listening to Real World, World Circuit and Rough Guide releases and compilations alongside a range of other music.

While these outfits continued to showcase international touring bands, a powerful grassroots movement provided opportunities for emerging UK musicians not only to see big ticket 'world music' acts on large festival stages but to meet them, jam with them and, in many cases, form bands with them. Focused around Dalston's Passing Clouds and offshoot the (New) Empowering Church, this scene had a focus not on 'world music' as a spectacle but on organic fusion between different musical styles, bringing them into twenty-first-century London. Musicians like Moroccan *gnawa* master Simo Lagnawi, Algerian Seddik Zebiri, Congolese guitarist Fiston Lusambo, Gambian kora player Jally Kebba Susso, Zimbabwean marimba player Kudaushe Matimba and Nigerian keys player/vocalist Dele Sosimi would regularly hang out there, meeting musicians from the UK and elsewhere – including jazz musicians of this wave like Shabaka Hutchings and Wayne Francis. Bringing a wealth of cultural experience but open to contemporary influences (Dele played with Fela Kuti, Kudaushe was the youngest member of the Bhundu Boys, Fiston had played with Kanda Bongo Man and Samba Mapangala), this scene was important in bringing together 'world', jazz and electronic influences and helping lay the template for an organic appreciation of African music.

'The whole world music as rare groove thing' (edits and reissues)

In contrast with the world music scene's emphasis on live performance by glamorous international stars and studio albums with high production values, the 'African rare groove' scene fetishised the raw and unpolished. Where world music seemed to oscillate between a quest for 'authentic' traditional recordings and the slick eighties pop of Salif Keita and Baaba Maal, the reissue world welcomed the in-between: experiments with outdated synthesisers and production techniques and flash-in-the-pan local obsessions with American styles. Compilations like *Nigeria 70: The Definitive Story of 1970s Funky Lagos* (Strut, 2001), *Nigeria Rock Special: Psychedelic Afro-Rock And Fuzz Funk in 1970s Nigeria* (Soundway, 2008) and *Racubah!: A Collection Of Modern Afro Rhythms* (Comet, 1999) emerged to showcase neglected pockets of global musical history.

Quinton Scott

The world music and jazz scenes in the eighties and nineties didn't tend to cross into each other's orbit too much until DJs began waking up to original rare grooves from Africa during the late nineties. After Fela Kuti died in 1997, New York DJs in particular began producing tracks in his spirit. Masters At Work released a whole series of Afrobeat singles for clubs, then Kerri Chandler and Jerome Sydenham on Ibadan Records, Joe Claussell, Dennis Ferrer. The reissues started then too. Universal released several box sets of Fela Kuti's albums and labels like Strut, Comet and Counterpoint started to look further into African music for the rare grooves that DJs might play in the West, specifically the time from the early seventies when African bands were being influenced by James Brown's funk and soul. There was a strong rare groove scene during the late eighties, especially in London, and it always surprised me that some of the DJs from that time didn't pick up more on that and track down some of the great African records that were being made during that era. But, beyond Fela and Manu Dibango, not much of it was being played and the world music DJs during the eighties and nineties didn't really value that side of the music so much. So, it took collectors like Duncan Brooker to break the mould – his *Afro Rock Vol. 1* album from 2001 is really the first to explore deeper African rare grooves from the seventies involving original African labels, producers and artists, and a lot of ripples were created from that release. Many more compilations followed in the years that followed and a whole new raft of labels came through.

While Polygram rapidly released box sets of Fela Kuti's work under the Kalakuta imprint specifically created for this purpose, independent labels popped up to shine a light on neglected African urban music including Comet (France, 1998), Strut (UK, 1999), Soundway (UK, 2002), Analog Africa (Germany, 2006) and Awesome Tapes From Africa (USA/Germany, 2011). This echoed parallel developments in Latin music, with labels like Soul Jazz (UK, 1992), Far Out (UK, 1994) and David Byrne's Luaka Bop (USA, 1988) issuing compilations like O *Samba* (Luaka Bop, 1989), *Brazilian Love Affair* (Far Out, 1998) and *Nu Yorica!: Culture Clash in New York City: Experiments in Latin Music 1970–1977* (Soul Jazz, 1996).

Although primarily a DJ and collector culture, the reissue scene, like trad jazz and Northern Soul before it, helped revitalise the careers of artists including Pat Thomas, Ebo Taylor, Orlando Julius, Mulatu Astatke and Tony Allen as they made the all-important transition from 'old musicians' to 'living legends'. While many of the American folklorists who helped repopularise the blues have been criticised for prioritising an infantilising vision of 'primitive' rural folk music as a political alternative to their distaste for modern, urban music, the narrative in this strand of revival was not for imagined purity but for a nostalgic vision of an earlier iteration of technological advancement that might be termed 'retro-futurism': the same fetishisation of earlier visions of the future to be found in the canonisation of eighties and nineties sci-fi films and series like *Blade Runner, Terminator 2* and *Red Dwarf.*

This aesthetic reached its apogee in the activities of Awesome Tapes From Africa (later just Awesome Tapes), the alter ego of American ethnomusicologist, DJ and journalist Brian Shimkovitz.[*] Shimkovitz won popularity from around 2010 initially through the Awesome Tapes From

---

[*] Brian changed his DJ name to simply 'Awesome Tapes' in 2022 'to avoid any confusion about where I'm from or who I am', though the label continues as Awesome Tapes From Africa. See awesometapes.com/about for more detail on the reasons behind this, and further comments on the label's ethics and inclusivity policy.

Africa blog, where he offered, for free download, MP3s converted from cassettes collected during his ethnomusicological expeditions around Africa. Like UK dancehall DJ Gabriel Myddelton, aka The Heatwave, who would host free downloads of the latest Jamaican and UK dancehall on his website, Shimkovitz amassed a huge following that he was able to convert to lucrative global DJ bookings. This popularity was enhanced by the novelty effect of performing exclusively with cassette decks, fetishising both the music and the retro technology that plays it.

Awesome Tapes and The Heatwave have been controversial figures: in both cases, the music they were offering for free download on the websites through which they built their popularity was music they did not own and had no legal right to distribute; yet it was equally clear they had a deep love of the music and the culture which helped introduce the music to a wider audience, creating ancillary benefits for some of the artists they featured.

As their popularity grew, both set up legitimate labels, with Myddelton's Heat Wax releasing contemporary dancehall and Shimkovitz's Awesome Tapes From Africa label releasing a combination of new African music and reissues. Awesome Tapes From Africa's spotlighting of forgotten African music resulted in new tours for Ghanaian singer Ata Kak, Somalian disco pioneers Dur-Dur Band, Ethiopian keyboardist Hailu Mergia and Ghanaian producer/radio presenter DJ Katapila. Ata Kak toured Europe in 2016–17, with a new band that included South African producer Esa and veteran Zimbabwean bassist Pax Nindi. While the band managed to pull together a solid show, it seemed to me that much of Ata Kak's popularity revolved around the very awkwardness of the thing: his vague, inconsistent vocals, awkward manner and the brash sonics of his vintage Casio keyboard. This point was made still more clearly when DJ Katapila played Cafe Oto, Dalston's respected centre for experimental music, in 2018. Accompanying his selections with esoteric vocalisations and live percussion played on a vintage drum machine, customised in primary colours using electrical tape,* the set reached a surreal crescendo with nineties pop trash 'We Like To Party' (Breakin', 1998) by Dutch act The Vengaboys. The hip, mostly white audience responded with a mixture of confusion and delight: this was a song that no self-respecting white DJ would play, under any circumstances, yet somehow, Katapila playing it almost made it alright. And yet everyone in that room, with the possible exception of Katapila himself, felt the song was still trash.

This was 100 per cent cultural meaning and 0 per cent musical, with any intrinsic pleasure coming from the awkwardness and ambiguity of the juxtaposition. Is Katapila launching into oblique musical meta-commentary on the Western gaze? Or does he just like the song? I found this moment deeply uncomfortable, sensing a patronising indulgence in the 'quaintness' of Katapila's tastes that was eerily reminiscent of the stereotyped hard living of the early blues artists; Lead Belly forced to perform for New York bohemians in prison clothes. Re-listening to Katapila's records, I began to wonder the same: are these being released for their musical merit or merely because they sound basic, fetishising the low production values of a 'poor' man making music in a 'poor' country with limited musical equipment?†

Despite these problematic wrinkles, the reissue/African rare groove movement helped to make many styles of African music accessible to

* The object in question inspired the cover of Katapila's *Aroo* (Awesome Tapes From Africa, 2018) and currently hangs in my studio in Camberwell, where Katapila left it after replacing it with a newer model he acquired in London, proving that what for a Western audience might be twee retro-fetishisation was, in his case, simply improvisation with limited resources, happily replaced as soon as newer technology became available.
† I checked with Brian what he thought about this paragraph, and he was eager to make a distinction between Katapila's productions and his DJing, commenting, 'I personally just like Katapila's music and I found that it fits sonically and musically with the popular music you hear a lot on the radio in Ghana (especially pre-Afrobeats). His DJing definitely ended up being a bit goofier than expected, but he is just playing the songs that he plays at Ghanaian weddings, etc., so it is what it is, depending on your worldview. The reason I began working with him is because of his compositions/recordings not because of his DJing which I hadn't even really heard before he visited. It wasn't a thing where I wanted to present something goofy to people as cute African culture or something.'

UK musicians, broadening their musical knowledge and helping to create a receptive, more knowledgeable public who would recognise and welcome elements of Afrobeat, highlife or Ethiopian jazz when they saw it in the live shows of Ezra Collective, Kokoroko and Nubiyan Twist.

The church of Fela Kuti began to attract an ever-increasing number of parishioners, and Africa 70/Egypt 80* alumni in the UK like Dele Sosimi and Bukky Leo enjoyed an improvement in their status based on their association with 'the Black President'. The revival in popularity of Afrobeat led to the creation of homegrown UK-based Afrobeat and highlife bands in the 2000s like Soothsayers, Yaaba Funk, Afrik Bawantu and London Afrobeat Collective, with horn sections featuring jazz musicians including Jason Yarde, Idris Rahman and Robin Hopcraft. Dele Sosimi's long-running Afrobeat Vibration night at the New Empowering Church in partnership with Japanese DJ/producer Koichi Sakai helped to bring the music to new, dancing audiences.

While not entirely white, this was definitely not a black scene. As per the pattern with both trad jazz and Northern Soul, black people in the capital would be more likely to dance to contemporary Afrobeats and grime than indulge in a retro fetish. Among the bands themselves, the common pattern would be to have one or two African bandleaders or singers like Dele Sosimi, Richmond Kessie (Yaaba Funk) and Afla Sackey (Afrik Bawantu) with a mostly white band. This provided the impetus for Sheila Maurice-Grey and her colleagues to start Kokoroko.

Sheila Maurice-Grey

The reason why we started Kokoroko: I remember playing in a few Afrobeat bands. And most of them had mainly white musicians playing, even Dele's band, not to throw him under the bus, but his band was mainly white as well. Which is not a problem. But the reason that was happening is because not a lot of the younger generation were interested in playing the music. There's a legacy that needs to continue.

* Fela's bands.

Kokoroko's rapid success can of course be attributed to a number of factors, not least the high quality of the playing and singing, the catchiness of 'Abussey Junction' and the support of Gilles Peterson's Brownswood Recordings. But the fact they rapidly leapfrogged most of the bands they decry indicates a clear appetite among the UK public for African music played by people of African extraction.

Similarly, Ezra Collective rapidly grew their following with their heavy, groove-based, London-centric version of the classic Afrobeat sound, given authenticity both by the Nigerian heritage of brothers Femi Koleoso (drums) and TJ (bass) and by their proud maintenance of the street swagger and style of Enfield, the North London suburb where they grew up. Femi was symbolically positioned as the holder of the Afrobeat torch-sticks when he interviewed Tony Allen for Worldwide FM in Gilles Peterson's Brownswood Basement in 2017.[*] This was by no means simply for the media – Femi had made several trips to Paris on the Megabus to study with Tony while a student at Trinity – but it set him down squarely as the living embodiment of the Afrobeat tradition. This status was affirmed by Femi's central role in the tribute to Tony that took place at the Royal Festival Hall as part of the 2021 London Jazz Festival. As well as playing drums in an all-star, thirty-strong ensemble that included Damon Albarn, Remi Kabaka, Ben Okri, Dave Okumu, the Kokoroko horns, Jimi Tenor, Lava La Rue, Nitin Sawhney, Andrew Ashong, Eska, K.O.G. and Wayne Snow, Femi delivered a moving, apparently improvised tribute speech at the start of the second half of the show.[†]

The combined effect of bands like Ezra Collective and Kokoroko in attracting younger, more melanated audiences and the availability of vintage African records, thanks to the reissue scene, was further enhanced by

[*] I was at that session as Tony Allen's agent, and remember enjoying the age dynamics at play, with Tony referring to Femi as 'dis boy', Femi addressing Tony as 'uncle' and me as 'cuz'.

[†] Tony Allen's speech is sampled on *Where I'm Meant to Be*, the Ezra Collective album which dropped just as I was making final edits to this book.

the opportunity to see many of the original artists live thanks to the new interest in their music. When veteran Ghanaian highlife guitarist Pat Thomas played Camden's Jazz Cafe in 2019, at least half of Kokoroko were in attendance, humbly paying homage to a respected elder.

Labels like Strut and Soundway have in recent years begun to release new music by UK-based artists Nubiyan Twist and Electric Jalaba alongside new releases by African artists like Pat Thomas and Seun Kuti and reissues of Sun Ra, Mulatu Astatke and Patrice Rushen, cementing the sense of a vital UK jazz scene, informed by the music of the past but clearly centred in twenty-first-century London.

'Every room had a stereo'
(calypso>reggae>bashment>dancehall> jungle>drum and bass>garage)

From mento, ska, calypso and bluebeat through reggae, lovers' rock, dancehall and dub to UK hip-hop, bashment, jungle, drum and bass, dubstep, garage and grime, Caribbean music has provided the sonics and swagger behind so much of London's music. These musical ideas have directly fed the new UK jazz scene, from the folkloric, calypso-influenced sound of Sons of Kemet, the dub- and garage-inflected sounds of Joe Armon-Jones and Henry Wu to the clear reggae influence on Nubya Garcia, Moses Boyd and Nubiyan Twist.

It is not just the heavy bassline of a Roots Manuva track being informed by sound system culture, or the rapid MCing of garage and jungle as an obvious continuation of the 'toaster' or 'deejay' at a dance, though it is all of that. It's an attitude of independence born of necessity against a background of everyday racism and police hostility. Can't rent a club? We'll run our own shebeens and house dances. Can't afford a sound system? We'll build our own. Can't get label deals, and when we do, we're always getting exploited? We'll run our own labels, set up our own distribution networks and record shops, press tiny runs of dubplates and white labels.

Adam Moses

What is often missed is that a lot of our clubbing as first- and second-generation people from the Caribbean or from Africa, we couldn't get clubs, so our parties took place in houses and warehouses. I'm from North-West London, from Harlesden, and that era, if you go to Harlesden, there's five parties a night. All night. Massive warehouse raves. And that was all reggae, soul, very Caribbean-, Jamaican-influenced way of presenting music. It was totally black, those events. So we came from that world to getting into jazz. Our thing was always like, man, this doesn't represent London. This is one of the most multicultural places in the world. And it just doesn't represent London at all.

It's about music occupying a central role in the fabric of people's lives, not only for twenty- and thirty-somethings going out but tiny children and old people too. Music as a fundamental communication tool, unifier of communities and bringer of meaning.

Wozzy Brewster

The Caribbean community back then, they would gather around each other's houses. That's the parties I grew up with, the music, the house parties. You would go to somebody's house and all the kids, we'd all be playing upstairs and running up and down, and the adults would be playing their tunes and dancing, there'd be curry goat and rice and chicken, rum cake and coconut bread, coconut ice and all the things. I grew up in that, house parties, blues parties. 'Shebeens' – Deptford High Street . . . Just going up the High Street and there's parties, underneath shops and you know people because we all grew up in Deptford.

Mickey Smith

I grew up in a house where there were blues parties every couple of weeks, so the whole Jamaican community used to come down. I grew up with such a rich background of music and sound systems and partying and dancing as part of life. Every room had a stereo, and every room had to have as big speakers as possible. So for me, my whole South London Soul Train thing was about that Jamaican party, about that idea of letting your hair down and just going for it, not giving a fuck, don't care how you look, don't care how you dance. All you care about is having a good time. A lot of my experience comes from that area.

The sonics of Caribbean sound system culture, too, have had a powerful influence on the way the new wave of UK jazz has been presented.

Wayne Francis

If you go to Total Refreshment Centre, that music's played on a big sound system, it's not played in a jazz club with a tiny sound system, the sound system is heavyweight! So everybody is used to playing with a big sound system. That's such a big difference to UK jazz and how it's presented is that it's come out of that sound system culture from Jamaica and the Caribbean and the musicians play live through that. And they're used to playing in those venues. And creating music for those venues.

The story of Caribbean music in London has been told in different ways. Lloyd Bradley's *Sounds Like London: One Hundred Years of Black Music in the Capital* gives a rapid historical overview. Caspar Melville's *It's a London Thing: How Rare Groove, Acid House and Jungle Remapped the City* offers a political analysis of how the central role of Caribbean sound system culture and the eighties warehouse party scene was marginalised in the acid house origin story only to resurface later as jungle. Kevin Legendre's *Don't Stop the Carnival: Black Music in Britain* gives a detailed, authoritative survey of African and Caribbean music in London, and Joe Muggs's *Bass, Mids, Tops: An Oral History of Sound System Culture* links early pioneers like Dennis Bovell, Norman Jay and Adrian Sherwood with contemporary artists like Shy One and Cooly G via Dego, Mala, Skream and DJ Storm.

All of these books are highly recommended. But although jazz is mentioned in all of them at different points, it is not the focus. Rather than replicate what's already been said, I want to speak about this from a jazz angle.

The present wave is not the first time that Caribbean musical ideas have informed London's jazz. As far back as the 1930s, British Guiana-born bandleader and dancer Ken 'Snakehips' Johnson was thrilling audiences with his West Indian Dance Orchestra before being tragically killed by a German bomb while performing at the Café de Paris in 1941. The Soho scene of the 1960s was infinitely enhanced by the creativity of Joe Harriott, Shake Keane, Coleridge Goode, Harold McNair and Frank Holder. And the Jazz Warriors generation – almost all of whom had come up playing in reggae bands – made their name through bringing their Caribbean heritage into the music.

Yet while the influence of Caribbean musical styles on UK jazz can be plainly heard by anyone willing to listen, less well documented is the circular influence of jazz on these styles: the presence of jazz musicians in mento, ska, rocksteady and calypso, and their influence on subsequent derivations, from two-tone right through to jungle and drum and bass.

Courtney Pine

My first time I listened to jazz was the ska records. You listen to the B-side, it's instrumental. Don Drummond. And Lester Sterling. And Tommy McCook. Roland Alphonso and Ernest Ranglin. These are jazz musicians. I didn't know I was listening to jazz – and to this day, people don't realise the B-sides of those records are jazz musicians improvising. This set the scene for what I'm doing.

Orphy Robinson

People need to know the proper history of jazz in the UK. We were all part of the Africa Centre. We all did the clubbing thing, we're all part of that scene. We played on all the records, even lovers' rock, the reggae scene. That was a lot of jazz musicians that did all the records. Cleveland Watkiss was a big part of that history. Which is why when he then went and did drum and bass and all that, it made sense because he's come from that history. He knows that thing inside out. You know, with Goldie and Steve [Williamson] – it was the jazz musicians that inhabited that world, jazz musicians who played in all the funk bands, all the Incognitos and the Jamiroquais – and pop bands that had horn sections, they were all jazz players as well. Even the Pet Shop Boys had jazz players!

The tribalism both around and within UK jazz from the 1950s onwards has frequently obscured the fact that for many people, especially within the black community, jazz is simply one black musical style among many. A Tribe Called Quest did not sample so many jazz records because Q-Tip was on a personal mission to rejuvenate jazz; they are just favourites in his record collection, in the same way that Dr. Dre sampled a lot of classic soul.

Mickey Smith

I always say that drum and bass and jungle is jazz; to me, it's all part of the same tree. Jazz is the trunk but every spiral that goes off, you can hear that jazz influence. Even when people are playing digitally and they're really good digital programmers, there's a flow of jazz. There's an improvisational element to it. There's a flow that reminds me of the core of where it is. You can't listen to jungle without hearing jazz and reggae fused together.

Jazz influence could be plainly heard in the 'intelligent' drum and bass of the late 1990s, particularly artists like LTJ Bukem, 4Hero, Goldie and Roni Size, where, as well as the producers being steeped in jazz music, jazz musicians often recorded and played live.

Steve Williamson

I got heavily involved in the drum and bass scene, I was recording with LTJ Bukem, recording with Dillinja. I was doing gigs where I was actually on stage with them, Fabio and Grooverider and I was on a plinth playing my horn. I recorded on Goldie's album *Timeless*, I went all over the bloody world with that. I was hitting drum and bass hard for years, and the music I was making then was sick because I was mixing it with the drum and bass programming and rinsing out beats. I was never about the whole idea of just playing jazz as a purist: I see jazz as way bigger than just wearing a suit and playing in a particular style.

Cleveland Watkiss, main vocalist for the Jazz Warriors, had been active on the lovers' rock scene of the late 1970s and early 1980s. In the 1990s, he was performing and releasing with Project 23, 'the first and only live Drum 'n Bass band',[8] and by 2006 he was MCing for twenty-five thousand people at Lovebox in Victoria Park on stage with Brazilian drum and bass pioneer DJ Patife.[*]

Roni Size's Mercury Prize-winning 1997 album *New Forms* was on Gilles Peterson's Talkin' Loud label, evidence of its jazz sensibilities; the deluxe double album even carries a track called 'It's Jazzy'. Indeed, jazz was central to the Bristol sound of the mid-1990s. The unique mix of jazz and reggae fed into the Wild Bunch sound system, which grew into Massive Attack after Nellee Hooper moved to London to join Jazzie B's Soul II Soul. Massive Attack's 'Safe From Harm' samples Billy Cobham's jazz funk monster 'Stratus'. Portishead's Adrian Utley was an established jazz musician who had toured with Art Blakey's Jazz Messengers and American bluesman Big John Patton. Even Neneh

---

[*] I know because, for two thrilling minutes, I was on stage with them, playing live drum and bass rhythms on my darbuka with Cleveland holding the mic, having been invited to guest after contriving to show Cleveland my skills backstage whilst volunteering at the Cheltenham Jazz Festival a month or two earlier. Although the episode makes me cringe a little now, it was at the time an incredible moment, playing with two of my heroes on the biggest stage I had ever been on. It remains an enduring monument to the power of the blag.

Cherry (initially of Bristol punk band Rip, Rig and Panic, before launching her solo career) had grown up as the step-daughter of pioneering trumpeter and free jazz hero Don Cherry.

It is a great historical irony that Massive Attack, Portishead, Tricky and Roni Size were dominating the UK music scene with demonstrably jazz-derived music in exactly the same period as *The Fast Show* was toxifying the word via the Jazz Club sketch; musical tribalism was such that if it wasn't labelled 'jazz', the jazz became almost inaudible.

Yet although they perhaps did not recognise it as jazz until years later, the jazz sensibilities that had informed drum and bass fed back into jazz via the raves which were formative musical experiences for many of this generation's musicians.

Oscar Jerome

A lot of it just comes from what you've been around growing up. You can tell a lot of people who are making waves now were influenced by British Caribbean bass culture. But I've always been a bit of a raver; at music college, I was practising four or five hours a day, and then going out to Bussey Building to Ray Keith nights with some of my friends from other places who weren't from my college, dancing to jungle and doing pills.

Tom Excell

I think I was actually into jazz for a long time before I knew I was into jazz. I came to it primarily through underground dance music of raves in East Anglia and didn't even realise that actually there was a lot of jazz used in that music. It was largely jungle music and there's loads of sampling of jazz records and minor nine chords being played on a sampler and moving around the keyboard, which is much of what the London jazz scene does today in a lot of ways! That kind of early nineties stuff is so full of jazz harmony and improv drums, although it's programmed. It just never really struck me actually how much I was enjoying the jazz elements of that music.

Ahmad Dayes

The only reason I ever wanted to do music or get into a studio or do any of that was to make drum and bass, I didn't give a fuck about anything else at that point. Me nineteen, eighteen, it was drum and bass, drum and bass, drum and bass. And looking back that is uniquely London. Okay, other places can claim it as well. But being in London in the nineties, that was like a tattoo! Identity. I had my moment in a club at some point and for four or five years straight, drum and bass was my life. These guys* were a bit too young for the raves at that time, but I like to think that them beats filtered into the psyche.

'This is the new dubstep' (dubstep)

The handful of people interviewed in this book who were closely involved with dubstep in the 2000s all see parallels between that movement and the UK jazz scene of the following decade, not so much musically but in its creation of a tight community around a particular club, with a network of producers, promoters, photographers, journalists and ravers all buzzing off each other.

Like grime, dubstep had grown out of garage and jungle, taking the deep sub bass of those genres (ultimately derived from Jamaican sound system culture) to a chest-pounding extreme. Mostly stripping out grime's hyped-up vocals, dubstep was bass music at its purest, combining the loneliness of a London night bus with the frenetic pulse of the entire city. While dancing to dubstep was essentially a disjointed, solitary musical experience, FWD at Plastic People in Shoreditch grew a powerful community of producers, DJs and ravers, with a small but highly connected number of producers releasing new music almost every week.

* Brothers and fellow United Vibrations members Yussef and Kareem Dayes, who were interviewed on a simultaneous Zoom call (between feeding the many infants who had appeared since I'd been their agent) on one of the best Dayes of my life.

This was in part a function of the fact that the scene was left alone for a long time to incubate: a close community often forms in a scene that exists outside of the mainstream, and that community tends to dissipate when the scene gets bigger. Like Minton's Playhouse for bebop, the Whisky a Go Go for punk, Paradise Garage for house, Dingwalls for acid jazz and Co-Op for broken beat, FWD at Plastic People was this place for dubstep.

Although dubstep as a scene petered out quite quickly (evidence of the vulnerability of 'new' musical terms like trip-hop and acid jazz once the first wave of excitement around them dissipates), its global impact was enormous, with some of its production values (the LFO or 'bass wobble' in particular) forming a massive part of what is known as EDM, the American term for the highly polished, aggressive post-dubstep of producers like Skrillex, Steve Aoki and Deadmau5 that began appearing in dubstep's wake from around 2010.

Claudio Lillo

The feeling of going to FWD every week, you'd listen to new music and you didn't care who was playing because everybody was sharing records, collaborating, every label was putting out new releases every week. And for a while that was kind of happening here, the Steam Down thing was dope, everybody was jumping on each other's gigs. I haven't been as excited by a scene since dubstep. I'd go to Plastic* loads, but it wasn't just Plastic.[9] It was everywhere. Online. There was just so much new music and it was cool and there was energy. And then since dubstep, everything was like, 'Oh, this is the new dubstep. This is the new dubstep'. It's the community, the sense of community which hasn't existed. And that's been the coolest thing.

* Plastic People, the now-defunct club in Shoreditch that was home to FWD, the legendary dubstep night run by Rinse founder Sarah Lockhart, not to mention seminal broken beat night Co-Op, CDR and residencies by Theo Parrish, Carl Craig, Four Tet and Floating Points.

'london town'

Kate Hutchinson

New subcultures have always excited me, especially when they're linked to the dance floor. The last clear example that we have of that was dubstep, certainly in terms of something that felt very mixed in terms of race and gender, and in terms of how organic it was. It was a scene that was, memorably, quite heavily populated by women, by clubbers, broadcasters, journalists and organisers like Sarah [Lockhart] at Rinse and FWD. That for me was the last tangible IRL club culture scene where there were specific nights that people would congregate at, like DMZ and FWD, and there was also an infrastructure around it coming up in terms of media – Rinse FM and *RWD Mag* – and the journalists associated with that, like Chantelle Fiddy or Melissa Bradshaw, and also Mary Anne Hobbs's *Breezeblock* shows on Radio 1. So when UK jazz started bubbling again and regular nights and radio shows started springing up, it was like, 'Wow, yes, amazing, something real is happening here!' Because the big argument after dubstep used to be that subculture's gone digital and something grassroots will never happen again.

With powerful scenes forming around Steez, Jazz Re:freshed, Church of Sound and TRC, UK jazz was the continuation of this communal energy, which provided a springboard outside of the community to international success.

'You'd need a maths degree'
(broken beat)

Beginning in the late 1990s in West London, broken beat – often shortened to 'broken' or 'bruk' and not to be confused with the drum and bass-derived 'breakbeat' or the heavy, four-to-the-floor 'breaks' of Freq Nasty and Krafty Kuts – was an attempt to synthesise house, garage and jazz, with a bass-heavy, sound system-derived sensibility.

Most closely associated with super-group Bugz in the Attic (so-named by much-loved producer, the late Phil Asher, in reference to how many people were crammed into Afronaut's attic studio in Richmond), and individual members Kaidi Tatham, Dego, IG Culture, Afronaut and Daz-I-Kue, broken beat was distinctive for chopped, stuttery drum rhythms,[*] jazzy chords, dirty, P-Funk-inspired basslines, frequently paired with soulful, jazzy vocals.

Daz-I-Kue

What you gotta understand is that all the people involved with broken beat were involved with the previous incarnation, IG Culture, that whole Ealing crew, Femi, Jamiroquai, Brand New Heavies. They all knew each other! Shake and Finger Pop, which Femi started, which was the funk night with Judge Jules. Doing that whole funk with the warehouse jams and all of that, bringing James Brown. And there was a whole crew of people before that who were jamming to jazz, dancing to jazz music. We were mashing it up, you know what I'm saying? I don't think the jazz thing ever really went away.

Associated artists included 4Hero, Atjazz and IG Culture's New Sector Movements, with more recent denizens EVM128 and WheelUp still flying the flag. Although primarily a DJ- and producer-led phenomenon focused around IG Culture's Co-Op nights at the Velvet Rooms and later Plastic People in Shoreditch (home also, in the same period, to seminal dubstep night FWD), Kaidi Tatham and Bugz in the Attic both had live bands for a time, which would have sounded, in many ways, like much of the electronic-infused jazz of today. A young Shabaka Hutchings even played in Kaidi Tatham's band, providing important experiences around the presentation of jazz.

Shabaka Hutchings

You could argue that whole broken beat scene like Kaidi Tatham and 4Hero was coming out of the jazz tradition, like seventies Herbie

---

[*] Not unlike grime: a similarity which may be more than coincidence; see below.

Hancock: that could be called jazz, but they weren't necessarily calling themselves jazz. They called themselves two-step and broken beat. So if you were to think about 'what does the word jazz mean', you wouldn't necessarily think of that in relation to jazz, you'd think the thing that's being told to you as being jazz, which is someone in a pub, in a suit. Playing standards.

The scene's biggest moment was probably Bugz in the Attic's remix of Fela Kuti's classic 'Zombie' for the *Red Hot and Riot** compilation (MCA, 2002), appearing alongside major artists including Nile Rodgers, Dead Prez, Baaba Maal and Jorge Ben Jor. This brought them international recognition and a slew of high-profile remix opportunities including Macy Gray, Amy Winehouse and D'Angelo, eventually signing to Richard Branson's V2.

However, their debut album *Back in the Doghouse* (V2, 2006) came out at the worst possible time in terms of the music piracy-driven crash of the record industry, and the album failed to make an impact, resulting shortly after in the group's separation and fragmentation of the scene. While it never grew beyond a small community of fervent enthusiasts, broken beat's impact on young musicians like Wayne Francis (United Vibrations, Steam Down) and Henry Wu (Yussef Kamaal, Kamaal Williams) was significant, highlighting the sonic possibilities of fusing jazz chord progressions with heavy basslines and electronic beats. This is reflected in the enduring affection for the scene and its pioneers. New 2021 albums by both Kaidi Tatham and IG Culture, as well as *Sankofa Season*, Kaidi's 2020 collaboration with much-loved UK/Ghanaian vocalist Andrew Ashong, indicate the continuing appetite for the music, at least among 'heads', with IG Culture's live band appearing at We Out Here 2021 and Church of Sound in February 2022, featuring respected musicians from the current crop.

Broken beat also serves as yet another example of jazz never going

* This was one of a series of records produced by the Red Hot Organisation to raise AIDS awareness. This particular album was a tribute to the music of Fela Kuti.

away; in this case neither smelling funny (à la Frank Zappa) nor changing address (Stuart Nicholson) but simply travelling incognito under another name until ready to be welcomed back into the family. Polarisation in the UK press between jazz, pop and electronic music meant that, as with the jazzy drum and bass of a few years before, what was essentially a form of jazz or at least jazz-adjacent music was branded 'electronic' or 'dance' and therefore not associated with jazz. This gave the misleading impression that UK jazz in this period was much more conventional or safe than it actually was, because many of the more electronic forms of jazz – now broadly accepted under the jazz banner – were being called other things.

Kees Heus

I've had this discussion with IG Culture a few times, of when broken was called broken, it was basically just seen as a club music. And that goes from hype to trend and hype to trend. But it was just a part of UK jazz history.

The musical debt owed to broken beat by some of the pioneers of the new wave of UK jazz has been repaid by the new attention and respect its instigators have received.

Emily Moxon

This new generation of jazz, it does feel like it's fulfilled some of that promise that broken beat had in a way. I think there's a big connection between those scenes.

'If Kamasi hadn't exploded'
(hip-hop and the USA)

Although not strictly a London style, hip-hop's global visibility combined with the close interpenetration between musical developments in the UK and USA mean it will not be out of place to say a few words on the role played by US hip-hop in preparing the ground for the new generation of UK jazz.

Hip-hop had played an important role in leading an older generation to jazz through tracing the samples in the 'golden era' early nineties hip-hop of A Tribe Called Quest, De La Soul, The Pharcyde, Digable Planets, Gang Starr and others. As the decade continued, artists like The Roots, Erykah Badu, D'Angelo, Common and Bilal – who owed no small debt to the intensely jazz-influenced productions of the late James Yancey (Jay Dee, aka J Dilla) – continued to provide a shining example of the musical commonalities between jazz, hip-hop, soul and R & B. Combined with the heavy influence of the UK's Jamaican sound system culture, jazz had fed into the output of UK hip-hop artists like London Posse, Roots Manuva, Ty, Jehst, Task Force, Skinnyman, DJ Vadim, The Herbaliser, Braintax and Wildflower. DJ Shadow's 1996 *Endtroducing* (released on James Lavelle's UK-based Mo' Wax label) was a major influence on the orchestral, sample-based music of producers like Mr. Scruff and live bands like The Cinematic Orchestra right through to GoGo Penguin.

With all these analogues, it would be extremely surprising if the emergence of a new generation of North American musicians exploring the liminal ground between jazz, hip-hop, Afrofuturism and electronics had no impact on UK musicians, particularly in the hyper-connected digital era of the 2010s. Like the UK jazz scene itself, the resurgence in popularity of a jazzier, soulful type of hip-hop in the 2010s did not come out of nowhere. Artists like Robert Glasper, Terrace Martin and Karriem Riggins all had multiple releases under their belts in both hip-hop and jazz dating back to the turn of the millennium. All three had at least one parent who was a jazz musician, and all were instrumentalists as well as producers, organically fusing America's two dominant black music traditions. The success of Glasper's *Black Radio* (Blue Note, 2012) was a major landmark after a decade's dominance of a more commercial, club-based hip-hop sound.

Femi Koleoso

I'm thinking of the big players in hip-hop in the 2000s, and 50 Cent wasn't sampling jazz. Sick music, but the golden age of hip-hop really had passed by then, and you're into this new wave, Eminem, hard, smacking beats like 'In Da Club' by 50 Cent. It left that Tribe, boom-bap thing of my older brother and it went like, 'This is a new ting now.' That was a bit of a gap in jazz hip-hop.

Featuring soul/hip-hop royalty Erykah Badu, Yasiin Bey (formerly known as Mos Def) and Bilal, soul/jazz singers Meshell Ndegeocello and Lalah Hathaway and newer names like Lupe Fiasco on top of instrumental samples from Glasper on keys, Casey Benjamin on sax, bassist Derrick Hodge and drummer Chris Dave, *Black Radio* won a Grammy for Best R & B album and became the first album ever to feature simultaneously in the top ten album charts of four different genres: hip-hop and R & B, urban contemporary, jazz and contemporary jazz. This feat was repeated by the follow-up *Black Radio II* (Blue Note, 2013), which reinforced the commonality between R & B, hip-hop, jazz and soul, adding Jill Scott, Snoop Dogg, Anthony Hamilton, Dwele and Norah Jones to the list of features.

Meanwhile in Toronto, white college students Badbadnotgood first attracted attention in 2011 through their YouTube cover of leftfield West Coast hip-hop collective Odd Future, which was tweeted by its founder Tyler, the Creator. Their self-released debut EP in the same year achieved prominence through covers of Wu-Tang Clan, Nas and Gang Starr, further blurring the boundaries between jazz and hip-hop, putting a hip-hop swagger back into jazz while re-injecting hip-hop with a virtuosic musicality. Their debut album *III* (2014) came not on a jazz label but on LA-based Innovative Leisure, founded by alumni of Peanut Butter Wolf's influential Stone's Throw and home to artists like LA beats pioneer Nosaj Thing; this helped further change the perceptions of where and how jazz could be presented.

'london town'

Kees Heus

How did it start? With groups like Badbadnotgood, probably. A younger generation knocking at the door. Badbadnotgood did it in a smart way doing the hip-hop classics like Robert Glasper did before. When I saw Badbadnotgood for the first time, I just immediately thought, 'Oh, something interesting is happening here.' There was this Badbadnotgood concert two or three years ago. It was sold out. Fifteen hundred. Mosh pits were going on! It's such a new energy that is projected into this new wave of jazz.

By 2015 their status was such that, rather than just covering their favourite hip-hop tracks, they were able to make a collaborative album with hip-hop legend Ghostface Killah of the Wu-Tang Clan, with guest appearances from Danny Brown and MF Doom (*Sour Soul*, Lex Records, 2015).

And on the West Coast, Flying Lotus (Steven Ellison) and Thundercat (Stephen Bruner) unashamedly brought jazz virtuosity into their electronic productions, and electronics into their jazz, taking the torch from Dilla to fuse jazz, hip-hop and electronics in awkwardly nuanced, stuttering rhythms. The great-nephew of pianist, spiritual jazz pioneer and mystic Alice Coltrane (second wife of John), Ellison had grown up surrounded by jazz, watching cousins Ravi, Oran and John Coltrane, Jr perform, attending the John Coltrane Jazz Festival his family organised, and visiting his great-aunt at her Malibu ashram. As a bored teenager growing up in the middle-class San Fernando Valley, just north of Hollywood, he started experimenting with LSD, so much so that he 'was relocated to a special school for "recovering addicts" where he was taught English by an ex-crack smoker'.[10]

The spiritual jazz heritage and formative psychedelic experiences were both powerful influences on his music. Whilst interning at Stone's Throw, Flying Lotus became heavily involved with what became known as the LA beat scene, where artists including The Gaslamp Killer,

Daedalus, Georgia Anne Muldrow, Ras G, Teebs, Afta-1, Nosaj Thing and TOKiMONSTA cohered first around Kutmah's Sketchbook night (from 2004), then (from 2006–18) at Daddy Kev's Low End Theory (named after A Tribe Called Quest's era-defining 1991 album). This creative, leftfield electronic scene provided the initial impetus for Ellison to set up Brainfeeder in 2008, releasing LA artists like Daedalus, Georgia Anne Muldrow and the late pianist Austin Peralta before signing a distribution deal with the UK's Ninja Tune in 2010.

Having released his own debut *1983* on independent LA label Plug Research in 2006, and participating in that year's Red Bull Music Academy in Melbourne, Flying Lotus signed to the UK's Warp Records in 2007 (home of Aphex Twin, Squarepusher, Autechre and Boards of Canada), with whom he released *Los Angeles* in 2008. While very much an electronic album, Ellison's musical lineage gave an immediate hook for those so inclined to present his stuttery, murky beats as pointing a new direction for twenty-first-century jazz. The backing of influential UK labels Warp for his own output and Ninja Tune as distributor for Brainfeeder made sure this new approach to jazz-influenced music reached UK musicians and audiences, and the fact that Warp was not a label anyone associated with jazz helped re-frame the music away from the stereotypes promulgated by *The Fast Show*.

Matthew Halsall

Flying Lotus is a really important figure in this scene. He set up his own record label and was sampling a lot of jazz music including his auntie, and he was working with Ravi Coltrane. And he was responsible for signing Kamasi Washington. And he was huge, Flying Lotus, when he went on to Warp Records and the album *LA*. So it started to open the doors to people thinking, 'This guy's bringing elements of jazz into electronic music and fusing it together.'

Flying Lotus's jazz roots showed even more clearly on second album *Cosmogramma* (Warp, 2010), which featured contributions on sax from his cousin Ravi Coltrane and marked the beginning of his collaboration with bassist and producer Stephen Bruner, aka Thundercat. Also from a musical family, Thundercat had played bass since the age of four, growing up listening to jazz funk artists like Stanley Clarke and George Duke. By his late teens he was coming into school bleary-eyed after joining his older brother Ronald in the crossover punk band Suicidal Tendencies and touring Europe with boy band No Curfew. Bruner went on to become one of the most sought-after session bassists in the world, touring with Snoop Dogg, Erykah Badu, J*Davey and progressive funk outfit Sa-Ra Creative Partners, where he met rapper Anderson .Paak, who was then the drummer in the group, and would himself go on to become an influential voice in the liminal space between jazz and hip-hop with albums like *Venice* (2014) and *Malibu* (2016).

From a chance meeting in the streets of Austin, Texas at SXSW 2008, Stephen and Steven went on to become one of the most important partnerships in twenty-first-century music. In addition to his contributions to Flying Lotus's own music, Thundercat was instrumental in the growth of Brainfeeder, which released all his music under his own name.

The Thundercat/Flying Lotus alliance also represented a continuation of a musical lineage of Afrofuturism that stretched from Sun Ra and Herbie Hancock to Erykah Badu via the cosmic funk of George Clinton, the ethereal techno of Drexciya and Jeff Mills and the deep Jamaican dub of Lee 'Scratch' Perry, underpinned by the literary Afrofuturism of writers like Octavia Butler and Samuel Delaney and the street art of Jean-Michel Basquiat. Coined by Mark Dery in his 1994 essay 'Black to the Future', Afrofuturism represents a convergence of science fiction, black power, cosmological speculation and psychedelics, using magical and cosmological themes to ask allegorical questions about the state of affairs in the real world, especially racism and the legacy of slavery. Alongside artists like Shabazz Palaces, Janelle Monáe and FKA Twigs, Flying Lotus and Thundercat helped repopularise

Afrofuturism, particularly after some of its visual cues were taken up by pop stars Rihanna, Beyoncé and her sister Solange Knowles, and brought to a wider public with the 2018 film *Black Panther*.[*]

Whether or not these aesthetic cues had any direct influence on the Afrofuturistic aesthetic choices of UK jazz artists like United Vibrations and The Comet Is Coming, they helped created a general visibility for these themes, which fans of the artists listed above could recognise and enjoy when they saw them in UK jazz.

Wayne Francis

Musicians that improvise and are looking to innovate by nature are futurists. So I would say Shabaka is a futurist, I would say Kamasi is a futurist. Anybody that innovates is a futurist, you're always thinking about what you can bring to the present and imagining what that's going to be. Exploring space or the deep ocean – it's all about exploration. Cosmic themes fit within that context and they are always trying to find another mode of expression. If I were to relate that to politics, my take would be: with the lack of representation for black people as a whole within the different areas of society, by being a so-called Afrofuturist you're creating a space where you can be whatever you want to be. Your art can replicate that.

At the same time, this cohort of US musicians helped bring unapologetic virtuosity well outside the realm of jazz. I remember hearing Thundercat remark charmingly (but with perhaps a hint of faux humility), 'That song doesn't get any easier,' after a note-perfect rendition of

---

[*] Kendrick Lamar was heavily involved in the score for this alongside producer Sounwave, but sadly did not bring Flying Lotus or Thundercat along with him: a missed opportunity. The main score was in fact composed somewhat underwhelmingly by Swedish composer Ludwig Göransson. Like the characters' accents (which were an exaggerated stereotype of whatever an 'African' accent sounded like to the actor – which tended to be Ghanaian/Nigerian, Senegalese or Ethiopian depending on whether the actor was British, French or American) Göransson's score was a pastiche of various elements of African music without feeling part of a unified whole.

'Them Changes' at Brainfeeder's ten-year anniversary show at Brixton Academy in December 2018, slyly drawing the audience's attention to his remarkable facility while creating a rapport by suggesting an endearing human fallibility. And, despite releasing most of his own music on Warp, Flying Lotus's communal thinking in using Brainfeeder as a hub to support the scene around him served as an important inspiration for the emerging UK jazz community.

By 2014, Flying Lotus's status allowed him to dig deeper into both jazz and hip-hop with *You're Dead* (Warp, 2014). In addition to heavy contributions by Thundercat, the album featured over twenty other jazz musicians including Kamasi Washington, Miguel Atwood-Ferguson and legendary pianist Herbie Hancock, who reportedly told Ellington and Bruner, 'If Miles was around today, he'd be hanging out with you guys.'[11] And if the presence of the world's biggest living jazz musician affirmed the record's jazz credentials, its featuring of nineties g-funk legend Snoop Dogg on 'Dead Man's Tetris' and torchbearer Kendrick Lamar on 'Can't Catch Me' did the same in the world of hip-hop.

The presence on *You're Dead* of saxophonist Kamasi Washington was no coincidence: he'd known Thundercat and his brother Ronald Bruner, Jr since their days playing jazz together at LA's Locke High School. Something like the US version of Tomorrow's Warriors, Washington, bassist Miles Mosley, pianist Cameron Graves, trombonist Ryan Porter and drummer Tony Austin had been playing together since their early teens via regional jazz programmes organised by London-born Barbara Sealy.

As the individual musicians came of age, they cohered as The West Coast Get Down, a twice-weekly jam organised by Mosley, with which producer Terrace Martin and both Bruners were loosely affiliated. Sealy set up SB Music Management (reversing her initials for obvious reasons), helping guide the careers of The West Coast Get Down as a whole, drummer Tony Austin, and eventually UK saxophonist and bandleader Nubya Garcia.

One of the West Coast Get Down's most decisive moments came in December 2013, when Mosley convinced the other members to clear their diaries and pool their resources to block book LA's Kingsize Soundlabs studio for the entire month, each agreeing to play on each other's albums for free.[*] Like the Soulquarians' first residency at Jimi Hendrix's crumbling Electric Lady Studios in 1997, which gave rise to major albums by Common, J Dilla, Erykah Badu, The Roots and D'Angelo, or Wiley's block-booking of a Bermondsey studio in summer 2004 in which 'the whole East London scene lived in that studio during the summer, forty-odd MCs and producers hanging out from 9 a.m. each morning, eating, drinking, smoking weed, and using the on-site games room',[12] this residency supported the creation of a phenomenal amount of new music, which remained in the vaults until the right time for it to be released.

All these strands – jazzy hip-hop, jazz with electronics, and a community of young musicians all coming up together – united spectacularly on Kendrick Lamar's 2015 album *To Pimp A Butterfly*, which featured live jazz from Kamasi Washington, Glasper, Thundercat, Mosley, trumpeter Ambrose Akinmusire and others on productions by Terrace Martin, Sounwave, Pharrell Williams, Flying Lotus, Thundercat and Knxwledge.

Having already established himself as one of the most exciting voices in hip-hop with *good kid, m.A.A.d city* (Top Dawg Entertainment, 2012), Kendrick's foregrounding of jazz on *To Pimp A Butterfly* was as much to do with his own taste as any deliberate attempt to reclaim it. Whereas conscious attempts to merge jazz and hip-hop like Stetsasonic's 1988 'Talkin' All That Jazz' or Miles Davis's 1992 'Doo-Bop' had often felt painfully clunky, this was the real thing.

[*] Various sources across the internet have reported this session happening in December 2010, 2011 and 2013 (although all agree it took place in December). I do not know the reason for the inconsistency and have been unable to establish a definitive answer, but 2013 seems the most likely to me. Five years would seem a very long time between recording and release.

As well as setting a new benchmark for hip-hop production, the album's effect on the global reputation of jazz was transformational. The record went straight in at No. 1 in the album charts in the USA, Canada, Australia, New Zealand and the UK, recording the highest number of release-day Spotify plays (9.6 million) of any album that year, and the second-highest first-week album sales (324,000),[13] going on to sell a million copies by the end of 2015. At a time when jazz had officially become the least popular genre in the USA, with just 1.4 per cent of the market (compared to 30 per cent for rock and 17 per cent for hip-hop),[14] and in which the charts were dominated by white musicians playing versions of black music (the biggest-selling artists of that year were Adele, Taylor Swift and Justin Bieber in the USA; Adele, Ed Sheeran and Sam Smith in the UK[15]), this foregrounding of jazz by one of the world's biggest artists was a massive boost. Like the support for grime by both Drake and Kanye that fed into the success of Grime 2.0,[16] the biggest hip-hop artist in the world coming out with an album that drew unapologetically on jazz was probably the most important single release in lighting the fire for the global jazz resurgence.

Femi Koleoso

People have been able to draw the line: Kendrick Lamar, hip-hop; Kamasi Washington, jazz; Kamasi was on Kendrick's record. That line there, it helps. And then they're like, 'Right, so jazz isn't that far away from stuff I do like: maybe it's for me.' The moment you kill that stigma that 'jazz isn't for me', then it just comes down to whether you're vibing or not, do you know what I'm saying? That *To Pimp a Butterfly* record was a big moment of marriage between hip-hop and jazz which had otherwise been lost. 'Cos beforehand, you would have a Herbie Hancock tune come out and Dilla would be sampling it. That line was quick, man! People were hearing hip-hop and they were hearing jazz. Ronnie Foster: 'Mystic Brew'. A Tribe Called Quest: 'Electric Relaxation'. It was clear, it was obvious. That had gone for a bit and then when Robert Glasper starts putting out tracks with Mos Def on it, Kendrick had Terrace Martin and Kamasi Washington on it, suddenly this idea that I had of Loyle Carner rapping over a jazz beat isn't that crazy. It suddenly makes sense to Loyle Carner and his fans, and Ezra Collective and our fans. It had a big effect, fam! I found that album empowering. I'm hearing a proper no-shame saxophone solo on a Kendrick record. And you've got to bear in mind that you're hearing this type of saxophone solo, and Kendrick's album before – *good kid, m.A.A.d city* – that was a good album. Kendrick's career was going fine. He did not need to break any boundaries. He's done his ting. Things were going great. And he still went there. That showed artistic bravery, and it showed freedom. And then the results for that album – that album went everywhere, man, people were going crazy for it.

The phenomenal reception of *To Pimp A Butterfly* created the perfect environment for the worldwide success of Kamasi Washington's *The Epic* on Flying Lotus's Brainfeeder label. It was released in May 2015, less than two months after *To Pimp A Butterfly*, despite having been recorded several years earlier – a very tactical harnessing of *To Pimp A Butterfly*'s halo effect. The record featured in end-of-year lists well outside of the traditional jazz press – *The Wire, Rolling Stone, Pitchfork, Rough Trade* and the *Guardian* – indicating that Kamasi, and by implication jazz as a whole, had broken through to a wider public, opening a portal for others to walk through.

Kerstan Mackness

People look at the success of Wynton [Marsalis] and it opens doors for Courtney [Pine] to step in. Without the success of Kamasi, Verve Records don't decide to breathe life into Impulse. They don't go looking for a headline artist to sign. They don't land on the idea of signing Shabaka [Hutchings]. None of that stuff happens. In the same way that the guy who signed GoGo Penguin to Blue Note had been looking for something in that kind of crossover space because Blue

Note had had a history of having success with things like Us3 and St Germain, which meant that the A & R was looking for something from the area and he hit upon GoGo Penguin. That's the cyclical nature of the industry, definitely.

I am not suggesting that UK musicians simply copied what was happening in America. Virtually all of the new generation of UK musicians had been honing their craft for years before the release of *To Pimp a Butterfly* and *The Epic,* and were already beginning to make waves locally. But the success of the new cohort of Americans helped open up a global market outside the jazz niche. The excitement around Flying Lotus, Thundercat, Kamasi Washington and the West Coast Get Down, Robert Glasper and Badbadnotgood did not create the jazz boom in the UK, but it amplified it and helped make it palatable to mainstream audiences.

Binker Golding

If Kamasi hadn't exploded on to the scene the way he did, we wouldn't be selling as many records now. I'd still be making albums, sure. I'd still be playing saxophone the same way. I heard Coltrane long before I'd heard Kamasi. He didn't introduce me to that way of playing. But truthfully, *Dem Ones* wouldn't have sold in the same way had that guy not had his success. It's that simple. And that's not just my records. That's everyone's records. Everybody you see that's riding this wave to whatever degree. The American explosion put a spotlight on the UK stuff. It always does.

5

'In Reference to Our Forefathers Fathers Dreams'

Jazz Warriors and the Continuum

Shabaka Hutchings

Anything that we are doing now literally comes off the back of what they did; it's not really possible to compare the two epochs, because one has led to the other.

Theon Cross

I'm aware that I'm standing on the shoulders of people before me. UK and US. I'm standing on the shoulders of people that have paved the way and maybe didn't have it as easy. Maybe didn't get into certain newspapers that I have or charted on billboards or had much of the attention that we have. We honour them as well. We are channelled through them.

The central ideas already discussed – jazz as the battleground for issues around cultural appropriation and ownership, jazz as the result of colonialism, slavery and globalisation, and London as the musical centre of the colonial nexus – cohere in the story of the generation before the present one: those who were born in the 1960s, the children of the Windrush generation. This is the 'Jazz Warriors' generation of Courtney Pine, Cleveland Watkiss, Orphy Robinson, Steve Williamson, one which played a vital role in opening space for the flourishing of the present generation.

The direct transmission of musical knowledge is only one part of the story. Learning musical technique without a meaningful political context to back it up is like agonising about a choice of sandwich when you have no stomach to digest it. The oral tradition is about far more than technique, more even than jazz itself: the music is a vehicle for the transmission of diasporic black experience, political consciousness and rebellion against a racist status quo in a world informed by slavery and its legacy.

Cleveland Watkiss

It's a continuum. And they've built on what we laid. So they're able to travel and spread the British experience further and wider than we were able to. We weren't able to do that because of loads of reasons. The climate, the time that we were in. You didn't have Ryanair and all that kind of stuff back in the eighties to be flying all around Europe. Different times. I just see it as a loop. It's a continuum. And it should be respected that way as well.

'London Is the Place For Me'

For many people, the era of modern multicultural Britain began on 21 June 1948, when Trinbagonian calypsonian Lord Kitchener descended the gangplank of the HMS *Windrush* at Tilbury Docks singing 'London is the Place for Me'.*

Built in Hamburg in 1930 as the cruise liner MV *Monte Rosa*, the ship had been used as a Nazi troopship during the Second World War before being taken in 1945 by the British as a prize of war and renamed the *Empire Windrush*. Although only one of several ships making the transatlantic crossing, and despite sinking to the bottom of the Mediterranean after a fire onboard in 1954, her name

* This was, of course, a highly choreographed routine for the benefit of Pathé News, and Kitch was already a well-known artist in the Caribbean. But it contributed to the idea of Caribbeans (and Trinidadians in particular, for those who bothered to notice the distinction) as high-spirited and full of impromptu music. Sam Selvon's *The Lonely Londoners* gives an equally stylised picture, with greater focus on their passion for 'sport' and its reciprocation by English ladies of all social classes.

became synonymous with the 'Windrush generation': the estimated two hundred thousand Caribbean immigrants who settled in the UK between 1948 and 1962. The British Nationality Act of 1948, in a sly PR manoeuvre, rebranded Britain's colonial 'subjects' as 'citizens of the UK and colonies', automatically granting them free movement between every territory in the British Empire, including the UK itself, and potentially opening the doors to 800 million people from British colonies in Africa, Asia, the Caribbean and the Mediterranean.

The dream of a better life at the centre of the colonial vortex was so compelling that *Windrush* passengers began to arrive in June 1948, six months before the Act even came into law on 1 January 1949. They were followed equally swiftly by racist backlash, with smouldering tensions around the UK bursting into open flame in August 1949 with the race riot at the Causeway Green Hostel in the West Midlands[1] and similar skirmishes in Leeds, Letchworth, Pontefract and West Bromwich. While the initial confrontations had primarily been between Polish, Irish and Jamaican migrant workers, far-right groups like the White Defence League and Oswald Mosley's Union Movement[*] fanned the flames of a general white working-class resentment towards Caribbeans that culminated in the large-scale race riots in Notting Hill in 1958, prompting activist Claudia Jones to launch the Caribbean Carnival – a direct precursor to the Notting Hill Carnival – the following year.

Evidently Britain had not expected so many of her citizens of colour to enter the mothership. Public hostility, violence and cries of 'Keep Britain White' culminated in the 1962 Commonwealth Immigrants Act, limiting immigration to those with work permits or whose parents and grandparents had been born in the United Kingdom.

The Windrush generation was the victim of multiple hypocrisies. The first, and most glaring, is contained within the late anti-racism

---

[*] This was a successor to Mosley's British Union of Fascists, which had its own paramilitary wing (the 'Blackshirts') and fought against Jews and left-wing groups in the famous Battle of Cable Street in 1936.

campaigner Ambalavaner Sivanandan's famous aphorism, 'We are here because you were there.' The colossal arrogance and monumental historical ignorance of the phrase 'go back to your own country' overlooks the fact that it was precisely the exploratory avarice of the British Empire that created a situation whereby descendants of Ibos, Yorubas, Bantus and Ashantis should have made their way, via the Caribbean, to the streets of Handsworth, Salford, Brixton and Westbourne Park. This empire did not hesitate to steal entire countries, with all the people and material resources contained within them; now its latter-day scions were expressing resentment that the very immigrants the NHS needed to function were making even the most perfunctory use of its services.

A second and related hypocrisy was the fact that the vast majority of the immigrants being stigmatised had entered Britain *legally* under their new status of 'citizens of the UK and colonies'. Challenging the 'half-truth' of Caribbean immigrants having been 'invited' to deal with labour shortages, historian Ian Sanjay Patel portrays the 1948 British Nationality Act and accompanying immigration as the inevitable consequence of Britain's unwillingness to relinquish her self-image as 'ruler of the waves'. The legal arrival of immigrants from across the Commonwealth was a direct result of Britain's rebarbative attempt to cling on to empire. Despite the legal obligations this new status created, British officials continually sought ways to refuse entry to non-white citizens; this was particularly acute in the Kenyan and Ugandan Asian crises of 1968 and 1972, when Britain did everything in her power to prevent British citizens of Indian extraction from exercising their legal right to take refuge in the UK after being persecuted by the new Afrocentric regimes in those countries.

The third was that stigmatisation of immigrants was often justified by the supposition that the UK's small land mass was infrastructurally unable to support a large influx of immigrants. In the immediate post-war years, Britain in fact had a shortage of workers estimated at between 600,000 and 1.3 million, and 200,000 'numerically surplus women'.[2] The issue of depopulation and a depleted workforce was so serious that the British government launched multiple schemes to attract white workers from other parts of Europe, including Bulgarians, Estonians, Latvians, Lithuanians, Poles, Romanians, Ukrainians and Czechoslovakians as well as German and Italian prisoners of war. The number of such European 'aliens' given nationality and settlement in the UK in the immediate post-war years is estimated at between 215,000 and 345,000. Yet by 1955, the total non-white population of Britain, most of whom had been born not 'aliens' but British subjects, stood at less than 100,000 (i.e. a miniscule 0.2 per cent of the population).[*] Given the very small numbers of immigrants of colour relative to white, and the abundance of jobs and single women, it seems clear that concerns about immigrants 'taking jobs and women' from locals had much more to do with said immigrants' skin colour than the actual overcrowding of the island.[†] This theme would recur again and again in the 1950s, 1960s and 1970s as Britain sought to have it both ways, maintaining its self-image as international custodian of fairness and good governance while discriminating savagely against its own non-white citizens.

The fact that there are now some black British people in positions of power in politics, the media and other professions should not be uncritically regarded as evidence of Britain's 'progress' toward a fairer,

[*] The differential treatment between white and non-white immigrants has persisted. In 2022, political pressure to expedite UK visas for Ukrainian refugees caused an enormous backlog for Africans, Asians and South Americans seeking UK visas. Many commentators pointed out the UK and Europe's utterly different attitude to refugees made homeless by the war in Ukraine compared to the apathy and even open hostility towards refugees of colour.

[†] Sexual anxiety from white males towards black has been one of the most common causes of racial tension globally: the fear that 'an old black ram / Is tupping your white ewe' dates back at least to Shakespeare's *Othello*. The Notting Hill riots of 1958 were sparked by a group of white Teddy boys attempting to intervene in an argument between a white Swedish woman, Majbritt Morisson, and her Jamaican husband, Raymond Morisson. The following day she was verbally and physically assaulted by a gang of white youths who threw milk bottles at her and called her racial slurs such as 'black man's trollop'.

more inclusive society, but as the hard-won spoils of a dangerous and painful battle for acceptance that continues today. Like all battles, it has its heroes: activist, writer and broadcaster Darcus Howe, leader of the Mangrove Nine, who was one of the first to expose institutional racism within London's Metropolitan Police, and would go on to edit *Race Today*, chair the Notting Hill Carnival and become an influential broadcaster and writer; Claudia Jones, who entered the UK in 1955 after being incarcerated and deported from the USA for her political activism, but went on to found the *West Indian Gazette* in 1958 and the Caribbean Carnival in 1959, campaigning tirelessly until her death in 1964; Leroy Logan, who left a successful career as a scientist to join the Metropolitan Police, fighting the force's intense racism from within, at great personal cost. And it had its martyrs: eighteen-year-old Stephen Lawrence, stabbed to death at a bus stop in Eltham, South-East London 'in a completely unprovoked racist attack by five white youths'* in 1993; the eleven black teenagers and two young adults who died at a house party fire on New Cross Road in 1981, in what the community has always believed to have been a racially motivated arson attack which the police totally failed to investigate until a twenty-thousand-strong march made the issue a national scandal.† But the battle's real foot-soldiers are ordinary people working long hours in menial jobs in the hope of creating better lives for themselves and their descendants,

---

* These were the words of the verdict reached by the jury of a 1997 inquest into the murder, but the principal killers, Gary Dobson and David Norris, did not stand trial until 2011, finally being found guilty in 2012, after nearly twenty years of intense campaigning by Doreen Lawrence, mother of the deceased, who was made Baroness Lawrence of Clarendon in 2013 in recognition of her efforts. The Macpherson Inquiry, launched in 1997 in response to the murder and the failure to convict Lawrence's killers, found the Metropolitan Police to be institutionally racist, and found the recommendations of the Scarman Report, launched in response to the 1981 riots, to have been ignored.

† In response to this political pressure, an inquest was launched in 1981, followed by a second inquest in 2004 in response to a High Court ruling. In both cases, an open verdict was returned due to insufficient evidence and it is probable that this will never change. Had the matter been immediately and thoroughly investigated, it is likely that this would not be the case.

often in the background of the most disgusting racism. The Windrush generation and their children rapidly discovered that the streets of Brixton, Tottenham, Toxteth, Moss Side and Digbeth were emphatically not paved with gold, but rather were grey, cold, expensive to live on, and illuminated by the bright blue light of police patrols.

Coming of age seeing the emptiness of their parents' dreams of being accepted by mainstream British society through hard work and Christian faith, the children of the Windrush generation found themselves mostly excluded from the middle-class jobs their parents had wished for them. Victimised by the police by the notorious 'sus law' (whereby they could be arrested merely on suspicion of being about to commit a crime, mostly just by being black), demonised by the media and vilified by politicians, this was a generation who very clearly perceived the multi-layered set of hypocrisies and injustices surrounding their presence in Britain. A generation who grew up with the 1981 riots in Brixton and on Tottenham's Broadwater Farm estate, accustomed not to be able to go to white clubs or venues, making their own scenes in shebeens and blues dances, playing reggae and lovers' rock, then soul, funk, acid house and jungle in warehouse parties, street parties and raves. Navigating racism at school, in clubs and in the streets was an experience familiar to almost everyone in this generation.

Claude Deppa

In the seventies and early eighties, there was no such thing as anti-racist. It just wasn't there. I remember days where I used to have a double case, trumpet and flugelhorn. If I saw somebody coming towards me – and you can spot a skinhead a mile off – you would just move.

Wozzy Brewster

I went to a school where there were ten black kids in my year. And seven of us were female. People would tell you to get in your banana boat and go back to wherever. And then you'd have to turn around and say, 'I don't know who you're talking to, but I'm born in South-East London, mate!' I'm very, very tolerant. You have three chances. So there's a point when somebody wants to call you a Nigger or tell you to get in your banana boat and go back where you came from, and do that monkey 'ooh ooh' noise that they used to do where in the end you just punch 'em out. At the end of the day, that's the only thing that's going to teach you. You're not going to call me a Nigger and think that I ain't gonna hit you, blonde little boy. I'll floor you and I'll batter you, and the teachers will have to come and get me off of you, which they did. You can call my mum into school, but my mum will tell you straight: 'The one thing I know, if she had to hit him, she had already given him his chances. And I don't expect my daughter to have to be called a Nigger in this school. So what are you going to do about it?' The racism was very blatant and, as a kid, you're only saying what's being said in your home.

'You could light a cigarette on people's foreheads' (Jazz Warriors)

It is essential to know this context in order to understand the meaning and significance of the Jazz Warriors: a group of young black musicians coming together in big band format to reclaim jazz as a black music, unapologetically and virtuosically celebrating themselves and their heritage. Independent in spirit, self-motivated, expecting absolutely nothing without fighting tooth and nail for it, the Jazz Warriors were emblematic of the defiance and confidence of second-generation black Britons who had no toleration for the compromises made by their parents.

Just like the present generation, most of the musicians who became Jazz Warriors had started to achieve recognition through running their own nights and jam sessions around London in the early 1980s, the most famous of which was Courtney Pine's session at the Atlantic in Brixton (now the Dogstar), just down the road from my house on Coldharbour Lane.

Courtney Pine

I got a start as a solo artist by playing in a pub in Coldharbour Lane. A trumpet player called Sonny was running the pub at the time, and he wanted to put jazz in his club to get rid of the coke dealers. It was so funny, using jazz to get rid of the drugs! We're talking about 1984, '85 kind of time. Just after the riots. Man used to try chop me up after I played there. I had to run for cover a couple of times.

Orphy Robinson

We'd all been playing in what's classed as Brit Funk bands now, a few of us had careers in other music before heading off into a more jazz territory. So we knew about hands-on approach, to create your own things, put on your own venue gigs. Flyer the barber's shop and the patty shop – we all knew to go and promote gigs there because we knew that our audience don't read the *Guardian*. Putting that information there for them is useless. All of those things that the establishment didn't want us involved in, they didn't want us at all their places. So we created our own scenes, which is what's happened now. Mau Mau and Steam Down – we did all of that, a long time ago!

By age twenty-two, Pine had already established himself as a major new figure in British jazz. His debut album *Journey to the Urge Within*, signed to Norman Granz's legendary Verve label (home of Ella Fitzgerald, Nina Simone, Billie Holiday, Stan Getz and Oscar Peterson), reached the UK all genres top forty chart in 1986, leading to national TV appearances including the coveted *Top of the Pops*.

Concerned about the lack of representation for musicians of colour in UK orchestras and big bands, Pine set up the Jazz Warriors in 1986 in collaboration with Abibi Jazz Arts, a community organisation for whom he had run a series of performances at the Royal Festival Hall for International Youth Year 1985.

Challenging the stereotype that black musicians could not read music, Jazz Warriors was envisaged both as a self-contained ensemble and as a vehicle to increase musical literacy. The band featured many of the most talented musicians of their generation, who would go on to become respected elders: Pine himself, multi-instrumentalist Orphy Robinson, vocalist Cleveland Watkiss, trumpeter Claude Deppa and bassist Gary Crosby, as well as names more shrouded in the mists of time, like saxophonist Steve Williamson and flautist Phillip Bent.

Claude Deppa

1984, '85, I started playing with Grand Union Orchestra. Courtney gets called in because Louise Elliott goes to Australia, and when we got to Grand Union, he saw all of this and said to me, 'Listen, man, the two of us are the only two black guys in this band! Why don't we have a black big band?' And that was the beginning of the Jazz Warriors.

Orphy Robinson

Creating the Warriors was fantastic because a lot of us were never included in the orchestras, we couldn't get a look-in. Warriors meant there was now a platform that you could actually come together. And it was frightening, there was so much energy coming from these people. We used to say that you could light a cigarette on people's foreheads because they were so hyper. It was that strong. Some wonderful, wonderful musicians and players and a lot of help that you were getting from each other as well.

Steve Williamson

The reason why I liken it to the big bang is because you had to have that huge ball of energy to create not just the great Shabaka, or the great Denys Baptiste, or the great Femi, or the great Moses, or the great Nubya, or the great Shirley Tetteh, all these cats. But ten years from now, twenty years from now, hundred years from now, it had to start somewhere with a huge big bang. And that's what the Jazz

Warriors was. That's exactly what happened. The world hasn't seen anything like it, I don't believe. At all.

Although primarily made up of musicians in their early twenties (and a sixteen-year-old Jason Yarde, rocking up in his school uniform), Warriors also included elders like thirty-one-year-old Gary Crosby and fifty-one-year-old Barbadian trumpeter Harry Beckett. As a mutual support network for black musicians to share knowledge, opportunities and advice, it plugged into a long tradition of community organisation, both within music – like Muhal Richard Abrams's AACM in Chicago and James Reese Europe's Clef Club in New York – and outside it, in the community education projects and after-school clubs of the Black Panthers. This tradition of mutual self-help can be traced back to the secret societies of nineteenth-century New Orleans, whose members would pay an annual stipend in order to guarantee a respectable funeral.[3]

As with the current wave of jazz musicians, a new group of young, well-presented, media-savvy musicians provided a perfect black British success story for the British media to latch on to. This would have been a welcome counterpoint to stories of racial tension and violence in the aftermath of the riots of 1981, 1982 and 1985.

Orphy Robinson

There was half a dozen of us that were kind of everywhere: the same sort of thing that's happening now, but on a larger scale, because at that time, it was very new for everyone. It was like, 'They're not playing reggae! What's going on?' So there was a move by all the popular style magazines: 'There's some black people! Bang!' So it meant we broke into other audiences. Our gigs were full of people that had never been to a jazz concert. Courtney's thing completely exploded in the charts. So he was on television, on chat shows – the *Graham Norton Show*, Jonathan Ross, and the Warriors would have popped up on some of those shows as well.

Many Warriors used the group's visibility as a springboard to sign individual record deals with major American labels: Pine was signed to Antilles, a subsidiary of Chris Blackwell's Island; Orphy Robinson to Blue Note; Cleveland Watkiss to Urban (a Polydor sublabel); Steve Williamson to Verve; and Phillip Bent to GRP. The individual members were flying high, with their faces on the covers of magazines like *The Face*, regular appearances on mainstream TV and radio, and sponsorships from designer fashion brands.

Claude Deppa

Steve Williamson was sponsored by Armani! I remember the jackets and suits he used to wear, he could stand up there with Wynton.

'Time to start takin' care of business'
(Wynton Marsalis)

It needs to be acknowledged that, for all their belief in the uniqueness and progressivity of what they were doing, the Jazz Warriors generation were operating in what might, from the vantage point of this generation, seem like a rather straight jazz idiom.

This was due in part to the explosive arrival on the global stage of trumpeter Wynton Marsalis. The son of New Orleans pianist Ellis, Wynton had dropped New York's prestigious Juilliard conservatoire in 1979 in favour of Art Blakey's informal, stage- and road-based finishing school, touring with his Jazz Messengers from 1980 to 1982. In that year, Marsalis won Musician of the Year, Best Trumpeter, and Album of the Year in *Downbeat* magazine for his eponymous debut. In 1983, at twenty-two, he became the first musician to win Grammys in the classical and jazz categories in the same year, going on to win at least one Grammy in each of the next four years. By 1987, still only twenty-six, he launched the Classical Jazz concert series at New York's bastion of high culture, the Lincoln Center, going on to lead its Jazz Orchestra and in 1991 becoming artistic director of Jazz at Lincoln Center, an independent entity that took its place alongside the New York Philharmonic and the Metropolitan Opera.

Steve Williamson

My life changed personally when I heard Wynton Marsalis for the first time. I saw Wynton and Branford [Marsalis] at the Capital Radio Jazz Festival in Knebworth. This young cat trumpet player, the same age as us, walked out there with Branford, and that was it for me, my whole life changed after that.

Jason Yarde

One of the albums that definitely changed things for me was *Black Codes from the Underground* by Wynton Marsalis. I remember my sister giving me the vinyl for my fifteenth birthday. That was when it changed, like, 'Oh, okay, there's some young guys nowadays playing this kind of music!'

Orphy Robinson

Wynton Marsalis and his brother Branford, Terence Blanchard – they were all coming through at the same time. Whenever they would come to the UK, you would chat. There was a real camaraderie and helpfulness with that generation of players. Remember, at the time, when people would play at Ronnie's, they'd play for a week or two weeks, even a month. So there's a lot of daytime to kill. So a lot of the musicians we got to really know well, and as our playing developed and as we became players on the scene, that continued. I'm sure that's happening now, here, with Kamasi Washington and Thundercat.

Philosophically underpinned by controversial writer and theorist Stanley Crouch, Marsalis' programme rejected both jazz funk and the avant-garde, staking a claim for jazz as the definitive black American music, rooted in swing and the blues. This musical neo-classicism came hand in hand with a social conservatism; Francis Davis describes the paradox of Marsalis as 'a rugged individualist out to restore traditional values with little tolerance for those who play by a looser set of rules; a straight arrow who talks like a rebel, though what he's rebelling against is non-conformity'.[4]

Wynton Marsalis

Everybody was saying that jazz was dead because no young black musicians wanted to play it any more, and because the established cats who should have been setting an example were bullshittin', wearing dresses and trying to act like rock stars. So when people heard me, they knew it was time to start takin' care of business again. I wasn't playing shit no one had ever heard before, but at least I was playing some real music.[5]

While they were unique in their organisational structure and in being the only black big band in the UK, the Marsalis influence may have been somewhat stylistically limiting to the Jazz Warriors, despite their attempts to bring their heritage into the music (e.g. taking the Jamaican national motto 'Out of Many, One People' as the title of their 1987 album, name-checking the Egyptian Saint Maurice of the martyred Theban Legion, and through the use of Caribbean and African percussion).

David Jones

We really disliked Wynton as a force. He defined himself as being against a lot of the figures like George Russell, who we thought were really important in the music. They didn't accept his vision of jazz. A lot of those figures were marginalised. They were not part of the canon of black American jazz. It was a very, very American view, there was no real understanding of a diaspora. There was no sense of what the music might be. It was seen as, 'This is the root. This is where it comes from. This is how it goes forward.' And it seemed rather narrow in its understanding of orchestral music. And then we met Wynton and we got to really like and respect him . . . It wasn't his fault that his vision had almost taken over.

Love him or hate him, Marsalis was important in stimulating debate, laying down a new (old) direction for jazz, rejuvenating record sales and gaining a respectability which could be used to acquire funding. While this mainstream respectability may have come at the expense of a certain subcultural kudos, there is no question that the success of Wynton and fellow 'Young Lions' Terence Blanchard, Marcus Roberts, Mulgrew Miller and Roy Hargrove helped create the conditions for so many of the Jazz Warriors alumni to get signed to American labels in the late 1980s and early 1990s.

'Maybe we had to be more evolved' (end of the Warriors)

The band's bright-burning flame exploded in a toxic fireball in 1990, due to the usual struggles around ego, money and power, leaving behind only *Out of Many, One People* (Island, 1987) as a testament to the group's energy.

Jason Yarde

People were flinging deals at us, sign this, do that. There was a lot going around and if you let those things get inside your head, like so-and-so is getting more opportunities than I'm getting, and all the rest of it, then it can lead to a lot of things imploding.

Claude Deppa

It went wrong when people started saying, 'No, this is my chair.' Even Courtney used to say, 'Look, man, I've got my gigs, somebody else come in, somebody else take that chair.' But there were certain people who just went, 'No, I'm not giving that up.' And that was hard because nobody else could come in and learn the parts. It was supposed to be a platform for anybody of colour to come through.

Steve Williamson

Maybe we had to be more evolved as people for something like that to have survived in the same form. We were all young. You know, without trying to place blame, when you throw a lot of trinkets people's way – and by that I mean you're getting deals, people are throwing all this money and all this stuff and this one's got a new car – when you're young, these things can get in the way of the actual purpose. When I say more evolved, when I'm looking at the younger generation now and looking at cats from Soweto and Shabaka to these cats: that mentality was weeded out. But it's only natural because you have to think about how long we've been in this country, our parents as a presence, and how relatively short a time after that presence was the beginning of the Jazz Warriors: we're just talking a couple of decades.

By 1992, virtually none of the Jazz Warriors alumni were still with their American labels, either having had their contracts discontinued, or choosing to leave after feeling that jazz was no longer a key focus: a stark warning to the present generation who are currently enjoying exactly the same kind of success.

Claude Deppa

They were all dropped literally within six months of each other. And you just go, 'Whoa, have we gone out of fashion?' I get a feeling the record companies were aware that the energy really came from the Warriors as a unit, and maybe they noticed that it was splintering. It was sad, because it wasn't just the people who were taking it further were dropped. The whole Warriors sort of disintegrated into nothingness.

Cleveland Watkiss

It was all about the moment and the moment went. Then there was another moment. It's a fleeting moment in time. You think you're going to be King Shit for ever? You're going to fall a long way, and a lot of us did.

For many of the young musicians who had tasted stardom and industry approval, having come of age in the brief jazz resurgence that followed Wynton Marsalis and the other Young Lions, this was deeply distressing. While some managed to maintain successful careers within jazz, with Courtney Pine maintaining popularity throughout the 1990s, many were forced to play other styles of music simply to make a living, while others left music and dropped off the radar altogether.

Nikki Yeoh

Loads of cats like Phillip Bent: no one's heard of Phillip any more. The music business is very fickle. Just because you have an amazing deal back in the day, it doesn't necessarily guarantee you have any future in music.

Steve Williamson

I've seen many people over the years in various fields of music that got dropped from record labels and they're all the same. Because they really raise you up very high before they drop you. Raise you into the bloody clouds, then they drop you. As a young person, it was a really powerful knock. You think to yourself, 'Well what's going on?', because I personally have only wanted to do that in my life. My ambition has never waned in any way. But you just find other things to do. All of a sudden, you see these young guys coming through, cats like Soweto who was just killing it. Then in a way you kind of make way for them. I've actually heard at times that you're not as relevant. I've heard those things over the years which is just silly, innit really. But that's how it is. They kind of just let a few people in and that's how it is. There were some lean years.

'We start with the first rung of the ladder' (Tomorrow's Warriors)

Most people agree that Courtney Pine was the leader and spokesperson of the 1980s black UK jazz scene, with Steve Williamson its tortured genius. But for most of the younger generation of musicians, by far the most important Jazz Warriors alumnus was bassist Gary Crosby.

While some Warriors chased individual deals, Crosby and his partner Janine Irons set up Tomorrow's Warriors in 1991 as a vehicle for passing on practical music business advice and political wisdom alongside musical knowledge and training. For Crosby, the disintegration of the Jazz Warriors was emblematic of the troubles of a generation who did not have role models to guide them, and Tomorrow's Warriors grew from the still-smouldering ashes of the Jazz Warriors to fill this void.

Gary Crosby

Sometimes we can look back at things through rose-tinted glasses. There was no success in the Warriors. Seriously. It was a one-year, two-year blip. It had introduced us to the music community, it had introduced some of us as musicians to the rest of the world. It was actually its demise that drove me and Janine to start Tomorrow's Warriors. Towards the end of the Jazz Warriors I met Janine, and I realised that if you're going to build a structure that claims that it's going to make a change, it has to make a change in itself. Organisations are made up of individuals. And what you need is a soul. You need an aim and an objective, and you have to stick to it. I mean, to show the attitude when we started Tomorrow's Warriors, we bought flour, beans, all these non-perishables. Hence why the company had that kind of military connection: Crosby Irons Associates, CIA, Nu Troop. We were going on a battle, an artistic battle. That's how we saw it. We were going to save our community from mediocrity and almost a deliberate backwardness in how our community saw the arts.

The nephew of Jamaican guitarist Ernest Ranglin, Gary had grown up inspired by the elder generation of British jazz musicians: Stan Tracey, Ronnie Scott, Tubby Hayes; the Jamaican Joe Harriott and Vincentian Shake Keane. This combined heritage of British and Caribbean jazz was central to Tomorrow's Warriors' identity in terms of both music and consciousness.

Hosting regular jam sessions throughout the nineties at Camden's Jazz Cafe,[*] Tomorrow's Warriors became a vital training ground for successive generations of primarily but not exclusively black jazz musicians: Byron Wallen, Dave Okumu, Tom Skinner, Nathaniel Facey, Peter Edwards and Eska right through to Moses Boyd, Nubya Garcia, Theon and Nathaniel Cross, Cassie Kinoshi, Femi Koleoso, Cherise, Camilla George, Yazz Ahmed, Shabaka Hutchings, Zara McFarlane, Binker Golding and Blue Lab Beats.

Conceived not only as a musical boot camp but also as a political and spiritual one, it gave many of the present generation of musicians a solid grounding in the traditions of jazz as a political music and a vehicle to identify and speak out against racism.

Shirley Tetteh

My awareness grew when I started hanging out with the Warriors. Nobody else in my life was really talking about race the way they were. My general consciousness around racism grew when I started hanging out with other black musicians, 'cos I'd been to a lot of predominantly white schools.

---

[*] This author even once took part, as a fresh-faced eighteen-year-old in 2001.

'in reference to our forefathers fathers dreams'

Nubya Garcia

Subtly it was incredibly spiritual and political and incredibly important for us, because we were a group of black kids playing jazz. It was way more black than any of the musical spaces I'd ever been in my life. You weren't scared to go there or felt like you didn't have a place. I think just by what they were doing, even as a sixteen-, seventeen-year-old, by osmosis, we were all thinking, 'Shit. Okay. We don't have many spaces to be like this, to be surrounded by people our own age who have as much love for so many other styles of music that are in the charts, and also music that's been around for a hundred years,' that wasn't cool at the time within groups of people that weren't at my school and weren't at Warriors.

Rooted in the Marxist concept of owning the means of production, Janine and Gary believed firmly in the importance of controlling their own infrastructure to prevent a repeat of the foamy mess most of the Jazz Warriors alumni found themselves in when the bubble burst in the early 1990s. They launched Dune Records in 1997 to release music from members of the Tomorrow's Warriors community including Soweto Kinch, Denys Baptiste, Jazz Jamaica, Abram Wilson, Nu Troop, Juliet Roberts and Robert Mitchell, with Jason Yarde as in-house producer.

Janine Irons

Denys Baptiste Quartet took over the jam. We recorded Denys and, lo and behold, he got a Mercury nomination. And that's when our little label, Dune Records, was sort of catapulted into being. It was there to create a high-quality marketing tool to get these young people out and about to send to promoters because everything was really scrappy. People would just do a really scrappy bio to send to a promoter. I really wanted to raise the standard, set the bar high. So we had nice design, used good studios, we had fantastic analogue recordings. We had to do it because there was nobody else there, and they needed those tools. The record companies weren't interested. You do what's necessary. So we did the recording. We needed press releases, so we did that and sent it out to the press, we did everything apart from play the music, really.

Gary Crosby

And even sometimes did that!

As Tomorrow's Warriors amassed an ever-increasing number of successful case histories, it developed from house band to a wider educational organisation, moving from the Jazz Cafe to Soho's Spice of Life in 2004, launching a weekend residency at the South Bank in 2010 and acquiring National Portfolio Organisation status from Arts Council England, generating regular funding to continue its activities.

The programme's support for young people of colour and female instrumentalists* can take much credit for the present generation's increased diversity. By the 1990s, as jazz had become increasingly accepted as part of the mainstream musical tradition, universities and conservatoires had begun to offer jazz courses, and tertiary education had become a standard route to professional musicianship. This naturally discriminated against people from working-class backgrounds, which often included people of colour. This gap became even more pronounced under the 'austerity governments' of 2010 onwards, as free musical provision in schools became increasingly rare. This made it difficult for aspiring musicians who were not from middle-class backgrounds to get hold of an instrument on which to practice. Tomorrow's Warriors was vital in developing and supporting musicians from teenagers to professionals, encouraging many of the most talented students to apply to conservatoires.

* i.e. as opposed to singers: the standard role for women in jazz.

'in reference to our forefathers fathers dreams'

Nubya Garcia

Gary was a huge role model in the years that I was preparing to go to college. He encouraged a lot of us to get together to practise and swap albums and 'have you learnt this tune?' in a really positive way. And we had so many other people slightly closer in age to us like Peter Edwards and James McKay and Nathaniel Facey . . . loads of people came in and did sessions, we had masterclasses, and now that we're older I realise how hard it is to do that, how hard it is to progress with late teenagers who are always coming and going, to progress with something like the big band, where you've got twenty young people coming every week or every other week, so I have even more respect and gratitude for the way that they managed to keep things going and how welcoming they were to everyone. They made space for you, gave you advice, if you ever needed anything they were always there.

The regular weekly sessions created a mutually supportive community that went well beyond the formal Warriors programme. Forming multiple bands with overlapping personnel, playing on each other's records, turning up at each other's gigs (sometimes ending up on stage), bigging each other up on social media: the sense of a close-knit community all coming of age at the same time was vital in creating the buzz and excitement around this wave of jazz.

Gary Crosby

We not only loved those people, but we also loved the environment they created. We were part of a communal thing. Janine puts aside her own creative ego for the community, and that is the key. That's why they still remember Janine Irons and Tomorrow's Warriors, because these young people, especially the last generation of young people, they're intelligent. They understand the difference between love and toleration, between people talking and actually doing things. Because they're living down in South London, Lewisham, Peckham. The sharp

189

end of life. They need help. They don't need words. And Janine uses her skills to help them. So obviously they're going to remember that.

Janine Irons

It's always been about building that community. Everyone supporting each other and building, so that we start with the first rung of the ladder. And then it's 'how do we get to the next bit, we have to put in another rung', and each time, each generation that we worked with was helping to put the next rung in. So they don't have to keep starting at square one, on that first rung. We've got people at all those different stages of the ladder and everyone can climb up.

Gary's conscious privileging of the jazz tradition meant that a new generation grew up with a strong sense of the music's heritage, and of their own role within the continuum. Most of the musicians who came up through Tomorrow's Warriors also listened to grime, hip-hop and other contemporary music through school and their peers, and many also had Caribbean and African musical influences from home. But the Tomorrow's Warriors influence meant that they knew standards and had a powerful grounding in the lineage of jazz, both musically and as a political force. This intersection of jazz, contemporary influences and influences from their heritage was the triangle that has informed so much of the music of this wave. Further, because of the strong friendships being formed, and diverse make-up of the programme's attendees, most musicians from this wave did not grow up with a sense of jazz being 'uncool'.

Femi Koleoso

Jazz became a word to be proud of. Warriors put that in me. It became a word to be proud to be associated with that wealth of history and knowledge. Tomorrow's Warriors, that is when I got introduced to hard, swinging, improvised push and pull, badman jazz, d'you know what I'm saying? That's where I got that from.

The difficult lessons of the end of the Jazz Warriors period meant that Gary and Janine made it a priority to instil business advice, moral values and a political angle as well as musical knowledge and skill. The importance of independence and owning your own infrastructure, being true to your heritage, maintaining community, and jazz's vital role as a political tool for social change, were all drummed into the Tomorrow's Warriors alumni from an early age, creating a generation steeped in this understanding and ready to put it into practice.

Moses Boyd

I take my hat off to all of them. I am grateful for the lessons of the things they did, that I can sit and be, like, 'Not going to do that, not going to do that.' And that's why you'll never hear me cuss 'em out because they had a different battlefield. They were ahead of their time, sadly, and bore the brunt of that responsibility and took the reward and the failures with it. Gary will always talk very openly about things that happened within the Warriors. It's like your parents say, 'Don't do this,' and if you do it, what d'you expect, d'you know what I mean? So I always hail them up, man, because they trod the path first.

Janine Irons

This latest cohort of our alumni have a really big sense of community. It's like this lot suddenly understood what Tomorrow's Warriors was all about. Because you have more strength when there's more of you working towards a common goal. You can change the world. And we are changing the world. It's not giant steps. It's tiny steps. That community spirit is key and I really hope they carry it on, because we've seen the power of it just by how their careers have blossomed.

unapologetic expression

'You got to spread the news'
(Kinetika Bloco)

Tomorrow's Warriors was not the only organisation providing early-stage support to young musicians. Kinetika Bloco, founded in 2000 by the late Mat Fox, combined New Orleans marching band music with African and Afro-Brazilian percussion arrangements and carnival costumes. Spearheaded by Jazz Warriors alumni Andy Grappy (tuba) and Claude Deppa (trumpet), Kinetika went into schools across South-East London, recruiting the most promising musicians and inviting them to join their summer school.

Multi-disciplinary and open-minded in their approach to genre, the summer schools combined horn players, percussionists, dancers and acrobats, playing a broad repertoire of black music that stretched from Duke Ellington to Fela Kuti, George Clinton to Dizzee Rascal.[6] This open-minded approach both to orchestration and repertoire can undoubtedly take some credit for the flexible approach to genre that is one of the hallmarks of the current wave of musicians. Developing the power needed to play outside in marching formation also contributed to the intense stamina of musicians like tuba player Theon Cross.

Based in the Southbank Centre, at the same rehearsal space as Tomorrow's Warriors, Kinetika Bloco served as a natural feeder for Tomorrow's Warriors, with many musicians coming through both programmes, including Theon and Nathaniel Cross, Sheila Maurice-Grey of Kokoroko and Femi Koleoso of Ezra Collective.

Claude Deppa

There is something to be said for really great, nice, delicate playing. But it's not for me. I mean, I grew up hard, like you got to hear me the other side of the river if I'm going to play. And I've instilled that in a lot of the kids that I teach, so Sheila has a big sound, Mark Kavuma: you can play outside and be heard. With Kinetika, you need to do that, we're a marching band, you got to spread the news!

'in reference to our forefathers fathers dreams'

Theon Cross

Bloco was this great thing to inspire the youth to be passionate about music and have fun, whilst also getting technical, because when you're playing for that long, you just build up your strength! But then Tomorrow's Warriors, Gary would come down and pick out the ones with potential, and carry them on to take that music a bit more seriously. Kinetika had people really serious, but it also catered for the people that weren't necessarily going to be musicians, that just wanted to dress up and be in parades. But Warriors was in the same space and took people that had the potential to be professional. Almost like the next level, it's like Bloco was primary, and Warriors was secondary.

Orphy Robinson

This scene that have all their bands, that's why they're into spiritual jazz, Sun Ra – because that's what they were taught. My own son did a little spot in Kinetika at some stage, and I still remember him and the younger one going around the house singing Sun Ra tunes. Nobody's said, 'That's not hip. Kids shouldn't sing that.' They just accept it as music.

The group have given many public performances, leading the Team GB 2012 Olympic parade and performing at Notting Hill Carnival, the 2022 Beijing Olympics, Bestival, London Jazz Festival and even my own free South-East London event, Camberwell Fair, giving young musicians confidence through playing, and being appreciated, in real-life festival situations.

Sheila Maurice-Grey

I remember being so overwhelmed when I heard all of these young people playing, there were so many female horn players who were so sick, much better than me. It was really inspirational, and to me, those people seemed cool, they were all super cool. Kinetika at the time was full of a lot of people who probably would have gotten in trouble in school, but they were all really musically talented. It was really inspiring.

'Space to make things happen' (the Midi Music Company)

In Deptford, South-East London, a stone's throw from Steam Down's original home at Buster Mantis, Wozzy Brewster's the Midi Music Company has been operating since 1995, providing vital early-stage support to musicians including the Dayes brothers, Kae Tempest, Moses Boyd, Poppy Ajudha, Katy B and Shingai Shoniwa (singer and bassist of platinum-selling band Noisettes).

Born in Camberwell, Brewster had cut her teeth as front of house manager at the Albany in the 1980s, hosting concerts by acts as varied as Courtney Pine and the Jazz Warriors, Elvis Costello, Vic Reeves and Bob Mortimer.

Wozzy Brewster

The Albany Theatre was set up by the late, great Jenny Harris and John Turner. They came up from Brighton and established the Albany Empire, and they were open to cultures, people, gender, diversity in every single way. And obviously in the seventies, with the National Front being quite prevalent, and also racism being quite prevalent, they ended up burning down the original Albany on Creek Road, which was an old workhouse from Prince Albert's days. And so the new Albany, where the Albany is now, was only opened in 1981. You have to remember: Deptford is the home of the migrant. And has been for hundreds of years. So, when racism raises its ugly head in an area that is culturally diverse historically, it didn't deter people. It didn't make people go, 'Oh no, they burnt it down, we'll have to stop.' All that happens is people house all the different projects that have been in that building whilst they fundraise, whilst they get the piece of land, which was actually behind my old Sunday school and where the market had always been, and they rebuilt the Albany. And actually, thank you very much for burning it down, now we get a purpose-built space and we get a community centre and we get a cafe. So these seeds were sown at the Albany – Deptford has that cultural seed bed. It was never going to kill off the Albany. If anything, it makes you stronger.

A testament to Harris and Turner's tenacity and the creativity and resilience of the area's communities, the new Albany Theatre was opened as a local community resource by Diana, Princess of Wales in 1982, including theatre spaces, a cafe, community rooms and offices. It was here that Wozzy met drummer and educator John Stevens; she left the Albany in 1988 to join his Community Music organisation, which practiced what were then revolutionary ideas about the use of music, and jazz in particular, in community development. A cornerstone of the UK's free jazz movement in the 1970s, Stevens was himself deeply indebted to the exiled South African musicians The Blue Notes, many of whom would later be involved in The Brotherhood of Breath.

Wozzy Brewster

I got to work with John for six years. The best time ever. He was the first jazz drummer I'd seen close up, played with Dudu Pukwana, Charlie Watts, John Lennon. He put on art exhibitions. He was the king. And he wrote books like *Search and Reflect*. The Community Music course that they run at Goldsmiths is based on John's beliefs and John's understanding that everybody could make music, everybody can sing – and jazz was his world.

These formative experiences were integral to the ethos of the Midi Music Company, which aimed not only to provide space for production, rehearsal, writing and recording, but also to provide business advice to its members, using the 'Music Explosion' sessions to connect them with music industry professionals. This support did a great deal to help emerging South-East London artists create real careers.

Ahmad Dayes

Somewhere for us to rehearse, somewhere for us to record. We had that base from the get-go, Midi has always had the doors open for us, so we never wanted for rehearsal space or recording space. Space to make things happen.

Wozzy Brewster

We're creating a platform for you to be creative in whatever way you like. We've got instruments, rehearsal space, a recording studio and a MIDI technology suite. There's a computer room where you can go and do research. We subscribe to *Music Week*, and we get calls from people. That has built up since 1997.

'We do literally share the bread'

In addition to the official activities of organisations like Tomorrow's Warriors, Kinetika and Midi, we cannot underestimate the role of informal development opportunities through musicians playing in each other's bands and on collaborative creative projects. This kind of informal apprenticeship is central to the history of jazz and the continuity between musicians that runs through it, with musicians playing in each other's bands until graduating to their own. Miles Davis learnt his chops playing with Billy Eckstine and Charlie Parker; Wayne Shorter, Herbie Hancock and Art Blakey with Miles Davis; Wynton Marsalis and Claude Deppa with Art Blakey. The cycle continues.

Nubya Garcia

That's always been a part of the jazz tradition. You always get people on the bandstand and bring them up with you.

'in reference to our forefathers fathers dreams'

Moses Boyd

It's always there, man, that's embedded in the culture of the music. You look at Art Blakey, Benny Carter, Miles Davis: it's not enough for me just to do what I do. I have to pass something on, you know?

Jean Toussaint

Once I joined Art Blakey and the Jazz Messengers, it was like plugging into a very rich vein of the history of that music, because that finishing school was one of the strongest and most well-known and well-established in the music. Art just taught us so much through the music. He let us know how he wanted us to play, by the way he played. I was incredibly fortunate to have gone through that. You couldn't pay for that kind of experience and that kind of training. That made me. Before that, I was a student, and then I became a musician.

Jason Yarde

I managed to sneak backstage, and I remember seeing Courtney in the corner with about seven nicely turned-out young ladies fawning all over him. And he saw me and he literally just parted them and said, 'No I've got to go and speak to this young guy.' I was like fifteen. He didn't know me. I was just some young black dude who'd come back, I was probably as wide-eyed as the young ladies he was speaking to. But the fact that he just parted these women out the way and was like, 'I'm going to speak to you.' I don't have a bad word to say about that dude. I mean, most musicians, I'd be surprised if they acted in the same way.

Courtney Pine

I know all of them. I think they're all brilliant. Not just the ones that came here and sit down on my couch and we shared bread. What they're doing now in terms of being able to be applicable in all styles of music is something that I was trying to do back in the day. There's too many musicians right now for me to name one or two. There's so many guys out here that want to do this thing. And I think it's now getting to an overwhelming number of musicians, in a good way. In a very good way. Some people brandish the word 'family' about, but it's very much like that. The connectivity between musicians, it's not just a paycheque at the end of a gig or an album session. We do literally share the bread. And we know each other's kids. We teach them how to swim. There is that level.

This tradition was very much alive in the current wave. It was playing in the band of Warriors alumna Zara McFarlane that Moses Boyd met Binker Golding, resulting eventually in the Binker and Moses album *Dem Ones*. It was through his teacher Oren Marshall that Theon Cross joined Sons of Kemet after Marshall left, providing a link from the present generation back to Marshall's via Shabaka Hutchings, Tom Skinner and Seb Rochford, who was himself replaced by drummer Eddie Wakili-Hick.

Shabaka had gained essential experience as a young musician playing in live electronic group Red Snapper, helping him aspire to a wider context for performance than the opportunities he saw in the jazz world at the time, which would be manifested in the trajectories of his bands Sons of Kemet and The Comet Is Coming.

Shabaka Hutchings

I knew that the music wouldn't necessarily be confined to just playing small clubs. I did some gigs with Red Snapper early on, a tour round Russia and dates round Europe. That was the first time I played proper big rave clubs on big stages. And it did show me a lot about what's possible in terms of being able to play creative music for large audiences.

Seb Rochford

Theon was twenty-one when he joined Sons of Kemet. And obviously 'cos I loved Theon and thought he was an amazing musician, I was interested in what he was doing, and I was listening to his first EP, which had Nubya on it, and there's one solo on that thing, I was like, 'This sax player's amazing!' She played one of the last Polar Bear gigs, in Istanbul. She was amazing.

Producers have also played a significant if less visible role in determining the sound of particular records and helping musicians shape their creative vision, often straddling generations and using knowledge accumulated from their experience with earlier forebears. Jason Yarde of the Jazz Warriors produced Cassie Kinoshi's SEED Ensemble's Mercury Prize-nominated *Driftglass* (Jazz Re:freshed, 2018); Malcolm Catto of the Heliocentrics produced Yussef Kamaal's *Black Focus* (Brownswood, 2016), using musical knowledge and hardware acquired in his long career to determine the sound of that record; and mix engineer Dilip Harris's discography reads like a chronology of UK jazz and related musics, working with artists from Galliano, Young Disciples and Jamiroquai right through to Sons of Kemet, Hello Skinny and Joe Armon-Jones, alongside international acts including The Roots and Japan's UFO (United Future Organisation, featuring acclaimed DJ/producer and future Worldwide FM regular Toshio Matsuura).

Cassie Kinoshi

Orphy, Steve Williamson – what they have done definitely set up the foundation for what we're pushing on and then we're going to be setting up the next foundation for the next upcoming people. But that's what jazz is all about: building blocks and regurgitation and mixing of all different genres so it can constantly become something new. Jason Yarde produced the SEED album because he's always been a huge inspiration of mine as an alto player and as a composer. And Soweto as well. And Nathaniel Facey. They've all been involved in my development and all of our development. Tom Skinner gave SEED Ensemble one of the gigs that he used to run in North London . . .

there's all that kind of support still there. I feel supported personally and I can see what they do for other people as well.

Jason Yarde

I produced Soweto's first album. I've done a lot of production for Dune, maybe two-thirds of the catalogue I've been involved in the production. I feel lucky in that a lot of this new generation – Nubya, Chelsea Carmichael, Femi Koleoso, Laura Jurd – all those guys were at Trinity. Not that I could make any great claims on their progression. But I took them all in ensembles, and mentored them in different groups. You try and teach people something and encourage them. But I remember even the first session I did with those guys, it was clear they were on to something already. Besides the teaching thing, I am also on the board of Jazz Re:freshed. And the other gig I did for the first time last year was taking over the Take Five mentoring scheme,* which a lot of those guys have come through. I did some arrangements for Zara McFarlane. And a lot of them, we've worked together in Jazz Jamaica All Stars. I feel lucky that I've got my toes and feelers in the scene in a lot of ways. And producing SEED Ensemble for Cassie; it's not like I put myself on these people. I guess she'd seen the progression of people like Soweto and Nathaniel Facey, so she thought of me in terms of producing her album. There's a lot of commonality, and that led on most recently to producing Cherise's EP. It's not got to the point where I feel like the old man in the dance yet! I feel quite connected to all those guys on the scene in some way.

'This whole thing of putting it into conservatoires'

The individual bond between student and teacher can be one of the most magical in the lives of many musicians, intensely rewarding for both parties. Virtuoso pianist Nikki Yeoh, an established educator

* A development scheme for young musicians run by long-running jazz producer/promoters and London Jazz Festival founders Serious.

herself as well as an award-winning musician, never forgot the generosity of one of her first teachers.[*]

Nikki Yeoh

Then there was another pianist who I should mention. Honestly, this guy's taught probably every jazz musician in North London. Chris Wilson, he never, ever gets name-checked, he's really not well known, but he is just the living don. The way he teaches harmony is amazing. He's a really shy guy and he doesn't push himself forward. I mentioned him on my album as a thank you. Basically he completely banged out the classes, he had no space. This is when I was at secondary school and I said, 'I really want to have lessons with you.' And he's like, 'Yeah, I don't have any space.' But he knew I was interested and he showed me some little blues lick and I could do it straight away and he said, 'Alright, come to me at Islington Sixth Form and have lessons. I have a dinner break between such and such time. But if you don't mind me eating a bag of chips during your lesson, then you can come.' He didn't charge me anything and he gave me a lesson during his dinner break. What a beautiful cat. I learnt all my harmony from him.

This experience was shared by guitarist Dave Okumu, whose experience at school in Pimlico with Loose Tubes guitarist John Parricelli left a lasting sense of wanting to pay it forward.[†]

Dave Okumu

It was so life-changing for me having lessons with my teacher John Parricelli at secondary school. It wasn't for a long time, but the tools

[*] Yeoh is leading the team for jazz, improvisation and pop at Guildhall's Music Education programme in Islington (the London borough in which she grew up), as well as working at schools and colleges around the UK, including Camden School for Girls, where she taught with Nubya Garcia.
[†] Which he did, marvellously. My good friend Tag Ara, now the bassist for Greentea Peng and Wu-Lu, gushed about his experience of studying with Okumu at Pimlico fifteen years before: 'He's the reason I started playing music. Favourite musician, man, teacher.'

he gave me were just absolutely life-changing. And I think from that, I carried this sense of 'one day I'd love to do the same'. I think I had a bit of a martyry, Messiah complex outlook on it. I thought it was gonna be quite hard work, that I wouldn't get anything out of it, but it'd be some way of giving back. But I couldn't believe just how rewarding the experience had become for me within just a few weeks. I had some really, really amazing experiences, seeing the impact that music can have on a person's life. I saw people change just through playing music. I mean, I really believe in that stuff, but I didn't expect it would be so immediate and so tangible.

This bond can exist in many different contexts: informal tuition through playing together; one-on-one tuition; in educational settings like those created by Tomorrow's Warriors, Kinetika Bloco and the Midi Music Company.

One such context is degree-level courses at universities and music schools, the most prestigious of which are known as conservatoires: finishing-schools for musicians of astounding promise. Taking their name from the Italian *conservatori* (orphanages) at which the *conservati* (the orphans 'conserved' or 'saved') were given musical as well as spiritual education, the term came to signify music schools in general. The world's oldest conservatoire is the Accademia Nazionale di Santa Cecilia in Rome, founded by papal bull in 1585. Yet although conservatoires have supported classical music for over four hundred years, jazz could not be formally studied at tertiary level until the University of North Texas offered the world's first jazz-specific degree in 1947, followed by Berklee College of Music (Boston) in 1954.

UK jazz courses are an even more recent phenomenon, with Leeds College of Music blazing the trail in 1965, followed by the Guildhall School of Music and Drama in 1982 and the Royal Academy of Music in 1987. Undergraduate jazz courses at Trinity College of Music, Birmingham Conservatoire and the Welsh College of Music & Drama did not appear until 2000, with the Royal Scottish Conservatoire introducing a jazz course in 2009 and Manchester's Royal Northern College of Music in 2015.[7]

Confirming the old adage that if you want to learn to swim, you need first to get into the water, the formation of jazz courses was clearly a necessary step in making jazz education more widely available. But there are many steps between forming the courses and diversifying the demographic of those who attend them.

These barriers meant that many of the Jazz Warriors generation did not study formally; and when they did, it was not always the most enjoyable experience.

Cleveland Watkiss

Most of us are from working-class black backgrounds, so we didn't have the finances to go to these places. And there was an emphasis on certain technical abilities that a lot of musicians didn't have i.e. reading. I mean, it's an important asset to have as a musician. But music is about listening and absorbing music. Reading is another facility and skill that we should add to our armoury. But when it becomes the primary focus, which it is in some institutions, then are we really talking about jazz? Are we really talking about improvising? Are we grooming them to be real improvisors in the tradition of all the greats that we know? Or are we talking about developing young musicians by numbers to play in orchestras and pit bands and reading for the rest of their life? I eventually did get into and go to Guildhall School of Music and Drama. But it was a lot of fight, man, it was a struggle. There was never anyone who looked like us who were teaching. So then you're getting a total European perspective on the music that comes from your culture. It felt all backwards. Certain people that were around at the time, Mulgrew Miller, Wynton Marsalis – why aren't we getting these people coming to tell us about the music and the culture? Why's it always white people telling us about our shit?

By the time the present generation left school, this had changed, with many musicians of colour taking places at conservatoires, especially Trinity Laban (Femi Koleoso, Nubya Garcia, Moses Boyd, Camilla George, Cherise), the Guildhall School of Music and Drama (Shabaka Hutchings, Yazz Ahmed, Theon Cross, Binker Golding) and Leeds College of Music (Ashley Henry, Tom Excell, Luke Wynter, Nick Richards, Eddie Wakili-Hick).

This development owed a lot not only to the outreach work undertaken by all the conservatoires as part of a wider trend in educational philosophy and accountability that dates back to the late 1970s, but also to the close friendship between Simon Purcell (head of jazz at Trinity, 2005–17) and Gary Crosby of Tomorrow's Warriors. Their close bond helped establish a route from Warriors to the conservatoires, both in terms of giving young musicians the confidence to apply and helping them prepare for the selection process.

But it is important not to overstate the case. Many of this generation's most successful musicians studied at Trinity and Guildhall, which may be creating a skewed picture of diversity in the student body. Or, put another way, the fact that so many musicians of colour have made a name for themselves within the London jazz scene might give the misleading impression that the jazz courses were much more diverse than they actually were – and are.

Further, while the increased number of students of colour inside the institutions is undoubtedly a form of progress, quantitative data on increased percentages of students of colour shed little light on their experiences whilst there, which in many cases were not uniformly positive.

Camilla George

Simon Purcell and Gary Crosby know each other and they were friendly. And Gary wanted to get more people from our backgrounds into conservatoires and Simon was probably the only one that was receptive to that, so props to him for that. But once we were in, it was not like it was portrayed, and their idea of jazz was very narrow. There was never any looking at where it came from, never any emphasis that it was music of black origin.

For some, this was a symptom of an approach to jazz that was embodied not in the institutions themselves but in the personal philosophies of those who taught in them, exacerbated by nepotistic recruitment policies.

Yazz Ahmed

I feel that the social history of jazz has been lost in our music education system, perhaps diluting the spirit behind jazz, which is protest, expressing your thoughts, feelings, and bringing awareness of the inequalities we face. I feel like sidelining these elements and focusing on intellectualising jazz in our conservatoires takes away the authenticity of the music. Obviously jazz is a discipline which requires skill and technical knowledge but a lot of music colleges seem to over-emphasise this aspect, analysing things to death and losing the spirit and message behind the music in the process. Maybe that's what punters pick up on, why jazz sometimes isn't very popular, because they're not feeling that personal connection and it's become an intellectual exercise. There's nothing wrong with writing music that is complex or challenging to listen to, but I like music with a message, that tells me something about the composer, rather than something over-intricate for the sake of being clever.

Nubya Garcia

I think they're still living out this 'employ your friends' kind of thing. It still feels very club heavy. It's getting much better even throughout the time that I was there and just after I left. I've seen a lot of faculties change for the better. Just to allow more diversity into the building, that's your first port of call and it doesn't just happen with the students because the students are looking up at people that have no idea about their experiences and aren't tackling the history of music because of uncomfortable situations. You have to learn about black history when you learn about jazz. And that doesn't happen in one week in a history lesson, do you know what I'm saying?

Oscar Jerome

This whole thing of putting it into conservatoires. A lot of the black musicians from that generation have been kept slightly out of that clique, in terms of the teaching staff and the teaching jobs for these conservatoires. I obviously went to a jazz conservatoire; I got so much invaluable information and techniques to go ahead with what I was doing musically. But I learnt so much more from going to the Haggerston and other jams where it was more of a party atmosphere. I mean, there's a lot of incredible musicians who went there, but a lot of those people were very drawn to the intellectual side of it. They enjoyed the accomplishment, the mathematical thing of it. And anything that wasn't straight-ahead jazz or in the tradition of jazz that had already happened, they would call it pop music. I was doing my own band with me singing and stuff throughout uni, slowly developing that thing, but I was very focused on just getting good at jazz guitar. But people would be like, 'Oh, it's your pop thing. Are you doing your pop thing?' But I'm like, 'This is not really pop. It's just not swing!' And I feel like that came also from the snobbishness and slight disillusion from a lot of the tutors there. Their music that they created struggled to connect to a wider audience just because they were slightly disconnected, and I feel like they created this culture within the uni and within the students that really looked up to them to put people down for getting involved with other stuff.

This experience of struggling for oxygen in a stifling educational context was not confined to the students.

Dave Okumu

I've taken ensembles at Trinity, quite a while ago. It was a really fascinating experience because it confirmed certain instincts I had about institutionalised learning around creative processes. What I encountered were these very, very accomplished musicians who were just incredibly inhibited. It was infuriating and I was trying to get them out of their comfort zone and doing repertoire they might not ordinarily play. I was just trying to think of all these different ways of engaging them. And it wasn't until the last session we had, like, suddenly, some sort of penny dropped . . . It was almost like it took them a long time to feel they had permission to explore themselves. It felt like I was dealing with people who had been told what they should be for quite a long time, and so they were in a particular headspace. I actually needed to be more compassionate. But I hadn't worked that out. I was just really baffled because they were obviously really capable musicians, but they were just all sitting there a bit freaked out. We did our performance and I got my feedback from the powers that be, and I definitely hadn't fulfilled the criteria, everything was quite rigid. We actually went on a journey, and I think it was a really valuable experience for the people involved. But in terms of the institution it was just not really what they were after.

Some of these criticisms are quite damning, and seem at odds with the educational philosophy of Simon Purcell. Having himself graduated from Trinity on the French horn in 1980, Purcell was professionally active throughout the 1980s, collaborating closely with musicians Martin Speake and Julian Arguelles of Loose Tubes, as well as running his own hard-bop sextet featuring future Jazz Warrior Cleveland Watkiss.

Simon Purcell

Music colleges have been doing very, very important work with high ethical motivation since the 1980s. They rarely get credit for it. But it's always within the financial model that is set by the government. To play a musical instrument to the level that's currently required to get into music college is expensive. You've got to own an instrument. You've got to have access to musical instruments and lessons which used to be free under the Inner London Education Authority, which Thatcher abolished. A lot of this goes back to Thatcher and Keith Joseph, it really does go back to that Tory shit. That political hegemony we've been living under for a long time. Blair improved it a bit but we're back really in the shit now.

And then you've got another aspect of diversity which is the curriculum offer, because to play classical music and to play jazz as it's generally taught in music colleges in most of Europe requires a particular skill set and familiarity with the canon. Which I'm not going to judge on, except to say that it is prescriptive. Of course, in terms of genre, most of those people who were prejudiced have left, and all the UK music colleges either have jazz courses or embrace jazz to an extent. But the demography is changing very slowly.

I was in a position of care. It's the first point of the job as an educator: 'educare' means to draw out that which lies within. So philosophically and personally, I felt my primary job to all of them was to steward their formation. The function of curriculum is to steward the formation of each individual. I honestly, deeply and profoundly believe that. Sometimes the students don't get it or they don't see it. I'm not into the notion of canon at all, but I'm interested in the idea of an evolving body of knowledge. So, yes, some people would have felt like outliers. Sometimes there might be some tension, and I openly regret that conservatoire curricula cannot be more diverse, but it's a complex set of issues. I used to say to them, I think that we need to have the imagination and the curiosity of the younger generation, and the younger generation needs to have the experience and perspective of the older generation. We need the ingenuity of an entrepreneur and you need the social conscience of a collectivist. You always need both. Diversity in music and education is not just seeing a range of faces on

MTV or on a panel. It's the diversity of the curriculum. It's not just the attendance of the curriculum. It's the diversity of the curriculum, it's not just the demography, it's the subject matter and the ways in which things are taught and learnt. It's not just the what and why, it's the how.

It is important to acknowledge that this is a story that is very much in development. Even in the time since Nubya, Femi, Moses and their cohort left Trinity, the institution has undergone significant changes. Pianist/composer Hans Koller replaced Purcell as head of jazz in 2017, making changes both to the curriculum and the teaching staff, which now includes a number of people of colour: Cleveland Watkiss, Byron Wallen, trombonists Winston Rollins (brother of Jazz Warriors trombonist Dennis Rollins) and Richard Henry, and writer/journalist Kevin Le Gendre, as well as long-standing sax teacher Jean Toussaint and Cuban violinist Omar Puente. It is notable, though, that these are all tutors and there is still no one of colour on the core staff.

Hans Koller

Things need refreshing, that's why they gave me the job in the first place. Simon did an amazing job there because he put it on the map, so I was happy to be in his footsteps; at the same time, this music is about change. This is not a traditional music. It was always an innovative music, so any programme needs to reflect that. Jazz has to be intergenerational and it's a truly global art form so we need to have different sorts of characters there. I wanted Trinity to reflect the London I know and love with the full monty, not just one smell!

I do not want to minimise the vast amount of work still necessary to level the playing field, or diminish the importance of the negative experiences at conservatoires shared by many of this generation, especially musicians of colour. At the same time, it is important to recognise gains where they have been made, and the fact that so many of this generation have been to music college has put them in a position where they are able to garner the respect of the global jazz establishment through their indisputably high level of musicianship and training, while also managing to connect with young audiences at street level. This is a remarkable achievement for which they have been justly praised and which will stand as an enduring monument to this generation. Musically literate but plugged into developments in both urban and electronic music, influenced by Dizzee, Skepta and Wiley as much as Bird, Diz and Duke, but equally respectful of both, they have been vital in reclaiming the image of jazz for their own generation and those coming up behind them.

Taken as a whole, the combination of direct advice and support, the structures put in place, the penetration of music colleges, and the ability to share both positive and negative stories meant that the Jazz Warriors generation helped create the perfect conditions for the present generation to thrive, in many ways realising their own dreams of independence. And in this they were helped by rapid and wide-reaching changes to the music industry, accelerated by technological developments.

6

Letting Go

New Industry Models and the End of Musical Tribalism

The emphasis on independence drummed into those musicians who had come up through Tomorrow's Warriors, Kinetika Bloco and Midi was facilitated by the growth of the internet and mobile technology. Whereas the Jazz Warriors generation, for all their collective spirit, had had to exist mostly within major label structures, the technological changes that turned the entire recording industry on its head by the first decade of the millennium threatened the dominance of these models, creating a space for artists and independent labels to operate with far greater power.

Courtney Pine

In those days, you have to go and get a gig, go and get a record deal. It's not like now, where you can just do it, put an EP out, set up your own gig. It's not that time like before where musicians were hoping that somebody would be interested in them. Musicians now, they're ready to go. And that's not just because they came out of university; we have a situation where you have now sons and daughters, nieces and nephews of jazz musicians who will just tell them the straight truth, how to deal with it right now. This didn't happen before. I was getting nothing but negative feedback from the jazz scene. Musicians that are out there now, they're getting nothing but encouragement, bare encouragement.

Gilles Peterson

What I am mostly excited about is the fact that there's a foundation that they've created themselves. They are in control, they don't feel that it belongs to anyone else or that they owe anything to anyone.

'Tom's Diner'
(birth of the MP3)

The 1990s were the peak of the old music industry model, with the arrival of the CD relegating vinyl to a DJ tool and specialist collector's item. A massive marketing campaign behind the shiny and cheaply manufactured new format caused many people to buy their favourite records all over again on CD, generating burgeoning profits throughout the decade. The recording industry hit an all-time high in 1999, with the CD representing 88 per cent of revenues.[1] This figure reached 95.5 per cent by 2002, as cassette sales also began to disappear.[2]

This all changed with the MP3, the format first released publicly by Germany's Fraunhofer Society in 1995. The team leader, Karlheinz Brandenburg, had been researching human perception of music since the early 1980s. Using Suzanne Vega's 1987 classic 'Tom's Diner' as a reference track, the team discovered that it was possible to make significant reductions in the size of music files without the human ear being able to perceive them, thus making it possible to store a large amount of music in a smaller space than ever thought possible.

This was not the first digital format: CDs had been around since 1982, with MiniDiscs and DATs shortly afterwards. But the drastically smaller file size of MP3s, combined with rapid developments in digital storage technology and internet speed, meant that from the launch of WinPlay3 in 1995 it was possible to copy, share and store vast amounts of music. The 1999 launch of peer-to-peer file-sharing network Napster, followed in the next couple of years by LimeWire and BitTorrent, cannibalised the CD market, as lifetime record collections from all over the world were shared in a matter of hours.

Although illegal, this practice was so widespread that the industry was in tatters by 2010, bearing witness to a decade of sharp decline that saw physical sales plummet by 60 per cent globally.[3] The digital music revolution annihilated the market for CDs so comprehensively that most laptops made after 2015 do not even have CD/DVD drives.

Whereas most people born before 1990 will have some sort of CD player lurking in a corner or cupboard, most younger people cannot even play a CD, and in most territories it has joined the MiniDisc, cassette, reel-to-reel tape and Betamax as yet another obsolete format.

For musicians like Shabaka, Wayne Francis and Henry Wu, old enough to have been profoundly influenced by the broken beat movement of the early to mid-2000s, the importance of independence from major label structures emphasised by the Jazz Warriors generation was reinforced by a whole new set of horror stories from the 'middle generation'.

Daz-I-Kue

We were right in the eye of the storm. All the independent labels, all the independent artists saw it coming. We were reading articles about Napster and what was going to go on and we told them, 'Look, Bugz in the Attic needs to be released worldwide. You can't go with the old model of releasing it in territories because people will already have the album downloaded from Napster, from other areas.' But they were slow to react to that, they wanted the old model: see how it goes in the UK, then see how it goes in Japan. When the album came out, it was just two territories, I don't think it was released properly in America at all. I think V2 were having problems, then they closed down the whole thing. It is what it is, it's the business of music. It's just one of those things.

Courtney Pine

Everybody thought the world was going to collapse. And the only thing of value would be gold and art. I took the publishing money, set up a record company, set up a recording studio and that was it. I just stood on my own two feet. I'm doing my own artwork. Started directing my own art sessions. That was 2004. And I've been doing it ever since.

The industry began to recover in 2014 due to the growth of subscription-based streaming platforms: Spotify, Apple Music, Deezer,

Tidal and others. This growth pattern has continued steadily, with the global recording industry hitting an all-time peak of $25.9 billion in 2021 after 18.5 per cent growth in that year, and streaming representing 65 per cent of global revenues.[4]

It is important to take this ebullience with a pinch of salt, noting that, once adjusted for inflation, the 2021 figure is still 37 per cent down on the 1999 peak.[5] Furthermore, growth in the size of the industry does not always equate to artists actually being able to make a living from recorded music. 90 per cent of artist royalties on Spotify go to 1.4 per cent of the artists (in real terms, 43,000 of the conservatively estimated 3 million artists using the platform).[6] Further, Spotify keeps a minimum of 48 per cent of moneys earned, conveying the remaining 52 per cent to major labels (and often even lower percentages to independent labels and artists). This 52 per cent is then split again between labels, distributors and managers, not to mention producers and performers, meaning that it can still be immensely difficult for individual artists to earn a living, even if they form part of the 43,000 artists within Stop-Tief-I's 'top tier'.* According to *Rolling Stone*'s calculations, Spotify founder Daniel Ek's grandiose mission statement 'to unlock the potential of human creativity by giving a million creative artists the opportunity to live off their art' would take seventy-four years to achieve.[7]

Despite these qualifiers, the artists who came of age in the latter part of the 2010s came into a time of immense opportunity, both in terms of the general resurgence of a recording industry that had been declining for nearly twenty years, and because the industry's changes shifted the centres of power and made possible models that the new group of savvy, independently minded artists could use to their advantage.

Aly Gillani

There are more choices for artists now. A major label isn't the only way to sustain a career. There are many artists who are now of a size where

* Stop-Tief-I: Orphy Robinson's pet name for Spotify – 'stop stealing from me' in Jamaican patois.

they can go and do live shows everywhere and bypass a lot of the traditional industry structures. You can be in direct contact with your fans, whether that's through social media, your Bandcamp page or just developing that big live following. So aside from a whacking advance, what's a major label going to give you that you can't get yourself?

David Jones

The creators, musicians, composers, however you define them, have more power now. They're smart and savvy and they understand publishing and they don't get ripped off. And they're sharing. There's so much cross-fertilisation and people are able to step forward when the time is right for them and do something that really takes them forward.

'Put some bass in it'
(production)

The two main expenses which any artist before the mid-1990s needed a label to cover were recording and production: the cost of renting a studio with the equipment necessary to record, and the cost of manu-facturing vinyl.

As the consumer technology revolution progressed throughout the 1990s, DAWs (digital audio workstations – essentially audio pro-grammes that could run on a computer) like Cubase, Logic, Reason, Pro Tools and Ableton Live became increasingly affordable, offering much of the functionality of traditional studio hardware set-ups at a fraction of the price. Apple even started issuing the GarageBand DAW with every machine in 2004, encouraging every Mac owner to exper-iment with making music. You didn't even need a computer: MPCs, a combination drum machine and sampler popularised by legendary hip-hop producer J Dilla, offered an entire workflow 'inside the box', and at its most extreme, you didn't need specialist musical equipment at all: many of the most popular grime beats of the early 2000s were, famously, made on a PlayStation.

While DAWs were initially more suited to electronic music producers, the increasing affordability of high-quality soundcards and microphones and the creation of digital plug-ins to replace bulky and expensive analogue processing equipment meant that bedroom studios were within the means of an unprecedented number of aspiring producers by the mid-2000s, and it was in such settings that musician/producers like Moses Boyd, Joe Armon-Jones, Emma-Jean Thackray and Tom Excell began working.

As well as providing an opportunity to hone one's craft away from the pressure of limited time in expensive studios, the bridge from bedroom electronic producer methods to live recording meant that the producers of this generation thought much more in terms of the sonics of the grime, drum and bass, hip-hop and deep dub they had grown up with.

Joe Armon-Jones

I try and not mix my tracks like jazz tracks; I put more bass in them than there would be in a jazz track, more effects than you would have in a normal jazz recording and just try and move it away sonically. It happened naturally. I'm not sat in the studio trying to make it sound less like jazz; whatever comes out comes out.

Moses Boyd

I was like, 'It just needs a bit of a rebrand and just looking at it from a different angle, because I've got all of these friends that are high-level jazz musicians. But they're not in the 1950s. They shouldn't be wearing Ray-Bans. They shouldn't be playing to people sitting down. They shouldn't be recording their album sounding tinny and weak.' I'm like, 'Roni Size exists, man, put some bass in it!' That was my philosophy. I was like, 'You've been to Carnival, man, why does your record sound like an ECM thing recorded by Manfred?'[8] Do it how it should be done if you were doing it now. Forget what Blue Note sounds like, forget what Impulse sounds like, I've got flippin' access to these amazing studios, these amazing plug-ins, all of this history that I've grown up with, grime, sound system culture. I'm like 'Put all of it together,' that's where my thing was.

'Get your music out to the people' (distribution)

Sheila Maurice-Grey

I love the independence. It's definitely hard because a lot of what we're doing, we're having to do by ourselves and figure things out as we go along. Whereas in a more traditional pop route, you have everything laid out for you, but then it's very hard to be like, 'No, this is what I want.'

On the distribution side, artists were more able than ever to share their music with peers and fans. While the major labels struggled to adjust to the new reality, a slew of new sites sprang up offering direct-to-consumer commerce, bypassing traditional distribution systems. Bandcamp emerged as the market leader in this field, offering an attractive, easy-to-use platform for music creators and independent labels to sell their music directly to fans in both digital and physical formats. Likewise, digital aggregators like CD Baby, TuneCore and DistroKid offered the ability for creators to get their songs on Spotify, Amazon, Apple Music and all other platforms for either a one-off fee or low percentage, bypassing both labels and traditional distributors.

Vinyl, like the T-1000 cyborg in cult 1991 film *Terminator 2,* stubbornly refuses to die, with its crisp analogue sound, satisfying weight and opportunity for powerful sleeve art maintaining an ongoing cultural resonance. By the late 2000s, the vinyl market was well on its way to recovery, hitting a twenty-five-year high in 2017.[9] This trend continued until now, with vinyl sales eclipsing CDs in 2020 for the first time since the early 1990s, hitting a new thirty-year peak in 2021 with 23 per cent of all UK album sales on vinyl.[10] Pressing plants reopened across Europe and Technics resumed manufacture of its iconic 1210 turntable. Wryly sensing the mood of exaggerated celebration, the *Daily Mash* ran the satirical headline: VINYL SALES OVERTAKE SALES OF FOOD.

But the new popularity of vinyl was due to a small number of collectors, willing to part with significant sums of money to own a physical copy of music that could be limitlessly streamed for free via a monthly Spotify subscription. Sales were nowhere near pre-CD levels, when vinyl was the only legal means of acquiring music for on-demand home consumption.[11]

Dom Servini

The resurgence of vinyl has been massively exaggerated. Vinyl fell off a cliff edge about the turn of the century, we went through a period of digital download, legal and illegal. And then vinyl had a comeback, became fashionable. It never has and it never will get to where it was in the mid-nineties. Never. And people are buying vinyl for all sorts of strange reasons these days. Half of them aren't even playing it. I've had people message me before, who bought a Wah Wah record, an album that's got a digital download code in it. And they've said, 'Yeah, I got the record, I didn't get a digital download code,' and I'm like, 'You need to open the record, it's inside it on a card.' They're like, 'Oh, I'm not opening the record. Can you send me the code, I don't open my vinyl, I leave it sealed.' That's happened a few times.

Caveats aside, vinyl has become a meaningful source of income for many musicians and producers, especially in jazz, Afrobeat, house and techno. And it is not only middle-aged men with walnut floor-standing speakers who buy it: the format has become increasingly popular with younger fans. According to a 2020 study, 15 per cent of Gen Z (b.1997–2012) music fans said they buy at least one vinyl album a year, in comparison with only 11 per cent of millennials (b.1981–96).[12]

Vinyl's new popularity presented a logistical challenge for artists both in finding the money to pay for the pressing and in getting the records into shops: both elements that would traditionally have been taken care of by labels and their distributors. The industry responded with 'label services' deals, whereby small, artist-owned imprints or individual artists could maintain their ownership and financial independence whilst using a label's infrastructure. In many cases, labels were cut out altogether, with digital distributors like Believe, AWAL and the Orchard striking direct deals with artists, distributing music both digitally and physically (via partnerships with physical distributors like Proper[13]) and in some cases even investing in recording and marketing (as a traditional label would have done), while leaving the artists in full control and with far higher shares than under traditional label models.

These were the kind of hybrid deals struck by Moses Boyd, Ezra Collective, Poppy Ajudha and Theon Cross: making use of major label infrastructure while maintaining creative control and majority ownership.

Poppy Ajudha

A lot of us in that crowd just started completely independent. So it's quite hard to go from independent into some all-encompassing deal, because they know you're self-sufficient and they know you know what you're doing. But there is always a place for structural support, because if you want to grow to that global scale, you need it.

Even for those artists who did decide to sign with majors, the abundance of alternative routes available obliged labels to make much more competitive offers than the exploitative, take-it-or-leave-it deals of some of their predecessors. Artists were able to sign deals allowing far greater creative freedom and flexibility, respecting the work already done at ground level.

Kerstan Mackness

One of the things I really like about Ezra and Shabaka: the music has
got nothing in common but they share something. Which is aggressive
ambition. And I think that unapologetic desire to smash it out of the
park is really important because there's nothing apologetic coming out
in this music. That sense of swag and that desire to do it on their own
terms is really important. So, yes, Shabaka is signed to a major record
label, but the music that he's delivering is fiercely on his own terms.
And the same is true of his project with Dan and Betamax, The Comet
Is Coming. I mean, can you imagine the response from their record
label when you tell them we want to call our album *Trust in the Life
Force of the Deep Mystery*. They're like 'Oh, that might be a bit long . . .'
And you're like, 'No, that is what it is.'

It is important to temper the optimism by stressing that actual
incomes from recording are still much lower for many artists than
they would have been in the glory days of the late twentieth century. But what has changed is the balance of power. In the 1980s or
1990s many signed artists became extremely wealthy but it was far
harder to make a living as an unsigned artist; today there are many
more access points and many more routes open to making a living
from music.

Nubya Garcia

It's so hard to compare because we're living in a different time, we
measure success in a very different way. In the nineties, they all came
home and bought houses and cars. We'd never be able to do that now.
I think we're fighting a different sort of fight in terms of being able to
make money from music. Doing the DIY versions of our own shit and
understanding what actually goes into running a label, putting a record
out and all of that stuff, I think puts us in a much better position to
actually make money from music. Just recording and releasing music,

because 100 per cent of the profits can go back to the person who's done it themselves.

While many artists chose to remain independent or sign deals with distribution partners, some set up their own labels both to release their own music and support other artists coming through, like Moses Boyd's Exodus Records, Emma-Jean Thackray's Movementt, Shabaka's Native Rebel Recordings and Matthew Halsall's Gondwana Records.

Credit must also be given to the independent labels that supported this new wave of jazz. Whilst there had long been specialist jazz labels like Naim Records and Edition Records, the 2000s and 2010s saw the growth of a whole cohort of independent labels releasing jazz alongside other styles including house, techno, hip-hop and a range of African styles: First Word, On the Corner, 22a, Rhythm Section, Gearbox, Wah Wah 45s, Olindo, Strut, Soundway, Brownswood; even my own Wormfood Records, which released debut albums and EPs by UK jazz stalwarts Nubiyan Twist.

Emma-Jean Thackray

Artists need autonomy to be able to do whatever they want. And that's how things stay real. Once suits start getting involved in a creative capacity – of course get involved in an ancillary capacity, that's what they are there for – but when they get involved in a creative capacity, I think that's when things fall down.

Naturally, not everyone was convinced.

Oli Reeves

The whole DIY thing feels likes a massive buzzword these days. People are always saying, 'Oh, it's a DIY/independent operation,' I'm like, 'Hang on, you're a fucking major label, it's bollocks.' Do it yourself or being independent means just that. It's using your own hard-earned money.

unapologetic expression

The first 22a record, that was Ed's[*] hard-earned money, from stacking shelves in fucking B&Q. It's not from some rich daddy handing him over some cash or because some A & R thinks you've got the right look. It was hard-earned cash, from doing shitty jobs. And that's how the label is still funded now. Obviously, it's turned over from selling records and putting out great music that people like and getting gigs off the back of it, but also fundamentally, still having to work and put hard-earned cash into it. To me, that's what DIY is. But it just seems like one of those words that a lot of people seem to use nowadays, everyone loves saying they're independent. Mate – you're not independent.

But taken together, there is no doubt that the artists of this wave have a far greater set of opportunities for recording and releasing music than previous generations: maintain independence (with direct distribution or label services deals where appropriate); sign a straight-forward, transparent 50/50 deal with an independent label that under-stands, supports and nourishes your creativity; set up your own label or sign with a major label with the increased bargaining power that comes from knowing you have a range of other options.

Joe Armon-Jones

Me talking about the DIY stuff is not to say that I would never sign with a label again or work with labels, but just to have that stuff, that infrastructure there. So that if everything else just crumbles away you can still do your stuff. Get your music out to the people, you know?

'Now, everyone listens to everything'
(an end of tribalism)

If the changes in the recording industry catalysed by the MP3 shifted the centre of power and opened up space for different models, the

* Ed Cawthorne aka Tenderlonious, Oli's partner in the label.

growth of 'playlist culture' engendered by iPod and Spotify promoted a broadness of taste that was completely different from twenty years before. Where admission of a fondness for jazz in the 1990s could have resulted in mockery and exile in certain circles, by the mid-2010s, having some jazz on your Spotify or iTunes playlist meant exactly that, and not necessarily anything more.

To appreciate how revolutionary this was, it is necessary to understand the fierce tribalism surrounding the UK music scene before the turn of the millennium. Mod, rocker, punk, soulboy, New Romantic, skinhead, raver, junglist: it was not simply a question of which record you saved up money each week to buy, which weekly music mag you read or which club you chose to go to: it was your clothes, your politics, your language, your tribe. Even as far back as the 1950s, lovers of trad jazz were being called 'mouldy figs' by the 'dirty boppers' who had embraced jazz modernism and were fighting pitched battles in the street in defence of their particular variant. And as late as 1998, UK garage fans were donning the iconic Moschino Off Key jackets and trousers alongside shiny white Reebok Classics in an instantly recognisable union of music and fashion.[14]

Steve Symons

Things were definitely more tribal. I think it's hard for people to realise that the tribalism was an investment. To like music was an economic investment because the only way you could listen to stuff at home or out was paying for a ticket, buying a record: there was no free streaming available apart from the radio. So people really invested in it. There was always a fashion element to it as well. And this kind of tribal sense was quite strong, even though we were supposed to be the open-minded ones!

Quinton Scott

Back in the eighties and nineties, pre-internet, there were strong scenes and communities based around vinyl, parties, DJs and specific music styles; solid scenes that all had a very tight culture and a loyal following. By the early 2000s, that had started to fragment. Early digital music sites and social media contributed to that as music became far more available and the whole way people consumed music changed. Scenes sort of dissipated, with the focus becoming more on individuals and specific events and festivals.

Bradley Zero

I don't think there's any one thing that created it, but I think generally there's an open-mindedness that wasn't around even ten, fifteen years ago. Twenty years ago for sure, you were a junglist or you were into your house or you were indie or you were jazz or you were rock. Now, everyone listens to everything.

It is tempting to see in this fierce tribalism the quintessentially British (and quintessentially male) mania for holding fearsomely strong opinions about fundamentally unimportant things. Milk first or tea first? Toilet roll under or over the roll? Blur or Oasis? Beatles or the Stones? Meanwhile seismic change happens all around uncontested, global and local inequality continues.

But this glib analysis masks some very real points about late twentieth-century culture that may be lost on anyone born after about 1988. As late as the mid-1990s, when I first started getting seriously into music, there was no internet and no smartphones. If you had Sky, you could watch MTV, but for many families, my own included, you had a choice of only four (later five) terrestrial TV channels. If you wanted to hear new music, there were three main methods: listen to the radio, go to a club or take a punt on a new record or CD at your local Our Price, possibly after listening in-store at one of their exciting headphone stations. Or, especially for the generations above me, go to your friend's house and cluster round the record player to listen to the new vinyl on which they'd just splurged all their money for the week, right down to the bus fare home.

letting go

Orphy Robinson

We were going to clubs, didn't have Shazam. We had to go and ask the DJ, 'What's that?'

And then you would go record-hunting down in Berwick Street, Hanway Street, that's where you got your cut-outs. I tell students how crazy we were at that time. I used to walk home: spend all my money on records, and walk home to Stoke Newington.* And I was quite happy, walking for an hour and a half with my bag of records. I need to hear this stuff! And we did our own trace history. Who's playing on a Herbie Hancock record – ah, Tony Williams, this guy. Let me check out his stuff. And then you would see who's on that, that's how you followed your thing. You want to reach a higher standard so you're searching out as much as possible.

'This iPod Shuffle generation'

Adam Moses

The young people coming through are all part of this iPod Shuffle generation, where people don't necessarily listen to albums any more in the way that they used to. You get your iPod, put it on shuffle, whatever's in your library is played. You might get a hip-hop tune, soul tune, whatever it is, right? You've got a generation of kids who are listening to music in that way. How do we take jazz music and make it just part of that playlist?

The concept of walking around listening to music only you could hear did not begin with the MP3 player. It had begun with the Sony Walkman in 1979, the same year Margaret Thatcher became prime

* I've heard this story several times from DJs and musicians of the same era, generating a charming image of a ragtaggle procession with Orphy, Cleveland, Trevor Nelson, DJ Hype, the Ragga Twins, etc. all trudging up to Hackney on a cold Saturday afternoon, proudly clutching their records.

minister of Britain, ushering in a new era of capitalist selfishness. (As she told *Women's Own* in 1987, 'There's no such thing as society. There are individual men and women and there are families.') This seems more than coincidental. Like all technological developments, Walkman began to change the way in which people consumed music; albeit in what would now be regarded as a charmingly analogue way.

Nikki Yeoh

I'd go to the library after school, go through the records and rent them out for ten pence each. Go home and tape them and bring them back. In the eighties Walkman was a new thing, right? So I had Phil Collins on one side of the tape. And the other side of the tape was blank. And I thought, 'Right, I'm going to record this album I've just got out of the library.' It was John Coltrane, *Africa/Brass*. Which is quite a mental album, quite free, and very long tunes. So I recorded it. I didn't understand it first of all, I was like, 'This is a little bit of a headache, this music.' So I'd listen to Phil Collins on the way to school because it was cheaper to listen to one side of a tape and then let it reverse than it was to wind it back. Because if you wind something back, it runs out of batteries. If you fast-forward, it runs 'em out less, but it still burns out the batteries unless you get your pen and put it in the middle and spin the tape round. But then that breaks the tape. So I'd be really wanting to hear Phil Collins, right? But the journey to school wasn't super long. So I'd have to endure *Africa/Brass* for like two days in order to hear Phil Collins. And the revelation came when suddenly one day I was fed up with Phil Collins and I actually couldn't wait to listen to *Africa/ Brass*. That taught me that familiarity and repetition can make a shift.

The Walkman was briefly supplanted in the mid-1990s by the deeply unreliable Discman, on which you could play one CD (if you could keep still long enough for it not to skip), and eventually the MiniDisc player, which offered the revolutionary capacity of storing several albums on one recordable MiniDisc. But the MP3 format offered storage capacity on a completely different scale. Where previously consumers had been able to listen to only one album, Steve Jobs vaunted iPod's ability to hold 'a thousand songs in your pocket'. A combination of slick design and Apple's powerful international marketing engine meant that, just as the 'Rollerblade' brand had become synonymous with 'in-line skates' earlier in the nineties, iPod became the definitive method of listening to music until supplanted by Apple's own iPhone, and competing Android smartphones, in 2007.

If the birth of the Walkman coincided with a new phase of capitalist individualism in the UK, iPod was consumer capitalism on steroids. But how to choose between the vast number of songs available? Rather than listen to whole albums, consumers were encouraged to use the 'shuffle' function, randomly playing individual songs from their collections. Many people began grouping songs into their own playlists – a technologically more advanced and much less fiddly version of the analogue mixtapes that most music lovers who grew up in the 1980s and 1990s will remember making.

The subscription streaming services that began to dominate in the mid-2010s accelerated this trend through official playlists curated by the platforms' editorial teams, and functionality for user-curated playlists to be easily made and shared. This helped diversify listeners' tastes, replacing the tribal culture around musical genres with a broader, more open-minded outlook, with many playlists curated by 'mood' rather than genre. In addition, most streaming services use algorithmic technology to make recommendations and autoplay music based on users' listening histories, a process known as 'scrobbling'.*

Dom Servini

People don't give a fuck as much about genres any more. It's just music. That generation are much more open to listening to what we

---

* The word comes from Audioscrobbler, Richard Jones's first-to-market 2002 system, which merged with Last.FM in 2003, pioneering the use of audio recommendations based on listening history. The word's gentle suggestion of crumpets and an afternoon of board games in an English country house masks the wide-reaching significance of this kind of auditory intrusiveness.

would call jazz, because it's a valid form of music that can be played by their peers. They might listen to Shabaka and they might listen to whoever the latest death metal band is. Thanks to the internet.

Kate Hutchinson

You just have to look at the Floating Points/Pharoah Sanders record that's just come out* . . . I mean, nine out of ten stars in *Pitchfork*?! That would never have happened ten, fifteen years ago; alternative music sites like *Pitchfork* didn't really touch genres like jazz. I feel like people's horizons are broadening music-wise. We used to be so tribal in our music tastes.

'This kind of religious experience' (live shows)

Coterminous with the MP3-driven recording industry crash of the early twenty-first century was the growth of the live music sector, with live shows overtaking physical sales in 2010 as the single biggest source of music industry revenue.[15] By 2012, 50 per cent of all music industry revenue in the EU came from live events.[16] Where previously artists had toured to promote records, often at a loss and accruing agonising levels of debt to their labels in the process, by the mid-2000s releasing music had become, for many artists, a loss-making promotional tool to generate lucrative headline shows and festival appearances.

The growth of the live sector and its increased importance as a revenue stream meant many of this generation's artists were playing more shows than their predecessors.

---

* *Promises* (Luaka Bop, 2021). As well as being a mystically magnetic piece of music in itself, this was a major record symbolically in that it brought together the worlds of jazz, electronic music and classical music as represented by Pharoah Sanders, Floating Points and the London Symphony Orchestra.

letting go

Gilles Peterson

What makes it really interesting now is that they are self-sufficient to the point that they can play every day and do gigs every day. That wasn't the case before; in the eighties and the nineties, it was like once a week. Most of them still had day jobs or they were teaching, this, that and the other. There was no sense that you could actually really practise to an audience, practise your craft and grow.

The shift from recordings to live is consistent with an emerging preference in the same period for 'experiences over things . . . access over ownership'.[17] Why amass a DVD or video collection when you can watch whatever you want on Netflix, Mubi or Amazon Prime? Why own a bulky and expensive record collection when you can stream much of the world's music on Spotify for £10 a month? And why own a car or bike when you can rent one just around the corner from Zipcar or Lime? Or, indeed, have Mohammed (4.8*) pick you up in an almost-new Toyota Prius?

Whether caused by fear of the insecurity of ownership, an emerging ecological consciousness eager to avoid filling the world with unnecessary objects, or simply the need for exciting experiences to post about on social media, this shift gave increasing value to going out to experience music. And if there was a general shift in preference to having a live experience over owning a recording, it is logical that this would also result in a preference for live musicians over DJs.

Bradley Zero

I started getting a sense of things coming back around and an excitement around people playing live music for a dance floor. Obviously I'm a DJ, but you can't really replace live music. But it had fallen out of favour a bit, so many festivals sprouting up where it was just three days of DJs. Even I think that's boring! I think it just kind of came around at the right time. People were ready for some live music.

unapologetic expression

People were ready for some musicianship and people had open minds and open ears to let something else in.

Kerstan Mackness

The internet has pushed the value of a lot of things to absolute zero. There's none of that thing you had when I was young where the music you liked defined how you dressed. And if everyone is listening on Spotify and everyone's playlists have got everything from Dave to Slipknot to all points in between, then there's nothing to identify with and music's become valueless. So this really important tribal thing suddenly has no meaning because it's just something that you consume on YouTube, something that you get on your family Spotify account. So you all dress like skateboarders, you all listen to the same music on streaming platforms. There's no value or ecosystem to this. And then suddenly you're a seventeen-year-old dragged to Steam Down in Peckham and you're like, 'Holy shit!' There's a feedback loop between the thing that's happening and the audience. It's pure soul music in that sense. It's trance music. And it's dance music. So you've got this kind of religious experience.

'Smeared over 2,000 acres of Somerset farmland' (festivals)

Do you remember the festivals, Miranda?
Do you remember the festivals?
Do you remember hairy smalltown freaks crammed
into a clapped out Escort van? Oil smeared Hawkwind
T-shirts, cut off sleeves and an overall smell of sandalwood?

Do you remember the festivals, Miranda?
Do you remember real Crusties?
No, not the soft & fluffy tofu-sniffing trustafarians
but the Real Deal: ragged, grey-skinned, glue-crazed
nihilists, terminally pissed with 'Punk's Not Dead' tattoos

syringes filled with Special Brew . . . they'd come up to you,
see the cider-vomit dripping from your chin & go
'Cor, Two's-up on that then, geezer . . .'

Do you remember that acid they called 'Window Pane'?
Stick it under your eyelid, next thing you know
your brain's smeared over 2,000 acres of Somerset farmland . . .
Do you remember Welsh hippies with tie-dye beards?
Eight-hour cosmic rock jams, loads of weird noises
that sound like aliens passing wind
down a wormhole in time and space?

from 'Summer Lament' by Jonny Fluffypunk[18]

The blurring of genres caused by the digital music revolution coincided with the exponential growth of the festival industry in the twenty-first century: the live experience *par excellence.*

Originally a countercultural phenomenon, era-defining 1960s rock festivals like Woodstock, the Isle of Wight Festival and the disastrous Altamont Free Concert* provided opportunities for young people to get together, far away from the controlling hands of their parents, generating potentially revolutionary energy. It has been suggested that UK festivals have their roots in much older, pre-Christian seasonal festivals, a continuity consciously drawn on by New Age festivals like the Windsor Free Festival and Stonehenge Free Festival in the 1970s and 1980s, both of which ended in brutal battles between attendees and police.

As electronic music grew in popularity in the late 1980s, the rave and free party scene generated a fresh wave of bacchanalian energy,

---

* This was the event that to many people marked the symbolic end of the sixties. Envisaged as 'Woodstock West', a massive free concert to mark the end of the Rolling Stones's US tour, multiple venue problems meant that event logistics were totally botched. Escalating tensions throughout the day between audience members and Hells Angels who had been paid in beer to guard the stage resulted in the fatal stabbing of eighteen-year-old African American Meredith Hunter, as well as three other accidental deaths. See the documentary *Gimme Shelter* (1970).

closely followed by state suppression. The notorious week-long rave at Castlemorton in 1992, where twenty-five thousand people descended on Worcestershire's Malvern Hills, led eventually to UK prime minister John Major's controversial 1994 Criminal Justice and Public Order Act. This gave the police power to break up gatherings of more than twenty people, with the legislation specifically clarifying that '"music" includes sounds wholly or predominantly characterised by the emission of a succession of repetitive beats'.

While it may have been heartening for electronic music producers to have their creativity officially recognised as music, the Act was doubtless less welcome to rave and festival organisers who risked having their rigs confiscated, being fined and even imprisoned, in a government move which reinforced the links between electronic music and criminality. Illegal raves continued throughout the 1990s, often unsafely and with strong links to the criminal underworld, generating a romantic lore which imbued late-night journeys around the M25 and frantic calls to mobile 'party lines' with unexpected glamour. These were gradually supplanted by legal events like James Perkins's Fantazia; these were so successful that Perkins now resides in the seventeenth-century mansion Aynhoe Park, an upmarket wedding venue adorned with stuffed African animals and complete with an underground club.

The political implications of the UK's rave heyday have been well documented, with books like John Godfrey and Matthew Collin's brilliantly titled *Altered State* giving an overview of the political background and ramifications. To my knowledge, no definitive study of the development of the UK festival industry exists.[*] What is clear is that, perhaps inevitably, the utopian spirit of the free festivals and raves of the 1970s, 1980s and 1990s was harnessed and monetised; the commodification and commercialisation of anything that has proven its popularity at a grassroots level is a standard feature of modern capitalism.

[*] A deep study of this phenomenon is outside the scope of this book, but would make a fantastic book in its own right and I hope somebody writes one soon!

In 2010, 670 festivals contributed an estimated £450 million to the UK economy; by 2019, before the Covid-19 pandemic micturated on the fireworks, this figure had risen to £1.76 billion across 975 festivals, with 5 million attendees: almost 10 per cent of the UK's total population. Research by Mintel for 2018–19 asserted that 26 per cent of UK adults had attended some kind of music festival that year.[19]

The commercial appropriation of what had been revolutionary understandably attracted scorn from certain corners, with 'boutique' festivals like Wilderness being singled out for criticism due to the high prices of food and drink and the attendance of former Tory prime minister, David Cameron.[20] Jonny Fluffypunk's lines at the start of this section express an older generation's horror at what festivals have become.

Whatever your views on the sanitisation and commercialisation of festivals – my own is that there is something inherently political and powerful about large groups of people gathering to listen to music which no amount of commercialisation can entirely stamp out – there is no question that festivals have contributed to a further blurring of genres through the juxtaposition of different musical styles in physical proximity.

While some are highly genre-specific, the majority, especially the new breed of boutique festivals, programme across genres, with attendees flowing freely between different musical styles. A generation raised on iPod Shuffle and Spotify would think nothing of raving it up to Modeselektor or HAAi, then ducking out to see Ezra Collective.

In addition to a general blurring of genres, the accessibility, sonic swagger and cross-fertilisation with other musical styles of this wave helped its artists get booked on pop and electronic festival line-ups as well as jazz ones.

Femi Koleoso

People being able to draw a line between grime music and jazz has helped expose it to festivals where otherwise you would have not had a jazz band at Boomtown, or it would have been hard to see a jazz band at Coachella.

unapologetic expression

Steve Symons

Up until three, four years ago, I would maybe put on one jazz act at Glastonbury every year. I'm planning about five for this summer. A lot of jazz can get blown away in a large outdoor environment like that, and if there's not a lot of love out for it in the crowd already, it's going to die, and I hate seeing that happen. [West Holts] is a twenty-five-thousand-capacity field, so it's a space for big, bold, punchy things, not too intricate and delicate. There's that kind of pop/dance edge to a lot of what's going on now, which gives it that much wider appeal.

'Those lines are definitely more blurred'

In addition to 'jazz' artists having far more opportunities to play within mainstream and boutique festivals, jazz festivals themselves had become both more open-minded in their programming and less stereotyped in their presentation.

Ciro Romano

We don't use any jazz iconography in our comms. If you look at many European jazz festivals – it's still the J with a sax, the T with a trumpet, and that caricature of a Dizzy Gillespie figure blowing a trumpet with his cheeks out. That was all out. We were going to have none of that.

Tom Excell

There's so many line-ups that have loads of jazz artists, or festivals that would get called a jazz festival with loads of bands that play a lot of African music. Those lines are definitely more blurred.

Shabaka Hutchings

In the eighties, when people were coming to jazz gigs, they were coming to music that was being defined as jazz. Someone would have to say, 'I am a jazz fan. I am going see this music.' But today you're getting the music not being plugged as jazz, which means the artists that are breaking out are becoming a little bit more mainstream. Which is not to say that Courtney Pine and those guys weren't very mainstream and they were on the cover of magazines, with massive record deals. But there's something about today where it feels like bands are just bands. So say with The Comet Is Coming, it's put across in the same realm as Tame Impala or Bonobo or whoever. As just a band that will play a festival as opposed to a jazz group. That's the essential difference. It's almost like jazz musicians are trying to permeate pop culture as opposed to take some of the people and bring them towards jazz.

And if a more open-minded approach among audiences meant they were more receptive to music categorised as 'jazz', the same open-mindedness among DJs, promoters and musicians meant that they were far more easy-going in their approach to genre than previous generations.

Bradley Zero

What I find really inspiring about this generation is the confidence to just do your thing and not really worry about whether it is or isn't getting accepted. They're not trying to reject the tradition of jazz, nor are they trying to strive for it. They're just doing their thing in reference to it and not really caring too much about if people use the term jazz or they don't. They're just doing it!

Adam Moses

I'm happy to call it jazz because, for a long time, you have people say, 'That's not jazz,' and that limited the scene until Jazz Re:freshed came in. And we're going, 'Yeah, that's jazz. That's jazz. And I don't care what person says it's not, I don't care if the great Branford Marsalis comes to me and says that's not jazz, because you've got no more authority on this than I do. If I think it's jazz, it's jazz – done.'

7

'Free My Skin'
Social Media, New Media, Old Media

The independent ecosystems that filled the space opened by the disruption to the recording industry were fertilised by a range of new channels of communication. Social media, blogs, video platforms and internet radio – and the ancillary effects of these new platforms on the traditional media – offered the generation of artists who came up in the 2010s a plethora of new ways to grow their audiences and express their identities, personalities and politics. While not without their dangers, these tools were vital for this generation to achieve Gary Crosby and Janine Irons's vision of independence.

Gilles Peterson

You've got this generation who can really speak for themselves. People have been asking me, 'Can we interview you about the scene? About this new thing?' I've literally said no to everyone. I just said, 'Look, to be honest with you, the last thing this generation needs is people like me bigging them up,' because it's not my scene, I'm part of what's come. I'm loving the fact that there's great music that I can play amongst all the other stuff that I play on the radio and in the clubs. But I don't want to be the spokesperson for it! The strength of that scene is that they are speaking for the first time, in a way. I mean, Courtney spoke for the scene, but there was a different element of what he was doing. This scene is more than just a sort of cultural thing. It's a movement.

'free my skin'

Camilla George

The difference now with this generation is that we have tools like social media. People can tell their story. We can create our own narrative.

'The renewable natural resource of our narcissism' (social media)

Go to a festival or live gig almost anywhere in the world and it is extremely likely that the most emotional crescendos and virtuosic musical moments will be accompanied by a forest of smartphones held aloft, recording. There is an eerie, digital beauty to this, and seen from far enough away, you could perhaps confuse the glare of screens and flashes with the lighter-raising moments of stadium rock or jungle: forty-thousand-strong crowds bearing tiny flames while swaying slowly to Aerosmith's 'I Don't Want To Miss a Thing'; gurning junglists finding their way out of the long dark tunnel in dank warehouse raves humid with sweat and ganja smoke, accompanied by Origin Unknown's 'Valley of the Shadows' and the raucous encouragement of MC Skibadee (RIP).* Yet while raising your lighter in a concert or rave was supposed to indicate deep connection and shared emotion with the rest of the crowd, raising your phone to record a clip to post as an Instagram story represents almost the exact opposite, taking your attention away from the moment and focusing instead on how it will be construed by your digital followers. As noted, one of the biggest reasons for the growth of the live music and festival industry is consumer desire for 'experiences' which can be shared on social media. Ironically though, being surrounded by people holding up their phones and filming can drastically reduce the value and meaning of the experience.

This paradox is at the heart of the social media revolution that in

---

* Skibadee, along with partner Shabba D, was one of the most respected jungle MCs until passing away unexpectedly aged forty-seven in February 2022.

twenty years has changed the way the majority of the world's population communicates with each other and understands themselves, powered by what writer Jia Tolentino brilliantly calls 'the renewable natural resource of our narcissim'.[1] By 2021, there were 4.62 billion monthly active users of social media worldwide: 58.4 per cent of the world's population.[2] Hike to the top of any mountain or waterfall and it is almost guaranteed someone will be perched on the edge, posing for the 'Gram. From street performers to eccentric animal behaviour, car crashes to police brutality, it is rare to see almost anything of interest occurring and not also see somebody filming it. Like the 'White Bear' episode in Charlie Brooker's *Black Mirror* (2013), where a woman flees sadistic attackers while zombified passers-by film her trauma instead of offering assistance, for much of the world's population, the recording and sharing of the experience has become almost indivisible from the experience itself. For all social media's promises of connection, a majority of the world's population spend a terrifying amount of time[3] glued to their phones and computer screens, watching other people have experiences – and often experiencing not connection but alienation in the process.

Cleveland Watkiss

We call it technological advancement, but we still don't even know how to deal with each other, so what are we talking about? We don't even know how to treat one another, and we're talking about we're so advanced technologically. Really?

While social media has rightly been criticised for its pernicious effects if misused, it provided the present generation of jazz artists with opportunities to curate their own image and connect directly with fans: opportunities rarely granted to earlier generations of artists.

Adam Moses

If you look back to the very early times of jazz, the presentation wasn't often done by the people who were making it. It's coming out of the hands of the creators. The presentation and how it's delivered to the mass audiences through mainstream media is always done by someone else who's given their own interpretation of how it should be presented, and it's not necessarily how it fits into the actual lifestyle of the artists performing.

Little had changed, in this regard, by the early 1990s, with the Jazz Warriors generation still presenting a public image moderated by labels and their media teams. By the time the present generation came of age, it was a totally different story.

Theon Cross

The means to promote yourself and put out your own content. Control your own branding, put out your own point of view. These are things we take for granted but [that] they didn't have, things they had to rely on other people for. The independent thing wasn't the way. But there have been people nowadays that have showed us that that can work.

The combination of genuine organic energy at a grassroots level, powerful live shows and a strong cohort of artists all coming through at the same time was amplified by the media savviness of a generation raised in an intensely visual and performative culture. Whereas in previous generations, a photo shoot would often only take place once a band had been signed, high-quality press photos became a standard requirement for even unsigned acts, with many artists understanding the curation of a coherent visual package as a core component of their artistry.

Shabaka Hutchings

The older generation are every bit as good at certain things, which people thought were the most important. Those things are your actual instrumental skill. What if they're not as good at everything around the music, the broad image? Some people might say that's not that important. But if it's not that important, you can't get mad if your music isn't popular. If you want your music to get accepted by the mainstream, you've got to give them what they want, which is an aesthetic package which is broader than the music itself. And I think the younger generation is a bit more savvy in presenting a package that just looks better. How the band looks on stage, the videos, press pictures: everything around the music. The brand. If you don't care about the brand, that's totally fine for me. And there's a lot to be said for that. But then you can't get mad at someone else who has more popularity because they do care about their brand!

Innately understanding the importance of branding and having already crafted powerful visual identities through years of social media activity, the new generation provided a ready-made story for the media to amplify. This readiness helped them receive years of sustained coverage, in some cases before even releasing debut albums.

Kerstan Mackness

You have a perfect synergy of the internet and social media, meaning that they don't need to rely on newspapers, magazines or tastemakers. This all happened away from and without the knowledge of jazz media or jazz broadcasters or anybody. Even Gilles only came to it after it was already a thing. People suddenly have the structures to be independent and to create their own scene and the means to promote it through social media.

Yet if it offered unprecedented opportunities for community creation, social media also represented the cynical transformation of the human need for connection and peer approval into a monetisable asset in which users become 'unwaged labourers who produce goods (data and content) that are then taken and sold by the companies to advertisers and other interested parties'.[4]

Web theorist Nick Srnicek brands Facebook (now called Meta),

Google and other companies that attract advertising revenue by selling user data 'surveillance capitalists', pointing out that 'the suppression of privacy is at the heart of this business model. This tendency involves constantly pressing against the limits of what is socially and legally acceptable in terms of data collection.'[5]

Tolentino goes further, asserting not only that Facebook's business model was based on exploiting its users but that 'what began as a way for Zuckerberg to harness collegiate misogyny and self-interest has become the fuel for our whole contemporary nightmare, for a world that fundamentally and systematically misrepresents human needs'.[6]

By the mid-2010s, many people suspected that, despite mission statements 'to give people the power to build community and bring the world closer together' (Facebook), 'to organise the world's information and make it universally accessible and useful' (Google), or 'to inspire creativity and bring joy' (TikTok), the true purpose of these megacorporations, like all megacorporations, was to make as much money as possible through the exploitation of resources: in this case, us.

Further, 'network effects' dictate that 'the more numerous the users who use a platform, the more valuable that platform becomes for everyone else . . . which leads to platforms having a natural tendency towards monopolisation'.[7] Media giant Rupert Murdoch's NewsCorp bought MySpace in 2005 (and sold it on for a multimillion-dollar loss in 2011 after it had been crushed by Facebook's popularity), Google owns YouTube, Meta (formerly Facebook) owns Instagram. In a world controlled by vast corporations getting vaster as 11 billion hours of human interactions are forced through the social media grinder each day and rendered as profit, authentic creative music played by real people in a live environment and released on independent record labels can seem like fresh salad after a week of cheap sausages.[8]

As an increasing number of scientific studies began exposing links between social media and anxiety, depression and even suicide,[9] the primacy of the live experience became an ever more important antidote to the hyper-stylisation and oversaturation of images and stimuli that social media can create. Steam Down insisted on no filming or photos, prioritising a raw, authentic experience; Church of Sound deliberately made space for a genuine community of people to eat, drink and socialise before the concert.

Here was another dimension to the 'perfect synergy of the internet and social media' described by Kerstan Mackness: not only does this generation have control over their infrastructure and the means to promote themselves, they can also position themselves as a symbolic antidote to the very forces which have supported their growth, using social media to offer real-life connection through intimate experiences of improvised music in DIY, non-commercial spaces.

Federico Bolza

What really connected with people is an organic experience where instead of scrolling through social media or streaming, people actually wanted to go to a gig and feel the communal experience of something with a bunch of other people, dance and have a good time.

'The bloggers were definitely the new sheriffs' (blogs and web publishing)

Orphy Robinson and Jason Yarde both told me that, for all the hype around the present generation, the new cohort have not yet received as much TV and mainstream radio exposure as the Jazz Warriors' generation. Even if they are right – and this is certainly changing* – this assessment does not take into account the diminished importance of these platforms in the new digital world. Just as social media offered artists increased opportunities to connect with fans via their own channels, technological advances in the same period shifted power away from TV, radio, newspapers and magazines. Generally independent, lean,

* Ezra Collective, for example, were made the house band for ITV's *The Jonathan Ross Show* in late 2022.

and rarely paying fees to contributors, blogs, internet radio stations and video content platforms were able to support a far wider range of music than had been possible via traditional media.

Hand in hand with the growth of social media and the MP3 and precipitated by the same forces was a new and influential format: the 'weblog', commonly known in its truncated form of 'blog'. Grandiosely taking its name from the nautical captain's log in which the events of the voyage were recorded, the blog cast internet users as intrepid explorers valiantly navigating the high seas of cyberspace from their living room, bedroom or Somali internet cafe, recording impressions, sharing feelings and opinions.

In many ways the emergence of blogs in the mid-1990s laid the template for the social media explosion of the following decade. Where the need to understand coding had previously limited blogging to serious tech enthusiasts, web publishing tools meant that anyone with internet access and an opinion could set up their own blog. And many did: by 2011 there were no fewer than 173 million public blogs in existence worldwide.[10] Most of the platforms on which blogs were hosted offered the opportunity for readers to comment and interact with each other as well as with the original post: the functionality known as Web 2.0 and out of which social media grew. This was not entirely different conceptually from the 'Readers' Letters' sections of traditional newspapers and magazines, but the possibility of immediate comment and conversation supported the rapid formation of communities around special interests of all kinds, from the mind-numbingly pedestrian to the mind-bendingly niche.

All over the world, individual music lovers began sharing their opinions on the music they loved, and in the heyday of music piracy in the 2000s, even MP3s of the music itself, until this practice was halted in what became known as Musicblogocide 2010, when hundreds of thousands of blogs were taken down after receiving stern letters from major label legal teams.[11]

The blogger was a hybrid, somewhere between a fan and a journalist, but without the commercial pressures, barriers to entry or pretence of objectivity faced by professional journalists. In this sense, blogs were closer to the fanzines of the seventies, eighties and nineties that sprang up not to criticise but to amplify marginalised music and galvanise a community around particular scenes, circumventing traditional media gatekeepers. Blogging represented a democratisation of music journalism analogous to the democratisation of music production and distribution that the internet also facilitated: anyone could set up a blog and express their opinions, just as anyone could release their music on to streaming sites. This meant vastly more product available, but much of it very low quality. Picking out the genuine needles in an ever-expanding haystack was one of blogs' key functions: respected bloggers, like tastemaker DJs, attracted committed communities that would trust their taste, giving them an important platform to help promote new music. As noted on *Stereofox*, 'If music had entered its wild, Wild West post-Napster, the bloggers were definitely the new sheriffs.'[12]

Paradoxically, the plummeting signal:noise ratio meant that music blogs themselves had to compete for readers' attention in a crowded digital marketplace. One solution was aggregators like Hype Machine, which rank blogs according to the total number of referrals from other blogs (the same principle on which all internet search engines work). But as with the 'network effects' described above, this system privileges the blogs which are already the biggest. Like Spotify, in which an artist's most popular two or three tunes become the most likely to be played by consumers seeking those artists, creating an ever-increasing inequality between these tunes and all the others, this tendency allowed some of the biggest blogs to grow exponentially, wielding significant power as platforms to promote new music. Just as social media 'influencers' are employed to sell product, the popularity of blogs inevitably attracted the attention and investment of the corporate music industry.

Pitchfork, launched as a personal music blog in 1996 by independent writer and Minneapolis record shop worker Ryan Schreiber, used its popularity to launch a festival in Chicago in 2011, hosting subsequent editions in Paris, London and Berlin. The platform grew so large that it was bought in 2015 by media giant Condé Nast, publishers of *GQ*, *Vogue*, the *New Yorker*, *Vanity Fair* and *Wired*. *Afropunk*, which started life as a comments board on the promotional website for James Spooner's 2002 documentary about black punks (*Afro-Punk*), similarly grew into a major international brand, with a 2005 festival in Brooklyn spiralling into an international business with editions in Paris, Johannesburg, London, Miami, Atlanta and Bahia, Brazil.

As high-quality web publishing tools became increasingly available to individual bloggers, and the decline in physical sales forced most print magazines online, it became difficult to differentiate 'true' blogs (i.e. sites set up by individual enthusiasts) from magazines which just happened to publish online. Additionally, many companies whose core business was elsewhere, like Bandcamp (distribution), the Vinyl Factory (vinyl plant and label), Red Bull (energy drinks) and Resident Advisor (event listings and ticketing) set up music blogs to increase engagement with users and grow brand loyalty.

The importance of blogs started to wane in the second half of the 2010s, as the dominance of artists' own social media and the growth of curated playlists and algorithmic recommendations within streaming platforms reduced the importance of support from individual enthusiasts. The biggest blogs were assimilated by the music industry, representing a shift in power back to the traditional gatekeepers.

Nevertheless, from American behemoths like *Pitchfork* and *XLR8R* to niche blogs like *Twisted Soul Music*, *Stamp the Wax*, *Soulmotion* and *Passion of the Weiss*, and blogs designed for particular communities like *Afropunk* and *gal-dem*, the 'blogosphere' played an important role in offering alternative channels for this generation of artists to get their music heard and their stories known. The new UK jazz artists benefited from support within the jazz community – long-running blogs like *LondonJazz News* and veteran music journalist, author and former *Guardian* football writer Richard Williams' *The Blue Moment* – but also from well outside it. Coverage in general art and culture blogs like *The Quietus*, *Vice*, *The Skinny* and *Bonafide Magazine*, blogs with a central non-jazz theme like SBTV's blog (grime), *Wordplay* (hip-hop) and *Sounds and Colours* (Caribbean and Latin American music) alongside niche blogs like *The Fragmented Flâneur* all helped the music reach a range of different audiences. And coverage in major international blogs like *Pigeons and Planes* and *Stereofox* helped the music translate internationally.

'A studio no bigger than a broom cupboard' (internet radio)

An important factor that empowered the new wave of music to travel outside the traditional jazz audience was the support from tastemaker DJs like Floating Points, Four Tet and Bradley Zero playing the music in their DJ sets: not only at venues and festivals but also through their regular shows on community radio station NTS. Founded in Dalston in 2011 by DJ Femi Adeyemi in a studio 'no bigger than a broom cupboard with the décor to match',[13] it was very much a DIY enterprise, with Femi and friends 'daisy-chaining ethernet cables from the Vortex Jazz Bar across Gillett Square into the studio'.[14] Ad-free, community-focused and volunteer-run, it was important both in exposing people to new music and in cementing communities around that music. One of the beautiful paradoxes of the internet is the ability for micro-communities to exist on a global scale: while NTS was a celebration of grassroots creativity and culture in the rapidly gentrifying area it was situated, the fact that it could be listened to anywhere in the world via an internet connection meant that that sense of hyper-local community could exist on a global scale.* The station boasts that it broadcasts from (i.e. with content created by artists based in) fifty cities worldwide – and is listened to in hundreds more.

* Not everyone, of course, would share this positive analysis; I've heard NTS criticised for fostering a community of 'rootless global hipsters'.

NTS was followed by a slew of other internet-only stations includ-ing Soho Radio (2014), Radar Radio (2014), Balamii (2014) and Worldwide (2016). Based just next to the Bussey Building in Peck-ham's Holdrons Arcade, Balamii, like NTS, began as a hyperlocal vehicle to promote the creativity of Peckham but has expanded to host shows from over thirty cities, as well as events and video streams. Worldwide FM, initially based off Stoke Newington Church Street, just a few hundred metres from the Total Refreshment Centre, was launched by Gilles Peterson's Mistral Productions team alongside longtime collaborator and protégé Thristian Richards (aka the bPm/ Thris Tian), providing a dedicated space for jazz and related music. Like NTS and Balamii, it grew rapidly, with regular shows by many of this book's contributors – Shabaka Hutchings, Tom Skinner, Femi Koleoso, Kate Hutchinson and Emma Warren – representing the UK community as part of a roster including international stars like NYC house legends Kenny Dope and Louie Vega (Masters at Work), Afro house master Osunlade, disco champion François Kevorkian and Jap-anese jazz pioneer Toshio Matsuura. This was supplemented by the Brownswood Basement YouTube channel, featuring live performances recorded in the basement of Brownswood Recordings HQ against a background of Gilles Peterson's enormous record collection.

Omar Lye-Fook

When I first started out, there were only a handful of radio stations that were national – forget about international – and to get on their playlists, you're battling a whole bunch of people. Whereas now, people don't need to go to those five stations, they can pretty much listen to anything that they want. So that puts less pressure on the people making the music to conform to something. Because the A & R pressures I remember hearing were, 'Are you going to make this kind of record? Because this daytime DJ will play it on his show, but if you don't, he won't play it.' Why the fuck am I making music for this DJ? That's not why I got into making music.

unapologetic expression

An ever-expanding repository of global culture
(video content platforms)

When I was growing up, opportunities to see live performances without actually going out were limited to mainstream TV programmes like *Top of the Pops, Later with Jools Holland* and Channel 4's hip-hop show *Flava*. By the following decade, the increased affordability of video recording and streaming hardware combined with the ubiquity of the internet saw a preponderance of 'content platforms'.

Broadcasting initially from the actual boiler room of co-founder Blaise Bellville's East London residence, the most influential of these was Boiler Room, which began as Platform, a mixtape concept featuring a live DJ mix by Thris Tian and Femi Adeyemi, streamed live on UStream.[15]

The concept was simple: a DJ playing for the camera, with friends, fans and miscellaneous hipsters dancing ostentatiously in the background while pretending to be unaware their moves were being broadcast not only internationally but deep into the future. Unlike terrestrial TV, where broadcasts would be kept in dusty BBC vaults and (if you were quick enough) on your own bootlegged VHS, the internet has become an ever-expanding (if commercially owned and unreliable) repository of global culture.[16] If you didn't see the original stream, it would quickly be up on YouTube, as well as entering the vast archive on Boiler Room's own website, providing unparalleled opportunities for fans and promoters to discover new artists as well as watch their established favourites on demand.

Moving first from the original boiler room to invite-only weekly Wednesday sessions at Elephant and Castle's Corsica Studios, Boiler Room rapidly expanded into a global brand, broadening its music policy to include live music in a range of genres, including jazz. Streams by UK artists including Yussef Kamaal, Al Dobson Jr, The Comet Is Coming and Ezra Collective were central to those artists' growth, particularly when placed alongside international stars like Hermeto

Pascoal and Badbadnotgood. Forming partnerships with global brands including Ray-Bans and Adidas, running its own festivals and hosting stages at tastemaker festivals Sonar, Dimensions, SXSW and Dekmantel, Boiler Room currently broadcasts thirty to thirty-five shows a month from Los Angeles, New York City, São Paulo, Amsterdam, Krakow, Sydney, Lisbon, Berlin and Lima.

Similar online platforms for live music include Balcony TV (Dublin, 2006), Tiny Desk Concerts (Washington, DC, 2008), Sofar Sounds (London, 2009), Mahogany Sessions (London, 2010) and Colors (Berlin, 2016). While each has a different style and aesthetic, taken as a whole these platforms have significantly increased artists' ability to reach audiences worldwide via a professionally shot live performance on a trusted platform.

As with social media, these platforms are not without their issues. Artists are often not paid for their participation, but rather paid in 'exposure' and a free high-quality live video, while many of the platforms themselves have grown into huge international businesses, pocketing advertising revenue and brand partnership fees and acquiring huge databases. Similarly, there is no guarantee of how many people will watch a stream; while well-timed performances on Colors or Boiler Room can give artists a significant boost, some of the smaller platforms often benefit much more from their access to an artist's following than the other way around. Nevertheless, these platforms have played an important role in helping artists connect with global audiences via intimate performances.

'A changing of the guard'
(old media)

Just as the range of options available to independent artists increased the amount of bargaining power held by those who *did* choose to sign with majors, the new opportunities offered by internet radio, content platforms, blogs and social media drove a concurrent democratisation of traditional media. This was manifested in changes in how these media were consumed, who was granted a platform and what they were saying.

The BBC launched two major new stations in 2002, Radio 1Xtra and Radio 6 Music.* 1Xtra, in the less nuanced parlance of 2002, was created very specifically to 'woo a young black audience', playing 'a mix of R & B, hip-hop, garage and reggae . . . presented with all the urgent fervour of a pirate station'.[17] 6 Music was branded as promoting 'alternative' music, which initially mostly meant 'indie', but in 2012 Gilles Peterson took up the three-hour Saturday afternoon primetime slot, giving him an opportunity to play new jazz and related music to a much wider audience than previous late-night shifts on Radio 1. His new show was scheduled just before *The Craig Charles Funk and Soul Show*, presented by the star of cult nineties sci-fi comedy *Red Dwarf*, which meant that six hours of primarily black music were now being broadcast to 6 Music's 3 million listeners every Saturday. Ex-Fun Lovin' Criminals frontman Huey Morgan and Welsh singer Cerys Matthews of Catatonia also used their shows to champion jazz alongside other genres.

Further, the switch from live to 'on-demand' meant that FM and digital as well as internet radio shows could be listened to and shared long after broadcast via the BBC's iPlayer and BBC Sounds app. This meant that even if jazz only occupied a small percentage of a station's output, it could be selectively listened to at any time throughout the week, making it feel more available (in comparison with the need to stay home or stay up to catch a particular show, familiar to earlier generations of enthusiasts).

This pattern was visible in the print media also, with every major newspaper now available online. Some were behind a paywall, but many, especially the *Guardian* – paper of choice for many lovers of the new jazz (i.e. the same kind of left-leaning young people who were into jazz in the 1950s and early 1960s) – left it up to the reader to

* Although digital stations rather than FM, I include them here as they are publicly funded and function very similarly to the BBC's FM stations.

contribute voluntarily. In addition to reducing the barrier to access, this was the best of both worlds in that articles could be found online and shared on social media while having legitimacy conferred upon them by virtue of being published by respected outlets.

Similarly, print magazines like *NME*, *Clash*, *Fact* and *i-D* all launched online editions in the latter part of the 2000s. As well as being readily shareable, the online format allowed scope to cover wider genres than previously. *Mojo* had traditionally been a classic rock magazine, and *Mixmag* focused on electronic music: both began covering the new jazz sound, reinforcing the breakdown of genre boundaries.

This increased coverage can sometimes produce tensions between media presentation and artistic intention, however.

Adam Moses

The other side of music is the sex appeal. Whether people want to acknowledge it or not, that is one of the things that sells the scene. Things need to look sexy. That's why advertisers spend billions of pounds per year on showing beautiful-looking people next to their product, because something within our subconscious works on that level. This scene, you've got these young, attractive people all getting into this music. I think that has a big impact. And also Moses and Binker, Shabaka, these guys had this raw kind of energy. Nubya. This is the energy. This is the vibe. And you can present that how you want it to be presented.

For all the control this changing world has given artists over presentation, the issue of media presentation vs artist choice has not totally disappeared. The difference is that artists now have more channels to voice their own reactions to exactly this kind of stereotyping.

Poppy Ajudha

The media will always create things in a certain way. I remember *i-D* did a ten-page spread and it platformed a whole bunch of jazz artists. It had Yussef in it, Blue Lab Beats, Tiana Major9. I was in it. Oscar was in it. Ezra was in it. Olivia Rose shot it, and I remember I was really excited to be in *i-D* magazine because I love *i-D*, I love fashion, and maybe for other jazz musicians it wasn't a big deal because they didn't really know *i-D* magazine. I was on the first page and it said, 'Jazz can be hot.' And it was like, it's really great that I look hot and I'm on the first page. But I remember that feeling of, 'Oh, she's just on the first page 'cos she looks good and she's not even a jazz musician.' The media will always choose the visual aesthetic, but that doesn't mean I shouldn't be there. There's always that double-edged thing that you can't escape. I don't choose the way that people present things. But we do live in a visual culture. So you have to take it with a pinch of salt, basically.

While jazz was being featured in a wider range of publications than previously, it was also being covered by a new generation of writers and broadcasters, many of whom were enthusiastic about jazz even if their background was in other music. This was a refreshing contrast to the way in which jazz had been discussed previously, which seemed to be mostly divided between dyed-in-the-wool jazz purists writing in specialist jazz columns and magazines, and mainstream commentators displaying open hostility and scorn.

David Jones

There was a die-hard jazz-defining audience in the eighties and nineties and a lot of the jazz critics who thought the same way would give us a regular roasting. There was a particular writer called Jack Massarik, who wrote for the *Evening Standard*, and when it came to joining jazz up to other musics, he felt incredibly protective of it, because he felt jazz is a vulnerable flower. Like it was something that had to be defended, had to be looked after and he felt that the people who tried to, as he put it, commercialise it, were going to trivialise it. They were going to create a horrible legion of smooth jazz and would drag the music off and sanitise it.

'free my skin'

Kerstan Mackness

The newspapers have had a changing of the guard in terms of who they get to write about stuff. For a long time, music magazines and the music pages were either edited by classical people who were predetermined to hate jazz, or by a certain generation of rock and pop writers who hate any music that actually involves playing instruments. They absolutely hated jazz on the idea that jazz was noodly. Prog has a lot to answer for, and bebop. They hated bebop and then they hated prog.

One of the key new voices championing the music was Kate Hutchinson, who wrote about the emerging UK jazz scene for the *Guardian*, *Observer*, *Independent*, *Sunday Times* and the *New York Times*, as well as hosting the podcast series *The Last Bohemians*, a regular show on Worldwide FM, and even DJing for Boiler Room. Yet she very much did not come from the jazz scene; her background was as clubbing editor for weekly London listings magazine *Time Out*.

Kate Hutchinson

I've always been interested in exciting things that are happening in youth culture and thinking, what new voices in music can I help bring to a wider audience? The way I write is to try and make something that might be perceived as niche or leftfield make sense to, say, my mum. So in that way, maybe I'm a bit of a bridge with the mainstream because, even though I was aware of jazz's place in UK club culture from my *Time Out* days, via people like Gilles Peterson and Perry Louis, I wouldn't say I was *in* this current jazz scene that's emerged more recently. I've never really been part of any scene. I've always been kind of teetering on the edge, looking in from the outside. I guess I see my job as trying to make underground culture resonate on a broader level and helping, I hope, to give it some sort of platform.

Just as the musicians of this generation were quite happy to be described as jazz and equally happy not being, drawing freely from a multitude of styles, so a new generation of journalists and presenters were increasingly happy to feature jazz as part of a range of different music. The combination of new voices talking about the music, new platforms on which to promote it, and an arsenal of social media, gave the new UK jazz generation an unprecedented freedom to curate their own image, tell their own story, and call out the bullshit.

And there seemed to be an ever-increasing amount of bullshit to call out.

8

'Wake (For Grenfell)'

Jazz, Politics and Identity

It was one of the defining images not only of Theresa May's disastrous prime ministership but of the entire decade: smoke billowing from an iconic brutalist tower block as seventy-two mostly non-white, working-class residents of the Grenfell Tower in North Kensington, West London died in their own homes on 14 June 2017. This utterly avoidable loss of life became symbolic of a deeply divided, unequal Britain, shining a harsh light on its hypocrisies, inequalities and racial tensions. The fire took place in one of the richest boroughs in the country, within shouting distance of multimillion-pound investment properties owned by Russian oligarchs and Saudi billionaires, compounding the sense of inequality and injustice. The borough's own report had noted in 2016 that life expectancy for men in its poorest part was sixteen years lower than in the richest.[1] Reviewing the effect of policy recommendations made ten years before, a 2020 report noted that ten years of Tory austerity had not only deepened inequality in society but generated a massive drop in life-expectancy increase, slowing a positive trend that had continued since the Second World War, with life expectancy actually decreasing in many of the country's poorest areas.[2]

Of course, it was a tragedy. But this was no freak accident. Indeed, it was an inevitability: the compound effect of a toxic cocktail of privatisation, corporate greed, slashed council budgets and savage inequality. The real question is perhaps not 'why did it happen?' but 'how far back do you want to go?' The immediate cause of the fire was a malfunctioning fridge-freezer in a fourth-floor flat, but its spread was caused by the highly flammable aluminium composite cladding which had been installed in a 2015–16 renovation. This cladding had been chosen over the more fire-resistant alternative proposed by the initial contractor simply because it was cheaper, despite the fact that similar cladding had been involved in multiple deadly fires dating as far back as the Summerland Fire of 1973, in which fifty people died in a leisure centre on the Isle of Man. In this sense, it is possible to see the fire as a direct result of the cuts to public spending under the austerity programme initiated by Conservative Chancellor George Osborne in 2010, which saw council budgets cut by an average of 40 per cent. This was part of a wider series of savage cuts to public spending, with eight hundred libraries (20 per cent of the country's total)[3] and 760 youth centres closing across the UK over the following decade, and government spending on youth provision slashed by a billion pounds (70 per cent).[4]

But the building's problems did not begin in 2010. As far back as 2005, twelve years before the fire, a report by engineering company Capita Symonds had expressed severe safety concerns about the building, criticising the lack of emergency lighting and accusing Kensington and Chelsea Tenant Management Organisation (KCTMO) of 'inadequate management', 'inadequate installation standards', a 'failure to acknowledge the importance of undertaking urgent remedial works' and a 'lack of communication' with residents.[5] Although nominally a vehicle for council tenants to make decisions about their own estates, in practice many tenant management organisations were simply corporate property management companies under another name, utterly divorced from the communities they were supposed to serve. KCTMO was a paragon of this type of organisation: the largest tenant management organisation in the country, managing Kensington and Chelsea's entire housing stock: a vast, unaccountable corporation masquerading as a democratically owned and run organisation.

The very existence of KCTMO was a product of a long programme of privatisation initiated by Margaret Thatcher's Conservative government in 1979, continuing throughout the 1980s, selling off a vast swathe of national resources: energy, water, transport and parts of the NHS. Justified as part of a drive to promote British entrepreneurship, create 'value for money' and give the people of Britain increased choice, privatisations continued in the 1990s under John Major's Conservative government and, from 1997, Tony Blair and Gordon Brown's Labour. The net effect was, predictably, the most expensive public transport system in Europe, one of the most expensive energy systems, and colossal mismanagement of public services including prisons, care homes, schools, hospitals, libraries and council housing as private companies extracted vast profits at the expense of taxpayers and service users.

It is significant that Cassie Kinoshi chose to put a song called 'Wake (For Grenfell)' on SEED Ensemble's Mercury Prize-nominated album *Driftglass* (Jazz Re:freshed, 2019), and that artists including Stormzy, Craig David and Jorja Smith took direct action in response to government inertia, recording a fundraiser for victims of the fire which went to No. 1 in the UK charts in June 2017. If the Grenfell fire was symbolic of an unequal, divided Britain, the artistic response heralded a new generation of socially engaged, politicised artists. Whereas their immediate predecessors had plied their trade in a background of New Labour's mixture of reasonably progressive social policies and neo-liberal economic ones under the guise of an inclusive multiculturalism, the barefaced corruption and aggressive erosion of public services under the post-2010 Conservative-led governments, as under the Thatcher government of the 1980s, galvanised the political consciousness not only of musicians but of young people in general.

Where it had become commonplace to justify a lack of interest in politics by citing New Labour's centrist economic policies and saying that all political parties were the same, a generation for whom Margaret Thatcher was less a personal memory than a mythical bogeyman left-wing parents would warn their children about now had first-hand experience of the sharp end of a brutal Tory government. The anxiety-inducing sense of an unaccountable leadership propped up by corporate interests was echoed around the world with the rise of right-wing populist leaders including Bolsonaro (Brazil), Erdoğan (Turkey), Orbán (Hungary), alongside Johnson, Trump and Putin.

Indeed, for many people, escalating environmental disaster, scarcity of resources and the renewed threat of nuclear war, with multiple countries ruled by borderline psychopaths with expansionary tendencies, characterised by xenophobia, homophobia, sexism and social conservatism, have contributed to a feeling that we are approaching the 'end of days' predicted for thousands of years by mythological and religious traditions across the world, in which humanity would finally destroy itself, and the entire planet along with it. Conversely, the last few years have seen significant progress around social issues, including feminism, anti-racism and trans rights, leading to the conflicting feeling that, despite everything, things are getting better.

This dizzying tension between two incompatible extremes has been reflected in the music, much of which, since 2010, has been characterised by an urgency that marks it out as very different from that of the previous fifteen years. Whereas for their immediate predecessors, politics felt like something one could choose to opt out of, this generation's output has been energised by the sense of being locked in an epic battle between good and evil in which every single act of kindness, generosity and truth feels like resistance to an increasingly terrifying world run by people in the grip of the worst kind of selfishness. There is also an increased understanding of the interconnectedness of different struggles: that the fight against racism, sexism and discrimination of all kinds is intimately bound up with the legacy of capitalism and colonialism and a fight for a fairer world. This renewed sense of political urgency in the UK created the perfect environment for jazz to reclaim its place as relevant, politically charged music.

Gilles Peterson

The last fifteen, twenty years have been a little bit confusing for people to really feel part of something, a real movement. I haven't really felt much of a subversive political subtext in music. It's almost not been fashionable, and suddenly when this happens, you go, 'Fucking hell, what've we been doing? We've just been getting stoned, just escaping into our own selves because we've all been so disillusioned and confused by the political world!' So I'd say that this is really, really an incredible moment. I can't wait to see what comes out of it. It's making me want to join a political party for the first time since I was standing outside the South African embassy back in the day . . . You know, I might go and give Alabaster DePlume a call in a minute and find out what I can do for the Labour Party! I can't speak for everyone and I'm sure that Shabaka might have a different answer, and Nubya, too. But I feel that the political message was almost like a secret. It wasn't at the front of the phrase. It was super subtle. And right now there's no room for subtlety. Right now, it's like, 'Let's go. Let's do what we can do.' Which is great.

Emily Moxon

In this time that we're living in, there's no point doing anything that's not really meaningful. You can't just put out a record for the sake of it. I think that the conditions that have created the Black Lives Matter movement have been real and present things in people's lives. And the music has naturally responded. So it's not surprising that it feels relevant now that everyone's paying attention. That music's been born out of that culture.

Huey Walker

So many of them have done songs about Grenfell or things that are political. A lot of it is very political and proudly so. And that's fantastic.

Dahlia Ambach Caplin

The political climate we're in might feed some pretty incredible music. There's a lot of reasons to be angry today. And there's a lot of reasons to feel vulnerable. And those two things feed creativity: vulnerability and anger. Creativity is a way to channel it. That's their weapon. That's their expression.

'You can't separate music and politics'

In being the unapologetic expression of an oppressed people, the roots of jazz are revolutionary, even when the music itself is not explicitly political. Telling your story and affirming your right to a voice is a deeply political act. In the current context, the simple fact of black and mixed-race people from working-class backgrounds expressing themselves through music is inherently political, as is the increased prevalence of female musicians.

Cleveland Watkiss

Regardless of how anyone wants to dice it, you can't separate music and politics. They are one and the same thing. From when we come out the womb we're making a political statement. By even coming out of the womb.

Shabaka Hutchings

We like to call certain parts of life political. But in some ways, everything is a political point. In the end, all the music adds up to give you a tapestry of what the landscape is. As opposed to some music being more valid because it's giving a certain perspective, which might be one of struggle against oppression. It all exists as one whole.

Likewise, context plays a major part in the music's political power. The decisions to launch Steam Down in Deptford, an ethnically and socially mixed area of South-East London, and to make it free entry, were innately political. Further, the general DIY ethos of this generation can be seen as a challenge to the rampant commercialisation of the capital, and a statement of solidarity with wider sustainability movements.

'wake (for grenfell)'

Federico Bolza

That kind of micro-promoter, micro-community based thing, it's in this generation's DNA. And it's the antidote to everything else. So on the one hand, they bring gentrification. But on the other hand, they stem the crass commercialisation of places. And I think, weirdly, this kind of thing is intrinsically linked to this organically made music. It's like people that are trying to do good for the planet through community schemes, grow their own vegetables, eat less meat, and listen to jazz, like real music made by real people.

Music operates on multiple levels simultaneously. Regardless of who is playing it, where it is being played, what they say about it, and what it is called, music can transmit an energy and understanding that can reach listeners on a subconscious, non-verbal level.

Cleveland Watkiss

The thing about music, it doesn't lie. Anyone that's got ears can hear, man. If you train your ears, you can hear. I can hear the bullshit even if I don't hear the lyrics. I don't need to hear the lyrics to hear the bullshit. Or I can hear the lyrics, and hear the bullshit. The music doesn't lie, man. Once you develop your ear to a certain degree and level, it's very clear what's being said. When you're listening.

The energy and spiritual message encoded in the music itself can be enhanced by song titles, which can be used as a further signpost to the music's political significance. This was extremely common during the civil rights era: song titles like Blue Mitchell's 'March on Selma', John Coltrane's 'Alabama' and Bobby Hutcherson's 'Poor People's March'; songs in support of African decolonisation like Lee Morgan's 'Zambia' and 'Mr Kenyatta', Wayne Shorter's 'Angola' and Sonny Rollins's 'Airegin' (Nigeria backwards). In the current wave, tracks like SEED Ensemble's 'The Darkies', Nubya Garcia's 'The Message Continues' and all of the tracks on Sons of Kemet's *Your Queen Is a Reptile* – each named after a powerful female of colour – use titles to help focus the appreciation of the music, even when no lyrics are involved.

Courtney Pine

Some people don't even know the title, they can just hear a tune and say, 'That's fighting music. That sound like a riot.' But if you're interested, you can go to the title and get a reference. If you want to go there, it will help you get closer to what the artist had in their mind at that time.

Cassie Kinoshi

It doesn't inherently have to sound like people marching and being angry to be protest music. Musically, even if you don't have rap lyrics or spoken word, I don't think that necessarily matters.

Vocals obviously offer an opportunity for more direct political expression. Like Gil Scott-Heron's caustic 'Whitey on the Moon' and Billie Holiday's terrifying 'Strange Fruit', tracks like United Vibrations' 'I Am We', Zara McFarlane's 'Black Treasure' and Poppy Ajudha's 'London's Burning' offer a direct political message.

Wayne Francis

Musicians reflect the time, amplify it or make it common knowledge. The discussions always start happening in the academic, intelligentsia kind of community. People are thinking about those things quite widely, then artists start hearing those conversations and find those ways of speaking, and when you write about it in a song it's a lot more simple and easier to digest. And it's a specifically visceral and emotional perspective where you listen to the song and all of a sudden you're feeling the emotion of it, rather than a lecture, which is like you're telling people all these facts and figures and perspectives and theories. Music goes straight to people's hearts – as it always has done. That's the reason we listen to music is how it makes us feel, you know?

'wake (for grenfell)'

Many musicians of this generation used their music to participate directly in political protests, including the People's Vote march (for a second Brexit referendum) in March 2019 and the Black Lives Matter protests in June 2020. They also sometimes chose *not* to play in certain spaces, like Shabaka Hutchings' refusal to play in Bristol's Colston Hall (until renamed) because of its association with slavery, and many musicians' refusal to play in Israel out of solidarity with Palestinians.

For some, the stage can also serve as a way to test and display political ideas. Individuals combining to create a collective sound but having space for their own voices can be a metaphor for a healthily functioning democracy.

Jean Toussaint

Jazz is the experience of the musicians playing it. So if they could move a lot of the people that are coming to see them, then right away, you know it's a democratic system. A band on stage is democratic, they're all doing it together. So it's like a snippet of real life. To make a concert successful, everyone on stage has to work together. And if the audience can feel that from the musician, then hopefully that will carry on into their daily lives. It's everyone together as one, trying to grow and enjoy that sound that's happening. And from that enjoyment, it just makes us understand each other more. So in that sense, it's political.

And of course, what a musician says in interviews, writings and on social media, and what they do in their personal life, can have an effect on how their music is interpreted. Many people will not listen to R. Kelly because he has been convicted for child sexual abuse, or Wagner because of his open anti-Semitism and subsequent adoption by the Nazis.

Conversely, the way that Shabaka Hutchings has positioned himself as an articulate spokesperson on not only musical but wider cultural and political issues (e.g. through his opinion pieces for the *Guardian*) has helped strengthen his position as the godfather of the new UK jazz scene, reflecting light back on to his music.

Beyond these specific examples, it's possible to see this generation and their actions as part of a wider set of cultural shifts.

'Things have become more sophisticated'
(identity politics)

The way in which many of us today dissect and analyse race, gender, sexuality and other related characteristics utilises the language of 'identity politics'. The term was first coined in the sense in which we know it today in 1977 by the Combahee River Collective, a black lesbian feminist socialist organisation active in Boston, MA between 1974 and 1980. Feeling left out by the racism of the mainstream feminist movement and the homophobia and sexism of the civil rights movement, the term was a recognition that different groups might need different kinds of support in order to achieve equality.

As discussed, the multiculturalism trumpeted in the New Labour era was supposed to indicate an inclusive cultural identity based on the diversity of the UK's population. By contrast, identity politics is about the recognition of differential needs and a specific focus on bringing marginalised voices to the fore: those of women, ethnic minorities, LGBTQ+ groups, people with disabilities, etc.

Like 'identity politics', the term 'intersectionality' originated in black radical thought, coined by Kimberlé Crenshaw in 1989 to refer to the range of interacting systems of oppression affecting the lives of different identity groups.

Both terms became increasingly mainstream during the 2010s, with 'intersectionality' entering the *Oxford English Dictionary* in 2015. An entire new lexicon migrated from cultural studies textbooks to common parlance, and with it an increased ability to articulate the experience of marginalised groups: *microaggressions, structural racism, patriarchy, toxic masculinity, normalise, triggering.*

'wake (for grenfell)'

Wayne Francis

There's been a lot of work happening within activist circles. And I think the language to even articulate that kind of intersectionality and code-switching is only emergent over the last six years. So a lot of musicians growing up now, ones that are younger than me, there's been a lot more digital publications, independent publications that informed that generation. They grew up when those conversations were being opened up in their developmental stages, learning how to play music while those things were going on. So because that conversation was emerging in their early development phase, that generation are probably much more open to speaking about those things. I think the music reflects that. And that's why a lot of young musicians are more comfortable aligning themselves politically.

Steve Williamson

Without a doubt, things have become more sophisticated. The terminology like 'microaggression': people are beginning to understand about these concepts that we've known about for bloody decades.

Closely tied in with the growth of smartphones and social media, it became commonplace to express one's identity and share stories of marginalisation in a way that simply was not the case for people who, like me, were born in the 1980s and earlier. Musicians of my age group all remember a time when their cultural heritage and any experience of racism needed to be suppressed in order to fit in rather than paraded as part of their identity.

Zara McFarlane

What I see of younger generations is that people are way more open about all different types of heritage, identity, sexuality. I don't think it was like that when I was younger.

Yazz Ahmed

I grew up in Bahrain and moved to London when I was nine years old. I adapted to British culture and tried to hide anything to do with my family and my dad being Muslim, because I felt I would be made fun of. Some of my sisters have darker skin than me and were racially abused because of this. So I just thought I'd keep it down, I kind of suppressed my culture – it's awful, actually.

An entire generation grew up with new ways to understand their experiences, and new platforms on which to articulate them, so it was perhaps inevitable that this was expressed in their music.

Poppy Ajudha

As a person of colour, as a woman, you're always aware of yourself because you're always being reminded of how your identity reflects the music you make. No one's ever saying, 'Oh, this white man won this because he's white,' but they're saying, 'This woman did this,' or, 'A woman of colour did that,' or whatever it is. So I think identity politics becomes a huge part of how we communicate who we are in society.

'That external oppression that you get from men' (#MeToo)

Almost none of the progressive agendas or social analyses that came to prominence in the period I am describing originated in that period. This has been levelled as a criticism of the political militancy of millennials and Gen Z, pointing out that the conversations that have now entered the mainstream are old news to many activists and academics.

I believe this sort of critique – often intermingled with a kind of competitive activist one-upmanship – is not only beside the point but a complete misunderstanding of how change actually works. It is precisely at the point that a minority agenda enters the mainstream that real change begins to happen. When I was growing up, vegetarianism was still seen as a minority concern in the UK, and veganism virtually non-existent apart from among practising Jains, Hindus, Buddhists and anarchists. Recycling was a conversation rather than a given. It takes a whole generation for cultural norms to change. Amid my parents' generation, it was common for women to have jobs but still do the bulk of the housework and childcare in a way that many people in my generation would find deeply unfair. Things were different again in the generation that came of age during the Second World War; a close friend's grandmother told her that she did not mind men patting her bum in the workplace as it was their way of showing that she had done a good job.

Change often coalesces around particular flashpoints, but these flashpoints are usually the work of years, decades and even centuries of tireless campaigning to ensure that progressive ideas are 'lying around'.[6] One such flashpoint was the successive revelations, from October 2017, of American movie executive Harvey Weinstein's serial sexual abuse of women. Almost ninety accusers came forward with harrowing stories of sexual intimidation, blackmail and rape. As more and more of his victims came out to testify, women all over the world took to social media to share stories of their own experiences of sexual abuse and unequal power relations using the #MeToo social handle. Like 'intersectionality' and 'identity politics', the phrase had been coined by a black female, sexual assault survivor and activist Tarana Burke, and had been 'lying around' since 2006, long before going viral in response to the Weinstein allegations.

The global social media outpouring, underpinned by the revelation of the scale of abuse, with a 2013 World Health Organisation report estimating one in three women globally to have suffered physical or sexual violence at some point in their lives,[7] caused a huge aftershock that made it instantly less acceptable to say things that would have been brushed under the carpet only a short while before. A series of public accusations created a culture which gave stark examples of the consequences of abusing women or making sexist remarks. This was generally understood by people on the left as a necessary clearing away of cobwebs but caused panic on the right as instances of a potentially never-ending 'cancel culture', in a modern echo of the nineties fear of 'political correctness gone mad'.

Local casualties included Radar Radio, 'arguably the most exciting digital radio station in the UK'[8] until it collapsed in a matter of hours after accusations emerged of sexual harassment at the studio, resulting in two of the major DJs leaving the station, closely followed by every other DJ.

The focus on sexual violence helped create a climate in which broader feminist issues could also be discussed, including gender representation on festival line-ups and the sexualisation of the female body. The communal solidarity offered by #MeToo provided an opportunity for many women to use social media to challenge blatant examples of daily sexism.

All this fuelled a growing conversation within the music industry about the importance of gender balance on festival line-ups. This had been a conversation for several years before #MeToo, with music blog *Crack in the Road* tweeting a version of the 2015 Reading and Leeds line-up poster with all the all-male bands removed: virtually blank. This was still a problem in 2018: Festival Republic director Melvin Benn maintained, in response to criticism of his Wireless Festival hosting only three female performers across three days of music, that 'within the genre, there are insufficient women across the board that are strong ticket sellers'. Green Man festival director Fiona Stewart claimed, 'We want to have more women at the top of the bill, but it has been hard this year and there is an industry-wide issue of fewer female acts available at all levels that has affected the booking process.'[9]

In the same year, the BBC posted an analysis of 756 acts on the posters of major UK festivals, showing that 77 per cent of advertised groups were all-male, a further 9 per cent mixed but more male than female, and only 13 per cent all-female. Questioned about the lack of gender balance on Glastonbury Festival's main Pyramid Stage in 2019, organiser Emily Eavis explained, 'The pool isn't big enough. It's time to nurture female talent. Everyone wants it, everyone's hungry for women, but they're just not there.'[10]

Her comments highlight the point that creating gender balance is not simply a question of fairness or positive discrimination at the festival programming level but of nurturing female talent at earlier stages in order to help artists grow to the point that they can become major headline artists years down the line. Vanessa Reed, former CEO of PRS for Music, began the Keychange Initiative in 2015, aiming for 50/50 gender balance by 2022.*

Barcelona's tastemaker festival Primavera Sound insisted on a 50/50 gender balance at the 2019 edition, with the slogan 'The New Normal' boldly displayed on every stage. By February 2020, pop band the 1975 were explaining that male artists can 'be true allies' by contractually refusing to play at festivals without an equitable gender balance.[11] While the very existence of initiatives like Keychange highlights the persisting inequality, there has been an undoubted cultural shift in consciousness around representation which makes it increasingly unacceptable for promoters to book disproportionately male line-ups.

Where female instrumentalists like Nikki Yeoh had previously been outliers, the new wave – Sheila Maurice-Grey, Cassie Kinoshi and Richie Seivwright of Kokoroko, saxophonists Nubya Garcia, Camilla George and Chelsea Carmichael, trumpeters Yazz Ahmed and Emma-Jean Thackray and guitarist Shirley Tetteh – left no doubt whatsoever about women's ability as instrumentalists, bandleaders, composers and producers, overturning many of the prejudices they themselves had grown up fighting.

* It is unclear where non-binary genders fit into the 50/50, with Read herself talking about 'female talent' whereas Keychange's official slogan is 'We Bring Under-Represented Genders in the Music Industry to the Main Stage'.

unapologetic expression

Yazz Ahmed

When I was studying music at high school, we didn't learn about any female composers, so I thought, 'Maybe women aren't intelligent enough to become composers.' That really stuck in my mind. It wasn't until I graduated from the Guildhall that I realised, 'Maybe I can write music.' It really affects people's confidence. I didn't have any female role models. I didn't know any professional female trumpet players who specialised in jazz. So obviously, that puts a lot of doubt in someone's mind. I had to work really hard because I had to break stereotypes. I had to show the guys that I could play and I wasn't inferior. I think it's much better now. A lot of young players are seeing more women, which is great. And hopefully it will give them the confidence that I never had. If you see someone that looks like you or comes from the same place as you, then you can imagine yourself doing that thing. And everybody has a story to tell, we're a better society if we promote other voices.

This generation are at the vanguard of a movement that is now beginning to be echoed elsewhere in Europe.

Emma-Jean Thackray

London is the place where I can see more female jazz instrumentalists being applauded than anywhere else. In Europe, there are several festivals I went to where I was not only the only female person that day playing, but I could have been the only female playing the whole festival. And that just stuck out as being really odd, because when you're in London all the time and around your peers, there are loads of female instrumentalists, you're not necessarily thinking about that because there is real change and real progression happening here, particularly in the UK, particularly in London.

'wake (for grenfell)'

This increased visibility creates a virtuous circle in which potential musicians 'see themselves' on stage, giving confidence that playing this music might be 'for them'.

Cassie Kinoshi

One of the things I constantly repeat is that representation is everything. So whilst historically there were jazz musicians and composers and bandleaders who were female, there wasn't necessarily that same amount of publicity for them. And now we are able to play: we're on social media, we're fronting bands and we get a little bit more presented and pushed forward. And young girls being able to see that: if you can see someone doing something like that, you can aspire to do it.

Shirley Tetteh

The aim is that it doesn't feel strange to see any kind of person on stage playing music. I went to a girls' school for about two years when I was eleven, and that's when I first started playing guitar. So I didn't know that it wasn't normal for women to not play until I switched schools. You start picking up subconscious cues and then you start looking around at the jazz community and realising that the impression is that all the people that improvise well are men. And that's not true. So if we can shine a spotlight on all different kinds of people it does make a difference.

While there is no doubt that this generation advanced the cause enormously through their brilliance, they also benefited from the wider conversation around the importance of gender balance on venue and festival line-ups. Furthermore, the abundance of female musicians helped reinforce the link between this wave of jazz and progressive politics: for many people, supporting UK jazz and these artists in particular could be a statement of feminism.

Similarly, #MeToo helped create a space for women to discuss their navigation of their image. Women's role in music had long been hyper-sexualised, with opportunities for female performers typically limited to singers and dancers rather than instrumentalists, and women feeling an extreme pressure to appear sexy. This moment provided opportunities for women to challenge this by showcasing a plethora of different female identities, from Poppy Ajudha's highly stylised reclamation of sexuality, Nubya Garcia's dignified elegance to Sheila Maurice-Grey's conscious refusal to be objectified.

Sheila Maurice-Grey

I'm very much in control of how I'm being perceived and viewed. The way that we have portrayed ourselves in Kokoroko and the other bands I am in is very much removed from being overly sexualised. And that is quite a step and a movement in itself. I think we are in a different time where you can do either one or the other, and hopefully we'll get to a time where it doesn't really matter and it doesn't determine your success.

It was not that the battle had been won – as Poppy's testimony below shows, there is a lot of work still to be done with many of the same issues recurring. But this moment provided a space to understand, discuss and challenge rather than simply accept.

Poppy Ajudha

You have to get over that external oppression that you get from men, where actually they're probably just jealous, or they want to diminish your artistry because they feel insecure about their own. And if I want to look good or present myself in a certain way, that shouldn't detract from how good my music is. But as a woman, you feel often like you have to choose. I'm sure Nubya's felt that pressure of being a female instrumentalist, a lot of people being like, 'Oh, she's only there because she's a woman or she's pretty.' And it's like, no, she's an incredible musician and she's also hot. Don't be a hater! It is what it is. She can't help that she was born that way!

'wake (for grenfell)'

Unpicking these subconscious assumptions can be a long and complicated process.

Poppy Ajudha

I made the choice to get an all-female band because I felt like it would be a safer space for me to actually grow as an artist. I got people to send in audition videos. But it was funny, I didn't think that they were going to be as good as they were. I remember when I had the actual rehearsals: they were never late, always knew what they were doing. You think I've ever played with a band of musicians that have actually practised the material I sent them? They were just on it, and they're such incredible musicians. And even as someone who is such a big feminist and such an advocate for women and equality, I still have that in my mind that male musicians might be better. And then we play together, and it was everything I wanted it to be for me as an artist. As we started doing shows live, people were like, 'It's so amazing that you've got an all-female band.' It was also amazing for the band members who had never played with an all-female band. So in the break, we'd be talking about gender issues and it would just come up because we'd all experienced these things, it became just such a safe space for us to talk about stuff. I didn't do it because I thought people would notice it, but it really did impact other people. I think we're from a very liberal intellectual space where feminism is much more normalised, and actually for the wider community and a lot of men, it's not that normal yet. I think there is still work to do. Seeing female musicians being really good at what they do and realising for men and women: one, you could be that yourself, but also women can be that and they can blow you away. And they're so much more than maybe what you see them as in your mind. I didn't realise it was going to have the impact that it had for me and for everybody else. Honestly the best thing I've done.

unapologetic expression

An opportunity to make real changes
(Black Lives Matter)

On 25 May 2020, Minneapolis policeman Derek Chauvin stopped George Floyd in his car on suspicion of having used a forged twenty-dollar bill in a local grocery store. When Floyd maintained his innocence, Chauvin subdued him by putting his knee on his neck for eight minutes and forty-six seconds, ignoring his strangled cries of, 'I can't breathe.' In a chilling image broadcast all over the world, Chauvin was seen grinning for the camera while Floyd gasped for breath. He was dead before he reached the hospital.

Floyd's death attracted worldwide condemnation, with protestors on the grass outside Chauvin's house calling for him to be tried for murder.* A twenty-four-hour police detail was deployed, creating another iconic image of a wall of white riot police defending a classic suburban American house from a sea of multi-ethnic protestors on the lawn: the American dream under threat from the miscegenated liberal masses.

The event brought renewed prominence to the Black Lives Matter movement, which had begun in 2013 in response to the failure of authorities to bring storekeeper George Zimmerman to justice after fatally shooting unarmed seventeen-year-old Trayvon Martin. Floyd's killing reopened old wounds all over the world, with a mass sharing of stories of police brutality and racial profiling that gave the lie to the idea that things were getting better. Actor Will Smith observed, 'Racism is not getting worse: it's getting filmed.'[12] Protests in Minneapolis turned into riots as the police department failed to make a proper apology or initiate an investigation.

Condemning the city's 'weak liberal mayor', President Trump threatened to send in the military, gleefully proclaiming on Twitter, 'When the looting starts, the shooting starts.' He was as good as his word, deploying forces in Atlanta, Georgia and Portland, Oregon

---

* Chauvin was eventually convicted of murder on 20 April 2021.

when demonstrations escalated into full-scale riots and fires. Rumours abounded that the CIA had used agents provocateurs to amplify the damage as an excuse for military action, with viral footage emerging of black protestors pleading with a white man dressed in full riot gear to stop after he went through Atlanta systematically and calmly smashing windows with a brand-new hammer.

Rather than apologising, Mike O'Meara, the head of the NY Association of Police Benevolent Associations, inflamed the situation in a televised address on 8 June 2020 where he denied that black people are in any danger from police, complaining: 'Everybody's trying to shame us into being embarrassed about our profession . . . Stop treating us like animals and thugs and start treating *us* with some respect. We've been left out of the conversation . . . We've been vilified . . . I'm proud to be a cop,' repeatedly claiming that their 375 million interactions with the public had been 'overwhelmingly positive' while surrounded by an intimidating all-male pack of mostly white police officers.

As with #MeToo in 2017 where the Weinstein revelations created a space for thousands of women to speak up about their experiences, not only of sexual violence but sexism in general, the George Floyd killing was the match that lit a global fire that cast a flickering light on the continued racism, prejudice and adverse life experiences that have affected black people ever since slavery. While police violence against black people was absolutely nothing new, the scale of the global reaction was unlike anything since the 1960s. Protests in cities all over the world were accompanied by an outpouring of testimony on social media.

In the UK, books including Reni Eddo-Lodge's *Why I'm No Longer Talking to White People about Race*, Robin DiAngelo's *White Fragility*, Afua Hirsch's *Brit(ish)* and Akala's *Natives* immediately sold out and were hurriedly reprinted as 'white allies' sought to inform themselves about the experiences of people of colour. Organisations hastily put together 'diversity committees' and 'diversity and inclusion policies', in many cases suddenly taking on initiatives to tackle issues that staff members had been trying to raise for years. The music industry observed a world-wide twenty-four-hour 'Blackout Tuesday' on 2 June 2020, in which participating individuals and organisations withdrew from work to 'educate themselves about race', and protestors pushed a statue of slaver William Colston into Bristol Harbour. Bristol Police did not intervene in order to avoid 'a very violent confrontation', and the iconic footage of protestors knocking the statue off its plinth, kneeling on Colston's neck for a symbolic eight minutes and forty-six seconds, then rolling him into the harbour from which Bristol ships had launched two thousand voyages between 1698 and 1807, transporting an estimated five hundred thousand Africans to slavery, sparked the predictable mix of jubilation and outcry.[13] Some celebrated this as a symbolic new chapter in world history and called for a review of the histories of all statues globally,[14] while for others, including Home Secretary Priti Patel, it was 'utterly disgraceful' and portended the end of society as we know it.[15]

Steve Williamson

I would say now is the first time I've felt something like this in this country, or in the world in fact. I don't think I've witnessed anything like this before.

The global prominence of Black Lives Matter in June 2020, of course, did not create the current wave of jazz. By this point, the scene had well and truly broken, and many of the artists had already had several years of international popularity, often with overt political themes. But like the Black Lives Matter movement itself, which had been building since 2013 on much older foundations, this seemed to be the culmination of a particular moment of interest in politicised, defiant music by people of colour. June 2020 simply provided the most visible expression of a political consciousness that has under-pinned the scene's success, as people celebrated a new-found con-fidence among young black musicians to embrace and reclaim the history of what had once been undeniably a black music.

'wake (for grenfell)'

Wozzy Brewster

I've been paying taxes towards slave owners up until 2015.[16] But there was no reparation for those slaves whose feet were cut off, hands cut off, their children murdered. And they took the music as well. The African rhythms, the chants, the storytelling. And then these things have been celebrated. It took that man's life for people to actually realise this is plain murder. Come on. It's been going on. We know it's been going on for decades and centuries. But this is like right in your face. The way that the police officers did it riled people in such a way because these people are supposed to be protecting us all. And actually, if they can just do that, what else can they do? We talk about music, they have taken black music and rinsed it and put it in all of its formats, but never, ever really given the true value to the Black artists who've created it. About time those slave owners were not celebrated. About time those statues are removed, about time that we pause, and about time that everybody stood up for the injustices against colour.

Nubya Garcia

Our generation are used to pushing the ceiling and breaking it and being like, 'Well I don't wanna do it like this so I'm going to do it this way,' and I think that's just part of the kind of youthful energy that happens every single generation, whatever you're fighting, the fight is different to the fight that's happened before, you feel like you can go further and you feel like you can change things.

'Just noise to me'
(performative wokeness)

Not everyone was convinced, and for different reasons.

Struck by the cleaner habits of many musicians of the younger generation in comparison with the hedonism of those who came of age in the 1980s or 1990s, some older musicians understood both the political self-expression and lifestyle choices as part of a performative 'wokeness' that was more important than the music itself.

The term 'woke' had been used as far back as 1938 in Lead Belly's 'Scottsboro Boys' to signify not only being awake but being 'woke' to racial injustice. African American novelist William Melvin Kelley, author of *A Different Drummer*, had called out the term's appropriation by white beatniks as early as 1962 in an article for the *New York Times*, 'If You're Woke You Dig It'. The term had been re-popularised by legendary Afrofuturist Erykah Badu with 2007's 'Master Teacher'; Badu used the phrase 'stay woke' in 2012 in a tweet in support of persecuted Russian feminist group Pussy Riot, and the term gained currency in the Black Lives Matter protests of 2014. But by the latter part of that decade, like 'cancel culture', it was being used mostly pejoratively by right-wing commentators to signify an 'overrighteous liberalism'.[17]

Binker Golding

The behaviour of jazz musicians is safer now than it ever was. I barely know a single jazz musician that takes drugs. Many of them don't even drink, they're far more likely to be a clean-living vegan type that gets up at 5 a.m. and has a gong bath than they are to be a coke-snorting, heavy drinker that stays up until 5 a.m. I'm not proud to admit it, but I still smoke, I still drink. That's just who I am. Few jazz musicians ten years younger than me do any of that shit. But that's also just people today in general. People want to look as though they're with the times. That they're up to date. They want to look 'woke'. What does that mean? I literally don't know how people would define it. What? You read a few specific books?

Oli Reeves

We're in an age where everything is based around image, and if you're marketing yourself in the right way, or if your profile is correct, then

'wake (for grenfell)'

it doesn't matter if you're not putting out records, you're still gonna get booked. Jazz music comes from black culture and was created by black people who used it as a way to express themselves. That is the heart and soul of the music we love, we have to embrace that and cherish it. The music that comes out on 22a is celebrating that, but we're coming at it from a musical perspective. When I'm listening to something, I don't think about what colour someone's skin is, what country they're from. What's your playing like? How does it sound? I'm not listening with my eyes. My ears are open. My eyes might as well be closed. That's where I come from on it. But I know in the world we're in right now, people are listening with their eyes.

For some, the platforming of black and female artists is evidence of a transitory faddishness. This position is not limited to those who may feel that this focus has not been to their personal advantage: there is also the fear that the temporary focus on an endemic, structural problem will not create lasting change.

Sheila Maurice-Grey

It's a great thing that people are thinking about it and reading about it, but it's just a fine line when things become a commodity, the thing to do and the thing to say, like people are riding a wave and when it's cool, then people want to do what's cool. It's not like all of these things didn't exist before, they have existed and people have been fighting for it, maybe in a more serious way, and now I just don't take it seriously. It's just noise to me. You can put people on the face of things and show that you are making change. But what is it really for? Is it just so you're visually ticking the box, or are you really trying to make change?

Wayne Francis

As the times change, I don't know if the same musicians that are aligning themselves politically will align themselves politically. I've seen that happen where people have aligned themselves politically and then

279

later on, maybe they went back to talking about love songs, or cosmic philosophy, whatever else.

These reservations are not unique to this generation. Indeed, if jazz has a long history as a political music and vehicle for black liberation, it has an equally long history of being adopted by white bohemians as a political statement and conscious lifestyle choice. This is not just a question of fashion; in many cases jazz, and black culture in general, has represented for young white bohemians a symbolic escape from the oppressive clutches of Western capitalism. This often involves a process of intense idealisation, with black musicians and black people in general standing in symbolic opposition to whatever white bohemians want to escape from.

LeRoi Jones/Amiri Baraka succinctly expresses the difference between jazz as played by black musicians and as adopted by white:

Jazz as played by white musicians was not the same as that played by black musicians, nor was there any reason for it to be. The music of the white jazz musicians did not issue from the same cultural circumstance; it was, at its most profound instance, a learned art . . . The white musicians and other young whites who associated themselves with this Negro music identified the Negro with his separation, this nonconformity, though, of course, the Negro himself had no choice. But the young Negro musician in the forties began to realise that merely by being a Negro in America, one *was* a nonconformist.[18]

The New Orleans revival in the US, which became known as trad in the UK, maintained strong links with Communist and left-wing groups, who saw in the music an inclusive opportunity for working-class self-expression. Marxist historian Eric Hobsbawm, writing under the pseudonym Francis Newton in *The Jazz Scene*, points out the 'disproportionately large number' of 'Communist jazz-lovers', describing jazz as 'a music of protest and rebellion', although he notes that 'it is not necessarily or always a music of conscious and overt *political* protest, let alone any particular brand of political protest'.[19] In Newton's analysis, jazz is less suited to alignment with political causes than as a general statement of protest and disaffection with the status quo, while its origins as a black art form naturally make it both anti-racist and unorthodox.

Jazz was central to the poetics of the post-war American beat generation, those 'who sank all night in submarine light of Bickford's . . . who barrelled down the highways of the past journeying to each other's hotrod-Golgotha jail-solitude watch or Birmingham jazz incarnation'. For them jazz – and bebop in particular – offered an alternative vision to post-war America's 'eyeball kicks and shocks of hospitals and jails and wars' and a powerful musical prosody that directly influenced both poetry and prose.[20]

Until edged out by 'pop' (i.e. white rhythm and blues) in the mid-1960s, jazz remained, even in the UK, the music of choice for young, left-leaning bohemians. Cheltenham Jazz Festival director Tony Dudley-Evans recalls his time as a student in London in the early 1960s.

Tony Dudley-Evans

It was a Monday night at UCL. There was a jam session that night, and Shake Keane, who played with Joe Harriott, used to be there most Mondays and it was packed. It was the place to be. People felt that they should know about jazz, and audiences were much younger. They were more like the current audiences, young, student-type audiences. I think those people that were following jazz in the sixties, in their twenties, grew up, remained left wing. Not necessarily active, some of them may have been active, some not – and jazz was a memory and they were still engaged with what was happening at a later time.

But in many cases the alliance between jazz, bohemianism and left-wing politics involved romanticisation and stereotyping. In *Black Skin, White Masks,* Fanon recalls being told by an American teacher friend that 'The presence of the Negroes beside the whites is, in a way, an insurance policy on humanness. When the whites feel that they have become too mechanised, they turn to the men of colour and ask them for a little human sustenance.'[21] The racist belief that black people are more in tune with nature has its roots in eugenicist pseudoscience and resurfaces in the idea of black people having 'natural rhythm': this is now often considered offensive even when meant in praise. And if on the one hand black musicians have been portrayed as close to the wellspring of autochthonous creativity, at another they have become fetishised as dissolute, hypersexual and criminal, again playing into a white fantasy. The white industry's fascination with this aspect of black marginality still exists in the popularity among white audiences of certain aspects of grime, drill and UK rap, as noted sadly by black UK soul artist Omar.

Omar Lye-Fook

It doesn't sit well with me, the fact that with a lot of the awards that I see, the grime, boys being bad boys or they're in gangs or talking badness and all that, they get awards. But when it comes to the soul category, I saw Adele, Sam Smith getting awards, I'm like, 'Hold on, where's the black soul artists?' And obviously, because we're singing about love and peace, they don't want to hear that, they want to hear about stabbing somebody in his throat. It's perpetuating a stereotype, it just perpetuates that thing of we're all bad and we're angry, want to have a fight and wanna cuss you at the slightest moment.

This idea of jazz being adopted as a bohemian affectation and statement of nonconformity resurfaced in Vice's satirical 'Nu Jazz Lad' 2019; he is 'the guy down the pub using (Theon) Cross as proof of how 'jazz is becoming the alternative music of the twenty-first century . . . He is impressed by *Crack* magazine's decision to put Shabaka Hutchings on the cover for their January edition, and let them know by quote-tweeting the image with the caption "long-overdue" and a clap emoji at least eight shades darker than his own hands.'[22]

If the article is to be believed, what began as the authentic expression of primarily non-white musicians from tough South London backgrounds, facilitated by grassroots community organisations like Tomorrow's Warriors and Kinetika Bloco, has been commodified, stereotyped and appropriated as a symbol of nonconformity, exactly as happened with the beats in the fifties and the trad jazz movement in the forties.

Binker Golding

Now for example, I'm sure Kamasi would've been dressing the way he does regardless, but it just so happens that that particular look is popular now. You go to these festivals and you see hipster-type guys in their early twenties absolutely draped in clothes and accessories that fit the look. I find it sort of hilarious. You just didn't see it to that extent ten years ago, but that's how fashion works, I guess.

Femi Koleoso of Ezra Collective talks about the success that followed the band's adoption of 'the uniform' – the sportswear associated with black urban youth – instead of the suits worn by their one-time heroes Empirical. The standard reading of this sartorial symbolism is that in so doing the band have made themselves, and therefore the music, relatable to young people of colour. This is undoubtedly the case, and one of the reasons why Ezra have attracted a wider following among this demographic than some of their peers. Yet an alternative reading might be that it's not only that they have worn clothes authentic to their background: they have also conformed to an image of how the music industry *expects* young black artists to look, and by conforming to this stereotype they have made themselves far easier to sell. Suddenly the 'swagger' praised by Kerstan Mackness or the 'energy' that is a central feature of virtually every excited media description of this wave of jazz begins to look like the twenty-first-century descendant of two long traditions of stereotyping of black music: as the natural creativity of a simpler people and the outpouring of expression of disaffected urban youth.

I do not wish to imply that Ezra and others owe their success only to the indulgence of white liberal posers or that their choice of dress was a calculated performance of a cultural stereotype rather than an authentic choice. Such a cynical perspective would do a gross injustice both to the skill and sincerity of this generation of artists and the integrity and aesthetic appreciation of their supporters. Nevertheless, it is impossible to separate the music from the political moment, which affects what music is created, how it is presented and how it is received. Success in popular music has never been only about how good you are: it is to do with the extent to which your music forms part of a cultural zeitgeist, catching the spirit of the age that amplifies what you do.

Beyond fears of faddishness and insincerity, identity politics can also be experienced as limiting by the very groups whose voices they are supposed to amplify.

Poppy Ajudha

Because we look a certain way, we get put in the same place, and that has maybe reduced the way I have expanded my music. As an artist, you are always reinventing yourself, always finding new influences. That's why jazz transcends so many genres now, because all of these artists that started playing straight jazz or learning straight jazz are being influenced all the time and changing who they are as they go. Part of being a musician is being able to explore and experiment and create new spaces to listen and new ways to think about music or the world. It's a constant thought process of unpacking who you are. Being an artist is part of that, trying to help your audience also unpack who they are by unpacking who you are, and being allowed the space to do that and the freedom to do that is the privilege of being an artist. We're often allowed to be a lot more uninhibited than other people.

'wake (for grenfell)'

'This is a worldwide movement'
(jazz and the ongoing struggle)

Despite the fears and caveats above, there is no question that global movements like #MeToo and Black Lives Matter, new conversations around race, gender, global power structures and the environment, the mainstreaming (and commodification) of lifestyle choices like veganism, and new language to articulate these intersecting struggles have created the perfect environment for jazz to renew its function as a vibrant, politically charged music. The music and the musicians who play it have both benefited from and helped to amplify these conversations, on the stage, on record and on social media.

But if now seems a politically progressive time, global news provides daily reminders that the world continues to be dominated by forces that represent the exact opposite. If progressive conversations are currently strong, it is in reaction to the strength of the agendas they are opposing.

It is in the context of this existential struggle that music can and must continue both to spread love and to amplify progressive agendas.

Emma-Jean Thackray

You can't always control what other people are doing. You can just set examples and focus on yourself. And if you're always doing as much as you can, always trying, that's all positive. Hopefully we'll be leading and then people will be following that example. And if some people are doing it for the sake of it to not look bad, maybe some good things will still come of that, and hopefully that will lead to some conversations that help structural change.

Nubya Garcia

I'm always happy to occupy spaces where people assume that I can't be. I think it's really good to challenge those stereotypes and images that people put out. It's encouraging more people like us to feel like they can do this and have a space that's not owned by white people at the top of the music industry pyramid. This is how it gets more diverse across the pyramid. This is a worldwide movement, and music is just one of those things that is getting reclaimed. Our parents' generation, they've wanted this for so long they probably didn't think it would ever happen. We still have a really, really, like reaaaaallly long way to go. But we are, just by existing and going to music college and making money from touring and being able to play our own music in the places we do. It's huge.

'Man Like GP'

Gilles Peterson: Forty Years of Jazz for the Dance Floor

We now know this generation: politically conscious, with the tools to control their own image, disseminate their own ideas and identities, independently networked, armed with the knowledge and support of their forebears, treading carefully over the debris of jazz's history. But who was their champion, and how did they fit into the wider history of UK music?

There were two types of dog walk I used to do as a teenager. In the first I would go out in the daytime in a tracksuit, sometimes with a football, and come back forty minutes later sweating and covered in mud. In the second, I would go out between 11 p.m. and midnight in my puffa jacket and beanie and come back twenty minutes later reeking of crystal-covered, late-nineties white widow. My mum was discreet enough to pretend not to notice the difference and it was only when she referred to it over a decade later that I realised she'd always known exactly what I was up to and judiciously refrained from comment. It may not have helped my emotional development and teenage paranoia but it definitely helped keep our relationship intact. Well done, Mum!

The most reliable time to find me doing the latter kind of walk would be on a Wednesday, returning to scuttle into my room as quickly as possible and tuning into Gilles Peterson's *Worldwide* show on Radio 1, which broadcast from 12 p.m.–2 a.m. every Wednesday night/Thursday morning. Needless to say this did not help me get up for school the next day, but it broadened my musical taste immeasurably. A quick glance at the 1999 Worldwide Award winners gives a tantalising taste of the musical diversity Gilles was championing at that time: The Cinematic Orchestra, Mos Def, London Elektricity, Nitin Sawhney, Peshay, Terry Callier, Innerzone Orchestra (an alias of Detroit techno legend Carl Craig).

I was not the only one.

Matthew Halsall

The two biggest influences in terms of introducing me to music would be Gilles Peterson and Mr. Scruff. From thirteen, fourteen onwards, I was listening to Gilles's show on Radio 1 . . . Late one! Cassette-tape recording it as well. So when I finally passed my driving test at a later date I had all these cassettes. I used to re-listen to his shows from like four years before. And I just loved it. I loved those shows.

I was then seventeen, I'm now forty. My life is different in almost every way, and my tastes have changed. I wouldn't go near that kind of skunk these days, no longer model myself on Dean Moriarty in Jack Kerouac's *On the Road,* no longer play *Tony Hawk's Pro Skater* or *Tekken 3* on the PlayStation, and imagine re-watching cult dark comedy *The League of Gentlemen* would be a cringe-inducing experience. But Gilles's show has remained a constant from that time until now, consistently evolving as the music did, whilst being a crucial catalyst for that evolution.

Whatever your first engagement, Gilles's combination of impeccable taste and endless yet discerning enthusiasm has meant that people who like and listen to him tend to keep liking and listening to him throughout their lives, which is one of the reasons why his fan base – and accordingly the fan base for the diverse musics he champions – has grown exponentially.

Dom Servini

When he was on Sunday mornings on Radio London, round about 1989, '90, it changed my world completely, just to hear someone playing jazz records alongside the kind of soul music that I was already into . . . It opened up a door; I could relate it to the standards and the crooner stuff that my mum influenced me with growing up. But hearing Willis Jackson's 'Nuther'n like Thuth'ern', it's just like, 'Wow, I can dance to this!' I mean, to use a very unfashionable word, this was music that was groovy.

Gilles has done a lot since teenaged-me used to listen to him well into the night, swapping the next morning's formal education for an informal one of a different kind. He has continued to give a platform to an extraordinarily wide range of artists, from Skream and Mosca, Jamie Woon and Floating Points, Romare and The Comet Is Coming, to Bugz in the Attic, Alabaster DePlume, Nubya Garcia, Ezra Collective and Moses Boyd right through to Sault and BCUC. He is one of the current jazz scene's most important champions, playing the music on his radio shows and in his club and festival sets, growing a community through Worldwide FM and the Worldwide and We Out Here festival brands, releasing music on his Brownswood label, and bigging up the scene both publicly and privately to his vast network of international industry players.

Noah Ball

Four Tet and Floating Points and Daphni, they all have to thank Gilles for being that person who to a mass audience would play mad jazz, mad music from all over the world as well as jungle or dubstep or hip-hop or house.

Naomi Palmer

Gilles is opening doors to all types of music. He loves jazz and his knowledge of jazz is vast. And he has some of the best ears in the game, so he's always been there pushing different sounds, which is hugely important and inspiring. Gilles has opened up people's ideas of which sounds can connect. In ten years of working with him, I never, ever, ever saw him lose his curiosity or his enthusiasm for new music:

he is a searcher and has an insatiable appetite for finding new artists and new sounds. He will see something extraordinary where everyone else is thinking, 'What the fuck is going on?' Gilles is very important when it comes to this particular movement, because he's been exposing us to these sounds for more than thirty years.

Just as the startling achievement of the generation that came up through Tomorrow's Warriors has been to rejuvenate jazz through its organic intersection with other music, Gilles has consistently managed to bring jazz into new contexts, repackaging it in a way that people can enjoy it without necessarily even realising it is jazz.

Gilles Peterson

My role has always been to subtly infiltrate the British media with music which someone will pick up without realising that they're picking it up. I've been fighting the fight amongst the media in an industry dominated by a status quo, which is looking at its own interests, which is making profit at the end of the year based on a history of rock 'n' roll, which is what this country is known for globally. So to be able to play whatever you love, you've got to play it within the fabric of that, which makes it more complicated. You have to be canny about it.

Paul Bradshaw

Gilles is canny, man, that's his skill. If there's something jazz in that piece of the tune, whether it's A Tribe Called Quest or a Public Enemy twelve inch or whatever, he will sneak that into the mix. Even if people are threatening to beat him up, he will sneak that shit into the mix, man, and gradually it changes the vibe. He finds a way to find a way. At the core of everything Gilles does is a jazz element.

By the point that I first came across him, Gilles already had almost two decades of important work behind him, going right back to the suburban funk and soul scene of the late seventies, via the warehouse party, club and pub scene of the mid-eighties, through late eighties jazz dance, early nineties acid jazz right through to trip-hop and drum and bass.

Not only does the present wave of jazz owe so much to the open-minded, dance-floor-driven approach to jazz he has embodied for over forty years, but Gilles's own story is one way of telling the story of jazz as a whole and understanding some of the other foundations on which this house was built.

'Donald Byrd Thanked Me'
(Northern Soul/Funk Mafia)

Britain in the late seventies was not a lovely place. The early years of the decade marked the end of the post-war global economic boom, and the UK had landed with a bump: a divided and poorly resourced island still coming to terms with the end of empire. Power cuts, a three-day week, mass unemployment, class war and seething racism against the country's black and brown population were the orders of the day.

It was against this background that Gilles's first musical heroes, the Funk Mafia[1] – Chris Hill, Robbie Vincent, Froggy and Greg Edwards (later Jeff Young and Pete Tong) – arose to provide a necessary escapism for young, predominantly white revellers. Primarily a suburban scene focused around the Home Counties of Essex, Kent and Surrey, these DJs could be seen playing a mixture of black American soul, jazz, funk and disco at clubs which 'read less like citadels of glamour than a particularly ribald pub crawl: Lacy Lady, the Orsett Cock, Frenchies, the Rio, Flicks, the Belvedere. If suburban jazz funk was born anywhere, it was in Canvey Island, an ugly lump on the Essex coastline with an oil refinery for a view'.[2]

The British white working-class obsession with black music was nothing new, even in 1979. The trend had shifted away from live performance and into clubs with Northern Soul, the DJ culture which erupted in Manchester's Twisted Wheel in the late 1960s, spreading across the

North and the Midlands. Based on an obsession with forgotten sixties soul records, most of which had been flops on first release, Northern Soul was characterised by sharp dressing and acrobatic, amphetamine-fuelled dancing. Young people would mission all over the North and Midlands for all-night sessions at Blackpool's Mecca, the Wigan Casino, the Torch in Tunstall and the Catacombs in Wolverhampton, some of them breaking into a chemist's on the way for supplies.

Both these movements foreshadowed the twenty-first-century interest in vintage African music stimulated by labels like Strut, Soundway and Analog Africa, characterised by a mythology around intrepid musical explorers digging deep to give new life to long-forgotten cultural treasures. Aspiring Northern Soul DJs would scrimp and save for a passage to the mythical promised land of America, unearthing rare and forgotten records in thrift shops and junk stores in Detroit, Philadelphia and Chicago. The 'discovery' of Bunk Johnson and Lead Belly had thrilled White America in the 1930s and 1940s, and recent tours by 'rediscovered' African artists like Ghana's Ata Kak, Ethiopia's Hailu Mergia and Somalia's Durdur Band hoped for the same effect on White Europe. Similarly, although primarily a DJ scene, the Northern Soul scene literally ran up the walls for rare live performances by rediscovered 'legends' like Major Lance, who was tracked down in Chicago and somehow persuaded to play at the Torch in Tunstall, Staffordshire, just north of Stoke-on-Trent.

Like Bunk Johnson, one of the heroes of the New Orleans revival who was working as a cowherd having long since sold his horn, most of the artists 'rediscovered' by Northern Soul were languishing in dead-end jobs and were utterly baffled to discover a new generation of fans in a faraway place erupting in enthusiasm for their forgotten work. Northern Soul began putting sixties records in the seventies charts with such regularity that Dave McAleer at Pye started the Disco Demand label in 1974 specifically to release this forgotten music. There is perhaps something archetypal in this redemptive fantasy of a forgotten artist suddenly discovering an obsessive following in a faraway land; a withered, bitter, alcoholic old hag is discovered to have been a beautiful princess all along.[*]

Whereas Northern Soul had been obsessed with forgotten records from a just-earlier period, scorning new releases, the 1970s Home Counties jazz funk scene was far more populist, and included new developments in jazz fusion, funk and disco: Chick Corea, Donald Byrd, Lonnie Liston Smith, Herbie Hancock, Miroslav Vitous, The O'Jays, War and Funkadelic alongside Miles Davis, Lee Morgan, McCoy Tyner and Sonny Stitt.

Godfather of the Funk Mafia was Essex boy Chris Hill, who had amassed a vast record collection with money earned while working at the Ford Factory in Dagenham. Having come of age in the Soho scene of the mid-sixties seeing artists like Joe Harriott in the Flamingo, and hearing jazz records played for dancing in between sets, he treated jazz as a form of dance music to be interspersed freely with other black music styles. In this regard he can be seen to have laid a template for Gilles's dance-floor-based approach to jazz. Although playing a lot of soul and Motown, he would start every set of his original late-sixties residency at the Cock in Orsett, Essex with Miles Davis's 'Milestones', and Blue Note tunes like Lee Morgan's 'The Sidewinder' and Don Wilkerson's 'Dem Tambourines' were a consistent part of his sound in the mid-1970s. A charismatic extrovert, he would routinely get on the mic not only telling audiences which record he was playing but insisting they go out and buy it.

Chris Hill

In the North, they kept the records to themselves – 'I've got this record and I'm going to cover it up so nobody else knows what it is' – but my attitude was 'I've found this record by Lonnie Liston Smith and you

---

[*] A version of this fantasy was at work in the enormous success of the 2012 documentary *Searching for Sugarman*, which to some extent reverses the usual racial narratives, showing the Mexican American artist Rodriguez uncovering a following amongst mostly black South Africans.

should buy it, and I'm going to keep on playing it until you do buy it and make it a hit – make the music bigger, make the scene bigger!' I've no sense of shame to keep on plugging the music rather than cover it up. Roy Ayers understood what we were doing. Donald Byrd thanked me – he was absolutely amazed. The payback was seeing these artists in the charts and knowing that our scene did it.[3]

Hill began a residency in 1973 at the Goldmine on Canvey Island, a backwoods corner of Essex which began attracting coachloads of music fans from all over the country, much to the annoyance of the locals. The club, and Hill, achieved national notoriety after a brief stint in 1976 playing 1940s swing records, which somehow kick-started a huge wave of press interest and even sent Glenn Miller to No. 13 in the charts in 1976, his first top forty position since 1954. Hill himself had No. 10 hits in both 1975 and 1976 with the novelty Christmas singles 'Renta Santa' and 'Bionic Santa'. Consciously retreating from the media hype, he began a new residency at the Lacy Lady in Ilford in 1976, moving back to the Goldmine in 1978. The scene continued to grow in popularity, attracting enormous media attention and migrating from the back rooms of regional pubs to all-dayers in Purley and Reading and full-on weekenders at 1930s holiday resorts. 1979 saw the launch of the Caister Soul Weekender, whose first two editions attracted three thousand and five thousand people to the Ladbrokes Holiday Centre in Great Yarmouth; the event still continues today, more than forty years later. The peak of the scene's popularity was the 1980 Knebworth Soul Festival – 'a much more agreeable use of Hertfordshire than heavy metal'[4] – which attracted a staggering (and staggering) fifteen thousand people to listen to the Funk Mafia DJs, Colin Curtis and Lonnie Liston Smith.

The scene's popularity and Hill's self-disclosed populist tendencies resulted in an inevitable dilution, with a combination of kitsch fashion, conga lines and beer-driven fighting causing many of the most serious music fans to form communities elsewhere. Just as a hardcore movement away from a populist dilution birthed bebop, free jazz, jungle and grime, this scene's version was the unlikely phenomenon that became known as the jazz dance scene, revolving around the central figure of Paul Murphy.

'I was one of the dancers'
(jazz dance)

Steve Symons

The other big difference between then and now was the jazz dance scene, the dancers. I haven't seen that come back, but that was quite magnificent. We'd get dancers from as far afield as Birmingham and Brighton coming up, and we'd have a dedicated hour at the beginning of the night for dancers. So they'd always turn up first thing and we'd play the stuff that nobody else could dance to, and people would come down early just to watch them.

Also from Essex, Murphy had grown up watching Hill at the Gold-mine in Canvey Island and Bob Jones at Deejays and the Countryman in neighbouring Chelmsford. Already well known on the suburban jazz funk scene through running the subscription-based Exodus Club, arranging coaches to other funk and soul clubs around the country, Murphy began his own DJ career when Bob Jones and Paul Gratue, residents at his Kingswood Club in Hornchuch, were unable to make it due to snow. With a spectacular record collection amassed through working as a buyer for Our Price and creating direct links with American distributors, Murphy carved out a reputation for himself playing intensely fast jazz fusion and Latin jazz for skilled, competitive dancers, both in Essex and at the 'Jazz Room' at the Caister Weekenders, where the serious music fans would retreat from the satin-shorted silliness.

In London, Greek Cypriot DJ Akis Eracleous, aka George Power, had amassed a huge following and, unlike the Funk Mafia Home Counties DJs, played for a mostly black crowd. The centre of this was

Crackers in Soho's Wardour Street, where he had been resident since 1976. Playing heavy jazz funk as well as soul, the club became the site for intense dance battles, particularly on the Sunday night and Friday daytime sessions. Many dancers at these sessions were underage, sneaking out of school for three hours of high-energy, acrobatic, combative dance. Among the teenage enthusiasts were future Jazz Warriors Courtney Pine and Orphy Robinson.

Courtney Pine

I used to go see Paul Murphy at Crackers, Friday afternoon session.[5] Paul Murphy was the instigator. The two scenes developed in parallel where you'd have clubs with dance troupes. And then you'd have a band come on. A lot of the venues when I started gigs, there'd be a DJ there. I can remember going to see Robbie Vincent down in Southend. I used to follow him around the country and he would play like half an hour of a jazz set and the real dancers would stay on the floor. I would be on the floor. I come from that perspective, I'm not some yout' that went college and came out the scale book. I was one of the dancers.

Orphy Robinson

The thing that I haven't seen in this generation so much is the emphasis on the dance side. A lot of ours came through the jazz dance scene, with Paul Murphy, who was a major influence; George Power at a club called Crackers in the West End.

If you ask most of my generation, they will say they heard about a lot of the music from going to clubnights at Crackers, and all the jazz there. The Hundred Club on a Saturday daytime, would you believe, you would go in at one and come out at four straight on to Oxford Street with all the people shopping, and you'd just been listening to Tito Puente and a world of music! Quite a few of us were skaters. The old skates, not the in-line ones. There was a skate dance scene as well. Heavy skate dance scene.

By 1980, both Power and Murphy were resident at the Horseshoe on Tottenham Court Road: Power on Fridays and Murphy on Saturdays. Essentially two function rooms on the first floor of the Horseshoe Hotel, this was not a purpose-built club, meaning that the DJs had to bring in a sound system and lighting rig each week. It was for this purpose that Power recruited two kids from Hackney and Islington, Colin Parnell and Bülent 'Boo' Mehmet. Although originally brought in to supply the sound systems, they played fast jazz dance in the smaller room, amassing a hardcore following who were able to dance to some quite challenging records – so challenging, according to dancer Seymour Nurse, that on seeing their charts listed in *Black Echoes*, many people didn't believe those records were really played.[6]

After the Horseshoe lost its licence in 1981, Power moved his 'Jazzifunk' night to the six-hundred-capacity Electric Ballroom in Camden, where he and Paul 'Trouble' Anderson would lay down funk, soul and jazz (later hip-hop and electro) every Friday, while Parnell and Boo played fast jazz for the dancers upstairs. In contrast to the suburban Funk Mafia scene, the clientele at the Electric Ballroom was almost totally black; the dancing in the jazz room was both impressive and deeply competitive.

By 1982, Murphy had replaced Colin and Boo and become a central figure not only for his DJ sets but because he supplied virtually every other DJ on the scene with obscure American imports via his Fusions record shop on Exmouth Market. The scene began attracting media attention, with journalist Robert Elms coming down with then-girlfriend Sade Adu and writing about it in *The Face*. Camden was then a rough and unfashionable area, and Murphy moved in 1984 to the trendier, more media-friendly Wag Club (formerly Whisky-A-Go-Go, a key Soho nightspot of the 1960s) and Fitzrovia's Sol Y Sombra, bringing in a young Gilles Peterson to take his place in the upstairs jazz room at Electric Ballroom. Gilles was deeply intimidated that first night and was virtually booed off stage, but in the long-term was saved by the different atmosphere and stricter door policies of the competing West End clubs, which in practice obliged much of Murphy's black fan base to return to the Electric Ballroom and give Gilles another chance.

Gilles Peterson

The scene was really heavy and a lot of people thought I couldn't hold it. I was this new kid on the block, to them Paul was God, he was the one who discovered those fusion tunes and had a wicked collection. It was the dancers who backed and supported me, gave me their confidence and allowed me to express myself as a DJ.[7]

Daz-I-Kue

I go back to a time when Gilles Peterson and Paul Murphy were doing Electric Ballroom. And this is the time you were born! Downstairs, Electric Ballroom on a Friday night was Trouble* playing all the latest electro, boogie, gogo music, all that stuff, and then upstairs in the small room, dark as hell, was all these jazz dancers dancing to jazz music. There was a whole movement going on. But it's also interlinked with how the whole warehouse jam was going, the jazz dancers were going to the house jams and the funk things as well. And that morphed into the whole Jazz Warriors and all of those people. And then that morphed into acid jazz. And there were people still doing the whole jazz thing as well. But it was in all of that context of acid jazz, hip-hop, house. We were mashing it up, you know what I'm saying?

Murphy set up the Paladin label, releasing the anthemic 'Vencer-emos' (1984) by Simon Booth's Working Week as well as records by Onward International, Harry Beckett, Tommy Chase and others in a brief flurry of prolific activity from 1983 to 1985 before selling his label to Richard Branson's Virgin and taking early retirement soon afterwards. He disappeared completely for several years from 1985,

* DJ and dancer Paul 'Trouble' Anderson.

closing his record shop and selling his personal collection.*

For many, the scene's final death knell was Julien Temple's film *Absolute Beginners* (1986), which features many dancers and 'faces' from the Wag Club. Ostensibly set in 1958 but with a background of racial tension insistently recognisable as a reference to the riots of 1985, the final result was hated by virtually everyone and marked the end of the golden era of hardcore jazz dance.

'We recorded in the garden shed' (jazz pirates)

While it was the Electric Ballroom where Gilles cemented his reputation as a club DJ, it was pirate radio stations that gave him his first taste of being on air. DIY, illegal enterprises run primarily for the love of music (plus the thrill of evading the authorities and a healthy dose of self-promotion), pirate stations were the platform on which many of the most influential DJs of the following decades gained broadcasting experience, while helping fill dance floors for the emerging scenes both as a means of announcing the jam and creating excitement for the tunes they'd hear there.

For most people, 'pirate radio' conjures images of youths in hoodies and Reebok classics climbing to the top of East London tower blocks with makeshift transmitters in the late 1990s, or, for those old enough to remember the first pirates, the romantic adventure of picking up Radio Caroline on a longwave radio from somewhere in the North Sea. Neither of these impressions has much association with jazz, but the 1980s were in fact a heyday of pirate radio stations playing jazz and related musics.

* In a cinematic scene undoubtedly more evocative than accurate, Peterson is said to have bought Murphy's entire collection, helping establish himself as the new king; Peterson himself denies this, saying in a comment on this chapter, 'I never bought Paul Murphy's record collection! I bought a few records that I could barely afford from his Paladin record shop in Berwick Street.' Pleasingly, Murphy is now back in the game, regularly DJing, and launched his new Jazz Room Records label in 2019.

The central role of pirate radio stations in the growth of jungle, garage and grime in the 1990s and 2000s has been well documented (for example, the BBC's *Tower Block Dreams* and *Radio Renegades*) and lovingly parodied in BBC mockumentary *People Just Do Nothing*. Similarly, the role of the original 1960s pirates in challenging the cultural hegemony of the BBC was glorified by Richard Curtis in *The Boat that Rocked* (2009), in which Philip Seymour Hoffman plays 'The Count' on Radio Rock; his character is based on Emperor Rosko, one of the first DJs on Radio Caroline, which circumvented the BBC's radio monopoly by broadcasting from a ship in the North Sea. It is this naval association from which 'pirate radio' takes its name. By broadcasting from international waters, Radio Caroline was able to offer the British public a youth-orientated programme not catered for by the stuffy BBC. The station attracted an estimated 10–15 million listeners per week (i.e. 15–25 per cent of the UK population) and, along with similar offshore stations Radio Atlanta and Radio London, gave broadcasting experience to major figures of British radio including Tony Blackburn, John Peel and Robbie Vincent. The clear demand for a different type of programming ultimately resulted in the creation of the BBC's Radio 1 in 1967. This apparent acknowledgement that the times were a-changin' coincided, as is often the case, with a tightening of broadcasting laws that effectively closed the loophole the offshore stations exploited.

Radio 1 was followed by BBC Radio London (no relation to the pirate) in 1970 as part of Frank Gillard's project to create regional BBC stations around the UK, in imitation of the American model, and by the launch of the UK's first two commercial radio stations, Capital FM and LBC (London Broadcasting), in 1973. Nevertheless, this increased offer still catered for an extremely limited array of music. Apart from the occasional mainstream soul track by Tony Blackburn and some jazz broadcasts by the BBC Concert Orchestra, the only credible black music shows to be heard on legal radio in the late 1970s were Robbie Vincent on Radio London (later, from 1983, Radio 1) and Greg Edwards on Capital. These would be listened to assiduously and taped to be squeezed out throughout the week.*

This left a void that was filled by multiple pirates. Radio Invicta 92.4 (1970–84) broadcast with the slogan 'Soul Over London', hosting jazz, funk and soul shows by Funk Mafia DJs Froggy and Chris Hill and launching the careers of Steve Walsh and Gilles Peterson. JFM (1980–5) – no relation to the later Jazz FM – hosted shows by Funk Mafia DJ Jeff Young (later host of Radio 1's first dance show), Steve Walsh and Pete Tong. Horizon (1981–5), broadcasting from Wyndham Road in Camberwell, served the airwaves with a similar mix of funk, soul and related styles.

These broadcasts were an inspiration to young Gilles, and his first route into music. Growing up on the borders of Sutton and Cheam on the outer reaches of south London, he had been collecting records since the age of thirteen, getting paid for DJing at under-fourteens discos as 'G+A Disco' with his mate Andrew and re-investing their earnings into growing their collection. By fourteen they were running their own pirate radio station, Civic Radio, from Gilles's garden shed, eventually upgrading to a transmitter on Epsom Downs with the assistance of his engineer father.

By 1985, Gilles was running his own pirate, KJazz, alongside Jez Nelson and Chris Philips, who would go on to found the production company Somethin' Else (which still produces his *Worldwide* show on 6 Music). Taking advantage of its elevated location and clear views over London, they paid £25 a week for the privilege of erecting a transmitter above the barber shop in Crystal Palace where Nelson's dad got his hair cut, on what became known as 'Pirate Row' for the sheer number of pirates operating from there.

---

* Robbie Vincent told Snowboy his show was 'the most taped in the history of radio', although it's not clear how he knew. But multiple people in Snowboy's book attest that local record stores were empty during his Saturday afternoon show and rammed immediately afterwards as listeners ran to seek out the latest imports he had just played on the radio.

Gilles continued to broadcast anonymously on KJazz even after securing a slot on a 'legal' station. If the idea of climbing up on to rooftops late at night with radio equipment, avoiding detection by both the police and the DTI, is an image that seems more closely suited to black yout's spitting fast lyrics over stark beats and heavy basslines than young white guys in Gabicci sweaters clutching copies of Lonnie Liston Smith's *Expansions*, that is perhaps testament more to selective media bias towards black criminality and a stereotyping of jazz as smooth and safe than any reflection of 1980s reality.

Indeed, most of these stations, although playing black music, were run by white people, with mostly white DJs. As Norman Jay asserted, 'they wanted the black without the blackness'.[8] This had been challenged by 'the UK's first black pirate station', DBC (Dread Broadcasting Corporation), which had broadcast from Neasden and Ladbroke Grove since 1980, but that station focused primarily on reggae and lovers' rock and ceased broadcasting in 1984. Promoter and entrepreneur Zak Dee stepped into that breach in September 1984, taking over pop pirate LWR (London Weekend Radio) and re-branding it as a station dedicated to black music, especially soul, hip-hop, funk, reggae and house. With both black and white DJs, many of the show's presenters would become major names in UK music, including Maxi Jazz of Faithless, The Shamen's Mr. C (future owner of seminal nineties club the End), the UK's first hip-hop star Derek B and the controversial hip-hop DJ Tim Westwood.

LWR was followed in October 1985 by Kiss FM, set up by the ubiquitous George Power alongside DJs Gordon 'Mac' McNamee and Tosca Jackson. Power soon sold his shares to Gordon Mac. Kiss FM DJs in this era included Norman Jay, Trevor Nelson, Jazzie B of Soul II Soul, Coldcut's Matt Black and Jonathan More, Paul 'Trouble' Anderson, future Dingwalls resident Patrick Forge and house pioneers Judge Jules, Danny Rampling, Colin Dale and Colin Faver. A struggle for dominance between the two stations developed into bitter rivalry; Anderson recalls having to guard the Kiss transmitter with a baseball bat to prevent sabotage from LWR, though it is notable that, unlike with mods vs rockers or trad vs modern jazz fans, it was a rivalry defined less by musical factionalism than simply wanting to be the most popular station on the airwaves.

Both were certainly popular, with Kiss commanding an estimated five hundred thousand listeners (more than one in every twenty Londoners) and coming second only to Capital as London's most popular station in a 1987 *Evening Standard* poll. As with the popularity of Radio Caroline, Radio Atlanta and Radio London pressuring the BBC to form Radio 1 in 1967, it was announced in 1988 that two new incremental licences would be granted for London, following George Power's success in gaining a licence for his London Greek Radio. Both Kiss FM and LWR came off air at the end of 1988 in order to apply for legitimate licences (in Kiss's case, accompanied by a massive New Year's Eve party at Dingwalls). Both were rebuffed, with the two licences being awarded to Jazz FM and Choice FM.[9] The choice of Jazz FM rankled for many in the Kiss camp, with Norman Jay opining that it had more to do with the personal tastes of the decision-makers than the station's value. This may have been a significant moment in the positioning of jazz as establishment music in the 1990s, not least after Gilles, a Jazz FM board member, was summarily dismissed from the station after promoting a demonstration against the Gulf War.

LWR had come off air once before in 1985 to attempt to gain a legitimate licence, investing heavily in a campaign only to find the promise of new licences cancelled altogether in 1986. They resumed illegal broadcasting after this second setback, finally coming off air permanently in 1990. Kiss persisted and were eventually awarded a licence in December 1989, beginning legal transmission in September 1990. The successful transition from pirate to legitimate commercial station is a phenomenal achievement, and one possible only through the vision, diplomacy and intensely hard work of Gordon Mac and his team, but it needs to be stressed that this success on the second attempt was possible only after significant investment from both Richard

Branson's Virgin (20 per cent) and EMAP (East Midlands Allied Press, 25 per cent), a media giant that had been publishing newspapers since 1887. This tension between pirate roots and corporate interests played out in predictable ways, with the station becoming increasingly commercial throughout the 1990s. By 1999 it was accused of outright racism, with presenter Steve Jackson claiming racial discrimination at an employment tribunal over his 1998 dismissal. He pointed out that the station had had a 50/50 balance between black and white presenters at its official opening in 1990; after the 1998 restructuring, every single peak-time presenter was white.[10]

This successive commercialisation and whitening of radio stations that had roots in their championing of black underground music is consistent with patterns discussed elsewhere in the book. Nevertheless, taken as a whole, pirate radio stations – like the legal community stations NTS and Worldwide FM – made an enormous contribution to the creation and cohesion of new scenes around jazz and related music.

'All these guys on the dance floor, letting off' (Dingwalls)

Having used pirate radio as a springboard, by 1986 Gilles was hosting a regular show on BBC Radio London, 'Mad on Jazz', using this platform to promote his Jazz Bops at the Town and Country Club in Kentish Town (now the Forum). That over two thousand people would cram in to see artists like Tommy Chase playing danceable, accessible jazz is indicative of a popularity jazz wouldn't have again in the UK until the present wave.

1986 also saw the birth of Gilles's Sunday afternoon session at Dingwalls in Camden Market, 'Talkin' Loud and Saying Something', a riff on James Brown's 'Talkin' Loud and Sayin' Nothing'. With a combination of hardcore jazz dance followed by an increasingly broad musical policy as the night (and the decade) progressed, 'Dingwalls' became one of the most celebrated sessions in club culture, still reminisced about by all those who were there and lovingly imagined by those who weren't. The concept was to combine the energy of the DJ-based jazz dance, rare groove and funk and soul scenes with live bands, and the appearances of jazz legends Roy Ayers, Pharoah Sanders, Poncho Sanchez and the Brazilians Flora Purim and Airto Moreira, often playing very different sets to those seen on the more conventional European jazz festival circuit, helped create the sense of something extremely unique and exciting.

Gilles Peterson

The great thing about Britain is that the audience is quite different. So when American musicians come in they're like, 'Fucking hell this is really interesting,' and when all those jazz legends would come to Dingwalls they'd be like, 'Wow, we never knew people liked our music for *these* reasons. We just thought they liked it for *those* reasons.' Whether it was Dave Valentin or Mongo Santamaria or Pharoah Sanders, they'd come and get a different hit and feedback from playing to our clubs and our audiences.

Paul Bradshaw

Gilles and Patrick and Janine were able to grab people coming into the country. Dave Valentin was a classic, because he was doing all these albums for GRP, just smooth Latin jazz. He had a wicked band, but he came into Dingwalls from probably playing in nice sit-down clubs in Europe, and they've walked through the door at Dingwalls at the beginning of that session, and thought, 'What the hell is this?' Walking from outside into this dark room where jazz was playing as loud as a funk session. All these guys on the dance floor, letting off. So they just thought, 'Shit, we need to change it up, man!' So they dropped a wicked set that day, no one else in Europe would have ever heard them play like that.

As with Jazz Re:freshed and Steam Down in the present wave, the regular weekly session was vital in consolidating a community around the music. The addition of Patrick Forge, then a DJ on Kiss FM, helped promote the session London-wide, and the sense of a global community was amplified by the 1988 launch of Paul Bradshaw's magazine *Straight No Chaser*, which ran uninterruptedly until 2007, uniting the London scene with kindred spirits and nights like Giant Step in NYC, Rude Movements in Atlanta, UFO in Tokyo, Kyoto Jazz Massive in Kyoto, Nicola Conte in Bari and Jazzanova in East Berlin.*

Dingwalls played host to most of the emerging eighties jazz musicians, including the nascent Jazz Warriors. But despite Courtney and Orphy's own claims to have come up as dancers in the clubs, Gilles experienced their sets as rather straight: 'jazz jazz'.

Gilles Peterson

I did a lot of work with people like Mark Murphy, Slim Gaillard, and Tommy Chase, the British drummer, was hugely important – not quite the schooled Guildhall set of black players that were coming out like Courtney. They didn't really fit – that whole scene didn't really have any roots in club culture. The people that did have the roots in club culture were more people like Tommy Chase, who could play bebop. There was a lot of the sort of post-punk new wave groups like Kalima, the Jazz Defektors, Marie Murphy, Team Ten, groups like that. Live music was an important part of it. It felt like we were the only people actually combining the two things. Of course I'd do a lot of DJ gigs where I was just playing as a DJ in a more traditional setting. Electric Ballroom didn't have bands upstairs in the jazz room, that was just dancing. But Dingwalls, I brought all the black British jazz musicians in at the time.

* Peterson described *Straight No Chaser* lovingly as 'the absolutely essential glue that gave context to the whole idea we were living'. The magazine was restarted as an annual edition in 2017, and was also responsible for the publication of Cotgrove's book, which provided a wealth of relevant information for this chapter.

But they were very conservative. Very straight. It was almost, 'We do the gig and we try and be American.' It took a few of them to slowly realise later on, people like Cleveland Watkiss kind of got it, but people like Julian Joseph and Phillip Bent, Steve Williamson, Courtney Pine: they were very straightforward jazz. And as much as I'd be playing that music on the radio – elements of it – it wasn't until quite a few years later that there was a generation of musicians who understood club culture, which is obviously where things like TRC come along and a generation of musicians like Shabaka. But in between those years, the Jason Yarde years and the Soweto Kinch years – Shabaka was the first one out of all those musicians who actually got it, creatively brought it into his music naturally, organically. All the others are great players but that . . . was jazz jazz. This was something different.

'The kind of decadent, left of centre, back room attitude that we had' (Acid Jazz)

Just as very few people are aware of the causal connections between trad jazz and the Beatles, not many people would link jazz with the UK's electronic music explosion of the late 1980s, which would continue right through the following decade, spawning a multitude of new genres and massively influencing music worldwide. Yet these connections are both real and direct.

It is 1987 and Gilles Peterson and DJ partner Chris Bangs are at a party at a *finca* outside San Antonio in Ibiza, observing the eclectic selections of DJ Alfredo with a friendly scepticism. Exiled from his native Argentina, Alfredo is combining the latest black Chicago house on Trax and DJ International with uplifting pop songs from Kate Bush and Queen, in an atmosphere of accepting, loved-up celebration. 'Avin it nearby are 'the Ibiza Four': Nicky Holloway, Paul Oakenfold, Danny Rampling and Johnny Walker, the DJ/promoters credited with kick-starting 'the Second Summer of Love' in 1988 and the genre that became known as 'acid house' when they brought this open-minded musical attitude back to the UK. Popularising the smiley face logo that has remained synonymous with rave, they introduced new generations of ordinary English people to the magical combination of 808 kick drums and MDMA at clubs like Holloway's the Trip, Rampling's Shoom and Oakenfold's Future.

But what brought them there in the first place? Holloway had been running weekly South-East London funk and soul sessions since 1983 under the Special Branch brand, most regularly at the Royal Oak off the Old Kent Road and the Swan and Sugarloaf in London Bridge. By 1985 he was bringing two thousand people to London Zoo every other month for the Doos at the Zoo to listen to funk, soul and jazz.

In a prefiguring of the package holidays to Cypriot beach resort Ayia Napa that marked the pinnacle of UK garage in the late 1990s, the entrepreneurial Holloway brought all of the core Special Branch DJs and three hundred punters to Ibiza in 1986, taking over clubs, bars and out-of-season Club 18–30 hotels for two weeks of partying. The 1986 trip was merely the consolidation of an existing jazz, funk and soul community. But on the return trip in 1987, everything changed. As percussionist and chronicler of that scene, Mark 'Snowboy' Cotgrove observed:

> By May the whole Special Branch scene had pulled itself apart. The second Ibiza trip had seen half of the DJs and punters discover the drug Ecstasy and they went off to the main clubs extolling the virtues of Balearic club music and house . . . On the flight home Nicky realised that there's been a big split, musically, and he decided to stop the Special Branch events and go off in the house music direction.[11]

Being five years old at the time, I spent most of this particular Summer of Love building fantasy kingdoms out of Lego on the floor of my parents' living room in Tufnell Park and bullying my two-year-old brother. By the time Pete Tong, Judge Jules, Danny Rampling and Paul

Oakenfold came into my consciousness, it was as the self-important voices behind a very white, very mainstream, hyped-up Friday Night BBC Radio 1 version of house music. But what happened in the ten years in between? Caspar Melville highlights a familiar pattern, arguing that 'the acid origin myth . . . has facilitated the "whitewashing" of rave . . . [fixing] the unstable histories of house music in the image of four white working-class lads living it large in Spain'.[12]

Melville argues that Alfredo's inspirational eclecticism and the accompanying chemicals were only one part of a rich cultural mix which already existed in London and which gave rise to the explosion of creativity in electronic music in the UK in the 1990s. He notes in particular the Jamaican sound system culture and the warehouse funk raves of the mid-1980s as powerful foundations for the UK's rave scene, influences which would re-emerge unmistakably in jungle: the fusion of acid house and hardcore with sound system culture and samples drawn from black music, not least the classic 'Amen break'.[13] Less interesting for Melville, but very interesting for our story, is the fact that Pete Tong and the 'Ibiza Four' all started their careers playing jazz, funk, soul and disco in suburban pubs and clubs. Before becoming the grandiose voice of the BBC Radio 1 Essential Mix and so famous that 'it's all gone a bit Pete Tong' became London slang for mishaps of all shapes and sizes, Tong 'had a reputation for being the hard-man of jazz with five DJ residencies in the Kent area alone'.[14]

While Tong, Holloway, Rampling and others threw themselves bodily into acid house, Gilles and Chris Bangs liked the party atmosphere while being unexcited by much of the music. For them, the music needed to be interesting enough that you could still dance to it even without the drugs, and jazz continued to tick this box.

Gilles Peterson

So we all went to Ibiza; '86, '87, Nicky would put on these events where they'd bring over five hundred English kids to Ibiza. We'd go and listen to DJ Alfredo, and that's when everyone took ecstasy for the first time. Suddenly all these boys from the suburbs got into ecstasy, and that's really where acid house happened. Then suddenly we were all doing a big event in 1987 in Brentford at the Steam Museum. I'm on after Paul Oakenfold with my partner at the time, Chris Bangs. So Oakey's on wearing his smiley T-shirt, and people are going bonkers, everyone's on ecstasy, it's the classic image that you've seen in the newspapers ever since then. And Chris and me are looking at each other going, 'What the fuck are we going to do? We gotta go on after this, it's going off!' So I pulled out a record by a group called Mickey and the Soul Generation called 'Iron Leg', and that record starts off with a twenty-second electric guitar riff at the beginning. So I put that on and basically used the vary speed on the 1200* just to give it this kind of wobbly sound. And then Chris said, 'Fuck acid house. This is acid jazz!' That's how acid jazz came about.†

While it's true that acid jazz began as a kind of joke, it was also a response to the idea that somehow jazz had to be abandoned simply because people were taking drugs and partying. Why would anybody think that? In this sense, 'acid jazz' was supposed to signify a dance-floor-focused, carnivalesque atmosphere and a new wave of jazz-influenced music that included and assimilated developments in hip-hop, house and electro as well as all the music that had been played in the Jazz Dance sessions: 'the drug culture energy, but mixed with a much more freaky soundtrack.'[15]

Gilles Peterson

That was basically a name to give the kind of decadent, left of centre, back room attitude that we had as DJs. And inevitably it led to Galliano

---

* Technics 1200: the industry standard vinyl deck.
† In Chris Bang's account in Snowboy's book, the event has moved a five-minute walk down Brentford High Street from the Steam Museum to Waterman's Art Centre, the tune has changed from 'Iron Leg' to an Art Blakey tune, and it's Gilles himself who coins the phrase on the mic. Oral history: a notoriously unreliable way to tell a story.

and Jamiroquai and all these groups being the first bands that were sort of half influenced by rare groove, half influenced by interesting jazz samples and very early hip-hop. That was really what acid jazz was, the true acid jazz, the groups that came out of that movement. And then the jazz groups, the more traditional ones; that was a different thing. It gave them a marketing lift, to be able to fit into some movement. So that's really how we all connected.

In the same period, purists like Wynton Marsalis were rejecting any developments in jazz that were not rooted in swing and the blues: whether the less rhythmic, European jazz as epitomised by Manfred Eicher's ECM label, or jazz and hip-hop fusions like Guru's *Jazzmatazz* albums, on which Wynton's own brother Branford would feature. Conversely, acid jazz was about accepting all developments as long as they worked on the dance floor.

Gilles and Chris Bangs began hosting Cock Happy parties, initially at the Cock Tavern in Spitalfields Market and later Lauderdale House in Highgate. Whereas some Dingwalls veterans would complain about the addition of hip-hop and electronic styles, the Cock Happy crowd were much more easy-going. Embodying the hedonistic attitude of acid house while maintaining leftfield credentials in comparison with its mainstream popularity, Bangs designed a logo that subverted the acid house smiley face, adding unfashionable glasses, cross-eyes, and buckteeth.* Badges were made for the first session at the Cock Tavern and worn with pride.

Symbolic of the maverick attitude and DIY spirit, the Cock Tavern didn't actually have a licence to charge on the door, so punters were sent round the corner where Gilles's long-standing facilitator Janine

* When I first saw this jazz take on the smiley face while researching this book, it reminded me, hilariously, of On The Corner Records boss Pete Buckenham. Gilles has been a big supporter of On The Corner, awarding them Best Label at the 2017 Worldwide Awards, playing their releases and giving Pete a regular show on Worldwide FM. It may be not so much a case of 'you remind me of a younger version of myself!' but 'you remind me of a comedy cartoon of my ideal fan!'

Neye would sell tickets from her car. And the split between acid house and acid jazz was not as clear cut as sometimes told; Gilles's long-running Sunday evening sessions at the Belvedere Arms in Richmond continued to attract a mixed crowd.

Gilles Peterson

Later, a lot of the big players in the acid-house scene were regulars; even when Shoom happened. That was where the jazz-heads and the e-heads mixed together.[16]

Gilles's talent for cross-branding has been a constant of his career. Harnessing the social currency of the term 'acid' from the hype around the emerging acid house scene, and the leftfield support for his acid jazz version, the name was used for the label he started with Eddie Piller in 1987.

The first single on the Acid Jazz label, 'Frederic Lies Still', was essentially a sample of Curtis Mayfield's 'Freddie's Dead' with Gilles's housemate Rob Gallagher – re-styled as the more exotic-sounding Galliano – ranting over the top in a style heavily influenced by Jalal Nuriddin of The Last Poets.

The acid jazz name was also used for four volumes of *Acid Jazz* compilations on BGP, the label Gilles had started with jazz dance DJ Baz Fe Jazz, as well as two albums of original music for Polydor: *Acid Jazz and Other Illicit Grooves* (1988) and *The Freedom Principle: Acid Jazz and other Illicit Grooves Volume 2* (1989).

If this sounds like way too many meanings for one term to sustain: it was. The acid jazz compilations on BGP were focused on re-releases of the 1960s and 1970s. As the Discogs entry notes: 'In spite of the title, the series focus is soul jazz and jazz funk from late 1960s and early 1970s, taken mainly from the Fantasy and Prestige catalogues.' The Polydor compilations, by contrast, were original recordings embodying Gilles's ethos. The producer was Simon Booth of the band Working Week, whose track 'Venceremos', inspired by the fast Latin

312

fusion Booth had heard Paul Murphy play at the Electric Ballroom, had become a staple of that scene. The whole record was introduced by Jalal Nuriddin of American proto-hip-hop group The Last Poets, whom Gilles idolised but Piller couldn't stand.

Part of the problem was Piller himself and the mod scene from which he had come.* When they met in the mid-1980s, Gilles and Chris Bangs were playing a lot of late-1960s/early-1970s organ jazz (Jimmy McGriff, Brother Jack MacDuff, Jimmy Smith) under the name the Baptist Brothers. This was where their musical world and Piller's crossed. Piller already held several years of label experience at Dave Robinson's Stiff Records, and it seemed natural for the two to collaborate after meeting at the Special Branch parties. But Piller's charisma and industry connections masked the fact that, musically, the two had little in common. Ironically, it was the very narrowness of the mod scene Piller had sought to escape that Gilles found too limiting. Gilles left the Acid Jazz label after only eighteen months, toward the tail end of 1989.

* Mod, short for 'modern', had originated in the 1950s to refer fans of modern jazz (as opposed to trad) and was associated with Soho clubs like the Flamingo and the Marquee, and later Manchester's Twisted Wheel (which would become the birthplace of Northern Soul). The original mods were characterised by a love of Italian fashion and design, manifested in sharp Italian suits and shoes, a penchant for Italian Vespa and Lambretta scooters, and espressos made by Italian machines in Soho cafes which, unlike pubs at that time, stayed open all night. This association with stimulants extended to 'purple hearts', the street name for the amphetamine/barbiturate called Drinamyl. By the early 1960s the subculture, like the music itself, had moved beyond jazz and become associated with early sixties rhythm and blues-influenced acts like The Who and Small Faces. As fashions became ever more flamboyant as the sixties wore on, and mods increasingly mainstream, 'hard mods' wanting to distance themselves from the art-school foppishness of mainstream mod culture appropriated elements of Jamaican culture to become 'skinheads', fusing Fred Perry and Ben Sherman shirts with braces, Dr. Martens boots and shaven heads, in what was originally a multi-racial movement that later became appropriated by far-right groups. A mod revival in the late 1970s was kick-started by Paul Weller's band The Jam and the release of the film *Quadrophenia*, which glorified the subculture of the early 1960s. Other bands contributing to this included the Specials, Secret Affair and, from 1982, Paul Weller's the Style Council. The mod aesthetic was central also to the 1990s Britpop bands Blur and Oasis.

Gilles Peterson

Eddie Piller's an Ace Face from the mod scene and it inspired him
and others for a new beginning, but fundamentally it wasn't coming
from them: they were mods playing Jimmy Smith records. Our only
connection with them and Paul Weller was Gabicci jumpers and Jimmy
Smith records. I'm very proud of my soul boy background and heritage,
and I'd be the first to shout about Chris Hill and Bob Jones and my
other influences, and when I finally got into a position where I could
shout about it and people would listen, the mod thing came in from
nowhere and took acid jazz away, and to where it went! Which is where
I fucking got out and formed Talkin' Loud records in late '89, and made
a progressive British black music label. The reason I survived acid jazz
was because I went beyond it. I was moving on all the time.[17]

Too many styles were being crammed into one brand. Piller's
interest was squarely in a certain type of Hammond-influenced soul
jazz and jazz funk sound as opposed to the broader approach Gilles
embodied in his DJ sets. Piller would go on to have huge success with
the Acid Jazz label, in particular with The Brand New Heavies, James
Taylor Quartet and Jamiroquai. Although Jamiroquai only released
one single on Acid Jazz, 'When You Gonna Learn', all three bands
helped create a sense of acid jazz the genre as smooth, mid-tempo,
middle-of-the-road jazz funk.

This is one of the reasons why the genre's reputation took such a
nosedive as the immediate excitement wore off, and acid jazz continues to be thought of by many, especially those who were not around
in its most exciting early days, as a highly embarrassing period and one
which helped tarnish the name of jazz in general.

Steve Symons

As soon as the term acid jazz became the designated moniker for it, it
was like the writing on the wall.

Lubi Jovanovic

Nineties acid jazz was a similar kind of thing to now. It was jazz-related music that got pretty big. A lot of people got into it, but maybe one-tenth or one-twentieth of the people were actually into the music. The rest of it is a hype thing and it's a fashion thing.

Noah Ball

After the UK jazz funk explosion, jazz was actually in the mainstream in a similar way to the current explosion of jazz. Gilles's Acid Jazz label and a lot of that stuff were incredibly popular for a short amount of time, and then it became a dirty word in the same way trip-hop became a dirty word.

Jazz being sullied by this association was made more painful by the fact that, for many jazz fans, it didn't even sound that much like jazz.

Adrian Gibson

The acid jazz scene had taken over all those column inches; it was Acid Jazz and Talkin' Loud and Dorado; you couldn't move for being written about if you were on one of those labels. The other styles of jazz were still going on and still had audiences. But if you were Us3 or the Brand New Heavies or Galliano then you were massive. Were they jazz acts? Not really, I mean, Us3 were probably the nearest to that, Brand New Heavies were always more of a funk, soul, disco band; Galliano were sampling jazz but they were more like a groove, rap thing. That whole thing of acid jazz was people calling it acid jazz and playing songs like, 'I really like this jazz track.' And then they'd play you a hip-hop song. You're like, 'Well, this isn't jazz at all.'

Binker Golding

Acid jazz. I don't know who coined that one or why. Were they trying to relate it to ecstasy culture or something? I have no idea what the goal was. But to this day when I hear that sort of music it's very false to me. It's very insincere music. I'm not saying that the musicians are bad. I just disagree with the choices that they made musically. And that's why it's dated so badly. It's so nineties. It was just such a poor decision. I mean, obviously, they were trying to make jazz cool, which is something that's been happening ever since the seventies. It doesn't work. I don't know why they couldn't see that. It's almost never cool when the older style tries to act more juvenile. It worked with Gang Starr and GURU, taking samples from Thelonious Monk: that works that way round. It doesn't work the other way around of the old guys trying to be young. It's like someone in their forties wearing dropped-down trousers with their boxer shorts showing. That's what fifteen-year-old kids do on the estate. You look like a fool at forty.

For Gilles, Piller's limited musical outlook was not the only reason for this: he also felt let down by what he saw as the musical conservatism of the Jazz Warriors generation, whose neo-classical, Marsalis-influenced approach to jazz meant most of the new music being created didn't match up to the boldness of the branding.

Gilles Peterson

That's why acid jazz never really happened, never really had its own music. If acid jazz at the time, as a term, had had the bands, and the DJ attitude and production – if we'd have been in the same place, we'd have created a music that would have been as powerful as 'Acid Tracks' by Phuture or whatever made acid house. But we basically didn't have that! We had the name and we had an attitude and we had a kind of crazy sort of avant-garde approach to putting it all together. And again, that got confused as well because Acid Jazz, the label, became something different to my thing – because acid jazz was basically closer to Working Week and the parties that we were having at Lauderdale House.

Nevertheless, while it may have ended up going down something of a blind alley, the acid jazz movement was important in proving that a version of jazz for the dance floor, influenced by contemporary developments in hip-hop and other styles, had the potential to break out of the box jazz was being squeezed into and connect authentically with a very wide range of people. For Gilles, the present wave is in many ways the realisation of this unfulfilled potential, which is one of the reasons he adopted it so enthusiastically.

'A progressive British black music label' (Talkin' Loud)

If Piller's mod-ish, organ-driven conception of acid jazz limited its musical development both as a genre and a label, it may be surprising that he was responsible for one of the clubs that did the most to break musical barriers: Hoxton's Blue Note. Opened in 1995 with earnings from the phenomenal success of Jamiroquai (whom Piller managed) on the site that had been jazz club the Bass Clef (run by bassist Peter Ind), Blue Note became one of the most important clubs of the 1990s. Despite the jazzy name, the Blue Note had a broad music policy that included Goldie's infamous Metalheadz session alongside nights by James Lavelle, Talvin Singh and Ninja Tune while keeping the flag flying for jazz with Snowboy and Phil Levene's Sunday lunchtime jazz dance session.

Mark Cotgrove

At the Blue Note every Sunday lunchtime before Metalheadz I had my heavy jazz dance session called the Hi-Hat with Phil Levene. Yes, Jazz Dance was virtually dead by then but not at the Hi-Hat, which had bigger weekly crowds than any jazz dance session before it or since, with people travelling from all over the country. It lasted eight years in total going from the Blue Note to the Jazz Cafe. It was interesting because many of my customers/dancers would leave my session at 6 pm and get in the queue to come back in to Metalheadz at 6.30.

Gilles, meanwhile, set up his own Talkin' Loud label in 1990, riding on the popularity of the long-running Dingwalls night. With industry credentials well established, he was able to sign a deal with Polygram for Talkin' Loud to be his own imprint, in theory being allowed a free hand in the A & R while benefiting from major label funding and architecture: a prefiguring of the 'best of both worlds' semi-independent scenarios many of this generation's musicians were able to create for themselves. It didn't always work out; Gilles resented needing to justify his aesthetic choices, being grilled at sales meetings and 'trodden on by horrendous A & R cliché people'.[18] Nevertheless, he was able to sign an amazing breadth of music that did much to join the dots between diverse musical styles and link them to jazz.

The label tends to be most commonly associated with the first three artists to release albums: Galliano, Young Disciples and Incognito. Already established on the Brit funk scene that pre-dated the acid jazz movement, Incognito had released their debut album on Chris Hill's Ensign label in 1981, a full decade before their first record for Talkin' Loud, *Inside Life*. This achieved chart success immediately with 'Always There' (featuring Jocelyn Brown), which went to No. 6 in the UK chart in summer 1991. Eight albums on Talkin' Loud yielded a further twelve singles in the top seventy-five.

Also strong out of the gates were Young Disciples, whose 'Apparently Nothin'' reached No. 13 in the UK singles chart in February 1991. Drawing on hip-hop, soul, funk and jazz, the project was a collaboration between vocalist Carleen Anderson, percussionist/producer Femi Williams (aka Femi Fem) and multi-instrumentalist Marco Nelson. Williams had been a key player on the mid-1980s warehouse funk scene, hosting parties under the names Family Funktion and Shake 'n' Fingerpop with Norman Jay and Jules O'Riordan (who would later find fame as BBC Radio 1 DJ Judge Jules, a reference to his law degree).

Meanwhile, Rob Gallagher (aka Galliano) had refined both delivery and recording techniques since 'Frederic Lies Still'. Having been the first artist to release on Acid Jazz, Galliano the band released four studio albums on Talkin' Loud between 1991 and 1997, plus a remix album and two live albums. Although not all of their output has aged brilliantly, the project was sustained by a powerful live show, with a band including percussionist Crispin 'Spry' Robinson, who as well as being an elder on the UK's Cuban *bata* scene now plays with Oscar Jerome and Balimaya, providing yet another link between this era and the present one.*

Yet the association with these three acts obscures the amazing breadth of music that the label released. Seminal albums touching a range of genres included *There's Nothing Like This* (1991), the debut album by UK soul legend Omar; and *Organix* (1993), the debut album by American hip-hop collective The Roots (who spent nine months in Peterson's office while building their brand, and were heavily influenced by the club culture they experienced during their year in the UK); French hip-hop master MC Solaar's heavily jazz-influenced *Prose Combat* (1994); the eponymous debut of US house dons Masters at Work's Nuyorican Soul project (1996), featuring the classic 'Black Gold of the Sun'; and Roni Size/Reprazent's Mercury-Award-winning drum and bass/live jazz album *New Forms* (1997).

By 1998 the label was on a roll, and the Mercury success supported Gilles's creative freedom. Highlights from that year alone include Courtney Pine's *Another Story*; 4Hero's immaculate *Two Pages* (featuring spoken word poet Ursula Rucker); Kruder and Dorfmeister's *K&D Sessions*, which helped introduce the world to the sound that became known as 'nu jazz', closely associated with Jazzanova and Munich's Compost label; and Terry Callier's enthralling folk/jazz fusion *Timepeace*. 1999 saw the release of Carl Craig's techno-influenced but highly experimental *Programmed*, under the moniker Innerzone Orchestra, and 2000 was the year of *Sincere*, the Mercury-nominated debut album by classically trained garage producer MJ Cole. As well as

* Galliano did in fact reunite for a live tour in summer 2023, playing at We Out Here, London's Village Underground and Bristol's Thekla.

reaching No. 10 in the UK singles chart with 'Crazy Love' and No. 13 with Sincere, Cole beat Dr. Dre to win 'Best Producer' at the 2001 MOBO (Music of Black Origin) Awards.

Naturally, not everything was a success. Some artists have sunk virtually without a trace, like communist hip-hop crew Marxman ('the Anglo-Irish answer to Public Enemy') and The K-Creative (who sound like a bunch of young Tim Westwoods trying and failing not to sound American). But the label fulfilled a crucial function in introducing jazz-influenced sounds to new generations – even if they were not aware they were listening to jazz. Yet it is remarkable how little credit jazz in general got for these successes, considering how obviously it was the glue holding together the label's diverse output. Who was talking about *New Forms* in terms of jazz in 1997, or *Sincere* in 2000?

Tom Excell

What is considered jazz now is so broad. You know, back when I was listening to all these different styles of electronic music and not really knowing that they had their roots in jazz, I think if that was now, I'd have just grown up being like, 'I love jazz music.' Whereas back then it didn't seem like anyone was talking about those styles being jazz. You mentioned the Roni Size album: there's so much jazz in that record, but I never heard anyone talking about it in the perspective of jazz, and now it would be completely different. It's just interesting what the trend of the time is, the hot topics and buzzwords.

The open-minded musical approach on which the label's output was based had crystallised at Dingwalls between 1986 and 1991, and after Dingwalls closed, at the Monday night 'That's How It Is' session at Bar Rumba on Shaftesbury Avenue (1993–2005), run in collaboration with Mo' Wax label boss James Lavelle (who had released, among others, DJ Shadow, DJ Krush and UNKLE). The impact of both the label and the clubnights was enormous, not only in spawning new nights around the world by people who had been directly influenced by Dingwalls – such as the vibrant scenes in Japan, Amsterdam, Munich and the Giant Step nights in New York – but through the dissemination of an inclusive, dance-floor-driven attitude to jazz that allows the music to change organically alongside other developments in contemporary music, renewing its audience in the process.

Gilles Peterson

All the festivals now, if you're marketing the Montreux Jazz Festival or this, that or the other anywhere in the world, they will all be looking towards that kind of idea that we've been pushing here, because that's the only way that you can bring in a new audience. The whole thing was dying! I did Montreux for ten years. I curated for them up until the first year of the Worldwide festival. And that's been fifteen years. So twenty-five years ago, Montreux asked me, 'Can you put on a Talkin' Loud night in the back room of the casino,' which is where the main festival was at the time, because Talkin' Loud was quite popular in Switzerland, believe it or not. In fact Switzerland was our number-one territory per capita. So I brought over Galliano and Omar and Incognito. And that was the little room, held maybe three hundred people, and the main auditorium next door had like two thousand people. And on the night itself, the main auditorium was empty pretty much. And our room, you just couldn't get in, the queue went round the block. It was crazy.

And okay, it was acid jazz, but it was jazz! It was an amazing night and we all took loads of ecstasy. And suddenly, as Galliano are doing their encore, I'm in the changing room and I get a knock on the door and it's Quincy Jones with a bottle of champagne and two beautiful women either side of him. And he says, 'I understand you're the guy responsible for this.' I said, 'oh, well—' And he goes, 'Yeah, I understand this is acid jazz. It's amazing. Tell me all about it.' And then the next day I'm up in his hotel suite for the whole afternoon, literally four hours, this is the first big A & R mistake I made in my life. I basically told him everything, what the reference points were, what the music was, what it was about. And then within six months he set up *Vibe* magazine, and a few months later, he was doing *Back on the Block* and trying to get me to work for him. He was trying to sign Galliano to Qwest at the time. So it's interesting, we found the formula to introduce an entire history of music to a new audience in a way that they could get it. You know, of course jazz will always survive because it's an art form, and there are universities that are dedicated to it. But to make it exciting: around the world, what we were doing had a very big impact. More of an impact than it was having in the UK, within the media and within the industry. Whereas in France, in Germany, in the States and in Japan, they were taking this movement very, very seriously.

'Just into making interesting records' (Brownswood)

In 2004, Peterson was honoured with an MBE, a fitting accolade for someone already revered both in the UK and internationally. By this point he had over twenty years of professional DJ experience, nearly twenty years of releases on BGP/Ace Records, Polydor, Acid Jazz and Talkin' Loud, and well over twenty years of radio experience, including six years of introducing the nation to diverse music every Wednesday night with his *Worldwide* show on BBC Radio 1.

But almost twenty years since that award, everything leading up to that point just looks like the first phase. Having left Talkin' Loud in 2004, Gilles set up his own Brownswood Recordings in 2006; unlike Talkin' Loud, this was a truly independent label of which he would have full creative control.

Brownswood's commitment to representing a broad cross-section of music could be seen from the start, with 2006/7 releases including Japan's Soil and Pimp Sessions' *Pimp Master*, the self-titled debut by the UK's forty-strong Heritage Orchestra, Ben Westbeech's questionably titled *Welcome to the Best Years of Your Life* and José James's jazz hip-hop album *The Dreamer*. The label also indicated its commitment to supporting new talent through the *Brownswood Bubblers* compilations. The first two editions in 2006 and 2007 featured tracks by esteemed remixer and jazz/house pioneer Eric Lau, new generation soul singer Nicole Willis, longtime Peterson collaborator Simbad, Jamie Woon, Flying Lotus, Tawiah and Taylor McFerrin.

The label found its stride in 2009 with the Havana Cultura Project, which showcased Cuban musicians including Yelfris Valdés (who would later appear on Yussef Kamaal's *Black Focus*). 2010 releases included Owiny Sigoma Band, a collaboration between Kenyan musicians Joseph Nyamungu and Charles Owoko and UK musicians Tom Skinner (later of Sons of Kemet) and the Kentish town brothers Jesse and Louis Hackett; Louis had been influential in the UK hip-hop of the early 2000s, producing beats for Task Force, Jehst and others as Louis Slipperz.

Brownswood got its first (and, to date, only) Mercury nomination in 2011 with Ghostpoet's *Peanut Butter Blues and Melancholy Jam*, combining the eerie 4 a.m. night-bus post-rave glow of artists like Burial with jazzy chords and dispassionate hip-hop slurry. 2011 also saw the release of Zara McFarlane's *Until Tomorrow*. Zara, like United Vibrations, heralded the beginning of the present wave of jazz, not only through her own releases but through the combination of personnel in her live band, which included Moses Boyd and Binker Golding.

Matthew Halsall

Zara McFarlane was working with Moses before he was known as another figure of the UK jazz scene, and Moses was wicked even at that early stage. I remember her showing me a track on her second album and I was like, 'Oh, that drumming's wicked on that track.' And he was super young then. Gilles took him immediately under his wing, realising there was this cool young guy doing not just the drum side of it, also interested in producing and collaborating outside of jazz, interested in all sorts of other stuff. Moses is definitely the son of Gilles Peterson's sort of UK jazz scene.

The Havana Club-sponsored Cuban connection continued with *Mala in Cuba* (2012), an experimental album where Mala, one of dubstep's pioneers and co-owner of the influential DMZ label and clubnight, was invited to Havana to collaborate with Cuban musicians, making some genuinely interesting, polyrhythmic Black Atlantic music in the process. A similar transatlantic approach combining electronic producers and live musicians was taken in Sonzeira's *Brasil Bam Bam Bam* (2014), where Floating Points, Rob G. from Galliano and Dilip Harris held a residency in Rio along with Gilles himself, creating original music with Brazilian artists including Seu Jorge and Elza Soares.

2015 continued the theme of international, jazz and electronic experimentation with albums by Cuban singer Daymé Arocena, producers LV (featuring Armenian pianist Tigran Hamasyan) and drummer/producer Emanative, whose *The Light Years of the Darkness* was the first album sponsored by the Steve Reid foundation and featured diverse guests including United Vibrations, Kieran Hebden (Four Tet), Earl Zinger (another alter ego of Rob G./Galliano) and Idris Ackamoor's 1970s free jazz ensemble The Pyramids.

2016 was a key year for what might be considered the current era of jazz, with releases including Shabaka and the Ancestors' *Wisdom of Elders* and Yussef Kamaal's *Black Focus*. The label has continued to provide a platform for diverse and interesting music, deepening its support for the UK jazz movement with albums like Joe Armon-Jones's *Starting Today* (2018), Maisha's *There is a Place* (2018) and the *We Out Here* compilation (2018) while continuing to release a range of different styles including Scottish Afro/electronic producer Auntie Flo's *Radio Highlife* (2018), grime/hip-hop producer Swindle's *No More Normal* (2019), Brooklyn-based jazz drummer/MC Kassa Overall's *I Think I'm Good* (2020) and South Africa-born, Doncaster-raised hip-hop misfit Skinny Pelembe's *Dreaming Is Dead Now*, right through to STR4TA's *Aspects* (2020), Peterson's collaboration with Incognito founder Bluey, and the eponymous 2021 album by Secret Night Gang.

Emily Moxon

Brownswood's never tried to be a jazz label. We've always done jazz records, but we've definitely done records that aren't jazz. We're just into making interesting records and I like working with artists that have something to say and I like working on records that feel like they're culturally relevant and resonant.

'A perfect, fantastic, perfect storm' (Worldwide)

The formation of Brownswood was not the only major event for Peterson in 2006. That year also saw the first edition of the Worldwide Festival in Sète, a picturesque town just west of Montpelier on France's Mediterranean coast. With just one stage, this was a vital space for fusing fan bases for jazz and electronic music. The importance of community is embodied in the name chosen for the 2010 compilation, *Worldwide Family*, mixed by Simbad and Lefto. Still held annually sixteen years later, as well as hosting an Alpine winter edition in Leysin, Worldwide has become one of the world's most important tastemaker festivals.

Bradley Zero

One place for me that was really key outside of Rhythm Section was Worldwide Festival. The way that it's this week-long gathering with only one stage at a time: the musicians are watching the DJs, the DJs are watching the musicians and everyone parties together afterwards. It just bred this really tight-knit, extended family appreciating each other's art forms. That's a key part of it.

Equally important are Gilles's Worldwide Awards. Begun simply as an award category on his radio show, the first physical event was held in 2004 at Cargo, East London, and moved venues for the next few years before settling on Koko (formerly the Camden Palace), held each January since 2010 until Covid-19 disrupted proceedings. This event has become a key fixture of many people's annual calendar and a reliable place to discover new music.

Both the festival and the awards ceremony were supported by the strength of the Worldwide brand established through the *Worldwide* radio show and the many Worldwide compilations on Talkin' Loud. After eight years on late but acceptable Radio 1 slots, the show was relegated to 2–4 a.m. Tuesday night/Wednesday morning in 2006, something of a graveyard slot even for the most hardcore. While this was indicative of a particularly low ebb for jazz at this point, it served as the catalyst for Gilles to launch both Brownswood and the World-wide Festival at a time when there was a little less hype, allowing this second phase of his career to build organically on a strong foundation.

This changed with his 2011 move to a primetime Saturday after-noon slot on 6 Music, reaching a far wider audience than the Radio 1 graveyard shift: a harbinger for the decade's developments.

Kerstan Mackness

I do just think a lot of it is a perfect, fantastic, perfect storm. Gilles moving from Radio 1 to 6 Music and having complete freedom to do whatever he wanted to do suddenly meant that he was in a position to support that music. Worldwide as well. And also Bradley Zero. It's that perfect combination of the internet and a cool scene somewhere like Peckham. And before you know it, you've got a scene. And then because jazz had become so moribund and boring, suddenly that scene has been able to translate itself abroad really quickly.

Not content with a radio show, two festivals and countless com-pilations, in 2016 the Worldwide brand was expanded to include an entire radio station, galvanising a community around the diverse musics Peterson champions. As well as offering extremely diverse pro-gramming, it represented a chance for many of the artists Peterson had always supported to have their own shows, deepening not only the opportunities to hear the music itself but also the communities around that music.[*]

We Out Here

The launch of We Out Here festival in 2019 can be seen as the unification of Gilles's entire career and a physical embodiment of the diverse musical communities he champions.

Like Gilles's own career, the festival is rooted in jazz but open to other music, always making space for contemporary developments, with enough accessibility to keep casual fans interested and enough progressive music to stop the fanatics from getting bored. It is the jewel in a crown earned by forty years of tirelessly promoting a forward-thinking, dance-floor-driven approach to jazz, from pirate radio to the BBC, suburban jazz funk sessions to the Montreux Jazz Festival.

Gearing up for its fourth edition in 2023, the festival foregrounds new jazz and jazz-related music alongside a powerful electronic programme, in no small part due to the fact that it is produced by NVS (the team behind Outlook and Dimensions). Yet it also makes space for the music's heritage, with stages given over to jazz dance and a special 'Sunday Afternoon at Dingwalls' session to bring the old heads back together. From jazz dancers at the Electric Ballroom, original ravers at Dingwalls, the Cock Tavern and Bar Rumba to Dimensions alumni and nineteen-year-old fans of Ezra Collective, it feels like a magical gathering across styles and generations. The wheel has truly come full circle.

---

[*] In a sad coda, Worldwide FM ceased regularly broadcasting in October 2022. But its impact on the scene was huge.

THE REMIX

'Because the End Is Really the Beginning'
Where Do We Go from Here?

It is to be hoped that, in a more reflective, accountable, post-2020 world, the new wave of UK jazz is in less danger from the kind of savage attacks by *The Fast Show*, *Bo' Selecta!* and Disco Demolition which decimated many people's opinion of jazz, garage and disco.

Bradley Zero

I don't think there's gonna be a crash. I think there's always gonna be people who are complaining about things or poking fun at things, like the *Vice* article. But there's still room for the cream of the crop to carry on. It doesn't feel so faddy. It's not like Moombahton or some kind of flash in the pan. And even if jazz seemed to be cheesy and uncool and a bit of a fad next year, there's still going to be loads of people listening, and there's still going to be people who care.

Similarly, in a less tribal musical universe, the regular, ignominious disappearance of genres like acid jazz, trip-hop and broken beat may have been replaced by something more stable.

Steve Symons

One good thing about this time is that we seem to have got out of the habit of naming and shaming a genre. The nineties was such an inventive era for music, particularly in this country, with stuff that you could file under trip-hop or big beat or acid jazz. And in a way, it was the terms that killed them: a few naff records and they're genres that may never speak their name again. It's really nice to see things coming back now without that kind of inbuilt peril. That first jazz period* was the culmination of fifty, sixty years of youth culture after youth culture after youth culture. And everybody expected the next year is going to herald the next big thing and it will have a name and it will have people that all dress the same and listen to the same music, and then we will have to bring it down to make room for something else. That doesn't happen any more. Thank God, it just seems a lot calmer. So I don't think people are going to be putting up the middle finger as they look backwards to this period in quite the same way as they did last time because people are just a little bit more chilled and a little bit more honest in the sense of looking back at music.

Nevertheless, history – and in particular the experience of the Jazz Warriors generation – tells us that popularity is cyclical, and that scenes rarely stay on top for ever. The fear of jazz suddenly becoming uncool and marginalised is part of the fundamental understanding of many jazz musicians, and not only those who, like the Jazz Warriors, actually experienced this fall from grace themselves.

Binker Golding

Jazz will always be there, I think we can expect that now. We've lasted since 1903 to the present day. And we've even been in the universities for a while. So I think we're probably going to survive, just like classical music. But this wave has definitely got a sell-by date. I don't know what that sell-by date is and what it gets replaced by, but it's definitely going to have a sell-by date, just like fifteen years prior did and fifteen years before that. This will come and go. People get bored of it.

Jean Toussaint

Jazz moves in waves. Wynton Marsalis joined Art Blakey, *Time* magazine started writing about him, *New York Times*, *New Yorker*. That

* Steve is referring to the late eighties/early nineties jazz boom, in which he was a significant player, at least in Bristol, both as promoter and DJ, under the name 'Tintin'.

was a wave in America in the early eighties, and in the mid-eighties, that wave moved over here. And then it died down, and virtually disappeared. And now that wave's come back around like waves do, and now people like Shabaka and Nubya, Moses Boyd and Binker and Cassie are getting that attention. That wave will die down again and then eventually it'll come again. I've seen three or four different waves.

Kerstan Mackness

When the scene comes down, when people move on to the next thing as we know that they do: let's see how deep the roots are. There will be a perfect tipping point, the mainstream music industry will sign as many of these acts as they can. They'll fuck some of them up. People will lose interest and move on to the next thing that's important. So Nubya's record will be everywhere because everyone's been waiting for it. And then the next Shabaka album or the next Comet album will get a little bit less hype than the one before, because people will be like, 'What's new? What's the new story?'

The media can have a very short attention span. After so many years of coverage for this wave, is another crash just around the corner? Time moves fast, and the sheer volume of cultural production fighting for attention almost guarantees that the present wave will not last for ever. Indeed, even in the three years between my first starting to research this book and finishing the final draft, the events described feel increasingly and irretrievably like the past. This lag will, presumably, feel even more pronounced by the time you read this sentence. What can this generation of musicians do to make sure they continue to ride the wave rather than being washed away by it?

This book has primarily been occupied with what came before: the struggles of previous generations to build the foundations upon which the present generation's success was built. But this success has played a vital role in reclaiming jazz as a youth music, making it far more likely that those coming up behind will choose to express themselves in this idiom. Further, this era's diversity – with many more musicians of colour, female and working-class musicians than previous generations – can inspire future generations to feel jazz might be 'for them'.

But what factors affect the music's future, and what can the current wave of musicians do to sustain their longevity?

'Listening for the potential'

Shabaka Hutchings

A lot of the people that started to get hyped five years ago, they were really young. They were just out of college a few years, had some bands, done some gigs locally, and then pushed out on to the road. So what they were doing was the first manifestation of what they can do. Now the exciting thing is that this is giving a scene a push. It's about seeing how far it goes. For me, when I listen to a lot of the UK jazz scene I'm not listening to them for what they're giving, I'm listening for the potential.

An explosion of media interest in a vibrant live scene meant that many of the people who were following 'the new UK jazz' were not traditional jazz fans. This left many older musicians, fans and observers somewhat bewildered about all the excitement. I will admit that even I felt that way about some of the music when it first started to emerge. I liked the energy around it but not all of it sounded fresh to me and I wasn't sure it justified the hype. Indeed, I used to refer to it privately (in my own head: I don't think I ever shared this term with anyone) as the Emperor's New Jazz.

The metaphor is apt – though not as pejorative as it might initially seem. While it would be wrong to characterise the new scene as utterly naked, even in its infancy, it is probably true that the new clothes for jazz about which the media was so excited had not fully materialised when the excitement began. But it is from this position of confidence that true innovation and development can come.

'because the end is really the beginning'

Dave Okumu

We have to keep supporting people who are trying to do authentic things and supporting evolution. Whenever something takes on a momentum, there will be an aspect of bullshit to it. It's not really the fault of the leaders of those movements necessarily. It's just human nature. It would be so easy to stand in judgement of what's happening now; these are just all people trying to find their way and given an opportunity to have a platform, they'll grow, they'll evolve and they'll figure things out.

It is not necessarily that those older musicians, critics, fans and observers who cried naked were wrong in their assessment of many of the musicians' development and originality at that time, so much as that they – and I – were missing the point. The startling achievement of the new scene was perhaps not creating something totally new but making the old music feel new again by dynamically recombining diverse aspects of jazz's heritage with the sound of urban London. This was enhanced by the creation of a celebratory context around the music in non-traditional jazz spaces, with far greater diversity both among artists and audiences than just a few years previously. From this starting point, musicians have their whole careers to tour and record, evolve and develop, learning and improving in the process. Even more importantly, their achievement in making jazz attractive for even younger musicians means a new generation will grow up with jazz as a reference point in a way they wouldn't have if it weren't for this generation.

This process of turning the Emperor's New Jazz into a suit as truly regal as the media suggested is central to this scene's meaning. Jazz in the UK is in a better place than it has been at any time since the 1960s and perhaps ever, with a young, engaged fan base who listen to jazz alongside other music, more diverse musicians, and supportive media, labels, promoters and festivals that are open-minded about what jazz is and can be rather than trying to force it to wear a restrictive uniform. This is the perfect base for the music to grow and develop, and it may be that the most important music to come out of this wave hasn't yet been made. It might not even come from the generation currently enjoying success but from artists still in their teens or pre-teens who have grown up absorbing Nubya Garcia, Ezra Collective, Kokoroko, Sons of Kemet and Nubiyan Twist, whose example will inspire them to create music in this idiom.

Shabaka Hutchings

Regardless of what anyone else says, 'jazz musicians' are funny creatures. For so long they were saying, 'Is jazz dead? Is it not?', trying to get audiences, or a wider, more diverse audience, then someone comes along that basically gets that audience for them, the streaming goes up. Everything goes up. The scene gets revived because the media can put them in the magazines without them looking like anomalies. And everyone's going, 'Oh no, they're not as innovative as they were back in the day!' You can't have it both ways!

This is something that a lot of older jazz musicians have a problem with, that humility of realising that even though some of the younger jazz scene might not have the attitudes that you think are important, there's always stuff to learn. Ezra, there is that enthusiasm that you know they are going to smash every single gig without fail and connect with the audience on an actual personal level. Which you can't necessarily say about all types of jazz that might be more proficient if you're looking at it purely from an instrumental context. If they hadn't been given the opportunity at the point where people might have been saying, 'Well they've not earned this,' then they wouldn't have got to the point where they are now. Sometimes you just gotta give artists a show and reserve judgement until you've seen them after a couple of years. For me the problem is if you see some artists and they're not going forward. It might be that the scene that we call the UK jazz scene is actually going to fully mature in the next five years. But that might not have been possible without the touring that they've been doing the last five years. You just never know what the historical trajectory is.

Wayne Francis

'UK jazz' is kind of a misfit terminology for a lot of people that have come from a similar background and are all exploring variations of improvised music. And I think if it continues then in five years there will be something that is more of a coherent form of music. The amalgamation of all of the different elements and all the different people is going to emerge into something very specific that's going to have a kind of replicable language that other musicians are going to copy. It's so young that you need to allow some of these musicians to write albums for ten years, and by the time they do that there's going to be a younger generation influenced by them and there's going to be a dominant sound that's going to come out.

'Making records is hard'

What the music currently has is a powerful platform from which to grow. Whether or not it achieves its potential, touching more people and opening up new forms of musical and political expression will have a lot to do with the kind of records people make. To experienced industry heads, whether or not this generation can convert the energy of a buzzing live scene into meaningful records that will still be listened to long after the Nu Jazz Lad has moved on to the next thing, is the challenge that will define their future impact.

Aly Gillani

Making records is hard. It takes a long time to perfect that studio craft. There's a lot of good records, but compared to how many good live bands there are, there aren't that many real classic albums. When you come from that live environment, it's a hard thing to make that transition – particularly if you come from that bedroom-DIY sort of vibe. It's easier to make it sound really professional if you're making electronic music or sample-based music. But if you're recording a whole live band, it's difficult. That's why someone like Shabaka, who's been doing it that much longer, can make great records – because he has the experience. He's been around other sessions and absorbed it all, and then channels that into all the projects he does. I think he's a cut above most – and it's not a judgement on the songwriting or the composition or the bands or anything, it's just experience in the studio. But that will come with time, if people are given the right time to develop.

Lex Blondin

Making records is a craft. You got to really know how you want to make your shit sound. Unlike the live realm, it's not just about the performance. The best results for me happen when great musicians with great musical ideas hook up with a wicked producer who guides them into a sound that works with their music. I think the ones that go the distance are the Beastie Boys of jazz. They'll be like, 'Cool, now we've got some experience with some wild live gigs, let's just lock ourselves up in a studio with loads of weed and all the pizzas and fuck around throwing new sounds and influences, reinvent ourselves.' Some of these cats have gone through their 'fight for the right to party' phase. Like, 'Cool, we're blowing up, people are injecting money, we've done tours, etc.' And they look back and be like, 'Mmmm, I'm thirty-something now, what am I trying to say, express?' and with a more focused intention and production in mind they tend to make even better music that speaks to an even wider audience. To me, some of the bands weren't completely mature when the genre exploded. It's great that it's given them a platform to get started as professional musicians and now they can go off and do even better albums and reinvent themselves.'

Emily Moxon

The thing with this scene is that the music was being made for the live context. When we made *We Out Here*, I think there were twenty-seven musicians who came through in the three days that we recorded that. Making great records, or making great albums, is a different craft to how the music lives in a live space. Nubya's record on *We Out Here* is called 'Once', and it's about that. Every time is different. That's the difficulty with jazz and what is magical about jazz: what happens in a live setting in front of an audience is not necessarily always how it is in the studio. As a record company, what you are into is amazing-sounding recordings. And it's not necessarily where the focus has been.

For some, the ability of this generation to reach bigger audiences will rely on stepping outside jazz, whether through collaborations with grime and pop artists or simply a more commercial, vocal-driven approach to the music. This has already begun to happen: Ezra Collective have released tunes with grime artist Jme and rapper Loyle Carner and feature Sampa the Great, Emeli Sandé, Kojey Radical and Nao on *Where I'm Meant To Be* (Partisan, 2022); Sons of Kemet have worked with Kojey Radical and D Double E;[*] and Poppy Ajudha has begun collaborating with acclaimed electronic band Jungle.

Claudio Lillo

Not everyone is going to be Thundercat. Maybe there is not going to be a UK Kamasi Washington. Maybe there isn't going to be a UK Thundercat because they really happened because of Flying Lotus

---

[*] I loved D Double E's unique delivery and leftfield sense of humour ever since 'Come to My House', a bonus track that appears on the bonus DVD for 2006 grime compilation *Run the Road Volume 2*. His contribution to both grime and dubstep has been enormous, under his own name and with the Newham Generals, as well as countless features. But whereas other artists have evolved a lot in the past two decades, both through taking on board wider political changes and through personal growth and the natural aging process, Dee didn't seem to get the memo. His feature on 'For the Culture' on Sons of Kemet's 2021 album *Black to the Future* struck me as something of a missed opportunity. Whereas it could have been a powerful union of two important Afro-diasporic scenes, it felt very much like Dee just took the money and rattled off some standard bars about 'looking for the dancehall queen', without engaging with the music or its context.

and Kendrick Lamar. So unless Skepta made a record with Nubya Garcia or Moses Boyd, that would maybe take it up. But also grime isn't rap, right? Skepta is not as big as Kendrick. For a UK artist to properly blow up, they'd have to do something with someone American or some big, big, big pop thing.

The backing of both major and independent labels that many of the artists of this wave currently enjoy alongside the plethora of independent options to reach their growing fan bases mean this generation is in a perfect position to make those meaningful records. It is not only a question of studio experience but also of access to professional studios, money for mixing, mastering, remixing and featured guests who could make the music connect with different audiences. And all this simply on the production side, before even considering artwork, videos, marketing budgets and distribution. *To Pimp a Butterfly* was exceptional not only because of Kendrick's individual genius but also thanks to nearly a hundred other creative contributors;[1] but those people all need to be paid. And while the financial backing of major labels can potentially open the doors to greater creativity, it can also impose creative limits and homogeneity. This generation's ability to use those forces without being crushed by them will determine their true artistic impact.

'It might help make the next Beyoncé' (representation)

This cohort's spectacular achievement of making jazz attractive for a younger, more diverse audience can lead to greater diversity both on and off the stage and a new fan base that will age alongside the music, continuing to support it by buying records, listening on platforms and continuing to turn up to shows long after the media hype has died down.

'because the end is really the beginning'

Aly Gillani

For me one of the most powerful things to come from this recent boom was the jazz special they did in the [8 April 2018] *Observer* magazine. The cover had a picture of Nubya playing sax on the front page. For young black kids, seeing someone that looks like them, playing those instruments, and being amazing at it: that's massively inspiring. If you ask a musician or producer or DJ how they got into music, they won't say, 'Oh, when I was twelve, I heard someone play a diminished seventh chord and that's it, I was in.' They say, 'I saw Kurt Cobain on the TV, and thought I want to be that guy,' or, 'I saw Dizzee Rascal and I was like, what the hell is that sound? I want to do what he does.' You need those touchstones. You get into something on a surface level and then you can discover the depth of it and get into the craft.

Sheila Maurice-Grey

I'm very conscious of being a role model because especially here in the UK, I'm one of very few black female horn players and trumpet players in particular. I've always been aware of that responsibility and I hope to see more black female trumpet players and horn players come up. A big thing about Kokoroko that people look at is the fact that it's a black female-led horn section; Nerija as well. It speaks volumes. It might help make the next Beyoncé!

It is important to note that female musicians remain in the minority, even in the present UK wave. And though most celebrate an increased focus on diversity, there is a fear in some corners of tokenism and insincerity, and a concern that positive discrimination should not replace critical assessment.

Nikki Yeoh

All of a sudden, now it's on the agenda: 'Let's create a woman band, let's create this woman flagship la dee dah.' And I'm just like, a minute ago you didn't really give a damn about us women musicians. Soon as money's involved, people start changing. It is a good thing, if it creates *good* female musicians, you can't just have female musicians for having female musicians' sake. There's one thing to have tokenism and check a box, it's another thing to just actually be badass. I'm not anti all the support for women, far from it. But I am anti giving too much praise to mediocrity when it's not valid. And then people not feeling like they have to strive.

Diversity is a question not only of the musicians on the stage but the labels, agencies and management companies that represent them, the promoters and arts organisations that support them, and the bodies that fund and regulate them. Most arts organisations have incorporated a commitment to diversity into their official mission statements, especially in the wake of the Black Lives Matter events of 2020. But there is a fear that many initiatives promote only the most visible manifestations of diversity while leaving the central power structures unchanged.

Huey Walker

If you look at the publicly funded sector, the diversity in the leadership, even though some of the programmes might be a bit more black, the people who are making the decisions on who gets to be programmed are still very unrepresentative. London is 50 per cent BAME.* If you want to be representative of your community, that's what it should be.

Janine Irons

Don't try and go to one of these institutions and try and change them. They won't change because for them to change, it means some of them have to give up their seats and they're not going to do that. You want a more diverse board? Somebody needs to leave the board.

* Until 2021, this was the UK government's standard demographic acronym meaning 'Black, Asian and minority ethnic'.

Who's leaving? Not me. So they create these fake posts, fake seats, fake roles, to tick a box and get some extra funding. They bring you in and then you become the poster boy or girl for the organisation. But actually, you have no power. You're not changing anything, you're not opening the door for all your brothers and sisters coming behind you or making it a level playing field. Instead of supporting the organisations and ticking everybody's box, why are you not building your foundations so that you can say how you want things to run? You get your vision of what does equality, equity, inclusion, diversity look like for you? And then you create that. I just think we can do it more quickly if it's your organisation, your vision, your rules.

This mantra of independence saw the Tomorrow's Warriors alumni running their own nights, controlling their own image, interacting directly with fans on social media, hosting radio shows and writing articles. But it applies also on an organisational level, and for Tomorrow's Warriors' founders, this increased independence needs to translate into a lasting framework to continue to amplify this generation's voices and those of their successors.

Gary Crosby

You have to leave some structure. Or if not structure, an opportunity for others to progress. A lot of the older jazz musicians have reached a height and a position: they don't really want anybody else coming in there. Hence, 'They're not good enough yet.' 'They haven't paid their dues.' 'We were there before them.' That kind of language. It's not how it goes. Hence why I'm quite reluctant. When people ask me about the future, I tend to say, 'Don't ask me, I'm the past!' And it was never based only on a financial model. Or an artistic model, although these are important things to what we do. The main thing was we saw ourselves in those young people. This is what we would want for ourselves and our children.

'Bigger than jazz'
(community)

One factor repeatedly mentioned in the origin story of this wave of musicians has been the power of community: a strong, mutually supportive cohort all coming of age at the same time, playing on each other's records, supporting each other physically and on social media, exchanging advice and enthusiasm. Musical community and communality is credited not only as a practical tool to ensure musical survival but as a tool for a better world.

Dave Okumu

The democratisation of creative processes through technology is like this double-edged sword. It's been amazing for me, because it's allowed me to make records that I wouldn't have been able to make. But it's also fed into this idea that we don't need people; we can just do everything ourselves. All I need is a laptop and I can play things and edit them and fix them. There's a dismissal of the importance of relationships and of what happens between the cracks and in the dialogue, or when you're in a room with someone trying to work out how to play something and why it feels a certain way. So much of my learning happened in those interactions. So it really excites me that there's people trying to find their way together and reclaiming the value of that aspect of music making.

Cassie Kinoshi

Jazz is a community thing. It's a way of sharing things. It's a way of connecting with people. And it's a way of expressing yourself authentically. That's what makes jazz such an amazing genre: that connection not just musically but personally. That is such an integral part of it. It's all about expression.

'because the end is really the beginning'

Moses Boyd

There's a difference with them and us, like, them: the King was Courtney and the Jazz Warriors. There was one ecosystem, one band, one unit. Whereas today the beauty is it's not just me, it's Shabaka. It's Theon. It's Nubya. It's Femi, it's Yussef, it's Cassie. We're all close. We are actually friends and because we're not in each other's face all the time, a lot of stuff doesn't cop its head. I haven't gotta stress about Theon's ego's getting too big: he's not even in my band! But when it comes to the studio, the creative part that matters, he's there, and that is a beautiful thing. We've learnt some of them lessons because I've been with Gary for how many years hearing what went wrong and what not to do. And you also compare with how the music industry has changed: I'm independent, Theon's still independent. Nubya's signed to a big major label in America, Shabaka also; there's so many different independent ecosystems happening, which is how it should be.

Conversely, for many inside the music industry, it is only when the leading artists of a given scene break out that they can reach truly significant audiences.

Claudio Lillo

I made a conscious decision not really to sign many jazz acts, because once I signed a couple, I had everyone under the sun being like, 'Hey, we want you to be our agent.' I just said no, because I don't want to be a jazz agent. I just want to have these acts who are bigger than jazz. Maybe not everyone that everyone has been talking about is going to make it. But that's just the way it is, right? The great ones are going to separate themselves from the pack. Just becoming a show that anybody would want to see. It'll be this moment that this was the beginning and then things blossom out of it.

How can individual artists continue to progress without forgetting where they came from? Can individual greatness and success open the door still wider for everyone, or can it only be achieved by consciously distancing oneself from one's peers?

One way of thinking about this is looking at material conditions. The vast difference between the black populations of the USA and UK (in 2021, roughly 47 million (14 per cent) in the USA compared to 2.4 million (4 per cent) in the UK[2]) have meant that the US has a far more established black middle class, as well as numerous black millionaires and even billionaires, able to re-invest in black culture. Many of these have come from hip-hop, with moguls like Dr. Dre, Jay-Z, Nas and Drake using their wealth and celebrity to invest in bringing through younger artists as well as diversifying into clothing brands and tech businesses.

Courtney Pine

Branford has the black dollar. He has a huge black audience that will make him a millionaire. We don't have that here. You look at BET,[3] how far are we from having a BET TV station? That's like in the next galaxy. Not even next century. That will never happen in this country. But America . . . they have been given things, but they have paid the price as well.

Bradley Zero

That's a critical difference between the UK and the US: not to say there aren't middle-class black people in the UK, there clearly are, but not in the same way. There's not middle-class black areas, black suburbs with big gardens and good schools in Essex or Surrey. People exist in bubbles, I don't think there's a community in the same way as there is in America.

I was in New York once and visiting my dad's friend, I must have been twenty-one. And we went to see Chick Corea in New Jersey, and I thought, 'Wow, this is it, we're going to a really cool jazz gig in America!' And it was so odd because it was like a recital, and it was packed with middle-aged, middle-class black people. A thousand

African American jazz enthusiasts sat down, clapping in between movements. It was like going to a classical concert! It was just so formal. That would not happen here. You would not go to a jazz gig and see a majority black middle-class crowd dressed in suits, wearing bow ties, talking about the art show that they'd just seen at the MOMA last week. It just wouldn't happen here. You'd have pockets. And I'm not saying it would be all white. But America is just this weird mix of the best and the worst of everything. In many ways it's way behind in civil rights, equality and oppression, as we all know, but in many ways it's also way ahead. It's just a lot more complex.

While it is comforting to imagine an alternative reality in which Roots Manuva makes a failed run for prime minister ('it's all gone higgledy-piggledy'), Dizzee Rascal is a host on *The Apprentice* and Tricky is 'where he deserved to be, a glamorous gargoyle on the edifice of twenty-first-century pop',[4] the UK's structural racism and proportionately tiny black population have consigned such visions to the realm of fantasy. Of the generation that came to prominence in the 1990s and early 2000s, Roots Manuva has all but disappeared after multiple mental health issues, Dizzee Rascal has been found guilty of assaulting his former partner,[5] and grime godfather Wiley has been quasi-cancelled after his anti-Semitic rant on Twitter in July 2021. While elder musicians born in the 1950s and 1960s like Jazzie B, Omar, Norman Jay, Trevor Nelson and Courtney Pine have all become respected figures and been granted honorific titles by the establishment, this has rarely translated to the level of financial success that would allow them to make meaningful infrastructural contributions.

There are signs of positive change – the Stormzy Scholarship provides financial support to two black students each year at the University of Cambridge, and his Merky Books collaboration with Penguin Random House is supporting black voices in literature; Tinchy Stryder's Star in the Hood clothing brand, founded 2006, has become an international success, partnering with JD Sports and taking investment from Jay-Z's

Roc Nation; rapper Loyle Carner has set up a cookery school for teen-agers with ADHD (the brilliantly named Chilli Con Carner); and Roll Deep's DJ Target hosts *The Rap Game UK* (with Krept and Konan), a BBC show dedicated to supporting young black British MCs, as well as hosting five shows a week on 1Xtra and his own chat show, *Tonight With Target*, on BBC Three. Grime/garage stars Kano and Ashley Wal-ters have reached new audiences through their lead roles in the Drake-owned series *Top Boy* (even UK rapper Dave appears as psychopathic gangster Modie, and Little Simz as Walters's love interest). Nevertheless, Gary Crosby and Janine Irons's emphasis on ownership is a long way from being realised in the UK as a whole.

For Courtney and Moses, the answer lies in proactively signposting black success stories.

Courtney Pine

We have this weird thing – and I think it's an overthrow from slavery – where if you are in a community, you don't really rate anybody else in that community. I come from a community with Aswad, Omar, King Sounds. And nobody really rates each other. No one talks about anybody else. I remember when I met Omar, because a journalist asked, 'Who would you like to work with next week?' And I said, 'Well, Omar.' And he heard it. And he was like, 'Why did you mention me?' We don't rate each other. We really don't.

Moses Boyd

Omar should be like an Erykah Badu, or a Maxwell or a D'Angelo. The UK need to adopt a bit of Americanism and be like, 'These are our heroes.' It should be, 'Look at Nubya, this Camden girl that's gone to do this and maybe she'll work with Beyoncé one day.' She's a UK hero! We should be talking about Little Simz like that. We should be talking about Sampha like that. But we don't. I don't know why, but I think that also needs to change. We need to make superstars out of our people before they leave. A Daniel Kaluuya, a John Boyega, not just music. If Daniel stayed here, he wouldn't have got the Oscar. It's only America that's celebrating him for the artist he is. Ella Mai, Jay Prince, the list goes on. As much as we can do what we do, there's another part of it that is beyond our control that I think the wider public needs to get behind. Because otherwise it just gets stale. You're just forever going to be talking about Britpop and how amazing that was, or wasn't. Nothing against Blur and Oasis. But I'm like, come on, guys, it's not that many songs! Speaking on behalf of the black community, I think culturally we're not as good as our cousins across the sea at championing stuff and making heroes of our people. Like Herbie Hancock: Herbie's done his thing, I'm not saying he hasn't, but why isn't Kaidi there, why isn't Dego there, why isn't Roni Size there?

They've had a longer history there. We will see that black middle class of our generation when we hit forty and things may change, but if we don't speak about it now, we don't want to get there and be like, 'Oh shit. What should we do?' I'm like, no, no, it starts from now. It starts with us, man, we've got to do something. There should be a Nubya Garcia regularly on *The Graham Norton Show,* on flipping *Match of the Day*, man, just because she's important. America has that, and we need to adopt some of that, because we've got so much here that has to leave just to eat.

Paradoxically the lack of an established black middle class may have contributed to the new UK jazz scene's dynamism. Whereas for years, US jazz artists had been able to eke out a moderate living without changing the paradigm, the very need to innovate and exist outside the UK's extremely limited jazz market pushed many musicians of this generation to intersect with other genres.

'I don't think the doors are as open' (venues and gentrification)

We have learnt how this wave of jazz was incubated by a vibrant underground live scene: Steez, Steam Down, Jazz Re:freshed at Mau

Mau, Total Refreshment Centre, Church of Sound. Just like the twice-weekly jam sessions at LA's Piano Bar where The West Coast Get Down came of age, Low End Theory for the LA beats scene, FWD for dubstep, or Movement and Metalheadz for drum and bass, scenes need regular live nights at sympathetic venues in order for the musicians to improve, test repertoire on writhing audiences, and cohere as a community.

Those musicians that have already reached a worldwide audience can perform on the established venue and festival circuit, which seems to have returned to good health despite the devastation caused by the Covid-19 pandemic, the global surge in the cost of touring and severe cost of living crisis it left in its wake, to say nothing of the ongoing complications caused by war in Ukraine. But the sad reality is that TRC has shut its doors to the public, Jazz Re:freshed has been exiled from Mau Mau, Steez is long gone and Steam Down at Buster Mantis is no more. Even Worldwide FM is no longer broadcasting new shows.

Aly Gillani

There are a bunch of people that have come through that now will have long, fruitful careers making the music they want to make. But the fact that you now don't have Total Refreshment Centre, that Buster Mantis can't hold Steam Down any more because it's too small, Ghost Notes was there and then was gone; that really makes it hard for those scenes to survive without those venues. It's much harder now for smaller acts coming through because I don't think the doors are as open. The Jazz Cafe does a good job for sure, but that's only for acts that have reached a certain level. Those that have got their foot in the door and got an album out: If they're smart and if they get the right backing, they can keep going. You've got great labels like Brownswood who are supporting that music and will continue to do so I'm sure. But I think that initial bubble has burst, and what happens next is anybody's guess.

To an extent this is part of a music scene's natural life cycle: a meadow of creative wildflowers appears in the spring and you can enjoy some beautiful moments there until they start looking shabby by late summer, only to spread their seeds for next year in the autumn. But the new scene won't blossom next spring if the meadow has been turned into flats by a developer, and young professionals attracted by the bohemian energy the music has helped to create move in next door and complain about the noise until the venue gets shut down.

Eddie Piller

The people that kick down the doors get arrested. They don't get to move in. This is how life works. But the horrible Hoxton story: look at it now, it's disgusting. Have you been there recently? It's just a travesty. A fucking disgrace actually. And the same will happen to Peckham. They tried to get rid of the Bussey Building the other year, didn't they? They'll get there in the end, don't worry. You couldn't make it up, how totally corrupt the destruction of the East End of London has been.

Technically venues can exist anywhere with enough young people to go to them; the survival of venues like the Fox and Firkin in Lewisham, Matchstick Piehouse in Deptford, MOT in Bermondsey and Studio 9294 in Hackney Wick is testament to this. Anyone who prophesies the end of grassroots creativity will be laughed at by history: it will come up like flowers through the cracked cement of the most industrial landscape. Despite the prevailing conditions, new venues are appearing all the time. But by the time you read this, it is likely that most of the venues listed above will no longer exist, closed due to a combination of rent increases, expired leases for meanwhile use, and the vagaries of simply keeping the doors open in an intensely competitive and unstable environment.

It is almost impossible for live music venues to compete on a commercial basis with residential developments. Protections need to be introduced at a government level. Responding to the closure

of much-loved community venue Passing Clouds, co-founder Eleanor Wilson fought tooth and nail for two years at great personal cost
to prevent the venue (an old printworks in Haggerston, Hackney)
being turned into flats, and the building was eventually awarded
'Asset of Community Value' status, helping it to remain a music venue
(although the licence was not returned to Wilson and the venue was
reborn, under new management, as the Jago). But legislation needs to
go further, otherwise the potential for venues to help attract people to
an area only to fall foul of noise complaints and raised rents is huge.
Nor are the consequences limited simply to venues being priced out: a
successful arts venue can be a major trigger for the gentrification of an
area as a whole, displacing entire communities.

Mickey Smith

It's hard to know how the local people can actually afford to stay here,
and the obvious answer is they can't. And that is a bit of a problem,
but people are becoming their own enemies by black people moving
out, selling their houses to rich people. But you couldn't leave Peckham
the way it was. We had our fucking MP turn up with a stab-proof vest
on back in the day, and before that, there was a ten-year period where
the Lib Dems had control of Peckham and they gave up on it. Didn't
give a fuck. There was no investment. Everything went down. I think
lots of artists and creatives and things like the Bussey have helped
lift Peckham up. But in a way it's become a bit of a victim of its own
success. It's a tricky one.

Beyond protecting their basic existence, government funding for
grassroots UK venues similar to that enjoyed by many in Europe would
support more experimental programming. Even those UK venues that
have managed to survive the glass, chrome and bulldozers can rarely
afford much risk, meaning there is huge pressure on artists to fill the
venue. This wave, through its creation of a celebratory atmosphere, can
do just that – a major achievement. But this need for popularity may

also be responsible for some of the more cautious artistic choices made by its practitioners. While I would not advocate the esoteric opposite extreme with more people on stage than in the audience, having a balance between commercial and artistic pressures, and an understanding that some of the most important art might not necessarily 'wash its face', would support more progressive artistic endeavours.

It has also been suggested that the greed of agents is squeezing the life out of the scene, charging extortionately high fees that make it unsustainable for promoters to continue booking artists whose growth they have supported.

Lex Blondin

The fees are going up and up and up. The hype created by the industry pushes artists to a certain level at rocket speed and before you know it you can't afford them any more. I'm all for artists getting good fees obviously, the only thing that's a bit troubling is how quickly things have got out of hand. The result is that a lot of promoters and venues who helped grow the artists' audience get replaced by a big fish that capitalises on the hard work made at the grassroots level. It's a shame that there's such a gap between the grassroots level and the touring circuit. Some agents are quite detached from the scene they work with and treat DIY promoters in the same way they deal with mainstream venues, asking disproportionate fees. They're such different beasts and should be dealt with accordingly really. There are healthy examples where the bigger help the smaller ones by including them in the process, but they're few and far between.

Also, all this hype focused on a few kinda creates a canon for what the new genre sounds like and it doesn't really leave much space for the other ones. So it's not the healthiest thing. That said, good music always finds a way to people who have their ears to the ground!

Blaming the greed of agents and managers for the failure to create a healthy ecosystem is a very old trope. While there is probably some truth in this old-fashioned slander – not only are some agents greedy but most also have a strong desire to *win*, which often plays out in financial terms even if money is not the primary focus – the situation is complicated and agents are an easy but sometimes unfair target. As an agent myself who has also spent a lot of time as both artist and promoter, I see the situation from various angles, one of which is that even apparently high fees rarely translate into significant individual wages once tour costs, crew, session players and commissions are paid, particularly for large groups.* Even more starkly, for all the focus on a continuum, most artists have a limited time in which to earn as much money as possible to create some kind of financial future for themselves and their families. Agents have a fiduciary duty to raise fees high enough to enable artists to have sustainable careers. If artists are not making enough money, it becomes increasingly hard for them to continue creating. As they get older, especially if they have dependents, the need to conform to commercial pressures becomes less an artistic choice than a survival strategy.

'The Tories slashed all of that'
(Making a living through music)

Even reasonably successful artists earn much lower wages than people of equivalent levels of seniority in other professions. Essentially, many artists subsidise live music venues and promoters through the frugality of their own lifestyles. One key area where artists have traditionally made savings to support their creativity is rent. Throughout the 1970s, 1980s, 1990s and even into the 2000s, many artists saved money by squatting abandoned properties. As well as providing space in which to make art and clothes, rehearse, host events and grow community,

---

* It is probably true that, even at a reasonable level of commission, many agents make more money than the artists they represent, a fact which has contributed to the stereotype of the hard-bargaining, wheeler-dealing, money-obsessed agent, and frequent clashes between agents, managers and 'the talent'.

squats gave artists the time to develop their craft without working constantly to pay rent to 'the man'.

Squatting residential property was officially made illegal in 2012, strengthening companies like Camelot and Ad Hoc that had sprung up to guard properties against squatters by licensing mostly middle-class squatters to live there as 'guardians', charging fees both to the 'licensees' and the owners.[6] The transition from squatting to guardian-ship is yet another example, like the mutation of raves and free parties into 'the festival industry', of wild unregulated space being monetised and controlled by corporate interests. For writer and cultural com-mentator Mark Fisher, the diminished opportunities for cheap hous-ing deprives artists of vital opportunities to hone their craft:

> If there's one factor above all else which contributes to cultural conservatism, it is the vast inflation of the cost of rent and mort-gages. It's no accident that the efflorescence of cultural invention in London and New York in the late 1970s and early 1980s (in the punk and post-punk scenes) coincided with the availability of squatted and cheap property in those cities.[7]

Another difference between the 1980s and now is that university tuition was then free in the UK, with students even claiming grants towards their living costs (and vinyl addictions). The disappearance of grants and exponential rises in tuition fees have meant all but the most privileged UK students leave university carrying intense debt. This financial pressure means university is necessarily understood more as a means to a financial end than a time to explore creativity, with most music graduates obliged to make immediate money by any means necessary, often at the expense of musical experimentation.

For all the attacks on industry and the unions for which the Thatcher government has been justly criticised, that regime's promotion of entrepreneurship in the 1980s saw the Enterprise Allowance offering unemployed people £40 per week to start their own business upon pre-sentation of a very basic business plan. For many people this represented an opportunity for state-sponsored creativity under another name; poet Mark Gwynne Jones used the money to take magic mushrooms at every stone circle in the UK, and write poems about his experiences.*

Paradoxically, for all Thatcher's attempt to obliterate the working class, it was probably easier to live as an artist or student in the 1980s than now; unless you were black, of course.[8] The Thatcher government's destruction of the welfare state and privatisation of national assets continued throughout the New Labour years. As chronicled by Owen Jones's 2011 book *Chavs*, the demonisation of those on benefits supported a shrinking of the welfare state that has made it increasingly difficult to live without work, with 22 per cent of the UK population living in poverty, including 4.3 million children, with black and minority ethnic children disproportionately affected.[9]

While some Conservatives might celebrate a shrunken welfare state, it is necessarily discriminatory against those less able to earn a living, particularly in a climate of economic uncertainty exacerbated by ten years of austerity alongside external factors like the global financial crash of 2007–8, the Covid-19 lockdowns of 2020–1 and the rising prices of fuel amid an escalating climate emergency. Furthermore, the arts have always needed external support, whether in the form of aristocratic patronage or state sponsorship. It is in recognition of this basic fact that the French system of *intermittence* exists, whereby recognised artistic professionals are paid by the state for any weeks they don't have enough shows to make ends meet.

This support allows French musicians to make a much more consistent living than those in the UK, especially since 2010, when the removal of vast swathes of public funding under the name of austerity forced many musicians to find new ways of connecting with audiences: classic neo-liberal economics. Even Shabaka – absolutely no

---

* The system was glorified by cult band Half Man Half Biscuit: 'On board the Enterprise Allowance / we could do whatever we liked'. When I called M.G.J. to ask if he was okay with me printing the above anecdote, he joyously affirmed, 'I was on board the Enterprise Allowance!'

Tory – credits this musical Darwinism with forcing the present generation to connect with new audiences outside traditional jazz spaces.

Shabaka Hutchings

When I was in college in the early 2000s, there was a lot of money being given to musicians through the Arts Council, coming out of college, to just go on tours all round England, like the Rural Development Fund. You came out of college, you could get funding to make an album, do lots of gigs; lots of venues were funded, places like the Forge:* government funding was around. The Tories came in and just slashed all of that; and what results is if you want to play you've got to find a way to relate to an audience – obviously it's not as clean as that, but it means that you're not getting musicians who can survive from being subsidised.

When there's less spaces to play because there's not enough stuff that can get subsidised for music that is not mainstream popular, it means that musicians are going to start to play in alternate venues like TRC or Steez, they might see if they can get a gig at Passing Clouds in amongst music that's not like theirs.[†] That wasn't necessarily happening when you had a lot of places that were identified as cultural jazz or cultural practical spaces. So that would push the music forward.

But for every musician who has developed a successful career by adapting their craft to economic realities, there are many more who have abandoned music altogether in favour of a more reliable source of income. Furthermore, making a living and actually pushing the music forward are not always the same thing.

* A music venue on Delancey Street in Camden, just around the corner from the Jazz Cafe. The venue opened in 2009 and suddenly closed its doors in 2017, saying that 'running a music venue in these times is exceptionally tough' (Tom Foot, 'Owners Announce Sudden Closure of the Forge Music Venue in Camden Town', *Camden New Journal*, 30 March 2017). The Forge reopened in 2023 under the stewardship of former Jazz Cafe programmer Adrian Gibson: another pleasing full circle.
† It was, indeed, at Passing Clouds in 2015 that The Comet Is Coming played their first proper show.

The lack of support for musicians in an aggressively capitalist society is also one of the main reasons why so many of the UK's most successful musicians come from middle-class or upper-middle-class backgrounds. Although this wave of jazz has gone some way to changing that, it is nowhere near a level playing field, and even some of the best-known artists of this wave come from much posher backgrounds than they may want people to think.

'Teachers are under such insane pressure' (musical education)

In addition to support for venues and musicians themselves, musical education at an early stage is crucial in creating future generations of musicians. Learning to play a musical instrument to a high standard is expensive. You need an instrument, a teacher and a place to practice without disturbing the people you live with, none of which would be available to most children from working-class backgrounds without support in school and through the valiant work of organisations like Tomorrow's Warriors, Kinetika Bloco and similar groups across the country. Without the removal of this basic barrier to entry, debating the nuances of originality and tone is reminiscent of the 'great princess who, when told that the peasants had no bread, replied: "Then let them eat brioches."'[10]

For all the criticism faced by Blair and Brown's New Labour governments of 1997–2010 for endorsing market economics, lying to the British public about weapons of mass destruction and following the USA into wars in Iraq and Afghanistan, they provided a meaningful level of support for music education for the generation of musicians currently enjoying success. This support was attacked immediately by Cameron and Clegg's 2010 Conservative–Liberal Democrat coalition, which slashed public sector spending in the name of austerity, going even deeper in 2015 once the Conservatives were ruling without the (partial) check of the Liberal Democrats.

The 2011 National Plan for Music Education had announced that 'children from all backgrounds and every part of England should have the opportunity to learn a musical instrument; to make music with others; to learn to sing; and to have the opportunity to progress to the next level of excellence if they wish to'.[11] No problem with any of that in theory – but, in practice, it failed to deliver on these promises. By 2019, children from families with an annual income of under £28,000 were half as likely to learn an instrument as those from families with an annual income of more than £48,000.[12] Budget cuts, a change in emphasis from music teachers in schools to third-party 'music hubs' and a devolved curriculum meant that music provision in schools varied wildly depending on the priorities of individual head teachers. The total number of secondary school music teachers in the UK fell from 7,500 in 2010 to 6,500 in 2017.

The *Exchanging Notes* report summarised in 2019: 'It's a tough time for music in schools, with budget cuts, staff cuts, a devalued music curriculum and decreasing numbers of young people studying the subject. Music teachers work long hours, often in isolation while juggling many competing demands',[13] while noting that 97 per cent of young people surveyed had listened to music in the past week and wanted to learn more. In other words, musical provision was woefully inadequate relative to music's importance in people's lives.

The Musicians' Union's report was even more stark:

> The vast majority of instrumental teachers are self-employed with none of the benefits of employment and many of the disadvantages of a complex web of poorly designed and implemented contractual arrangements. New instrumental teachers are significantly disadvantaged and prone to exploitation. There is little, if any, substantive professional development for these teachers and existing opportunities have been haphazard in their design and implementation.[14]

There is a paradox in the fact that the music industry is one of very few in the tiny island nation of the UK that continues to exert a disproportionate global influence, but that it is no longer properly supported at early stages. As Matt Griffiths, CEO of Youth Music, wrote sadly in 2020, 'Children and young people will simply not benefit from a regular high-quality arts curriculum in their school without the teachers to deliver it . . . Music is one of the country's greatest international success stories both creatively and economically, but this must be backed up with ongoing support at the grass roots. The alternative is a "Global Britain" diminished as its music continues to be slowly silenced.'[15]

Nubya Garcia

A lot of these teachers are under such insane pressure. I never had a group lesson in my life until I got to university, or until I got to Warriors. I was on scholarships to help pay for those lessons. I learnt very quickly because I had forty-five minutes to an hour of multiple instrument lessons at school. And also, I went to a Saturday school, which happened to be at my secondary school. So I had viola lessons, piano lessons and saxophone lessons for a really long time. It changed so quickly in less than ten years. It was insane, and I realised then that most people didn't have access to instruments. I got funding to get my saxophone and funding to get a viola; it seemed that all this stuff that was available. What I saw in the Saturday school I taught at [recently] was just really heartbreaking because I'd be sent three kids at a time who would be completely at different levels. There's no joy for the music any more because all the kids know is, 'I have an exam and I need to do really well because I have to get into the school because my parents want me to. But I don't have an instrument that can come home with me.' And then in secondary school, kids were under so much pressure in exams that nobody cared about music. It was insane.

It is often said that some of the most creative music emerges at times of intense political turmoil, voicing frustration with conservative or repressive governments. Thus the creative outpouring in electronic music of the late 1980s and early 1990s is understood as a response to the Thatcher government of the late 1980s: ecstasy-driven communal oneness in a field or warehouse as a response to state-sanctioned individualism. Similarly, the outpouring of politicised creativity in the late 2010s can be read as a response to the many frustrations of ten years of Tory rule: austerity, Brexit, the Grenfell fire, the Windrush scandal, the hostile environment to immigration and the rise of ethnic nationalism.

But the social and political conditions at the time when the music is being made are only one part of the picture. The other part is the educational situation at the time when the musicians making the music were growing up, and this time lag must be considered. Many of the musicians and producers making music in the 1980s and early 1990s would have benefited from the support for creativity in Wilson and Callaghan's Labour governments of 1974–9. Most of the musicians using their music to rail against political injustice in the late 2010s had the benefit of better music provision in their formative years under New Labour. According to this theory, we should expect a lull in creativity if a progressive Labour government ever manages to dislodge the Conservatives: a lull caused not only by musicians' relative satisfaction with the status quo but by years of under-investment in musical education under the previous regime.

This is, of course, just a theory. Music and politics are so complicated and a controlled experiment so impossible that such neat mirroring must remain an enticing conjecture. Similarly, although playing jazz on saxophones, trumpets, trombones and tubas requires access to an instrument, tuition and a lot of practice, there are many forms of musical expression. It might well be that the outpouring of digital creativity in grime and dubstep of the 2000s was stimulated by a lack of access to instruments, and I would not begin to argue that in some absolute way those are less valid forms of expression than jazz. But what is beyond doubt is that musical education is currently under threat; it is vital that it is supported for new generations of instrumental musicians to come through.

unapologetic expression

'Always feeding your own momentum'

Individual creativity does not exist in a vacuum: external conditions must be right in order for a spark to turn into a fire. At the same time, a perfectly built bonfire without a spark to ignite it is just a pile of wood. For all the importance of material conditions, the ability of this and any generation of musicians to find authenticity through digging deep into themselves, in order to capture the spirit of the times, will be central to determining their true artistic impact.

This generation of artists now have established fan bases and substantial support both in the industry and the media; this puts them in perfect position to continue to grow and innovate. The extent to which they are able to do this will determine whether this moment becomes the jumping-off point for still greater creative successes and the increasing fortification of jazz's position as a vital, unapologetic expression of spiritual and political truths, or just another crest on an endless wave.

Jean Toussaint

This is the biggest wave since the Courtney [Pine] wave, definitely. And the musicians that are enjoying that wave at the moment, they need to pay attention. Because it's not going to last. That's guaranteed. In three, four, five years, it's not going to be like this. It'll be uncool again. And then it'll come back around and be cool again. So it's about sustaining your profession. Think about the long run. Think about being here for as long as you can be. That's what I would say to the younger musicians who are enjoying that interest at the moment: take care of that business in every aspect. Make sure that they own their work. Make sure that whatever they put out, they own it and [don't] give it up. Make sure they continue to develop their craft. It's an ongoing thing and it continuously changes, and you need to be adding new material to your understanding, opening your mind to new possibilities. It's an ever-growing and ever-changing art form. And you just gotta keep on it.

'because the end is really the beginning'

Orphy Robinson

They have to keep moving. Don't stand still, work on that stuff and just keep going, and don't sit around hoping that everybody gives you things, because if you do that, when the focus does shift again, which it will do – you'll be left there with nothing.

Gilles Peterson

A lot of it is timing. That's why a lot of these musicians who don't hit it first time around, I always say to them to just keep going. Go round and round and round, and then the timing will hit you and you'll be fine. It might take you five circuits to get round so that your timing's right. Someone like Kamasi is probably on his second or third circuit, doing what he's doing, putting out records. And then in connection with the right label and playing the right kind of music at the right time, with really good artwork and an idea and the way the world was, all those things together just hit!

Byron Wallen

It's important that you build for your own future, because there's going to be a moment where you're not flavour of the month any more. And that's going to come very soon. And then what's going to happen to you? You've got to be true to yourself. The most important thing is to be the best person and the best musician you can be in your time rather than a copy of someone before. You will always have people who you were influenced by, your mentors, people who have paved your way. It's your goal to take the baton and move it to the next level. And if you can produce music that is completely of the time that you're making and you're making a statement you want to make, then that statement will be valid going forward, it's not going to be dated because that time is cemented. I remember something that Evan Parker said to me recently, he said if you make sure that your own momentum is always pure and you make sure that you're always feeding your own momentum, then it's something that can then always get bigger into the world. Whereas if you lose that momentum . . . then you've got nothing. And the other thing is that this music business that we're involved in is not a sprint for the people who are genuine musicians. This is a marathon. So we have to pace ourselves and be able to sustain the momentum and sustain the passion.

Nick Lewis

My way of staying sane in this industry is just don't expect anything. Just do what you think's right. Don't expect anything or any praise or anything like that, just get on with it.

Poppy Ajudha

Your legacy will not come from what people say in the moment. It comes from the way you create over time and the way you release music and how it develops as a body of work throughout your life. I think you tend to inspire other people when you are unapologetically yourself because a lot of people don't know how to be themselves, haven't been allowed to be themselves or have experienced trauma that stops them from doing whatever they want to do. I made that my focus from last year, and for the first time going on stage, I wasn't nervous because now I'm just doing my thing, and I don't give a fuck. You either like it or you don't like it. And as a woman, it takes quite a while to get to that place where you're not worried what other people think all the time, because there's just so much external pressure that it's hard to not have those voices in your head. It's just so much peace. I can't even describe it. It's crazy how much your perspective and your headspace can change completely who you are and what you see for yourself and your future.

Kees Heus

You never know what happens to music when it goes into the universe. That's how Sun Ra always talked about these things. You can go two ways: you can conform to the market, but the chance that you'll blow up is small, because there is no magic potion. But you also can just follow your heart and see what happens.

Sheila Maurice-Grey

The whole point of being a creative is that you're supposed to be pushing things forward. The main aim is just to make music that we love. If you're making music, the best thing you can do is like, 'Look, I love that sound. I'm going to try and make something that sounds like that, I'm not going to completely imitate it. I want to put my own spin on it.' Then I think you've already done the job. Not being too precious about trying to be a purist. But you have to get the balance right.

Oscar Jerome

Continuing to support each other, because there's this power in numbers. To have the younger generation getting involved, and also just staying relevant, keeping your ears open and not being snobbish. I love loads of different styles that are coming out at the moment. Just trying to keep interested in other things, always having an outward looking perspective.

Oli Reeves

From a 22a perspective, it's always just been about expression. It's never been about trying to be the same as anything else. We don't feel like we're part of the scene that's around. We're out on our own, doing our own thing. We just wanna make and put out great records. That's all it's ever been for us. Social media, fashion shoots, chasing the fame, none of that ever appealed to us. The dream was always to make records. Music is always just about feeling and expression. It's not a commodity. The records that we're putting out: these are just things that us and our friends have made that we love. It's not really about making money or about getting coverage from this newspaper or support from that DJ. Once we put it out there, we're like, 'Right, it's gone out to the world now, now we can move on to the next thing.'

It's like a never-ending process we've got ourselves into that we can't break out of now. It's great!

Omar Lye-Fook

My thing is just to be current at all times, and the way I think of that is not by following any trends. Because we're still listening to Marvin, we're still listening to James, we're still listening to Donny, you know what I mean? I just want to create music that people will still want to listen to years down the line. And I seem to have done that, because I get all different generations. It started off with, 'My sister likes your music.' Then it's, 'My mum likes your music.' Now it's, 'My nan likes your music,' because that's the age bracket that I'm in. But I had an eighteen-year-old girl come up to me the other day, and she showed me that she was actually playing one of my tunes on her phone. So I know I've managed to cross the generations. I think I've managed to set up a legacy that people can just enjoy. I just hope I've made little capsules of time that transport people back to certain parts of their life. And good parts. I don't start off thinking, 'This is the chart I want to get in.' I just come out with a groove. I don't really care about where it's going. I just want to come up with something that's going to be catchy, vibey. Something that people can dance to, bounce up and down to, sing to, all that kind of stuff. That's what I'm thinking about.

Steve Williamson

A jazz musician can play 'Mary had a Little Lamb' in about fifty different ways because of their musical understanding. They have a really broad sense of how music should be played and what you can do with tones, what you can do with chords and colours and it's amazing. Essentially what it's about is just translating what you do to other people. That's basically what I'm working on. That's the reason why I live, I swear to God, is to improve, improve, improve. Endlessly. Then by the time you're seventy or eighty you're just like . . . Jesus Christ! Me and Courtney Pine used to have conversations back in the days man, in the eighties, and we'd speak for hours on the phone. And I'd say to him, 'Man, God, imagine how we're gonna sound when we're forty.' I've always been fascinated by that, like if you just keep doing the same thing, how you gonna sound in ten years from now. And, really, wait till you hear this shit that I'm writing now.

Shirley Tetteh

For things to survive, they have to shift and change somehow, for the music to keep evolving. As long as a musician stays committed to their growth there's no such thing as them not being relevant.

Jason Yarde

Maybe if I was born and bred in New Orleans my opinion would be different, but for me, the whole thing with jazz, arguably more than other areas of music, it's been about self-expression and finding your own voice, and channelling that. I wouldn't even pretend for a minute I'm going to better what Charlie Parker did or John Coltrane or any number of people you could name. So then why am I pursuing this music? Why am I even trying to say something in this field? Well, it must be because I feel there's space for me to be creative and communicate with people in a way that they might like. And with the younger generation now, because they have more access points to the music, it's not being filtered so much through things like *The Fast Show*, all these negative kind of things; they're finding their own way to it. And ultimately finding it's valid. And it's something they can get into and use for their expression.

Femi Koleoso

The way to make sure the thing comes forward is stripping your ego out and making sure your mind is focused on the bigger picture. Jazz is bigger than Ezra Collective, music is bigger than Femi, the drums is bigger than me. The future is more important than my present. It's all about how do I translate the greatness that I inherited from Tomorrow's

Warriors, from uni, from school, from everything, how do I put that into people younger than me so that they put that into people younger than them? That's what a legacy is.

When I did Roundhouse with the Ezra Collective last year, I walked out and I saw a bunch of teenagers. And that gave me hope for the future. Because hipsters are fickle, man, when the next pair of shoes come out, they're all there: the other ones are getting thrown away.

Moses Boyd

The other side of this renaissance is musicianship has become cool again. It's not stopping with us, if people are picking up an instrument now in secondary school, in five years' time, I'm going to be interested to see what happens. I want to know and I want to be a part of it, as much as I still want to track down Wynton or Steve Coleman, I'm like, nah nah nah, what is on the ground is really interesting and really fruitful at the moment.

Matthew Halsall

My experience in jazz is, you take your chances when they come. It might not happen for another twenty years, or it might never happen. I certainly couldn't say to any of those young London artists, be careful and don't take opportunities, because they might wait ten, fifteen years and nothing happens.

Bradley Zero

Any movement comes with a certain cohort of people coming through and lifting each other up. Time will tell who continues around to the next circle. Who's gonna be the elders of the scene in twenty, thirty years from now, talking about the good old days when the kids knew what jazz was? Obviously not everyone's going to make it through. But time is also a great filter. And the people who speak the most truth and connect most intimately with their audience will continue to have one.

'because the end is really the beginning'

Dave Okumu

There's a phrase that I coined for myself in trying to understand what I really identify with musically. It's a sort of 'studied liberation'. So a lot of the music that I feel undoubtedly will last for ever and has changed my life comes from people who are really, really connected to their heritage and who have studied that heritage deeply. But they find liberation in that, they're not confined by that. They haven't been institutionalised by that knowledge; it's actually been their route to freedom. That's something that really inspires me about what I understand to be true jazz. Just when I thought I had a grasp of what that was about, someone would show me something else. And that's what keeps me going. I still have that feeling now.

Binker Golding

At the core of any good art, when you strip all the periphery away, is the meaning of existence. I personally think the job of the artist is to give the listener a higher perception of what it means to exist. It's the same if you're watching an Ingmar Bergman film or you're listening to some shit by Coltrane or you're looking at a painting by Mark Rothko. There's at least one archetypal element across all of those things. And that's why people keep coming back to them. Because they give human beings a higher perception of what it actually means to exist. That's what I'm interested in. The periphery, people are going to make up whatever myths about me or about Kamasi or about Moses that they want. I don't give a shit about any of that, man. As long as the record sells and some people are moved by it.

Hans Koller

My advice to the kids now is just be smart and don't say yes to everything. It's good to be set up for lifelong learning, because there's gonna be hard times. Try to be yourself, but to be yourself, you've got to really look inward as well as outwards, and learn who you are.

unapologetic expression

So you try to learn all the history of this thing, because jazz is an established art form. You're not going to reinvent the wheel; you've got to learn what's there before you could attempt to make anything new out of it. Not to copy it, but to try to see yourself in it and develop yourself out of it and see how you want to do it in your own way, in your own voice, in your own experience. That's what I try to impart on my students. And it's great what they're doing, because they're doing it in their own voice. We don't go out and play like Parker, but we can study it. You must do your own thing. You can't go out and play bebop verbatim. You can't because you are not Charlie Parker. At the same time, you have to understand that because otherwise it's very naive. You have to know the field you're operating in but you must not become that person. You must become you.

Seb Rochford

I just feel excited for that generation because they're still young, the best is yet to come. All this hype: they deserve it, it wasn't fabricated, it came up because they started their own nights, and they were packed! Their music is coming from a true place, and that's what will carry it. All these people writing about them or sharing the music, it's because of what they've done, they're not just plucking it out of the air and trying to present it as something that it's not. That's what it is and people love it.

Gary Crosby

This music is the future of the human race. This is the folk music for the future. This is the equivalent of urban folk music. This is our music. And deep down, me and Janine believe that art is the only thing that's going to change the human race. No amount of me talking politics or advice to young people is going to help. It's individual advice and help that possibly have nothing to do with changing the world but change you, the individual. Aside from that, it's pure love that we've given out, that's been coming back.

'because the end is really the beginning'

Nikki Yeoh

Always stay true to the music. Don't believe the hype. Be confident but open. And treat people nicely.

Wozzy Brewster

Evolve with their music and make the music that they love, music that people love survives all time, doesn't it? Don't even try to be trendy. Just do the music that you love. Believe me. And I don't think that the bubble has burst because I think it's just it finally has come to rise.

Courtney Pine

One of the things about playing jazz is that you have to stand on the shoulders of giants. Jazz is from the community, showing a legacy that comes before you. I think the worstest thing would be if there were no young artists out there right now, no evolution. That would have showed me that what I was doing then was a waste of time. But what's happened now is proof positive. I talk about roots and being a part of a chain; it's just one of those things where the music is more powerful than the individual and it's proved itself. And that's what I'd like to let be known. It's not about just one person. It's actually about the music called jazz and what it does. It's supposed to give birth to the next level. Next generation. The next chapter.

Afterword

Most of the interviews in this book were conducted in 2020 and 2021, with the bulk of the writing completed by April 2022. That time already feels a very long way away. This book is an exploration of a particular period in UK jazz, politics and postcolonial history; a handful of snapshots of a few episodes of a much longer series. The vitality of the scene itself and the rapid pace of events in our hyper-active, interconnected world mean that at whatever time in the future you read this, you will have access to knowledge that I do not, and this will inevitably shape and colour your interpretation of what you read here.

I am reminded of Blake's axiom in the suitably titled 'Eternity': 'He who binds to himself a joy / Does the winged life destroy: / But he who kisses the joy as it flies / Lives in eternity's sun rise.' Or as Cleveland Watkiss so succinctly put it (p. 18): 'being able to flow in the moment and let that moment be what it is. Let it be what it is and then let it go: "That's what it was. But this is what it is now."'

Nevertheless, the long gap between research, writing and publication presents me with an opportunity to close with some comments on recent events, both in jazz and outside.

* * *

In the few months since the submission of the final draft of this book, Ezra Collective have won the Mercury Prize, just recognition of their talent and hard work and a significant mainstream validation of the scene as a whole. Yussef Dayes has sold out the Royal Albert Hall in promotion of his long-awaited debut solo album *Black Classical Music*, and many of the artists interviewed in this book are now signed to major labels, just as their Jazz Warriors predecessors were before.

It would be wrong, though, to interpret this simply as 'the great ones [separating] themselves from the pack', as Claudio Lillo predicted (p. 345). Artists have remained conscious, cautious and connected, achieving ever greater growth without forgetting where they came from or turning their backs on their early enablers.

Despite now being an international headline artist, Nubya Garcia found time to perform at the Royal Festival Hall in September 2023 not alongside the next young hype artist but with Gary Crosby's Nu Civilisation Orchestra (packed full of Tomorrow's Warriors alumni), playing the 1962 Stan Getz masterwork *Focus* – not exactly a sell-out choice.

In recognition of Brownswood's importance, Yussef's album was released as a joint venture with Warner subsidiary Nonesuch Records, founded by none other than legendary executive producer Jac Holzman, the man who signed The Doors to Elektra Records.

And Shabaka Hutchings' commitment to furthering his own creativity and remaining fresh is so great that he publicly announced he would give up 'the big metal horn' after a final tour with The Comet Is Coming and Sons of Kemet, explaining: 'The safe option would be to just do less gigs on the sax and not take the extreme option of ending my association with it . . . Unfortunately I'm not that guy . . . I'm deeply grateful to be able to channel energy from a source that resides outside myself while undertaking the ceremony of ritual performance. I take my role in being a custodian of energy that rouses the spirit seriously and when called to make a sacrifice for an artistic purpose that I sense deep in my intuited mind's eye I choose to follow with humility and gratitude to a higher power.'[1]

* * *

afterword

Steam Down is back up and running weekly again, now on a Wednesday at Deptford's Matchstick Piehouse, keeping the vibes high and inclusive; Tomorrow's Warriors consistently nurture the next generation of players, with the success of their alumni only enhancing their mandate; Church of Sound continues to provide a platform for ever more creative shows.

Jazz Re:freshed are back running weekly sessions, now at the new Ninety One Living Room in East London (formerly the Vibe Bar, for anyone who remembers that far back), continuing to showcase the scene internationally in partnership with British Underground. The organisation is not just about musical development but creating a truly supportive community: when Jason Yarde had a severe stroke while on stage in France in October 2022, Jazz Re:freshed immediately stepped up, organising a GoFundMe page which raised almost £70,000, and counting, towards his rehabilitation journey.

* * *

Meanwhile, the world outside jazz is scary and getting scarier by the day. Vladimir Putin's colonial war in Ukraine has raged for nearly two years, with approximately ten thousand civilian deaths,[2] as Russia seeks once again to annex long-disputed territory. This aggression has disrupted the lives not only of Ukrainians but of hundreds of thousands of Russians, especially on the political left, who no longer feel able to remain in their own country.

Hamas terror attacks on a music festival, kibbutzim and towns inside Israel on 7 October 2023 killed an estimated fourteen hundred people, many of them in extremely brutal ways, causing existential horror for many Israelis and creating further division in Israel's already divided society. Israel's fierce retaliation has killed a reported eleven thousand Palestinian civilians, many of whom are said to be children.[3] The region looks utterly unstable, with fears of a full-fledged regional and ultimately global conflict should Hezbollah and Iran join

afterword

the fray. Discourse seems once again to be terrifyingly polarised, with many on the UK left casting Palestinians as 'indigenous' resisters against colonial oppression and Israel as a 'false state' operating as a vehicle of Western colonial powers, with its own illegal settlements in the West Bank reinforcing this image. Israeli officials are adding fuel to this fire, with Defence Minister Yoav Gallant describing Hamas as 'human animals'. As usual, the real winners are arms dealers, aerospace industries and mercenaries,[4] with civilians on both sides experiencing huge suffering.

The lack of a clear solution that will be satisfactory to both sides and their various constellations of international supporters – a solution that recognises the needs of both Palestinians and Israelis for statehood, autonomy and, above all, safety – has left many people in despair. We appear to have entered Stuart Hall's prophesied condition of 'permanent revolution':[5] crisis upon crisis upon crisis, all amplified by the ever-increasing roar of social media.

* * *

Why do I feel the need to mention these recent global events in the afterword to a book about the socio-cultural context of a particular moment in UK jazz?

Partly it is because they are on my mind – how could they not be? And yet it feels as though there is a powerful connection between the music and the circumstances we find ourselves in. It is not only that the music still known as jazz can provide respite and solace at the darkest of times, in solitary listening and in group communion, hearing musicians live; it is also that the forces which have shaped the music since its origin and continue to shape it are fundamentally the same forces that are shaping the conflicts. Jazz is the incidental product of geopolitical conflicts and movements of people, and an attempt to respond to these wider forces.

At its best, the process of the music's creation can be an example of collaboration in its truest form: collaboration between musicians on stage, between musicians and the audience, between the music and the city, between the city and its time. This reconciliation of disparate musical and cultural elements can, in its small way, not only respond to world events but give us the tiniest glimpse of a route through the madness.

André Marmot,
November 2023

Notes

Introduction

1 From the festival's own website, xthetracks.com.

2 Francesca Babb, 'How Jazz Got Cool — and the Names You Need on Your Playlist', *Sunday Times*, 20 Oct. 2019.

3 Niloufar Haidari, 'Introducing: The Nu Jazz Lad', *Vice*, 25 Jan. 2019.

4 A 1992 survey found that 74 per cent of rap sold in the first six months of that year was bought by whites (Clarence Lusane, 'Rap, Race and Politics', *Race and Class* 35:1, July 1993).

5 Michael Cragg, 'Craig David: "Bo' Selecta! was a blessing in disguise"', *Guardian*, 31 Aug. 2019.

6 This event first came on my radar thanks to Dave Randall's *Sound System: The Political Power of Music* (Pluto Press, 2017), but most of the details come from the short films cited below.

7 A lot more could, and has, been said about the origins of disco but space forbids me going further here. I would highly recommend Bill Brewster and Frank Broughton's *Last Night a DJ Saved My Life* (White Rabbit, 2022) for a general overview of disco's origins and role as the cornerstone of subsequent dance music genres. The *Saturday Night Fever* soundtrack sold 16 million units, made up primarily of new songs by Australian-born, UK-raised white band The Bee Gees, who went on become the sixth biggest-selling band of all time, shifting a mind-boggling 120 million records worldwide.

8 'Disco Demolition: From Riot to Rebirth', ep. 4 of *The Note*, Red Bull Music Academy (2016), youtube.com/watch?v=AiDYGlSJY1E.

9 Nat Shapiro and Nat Hentoff (eds), *Hear Me Talkin' to Ya: The Story of Jazz As Told by the Men Who Made It* (Dover, 1966); Arthur Taylor, *Notes and Tones: Musician-to-Musician Interviews* (Da Capo Press, 1993). Other books that have been especially helpful have been Mark Cotgrove (Snowboy), *From Jazz Funk and Fusion to Acid Jazz* (AuthorHouse, 2009),

Brian Belle-Fortune, *All Crews: Journeys Through Jungle/Drum and Bass Culture* (Vision, 2005) and Joe Muggs and Brian David Stevens, *Bass, Mids, Tops: An Oral History of Soundsystem Culture* (Strange Attractor Press, 2019).

10 One tragic exception to this was London Jazz Festival co-founder and former Serious director John Cumming, who was in hospital having treatment for cancer and asked for questions so that he could think about them in advance in order to maximise his energy in the interview. Sadly, he died a few days before our scheduled interview.

11 Not everyone took this chance, of course, but many did.

12 The London metropolitan area is much larger than the traditional M25, including the commutable towns of the Home Counties; its population is 14.8 million, after Moscow (17.3 million) and Istanbul (16 million). That's 3.4 million more than Paris and more than double the size of the next two, Madrid and Milan, with 6.55 and 6.2 million respectively (Thomas Brinkhoff, 'Major Agglomerations of the World', citypopulation. de/en/world/agglomerations).

1 'Rye Lane Shuffle'

1 Voter turnout did not fall below 70 per cent between 1922 and 1997; in the 2001 general election, four years into New Labour's rule, it plummeted to 59.4 per cent, the lowest since 1918. It did not pass 70 per cent again until the Brexit referendum of 2015, at which 72.2 per cent voted. Although voter turnout in the 2017 and 2019 general elections was higher than the previous four (68.8 per cent and 67.3 per cent), it was still lower than 1997 (71.4 per cent). (D. Clark, 'Voter Turnout in UK Elections 1918–2019, Statista, 22 June 2022, statista.com/statistics/1050929/voter-turnout-in-the-uk.)

2 Joseph E. Stiglitz, 'Of the 1%, by the 1%, for the 1%', *Vanity Fair*, 31 March 2011.

3 For an overview, see Gudrun Getz, 'Passing Clouds Made Dalston Culturally Rich . . .', *Independent*, 16 Sept. 2016. Running my Wormfood nights there from January 2007 (before it even had a licence) until it closed, I was privileged to witness the growth of a creative community up close, while also witnessing the terrifying life cycle of accelerated gentrification.

4 See (and buy) discography here: jazzrefreshed.bandcamp.com.

5 'The Steve Reid Foundation', accessed 4 Jan. 2022, stevereidfoundation.org.uk.

6 Anushree Majumdar, 'Meet the British-Chinese Muslim Man from South London Reinventing Jazz', *Indian Express*, 9 Dec. 2018.

2 'You Can't Steal My Joy'

1 American Dialect Society, '1999 Words of the Year, Word of the 1990s, Word of the 20th Century, Word of the Millennium', 13 Jan. 2000, americandialect.org/1999_words_of_the_year_word_of_the_1990s_word_of_the_20th_century.

2 Nina Simone once said, 'To most white people, jazz means black and jazz means dirt and that's not what I play. I play black classical music. That's why I don't like the term "jazz", and Duke Ellington didn't either – it's a term that's simply used to identify black people.' (In Brantley Bardin, 'Simone Says', *Details*, Jan. 1997.)

3 David Finkel, 'Genius at Work in Struggle', *Against the Current*, 144, Jan.–Feb. 2010, againstthecurrent.org/atc144/p2617.

4 The term 'Ebonics' was coined by African American psychologist Robert Williams in 1973 to claim ownership of the various forms of African American speech, privileging them as positive forms of expression as opposed to the deficiency suggested by then-current terms such as 'nonstandard Negro English'. It is likely that the roots of Ebonics lie in slavery, both in its importation of elements of syntax and vocabulary from African languages and in the need to create and maintain a private language that could not easily be understood by plantation overseers.

5 See Norman Mailer's famous essay 'The White Negro: Superficial Reflections on the Hipster' (*Dissent* magazine, New York, 1957).

6 Milton 'Mezz' Mezzrow and Bernard Wolfe, *Really the Blues* (Random House, 1946), p. 235.

7 Francis Newton (Eric Hobsbawm), *The Jazz Scene* (Penguin, 1959), p. 210.

8 LeRoi Jones (Amiri Baraka), *Blues People* (Harper Perennial, 1963, repr. 2002), p. 213.

9 Interestingly, their use of the word 'Original' in the title also linked them with the tradition of blackface minstrelsy. According to Strausbaugh: 'Borrowing or outright theft of another performer's work was considered fair, as long as you got away with it. You might see an act you liked in Buffalo, and next week copy it in Philadelphia – adding, of course, that

your version was "the original". In the post-Civil War years, there were dozens of travelling minstrel shows whose names began with the words "The Original".' John Strausbaugh, *Black Like You: Blackface, Whiteface, Insult and Imitation in American Popular Culture* (Tarcher/Penguin, 2007), p. 69.

10 Mezzrow and Wolfe, pp. 161–2.

11 Quoted in George McKay, *Circular Breathing: The Cultural Politics of Jazz in Britain* (Duke University Press, 2005), p. 315 n. 17.

12 Marshall W. Stearns, *The Story of Jazz* (Oxford University Press, 1956), p. 72.

13 Stearns, p. 158.

14 This is the reason given by William Russell and Stephen W. Smith in *Jazzmen*, ed. Frederic Ramsay, Jr, and Charles Edward Smith (Harcourt, Brace and Co., 1939), p. 22.

15 Stearns, p. 161.

16 Stearns, pp. 308, 320.

17 A reference to the docile old slave in Harriet Beecher Stowe's 1852 novel *Uncle Tom's Cabin*.

18 The 2015 film *Born to Be Blue* portrays the failure of Baker (Ethan Hawke) to win Miles Davis's respect as one of the principle reasons for him becoming addicted to heroin.

19 By (white) critic John Mehegan.

20 Valerie Wilmer, *As Serious As Your Life: Black Music and the Free Jazz Revolution, 1957–1977* (Serpent's Tale, 2018), p. 2.

21 'Stranger on the Shore', ep. 1 of *Jazz Britannia* (dir. Mike Connolly, 2005).

22 Billy Bragg, *Roots, Radicals and Rockers: How Skiffle Changed the World* (Faber, 2017), p. 388.

23 Bragg, pp. 388–91.

24 Alison Rapp, 'When Eric Clapton's Bigoted 1976 Rant Sparked Rock Against Racism', *Ultimate Classic Rock*, 5 Aug. 2021.

25 As the founders of Rock Against Racism wrote in an open letter to *NME*: 'Who shot the Sheriff, Eric? It sure as hell wasn't you, mate!' See the documentary *White Riot* (Smoking Bear Productions, 2020) for more on this movement and the racial context around it.

26 Jessica Lee, 'Did David Bowie Say He Supports Fascism and Call Hitler a "Rock Star"?', Snopes, 23 Dec. 2020, snopes.com/fact-check/rock-star-david-bowie.

27 DJ Rob, 'A History of Black-Owned Record Labels: Part II', 21 Feb. 2015, djrobblog.com/archives/105; Gerald Early, 'Motown', *Encyclopaedia Britannica*, 19 May 2023.

28 Dave Gelly, *Stan Getz: Nobody Else But Me* (Backbeat, 2002), p. 44.

3 'Movementt'

1 John Dankworth, *Jazz in Revolution* (Constable, 1998), p. 209.

2 The Institute of Jazz Studies was the first of its kind in the world, originally simply his private collection, housed in his Greenwich Village apartment and opened to researchers once a week, but moved to dedicated premises in Rutgers University in Newark in 1967. (Rutgers University Libraries, 'History of IJS', libraries.rutgers.edu/newark/visit-study/institute-jazz-studies/about-ijs/history-ijs.)

3 Elizabeth Fussell, 'Constructing New Orleans, Constructing Race: A Population History of New Orleans', *Journal of American History*, 94 (Dec. 2007), 846–55.

4 See C. L. R. James, *The Black Jacobins: Toussant l'Ouverture and the San Domingo Revolution* (Vintage, 1963), for a detailed analysis of this remarkable moment in global history. Needless to say, like Castro's Cuba and Chavez's Venezuela, Haiti paid dearly for its resistance to imperialism in the Caribbean, and this is one of the reasons why Haiti remains the poorest country in the Western hemisphere and one of the poorest countries in the world, with 59 per cent of its population living below the poverty line. ('IFRC Country Acceleration Plan 2019 – Haiti', 28 Feb. 2019, reliefweb.int/report/haiti/ifrc-country-acceleration-plan-2019-haiti.)

5 United States Census Bureau, 'Table 4. Population of the 46 Urban Places: 1810', internet release date: 15 June 1998, www2.census.gov/library/working-papers/1998/demo/pop-twps0027/tab04.txt; Robert K. Whelan and Alma H. Young, 'New Orleans: The Ambivalent City', in *Big City Politics in Transition*, ed. H. V. Savitch and John Clayton Thomas (Sage, 1991), p. 133.

6 A July 2022 estimate put 'Black or African American alone' at 58.1 per cent, with a further 4.1 per cent for 'Two or More Races' (United States Census Bureau, QuickFacts: New Orleans City, Louisiana, 1 July 2022', census.gov/quickfacts/neworleanscitylouisiana).

7 Marshall W. Stearns, *The Story of Jazz* (Oxford University Press, 1956), p. 42.

8   Stuart Nicholson, *Jazz and Culture in a Global Age* (Northeastern University Press, 2014), p. 75.

9   Nicholson, p. 77.

10 Chris Searle, *Forward Groove: Jazz and the Real World from Louis Armstrong to Gilad Atzmon* (Northway, 2008), p. 108.

11 John Dankworth, quoted in Nicholson, p. 56.

12 Nicholson, p. 87.

13 Kehinde Andrews, *Back to Black: Black Radicalism for the 21st Century* (Zed Books, 2019), p. 27.

14 David Owen, 'African Migration to the UK', University of Warwick, warwick.ac.uk/fac/soc/crer/events/african/abstract_david_owen.doc.

4 'London Town'

1   Jon Stratton and Nabeel Zuberi (eds), *Black Popular Music in Britain since 1945*, (Routledge, 2016), p. 43.

2   Louis Aragon, quoted in Merlin Coverley, *Psychogeography* (Oldcastle Books, 2018), p. 95.

3   Robert Elms, *London Made Us: A Memoir of a Shape-Shifting City* (Canongate, 2019), p. 22.

4   Marshall W. Stearns, *The Story of Jazz* (Oxford University Press, 1956), p. 23.

5   The phrase was coined by compiler Joe Muggs on his 2013 compilation album for Big Dada, *Grime 2.0*. As he explained to *Dummy Magazine*, 'People have realised that grime is not just another trend . . . It is now a settled part of the UK – and global – music ecosystem. But it's also grown up, its leaders are a bit older and more settled' ('Grime 2.0: Track By Track', *Dummy Magazine*, 1 May 2013).

6   A slight misquote of Skepta's 'Intensive Snare'.

7   See Frank Tenaille, *Music Is the Weapon of the Future: Fifty Years of African Popular Music* (Lawrence Hill Books, 2002), pp. 211–12.

8   As claimed on the Project's own Facebook page.

9   See Joe Muggs and Brian David Stevens, *Bass, Mids, Tops: An Oral History of Soundsystem Culture* (Strange Attractor Press, 2019) for a great interview with Lockhart, and for more on Plastic People see Tom Lea and Mr Beatnick, 'An Oral History of Plastic People', *Fact*, 17 Feb. 2015.

10 Joe Zadeh, 'The Evolution of Flying Lotus', *Vice*, 26 Sept. 2014.

11 Evan Minsker, 'Flying Lotus', *Pitchfork*, 10 Sept. 2014, pitchfork.com/features/update/9500-flying-lotus.

12 Dan Hancox, 'Wiley: The Enigmatic Godfather of Grime', *Guardian*, 24 Jan. 2017.

13 Julian Mitchell, 'Kendrick Lamar's "To Pimp a Butterfly" Proves a Challenging Narrative Is More than Profitable', *Forbes*, 26 Mar. 2015.

14 David La Rosa, 'Jazz Has become the Least-Popular Genre in the US', *Jazz Line News*, 9 Mar. 2015, news.jazzline.com/news/jazz-least-popular-music-genre.

15 Jessie L. Morris, 'Here Are the 10 Best-Selling Albums of 2015', *Complex*, 6 Jan. 2016; Rob Copsey, 'The Official Top Forty Biggest Artist Albums of 2015 revealed', Official UK Charts Company, 5 Jan. 2016, officialcharts.com/chart-news/the-official-top-40-biggest-artist-albums-of-2015-revealed__13273.

16 Kanye featured UK grime stars Skepta and Stormzy in his Brit Awards performance in 2015; Drake featured Skepta at his performances at Wireless 2015 and his own OVO festival in Toronto, both featured on the remix of Wizkid's 'Ojuelegba' and Drake even got BBK, the acronym of Skepta and Jme's label Boy Better Know, tattooed on his arm in 2015. (See, e.g., Aimee Cliff, 'A Brief History Of Drake's Relationship With Boy Better Know', *Fader*, 25 Feb. 2016.)

5 'In Reference to Our Forefathers Fathers Dreams'

1 Kevin Searle, 'Before Notting Hill: Causeway Green and Britain's Anti-Black Hostel Riots', blog, National Archives, 22 June 2020. nationalarchives.gov.uk/before-notting-hill-causeway-green-and-britains-anti-black-hostel-riots; Averill Earls, 'The Windrush Generation and the Mystique of British Anti-Racism', *Dig: A History Podcast*, 6 March 2022, digpodcast.org/2022/03/06/windrush-generation.

2 i.e. 200,000 more unmarried women of reproductive age than men available to impregnate them. Facts, figures and much of the insight in this section come from Ian Sanjay Patel's *We're Here Because You Were There* (Verso, 2021), which takes Sivanandan's aphorism as the schematic for a radical unpicking of the contradictions and hypocrisies with which Britain's postcolonial history is riddled.

3 See, e.g., Marshall W. Stearns, *The Story of Jazz* (Oxford University Press, 1956), pp. 57–63.

4 Francis Davis, 'The Right Stuff', from *Jazz and Its Discontents: A Francis Davis Reader* (Da Capo Press, 2004), p. 210.

5 Quoted in Davis, pp. 210–11.

6 Clinton visited the Kinetika Bloco summer school in 2015 and was visibly moved as the hundred-strong group of teenagers bashed out a rowdy version of Funkadelic's 'One Nation Under a Groove'. ('George Clinton Meets Kinetika Bloco – 2015', YouTube, youtube.com/watch?v=wtUu_EKLpzw.)

7 Information on UK jazz courses provided by Simon Purcell, and these universities' own prospectuses.

6 Letting Go

1 Mark J. Perry, 'Recorded Music Sales by Format 1973–2015, and What that Might Tell Us about the Limitations of GDP Accounting', AIEdeas, 15 Sept. 2016, aei.org/carpe-diem/annual-recorded-music-sales-by-format-from-1973-2015-and-what-that-tells-us-about-the-limitations-of-gdp-accounting. These are US figures; I was unable to find UK-specific figures but we can assume the pattern was widely replicated.

2 Nick Routley, 'Visualizing 40 Years of Music Industry Sales', *Visual Capitalist*, 6 Oct. 2018.

3 Felix Richter, 'Streaming Drives Global Music Industry Resurgence', Statista, 24 March 2023, statista.com/chart/4713/global-recorded-music-industry-revenues.

4 'IFPI Global Music Report: Global Recorded Music Revenues Grew 18.5% In 2021', IFPI press release, 22 March 2022, ifpi.org/ifpi-global-music-report-global-recorded-music-revenues-grew-18-5-in-2021.

5 Chris Cooke, 'US Recorded Music Market Grew 23% in 2021', *CMU*, 10 March 2022.

6 Tim Ingham, 'Spotify Dreams of Artists Making a Living. It Probably Won't Come True', *Rolling Stone*, 3 Aug. 2020.

7 Ingham.

8 Manfred Eicher, German record producer and founder of ECM Records.

9 Routley.

10 This figure, of course, does not include streaming, as this is not technically an 'album sale'. Will Richards, 'Vinyl Record Sales in 2021 at Highest Level for Thirty Years', *NME*, 29 Dec. 2021.

11 US vinyl sales, for example, reached 41.72 million LPs in 2021, compared with 530 million LPs per year at the format's peak in 1973. (See Lazlo Rugoff, 'US Vinyl Sales Reach Thirty-year High in 2021', Vinyl Factory,

14 Jan. 2022, thevinylfactory.com/news/us-vinyl-sales-2021-reach-thirty-year-high and Zachary Crockett, 'The Insane Resurgence of Vinyl Records', *The Hustle*, 4 Dec. 2021.)

12 Damian Jones, 'Gen Z Buy More Vinyl than Millennials, New Study Finds', *NME*, 16 Sept. 2021.

13 Daniel Sanchez, 'AWAL Signs Global Physical Distribution Agreement with Proper Music Group', *Digital Music News*, 5 June 2019.

14 The style of UK garage's heyday has been documented in numerous photo books and exhibitions including Ewen Spencer's *Brandy & Coke* photo-book and documentary (vimeo.com/94165736).

15 Kashif Naveed, Chihiro Watanabe and Pekka Neittaanmäki, 'Co-evolution between Streaming and Live Music Leads a Way to the Sustainable Growth of Music Industry: Lessons from the US Experiences', *Technology in Society*, 50, Aug. 2017, pp. 1–19.

16 Martijn Mulder, Erik Hitters and Paul Rutten, 'The Impact of Festivalization on the Dutch Live Music Action Field: A Thematic Analysis', *Creative Industries Journal*, 14:3, 2021, pp. 245–68.

17 Blake Morgan, 'NOwnership, No Problem: An Updated Look At Why Millennials Value Experiences Over Owning Things', *Forbes*, 2 Jan. 2019.

18 Reproduced by kind permission of the poet. Check him out: jonnyfluffypunk.co.uk.

19 Janice Warman, 'How Music Festivals Are Singing the Changes', *Guardian*, 27 Aug. 2010; House of Commons Digital, Culture, Media and Sport Committee, *The Future of UK Music Festivals: First Report of Session 2021–2022*, May 2021; Conor Hourihan, 'Why Festivals are More Popular than Ever', Gallowglass, 21 Feb. 2020, gallowglass.com/our-blog/festival-crewing/why-festivals-are-more-popular-than-ever.

20 'David Cameron at Wilderness: A Good Reason to Give Up Festivals', *Guardian*, 7 Aug. 2017.

7 'Free My Skin'

1 Jia Tolentino, *Trick Mirror: Reflections on Self-Delusion* (Fourth Estate, 2019), p. 163.

2 Simon Kemp, 'Digital 2022: Another Year of Bumper Growth', We Are Social, 26 Jan. 2022, wearesocial.com/uk/blog/2022/01/digital-2022-another-year-of-bumper-growth-2.

3 An average of two hours twenty-seven minutes *per day*. (Dave Chaffey,

'Global Social Media Statistics Research Summary 2023', Smart Insights, 11 May 2023, smartinsights.com/social-media-marketing/social-media-strategy/new-global-social-media-research.)

4 Nick Srnicek, *Platform Capitalism* (Polity, 2017), p. 53.

5 Srnicek, p. 101.

6 Tolentino, pp. 173–4.

7 Srnicek, p. 45.

8 My calculations from figures in Chaffey: 4.62 billion social media users worldwide multiplied by two hours and twenty-seven minutes' average time on social media per user per day: 11.319 billion hours per day on social media.

9 See, e.g., Caroline Miller, 'Does Social Media Use Cause Depression?', Child Mind Institute, 27 April 2023, childmind.org/article/is-social-media-use-causing-depression, which provides links to studies on this subject, and Josh Barrie, 'Suicide Rate Almost Doubles among Teenagers, as Social Media Giants Are Told They Have a "Duty of Care" to Tackle It', *i*, 3 Feb. 2019, which discusses social media's role in teen suicide nearly doubling between 2011 and 2019. Instagram and Pinterest were required to take part in legal proceedings after the death of fourteen-year-old Molly Russell in 2017 was closely linked to self-harm content she had seen online, and a 2022 report by British media regulator Ofcom concluded that one-third of online children aged between eight and fifteen have seen worrying or upsetting content online in the past twelve months. (Morgan Meaker, 'How A British Teen's Death Changed Social Media', *Wired*, 5 Oct. 2022.)

10 'Number of blogs worldwide from 2006 to 2011', Statista, 12 March 2012, www.statista.com/statistics/278527/number-of-blogs-worldwide.

11 Sean Michaels, 'Google Shuts Down Music Blogs Without Warning', *Guardian*, 11 Feb. 2010.

12 Lu Makoboka, 'Should Artists Give a F* * * About Music Blogs? Their Importance in 2021 Explained', *Stereofox*, June 2021.

13 Lorna Gangel, 'NTS Radio Founder Femi Adeyemi Can Be the Next John Peel – if He Wants To', *Hackney Gazette*, 31 Oct. 2013.

14 Josh Jones, 'Femi Adeyemi: Founder, NTS Radio, London', WeGotTickets INDIE50, Sept. 2016, indie50.wordpress.com/portfolio/femi-adeymi-founder-nts-radio.

15 *I-D* team and Francesca Dunn, 'Building a Music Empire with Boiler Room's Blaise and Sofie', *i-D*, 12 Feb. 2015.

16 There are of course huge risks associated with storing culture in this way. The internet so far lacks the equivalent of the British Library, which keeps one copy of every book published in the UK. After selling Balcony TV to the Orchard (a distribution platform owned by Sony), founder Stephen O'Regan was horrified to realise that the YouTube channel's 18,000-strong video archive had all been marked 'unlisted', becoming unsearchable and effectively making them invisible to anyone who didn't have the actual URL. He described this (commercially motivated) manoeuvre as 'an act of cultural desecration' (Pavel Barter, 'Musicians Pushed Off BalconyTV YouTube Platform', *The Times*, 18 Aug. 2019).

17 Matt Wells, 'BBC Enlists Raw Talent for Radio Station to Woo Black Audience', *Guardian*, 19 Aug. 2002.

8 'Wake (For Grenfell)'

1 Public Health England, 'Kensington and Chelsea Health Profile 2016', 6 Sept. 2016.

2 Michael Marmot et al., *Health Equity in England: The Marmot Review Ten Years On*, Institute of Health Equity, 2020. (In case you were wondering: yes, that's my old man.)

3 Alison Flood, 'Britain Has Closed almost 800 Libraries since 2010, Figures Show', *Guardian*, 6 Dec. 2019.

4 YMCA, 'Almost a Billion-pound Decline in Funding for Youth Services by Local Authorities across England and Wales', Jan. 2020, https://www.ymca.org.uk/outofservice.

5 Amelia Gentleman, 'Grenfell: Report Criticised "Inadequate" Management Twelve Years before Fire', *Guardian*, 1 Nov. 2017.

6 I have borrowed this term from the preface to Milton Friedman's *Capitalism and Freedom* (University of Chicago Press, 1962). I was made aware of this quotation by Naomi Klein's talk 'Coronavirus Capitalism – and How to Beat It', delivered at the beginning of the Covid-19 pandemic about the opportunities it offered for change and the importance of making sure that progressive agendas were heard. This can be seen at theintercept.com/2020/03/16/coronavirus-capitalism.

7 World Health Organisation, *Global and Regional Estimates of Violence Against Women*, 2013.

8 Poppy Noor, 'The Rise and Demise of Radar Radio', *Vice*, 11 May 2018.

9 Anna Codrea-Rado, 'There's Still a Big Imbalance: How Music Festivals

are Working on Gender Equality', *Guardian*, 11 May 2018.

10 Sarah Marsh, 'It's An Act of Defiance: The Rise of All-female Festival Lineups', *Guardian*, 20 Aug. 2019.

11 Vic Parsons, 'The 1975 Commit to Only Playing Festivals with an Equal Balance of Women and Non-binary Acts', *PinkNews*, 13 Feb. 2020.

12 This comment was actually made in a 2016 interview on the *Late Show* but resurfaced during the 2020 protests.

13 'Police Chief Defends Protest Tactics after Statue Torn Down', *Shropshire Star*, 8 June 2020; Sue Giles, 'Myths and Truths', Bristol Museums, June 2022, collections.bristolmuseums.org.uk/stories/transatlantic-traffic-enslaved-africans/myths-and-truths.

14 A statue of Belgian monarch Leopold II, who had been responsible for some of the worst colonial atrocities in Congo, was vandalised and removed in Antwerp; multiple statues of Confederate leaders and business people with links to slavery were attacked in the USA. ('How Statues Are Falling Around the World', *New York Times*, 2020.)

15 Patel made the pursuit of the vandals a personal priority, overstepping the traditional boundaries of her ministerial role by calling in the chief constable of Avon and Somerset Police to demand an explanation and personally intervening to make sure that the 'Colston Four' were tried. (Rajeev Syal, 'Did Priti Patel cross a line in urging pursuit of the Colston Four?', *Guardian*, 5 Jan. 2022.)

16 i.e. because of the 20 million pounds – 300 million in today's money – paid to slave owners as compensation after abolition. The United Kingdom took out a loan in 1833 to service this debt, which was only paid off in 2015. Naomi Fowler, 'Britain's Slave Owner Compensation Loan, Reparations and Tax Havenry', Tax Justice Network, 9 June 2020, taxjustice.net/2020/06/09/slavery-compensation-uk-questions.

17 Steven Poole, 'From Woke to Gammon: Buzzwords by the People Who Coined Them, *Guardian*, 25 Dec. 2019.

18 LeRoi Jones (Amiri Baraka), *Blues People* (Harper Perennial, 1963, repr. 2002), p. 153.

19 Francis Newton (Eric Hobsbawm), *The Jazz Scene* (Penguin, 1959), p. 253.

20 From Allen Ginsberg, 'Howl' (City Lights Publishers, 1986).

21 Frantz Fanon, *Black Skin, White Masks*, trans. Charles Lam Markmann (Pluto Press, 1986), p. 129.

22 Niloufar Haidari, 'Introducing: The Nu Jazz Lad', *Vice*, 25 Jan. 2019.

9 'Man Like GP'

1 I have followed Mark Cotgrove, aka Snowboy's *From Jazz Funk and Fusion to Acid Jazz* (Chaser Publications/AuthorHouse, 2009), in using the term 'Funk Mafia', but other sources including Bill Brewster and Frank Broughton's *Last Night a DJ Saved My Life* (White Rabbit Books, 2002) refer to them as the 'Soul Mafia'. The apparent interchangeability of these terms indicate both the close association between those two genres and the willingness of the DJs to play across them. Note the persistence of this association in *The Craig Charles Funk and Soul Show*.

2 Brewster and Broughton, p. 409.

3 Quoted in Cotgrove, p. 169.

4 From an article in *The Face* quoted in Brewer and Broughton.

5 Cotgrove, author of the definitive book on this scene, made various helpful factual clarifications on this chapter, including asserting that 'Murphy never played any lunchtime sessions', but since this quote comes direct from Courtney Pine I've chosen to leave it in.

6 Interview with Seymour Nurse, *The Bottom End*, Nov. 2010, thebottomend.co.uk/Bulent_Boo_Mehmet.php.

7 From Donald Palmer, 'Revibe: Gilles Peterson 1995', UK Vibe, Aug. 2019, ukvibe.org/archive/revibe/gilles-peterson_1995.

8 In *The Last Pirates: Britain's Rebel DJs* (BBCFour/Acme films, 2017).

9 See Jasmine Dotiwala, 'The Gentrification of ChoiceFM Killed It', *Huffington Post*, 23 Jan. 2014 for more on Choice's history and eventual evolution rebranding as Capital Xtra after being bought by Global in 2003.

10 Although it is only fair to point out that the tribunal found against him in this claim. See 'Radio DJ Was Sacked Unfairly', *Guardian*, 13 Nov. 1999.

11 Cotgrove, p. 60.

12 Caspar Melville, *It's a London Thing: How Rare Groove, Acid House and Jungle Remapped the City* (Manchester University Press, 2020), p. 146.

13 See p. 119.

14 Cotgrove, p. 27.

15 Gilles Peterson, in Jeff Mao, 'Interview: Gilles Peterson's Inspirations and Influences', *Red Bull Music Academy Daily*, 20 Nov. 2015, daily. redbullmusicacademy.com/2015/11/gilles-peterson-interview.

16 Cotgrove, p. 232.

17 Cotgrove, p. 235.

18 In Mao.

10 'Because the End Is Really the Beginning'

1 Lucas Garrison's 'All Seventy-one People on Kendrick Lamar's "To Pimp
A Butterfly" Album' (*DJ Booth*, 27 Aug. 2018, djbooth.net/features/2015-
03-18-kendrick-lamar-to-pimp-a-butterfly-album-credits) identifies the
credited contributors, but this doesn't even include uncredited session
players like most of the members of the West Coast Get Down.

2 Mohamad Moslimami et al., 'Facts About the US Black Population', Pew
Research, 2 March 2023, pewresearch.org/social-trends/fact-sheet/facts-
about-the-us-black-population; Office for National Statistics, 'Population
of England and Wales', 22 Dec. 2022, ethnicity-facts-figures.service.
gov.uk/uk-population-by-ethnicity/national-and-regional-populations/
population-of-england-and-wales/latest.

3 Black Entertainment Television, a black cable channel launched in 1980
and currently available to 75 per cent of American households with a
television.

4 This is Mark Fisher (in *Ghosts of My Life* (Zer0 Books, 2014), p. 41),
referring to Tricky's guest appearance with Beyoncé at Glastonbury's
Pyramid stage in 2011. As he points out sadly, 'Instead of taking up
his assigned role as the imp of the perverse in nineties mainstream pop,
though, Tricky sidled off into the sidelines, a half-forgotten figure. So
much so, that when he appeared as a guest at Beyoncé's 2011 Glastonbury
performance, it provoked a gasp of shock . . . All-too-symbolically,
however, Tricky's microphone didn't seem to be switched on, and he could
barely be heard.'

5 Hibaq Farah, 'Dizzee Rascal smashes photographer's camera after court's
guilty verdict', *Guardian*, 7 March 2022.

6 Katie Morley, 'Middle Classes Ditching Traditional Rental Properties to
become Guardians for Mansions and Stately Homes', *Telegraph*, 18 June
2016.

7 Fisher, p. 15.

8 Fisher (p. 50) notes the strange 1970s mix of savage racism and a stronger
welfare state.

9 Owen Jones, *Chavs: The Demonisation of the Working Class* (Verso, 2011);
'Tackling Child Poverty 2023' [abstract], Institute of Government and

Public Policy, [n.d.] igpp.org.uk/event/Tackling-Child-Poverty-2023, based on research from Joseph Rowntree Foundation, 'UK Poverty 2023', 2023.

10 Jean-Jacques Rousseau, *Confessions* (1782). Falsely attributed to Marie Antoinette, this is the quote most commonly rendered as 'let them eat cake'.

11 Quoted in Dr Jonathan Savage and David Barnard, *The State of Play: A Review of Music Education in England 2019* (Musicians' Union, 2019), p. 2.

12 Savage and Barnard, p. 2.

13 Youth Music/Birmingham City University, *Exchanging Notes: Research Summary Report*, 2019, p. 6.

14 Savage and Barnard.

15 Matt Griffiths, 'Save Music Education to Beat the Drum for "Global Britain"', *Schools Week*, 19 Jan. 2020.

Afterword

1 Instagram post, quoted in Andy Malt, 'Shabaka Hutchings Explains Decision to Stop Playing Saxophone at the End of 2023', *CMU*, 4 July 2023.

2 'Ukraine: Civilian casualties as of 8 October 2023', United Nations Office for the Coordination of Humanitarian Affairs, 9 Oct. 2023.

3 'Hostilities in the Gaza Strip and Israel: Flash Update 39', United Nations Office for the Coordination of Humanitarian Affairs, 14 Nov. 2023.

4 Eli Clifton, '"Hamas Has Created Additional Demand": Wall Street Eyes Big Profits from War', *Guardian*, 30 Oct. 2023.

5 See *The Stuart Hall Project*, dir. John Akomfrah (BFI, 2013).

Acknowledgements

The first thanks go to every one of the eighty-six interviewees who generously gave their time to speak to me with honesty, passion and integrity. This book could not exist without your work, and would be infinitely less rich without your voices. I hope you will feel I have done you justice. I would like to say a special thanks to Wayne Francis for coining the amazing phrase 'unapologetic expression' and granting permission for me to use it as this book's title; to Lev Harris, Dom Servini, Noah Ball, Janine Irons and Gary Crosby for going above and beyond making vital introductions when I needed them; to David Jones, Paul Bradshaw, Mark 'Snowboy' Cotgrove and Gilles Peterson for taking the time to give detailed feedback, to Gilles for special help with permissions, and to all the managers and other team members who facilitated these interviews.

To all my friends and family for their belief, support and encouragement. Particular thanks are due to my parents Michael and Alexi who have always believed in my creativity and encouraged me to find my voice, while providing shining examples that it's possible to do everything you want to do and still have time to be decent, kind, caring people. Special thanks to Holly for unwavering support both together and apart; to Nikhil Shah for encouragement and help with everything from music industry statistics to trigonometry, Sam Berkson for friendship, advice and support with the political sections of the book, and Dave Randall for kindness and political chats while pushing our infants round Myatt's Field during the pandemic. Thanks to Dad, Holly, Dan, Nix, Babbs, Rosie, Steve, Theo and Claudia for reading parts of the book at various stages and providing useful feedback. Thanks to Jonny

acknowledgements

Hyams for generously taking and editing my author photos, and to Tom Mustill for sharing your experience of the journey of a first time author.

To Jim, Shaggy, Asia, Maia, Shafa, Shakira, Aisling, Saff and all my Portuguese family for creating and maintaining a wonderful space for me to work on this book, and to Maggie, Sean, Alex and Emma for helping Holly take up the childcare slack while I did so.

To the SoA Authors' Foundation for my Michael Meyer Award, which helped me through a precarious post-Covid time while writing this book.

To Alexa at Faber for signing the book, to my editors Mo and Hannah for rough, medium and fine sandings delivered with patience and love, to Sam Matthews for the varnish, and everyone at Faber for bringing this project to completion. To Raimund Wong for the wonderful cover, and to all the artists who kindly allowed their images to be used on it. To my agent Becky for being on my side whatever happens.

To WOMEX for inviting me to present some of the ideas in this book on the 'Two Jazz Explosions' panel (October 2020), and to everyone who attended. To David Flower for encouragement and the introduction to Mark Ellingham, who first suggested I get in touch with Lee and Alexa, and to Simon Goffe for the same suggestions. To Bill Swainson for generous advice on how to approach publishers.

To Colin at Velocity and Lee at White Rabbit for validating that I had something here worth pursuing, and to Emma Warren, Caspar Melville and Kevin Le Gendre for their kind words.

To all my colleagues at Earth Agency for their support, and especially my long-suffering assistant Ben Haslett, who had my back when I needed to disappear for writing periods. To all the artists I represent, and their teams, for understanding my need to work on this project.

To Stathi, Prim, Philip Roe, Ben Aspill, and all the staff of Camberwell Leisure Centre, for keeping me (acceptably if not totally) sane, fit and healthy while writing this book.

To all the musicians whose work I have enjoyed while working on this book, and all the writers whose work has informed mine. Honoured to be part of the conversation.

Appendix: Full List of Interviews

For various reasons, not all those interviewed made their way into the final version of the book, but every interview informed my understanding of what happened, and I wish to thank everyone on this list for their time, energy, honesty and passion.

Adam Moses (co-founder, Jazz Re:freshed) – 7 April 2020
Adrian Gibson (promoter, AGMP; programmer, Jazz Cafe) – 16 June 2020
Ahmad Dayes (musician; trombonist, United Vibrations) – 23 Dec. 2021
Aly Gillani (DJ; founder, First Word Records) – 21 July 2020
Binker Golding (musician, educator; saxophonist, Binker and Moses) – 26
    May 2020
Bradley Zero (DJ; promoter, Rhythm Section; label owner, Rhythm Section
    International) – 24 April 2020
Byron Wallen (musician) – 6 Aug. 2020
Camilla George (musician) – 25 March 2021
Cassie Kinoshi (musician; bandleader, SEED Ensemble; saxophonist,
    Kokoroko) – 18 June 2020
Cherise Adams-Burnett (vocalist) – 6 April 2021
Chris Searle (writer; author, *Forward Groove*) – 22 June 2020
Ciro Romano (promoter; Love Supreme Festival) – 21 May 2020
Claude Deppa (musician, educator) – 2 Dec. 2020
Claudio Lillo (agent, CAA: Moses Boyd, Ezra Collective, Poppy Ajudha) – 20
    May 2020
Cleveland Watkiss (musician; vocalist, Jazz Warriors) – 12 May 2020
Courtney Pine (musician; bandleader, Jazz Warriors) – 6 May 2020
Crispin Parry (musician, journalist; founder, British Underground) – 3 June
    2020

appendix: full list of interviews

Dahlia Ambach Caplin (Universal Music) – 4 June 2020

Darrel Sheinman (founder, Gearbox Records) – 14 Dec. 2020

Dave Okumu (musician, producer) – 4 June 2020

David Jones (promoter; director, Serious, London Jazz Festival) – 2 Dec. 2020

Daz-I-Kue (producer, Bugz in the Attic) – 20 July 2020

Dilip Harris (producer, mix/mastering engineer) – 28 April 2020

Django Bates (musician, educator; bandleader, Loose Tubes) – 18 June 2020

Dom Servini (DJ; label owner, Wah Wah 45s) – 10 April 2020

Eddie Piller (DJ; label owner, Acid Jazz Records) – 22 July 2020

Emily Moxon (label manager, Brownswood) – 17 June 2020

Emma-Jean Thackray (musician, producer; label owner, Movementt) – 5 June 2020

Emma Warren (writer, broadcaster) – 17 April 2020

Eric Trosset (manager, Tony Allen; founder, Comet Records) – 11 Nov. 2020

Federico Bolza (manager, Theon Cross; founder, New Soil) – 21 April 2020

Femi Koleoso (musician, broadcaster; bandleader, Ezra Collective; drummer, Gorillaz, Jorja Smith) – 20 April 2020

Gary Crosby (musician; bassist, Jazz Warriors; co-founder, Tomorrow's Warriors) – 12 June 2020

Gilles Peterson (DJ, broadcaster; founder, Brownswood Recordings, Talkin' Loud) – 29 June 2020

Gordon Wedderburn (DJ, broadcaster, promoter) – 6 July 2020

Hans Koller (musician, educator; head of Jazz, Trinity College of Music) – 27 May 2020

Huey Walker (Senior Relationship Manager, Arts Council England; venue owner, the Flyover) – 12 June 2020

Jake Holloway (DJ; owner, Love Vinyl) – 5 May 2020

Janine Irons (co-founder, Tomorrow's Warriors) – 12 June 2020

Jason Yarde (musician, producer, educator) – 3 July 2020

Jean Toussaint (musician, educator; saxophonist: Jazz Messengers) – 8 June 2020

Joe Armon-Jones (musician; keyboard player, Ezra Collective) – 16 April 2020

Jonathan Dabner (founder, Jazz Cafe) – 8 April 2020

Kareem Dayes (musician; bassist, United Vibrations) – 23 Dec. 2021

Kate Hutchinson (writer, DJ, broadcaster) – 2 April 2021

Kees Heus (DJ; programmer: Paradiso, Supersonic Jazz, Amsterdam) – 10 Sept. 2020

appendix: full list of interviews

Kerstan Mackness (manager: The Comet Is Coming, GoGo Penguin) – 7 July 2020

Lev Harris (booker, Jazz Cafe) – 7 April 2020

Lex Blondin (DJ; promoter, founder: Total Refreshment Centre, Church of Sound) – 29 May 2020

Lubi Jovanovic (DJ, promoter) – 23 July 2020

Marina Blake (founder, Brainchild Festival) – 2 July 2020

Matthew Halsall (musician; label owner, Gondwana Records) – 11 Aug. 2020

Mickey Smith (DJ; director, CLF Art Café) – 14 Jan. 2022

Moses Boyd (musician, producer) – 20 May 2021

Naomi Palmer (agent, Earth Agency: Gilles Peterson, Yussef Kamaal) – 13 Nov. 2020

Nathan Graves (former Head of Jazz: Universal Music) – 21 May 2020

Nick Lewis (DJ, broadcaster; programmer: Ronnie Scott's, Koko) – 15 June 2020

Nikki Yeoh (musician, educator) – 16 July 2020

Noah Ball (promoter, programmer: We Out Here, Cross the Tracks, Dimensions, Outlook) – 27 May 2020

Nubya Garcia (musician) – 5 May 2020

Oli Reeves (label owner, 22a) – 7 May 2020

Oliver Weindling (promoter: Vortex Jazz Club; founder, Babel) – 21 April 2020

Omar Lye-Fook (vocalist) – 26 Jan. 2022

Orphy Robinson (musician: Jazz Warriors)

Oscar Jerome (musician; guitarist, Kokoroko) – 23 April 2020

Paul Bradshaw (writer, broadcaster; founder, Straight No Chaser) – 17 April 2020

Paula Henderson (programmer, WOMAD) – 6 Aug. 2021

Poppy Ajudha (vocalist) – 19 Jan. 2022

Quinton Scott (DJ, compiler; label manager, founder: Strut Records) – 23 June 2020

Russ Dewbury (DJ, compiler; promoter, the Jazz Rooms) – 1 May 2020

Seb Rochford (musician; drummer, Sons of Kemet, Basquiat Strings, Polar Bear, Pulled by Magnets) – 30 July 2020

Shabaka Hutchings (musician; bandleader, Sons of Kemet, The Comet Is Coming, Shabaka and the Ancestors) – 19 May 2020

Sheila Maurice-Grey (musician; bandleader, Kokoroko) – 19 Jan. 2022

appendix: full list of interviews

Shirley Tetteh (musician; guitarist: Maisha, Nerija) – 17 June 2020

Simon Purcell (musician; Head of Jazz, Trinity College of Music) – 28 July 2020

Steve Williamson (musician; saxophonist, Jazz Warriors) – 16 July 2020

Theon Cross (musician; tuba player, Sons of Kemet) – 28 May 2020

Tom Excell (musician, producer; bandleader: Nubiyan Twist, Onipa) – 5 March 2021

Tom Skinner (musician, producer; drummer, Sons of Kemet) – 27 July 2020

Tony Dudley-Evans (Cheltenham Jazz Festival) – 14 April 2020

Wayne Francis (musician; saxophonist: United Vibrations; bandleader: Steam Down Orchestra; co-founder, Steam Down) – 11 June 2020

Wilf Walker (promoter) – 12 June 2020

Wozzy Brewster (manager, United Vibrations; founder, the Midi Music Company) – 10 June 2020

Yazz Ahmed (musician) – 26 March 2021

Yussef Dayes (musician; drummer, Yussef Kamaal, United Vibrations) – 23 Dec. 2021

Zara McFarlane (vocalist) – 12 Aug. 2021

Bibliography

Akala, *Natives: Race and Class in the Ruins of Empire* (Two Roads, 2019)

Alexander, Michael, *Jazz Age Jews* (Princeton University Press, 2001)

Allen, Tony (with Michael E. Veal), *Tony Allen: An Autobiography of the Master Drummer of Afrobeat* (Duke University Press, 2013)

Amoruso, Sophia, *#GIRLBOSS* (Portfolio/Penguin, 2015)

Andrews, Kehinde, *Back to Black: Black Radicalism for the 21st Century* (Zed Books, 2019)

Appel, Alfred Jr., *Jazz Modernism: From Ellington and Armstrong to Matisse and Joyce* (Knopf, 2002)

Baldwin, James, *Another Country* (Penguin, 2001)

Belle-Fortune, Brian, *All Crews: Journeys Through Jungle/Drum and Bass Culture* (Vision, 2004)

Bolaño, Roberto, *The Savage Detectives* (Picador, 2008)

Bradley, Lloyd, *Sounds Like London: 100 Years of Black Music in the Capital* (Serpent's Tail, 2013)

Bragg, Billy, *Roots, Radicals and Rockers: How Skiffle Changed the World* (Faber & Faber, 2017)

Brewster, Bill and Broughton, Frank, *Last Night a DJ Saved My Life: The History of the Disc Jockey* (Headline, 2006)

Butler, Octavia, *Kindred* (Headline, 2014)

———, *Parable of the Sower* (Headline, 2019)

Cable, George Washington, *The Grandissimes* (Penguin, 1998)

Carr, Ian, *Music Outside: Contemporary Jazz in Britain* (Northway, 2008)

Charnas, Dan, *Dilla Time: The Life And Afterlife of J Dilla, the Hip-hop Producer Who Reinvented Rhythm* (Swift, 2023)

Chemam, Melissa, *Massive Attack: Out of the Comfort Zone: The Story of a Sound, a City and a Group of Revolutionary Artists* (Tangent Books/PC Press, 2019)

bibliography

Chinen, Nate, *Playing Changes* (Vintage, 2019)

Collin, Matthew, *Altered State: The Story of Ecstasy Culture and Acid House* (Serpent's Tail, 1998)

Collins, Patricia Hill, *Black Feminist Thought* (Routledge, 2009)

———, *Intersectionality as Critical Social Theory* (Duke University Press, 2019)

Cotgrove, Mark 'Snowboy', *From Jazz Funk and Fusion to Acid Jazz: The History of the UK Jazz Dance Scene* (Chaser Publications, 2009)

Coverley, Merlin, *Psychogeography* (Oldcastle, 2018)

Crowley, Roger, *Conquerors: How Portugal Forged the First Global Empire* (Faber & Faber, 2015)

Dankworth, John, *Jazz in Revolution* (Constable, 1998)

Davis, Angela, *Women, Race and Class* (Penguin, 1981)

Davis, Francis, *Jazz and Its Discontents: A Francis Davis Reader* (Da Capo, 2004)

Davis, Miles (with Quincy Troupe), *Miles: The Autobiography* (Picador, 1990)

DeVeaux, Scott, *The Birth of Bebop: A Social and Musical History* (University of California Press, 1997)

Dyer, Geoff, *But Beautiful* (Canongate, 2012)

Eddo-Lodge, Reni, *Why I'm No Longer Talking to White People About Race* (Bloomsbury, 2018)

Ellison, Ralph, *Shadow and Act* (Vintage, 1995)

Elms, Robert, *London Made Us: A Memoir of a Shape-Shifting City* (Canongate, 2020)

Fanon, Franz, *Black Skin, White Masks* (Grove, 1967)

———, *The Wretched of the Earth* (Grove, 2004)

Feather, Leonard, *The JAZZ Years: Earwitness to an Era* (Da Capo, 1987)

Fellezs, Kevin, *Birds of Fire: Jazz, Rock, Funk, and the Creation of Fusion* (Duke University Press, 2011)

Femi, Caleb, *Poor* (Penguin, 2020)

Fingas, Two and James T. Kirk, *Junglist* (Repeater, 2021)

Fisher, Mark, *Ghosts of My Life: Writings on Depression, Hauntology and Lost Futures* (Zer0 Books, 2014)

gal-dem, *'I Will Not Be Erased': Our Stories about Growing Up as People of Colour* (Walker, 2019)

Garratt, Sheryl, *Adventures in Wonderland: Acid House, Rave and the UK Club Explosion* (TCL, 2020)

Gelly, Dave, *Stan Getz: Nobody Else But Me* (Backbeat, 2002)

bibliography

Gerber, Mike, *Jazz Jews* (Five Leaves, 2009)

Gibson, William, *Neuromancer* (Voyager, 1995)

Giddins, Gary, *Visions of Jazz: The First Century* (Oxford University Press, 1998)

———, *Weather Bird: Jazz at the Dawn of its Second Century* (Oxford University Press, 2004)

Gilroy, Paul, *The Black Atlantic* (Verso, 1993)

Godbolt, Jim, *A History of Jazz in Britain 1919–1950* (Northway, 2010)

———, *All This and 10%* (Da Capo Press, 1976)

Goode, Coleridge (with Roger Cotterrell), *Bass Lines: A Life in Jazz* (Northway, 2002)

Gourse, Leslie, *Wynton Marsalis: Skain's Domain: A Biography* (Schirmer Books, 1999)

Grigg, Erik, *Mods: A Concise History* (Ed's Music, 2020)

Gruber, Brian, *Six Days at Ronnie Scott's: Billy Cobham on Jazz Fusion and the Act of Creation* (Gruber, 2018)

Hancock, Herbie, Daisaku Ikeda and Wayne Shorter, *Reaching Beyond: Improvisations on Jazz, Buddhism, and a Joyful Life* (World Tribune, 2017)

Hancox, Dan, *Inner City Pressure: The Story of Grime* (William Collins, 2019)

Hall, Stuart and Tony Jefferson, *Resistance Through Rituals: Youth Subcultures in Post-war Britain* (Routledge, 1993)

Hamilton, Marybeth, *In Search of the Blues: Black Voices, White Visions* (Jonathan Cape, 2007)

Hebditch, Steven, *London's Pirate Pioneers: The Illegal Broadcasters Who Changed British Radio* (TX Publications, 2015)

Higgs, John, *The KLF: Chaos, Magic and the Band Who Burned a Million Pounds* (Weidenfeld and Nicholson, 2012)

Hirsch, Afua, *BRIT (ish): On Race, Identity and Belonging* (Vintage, 2018)

Horne, Gerald, *Jazz and Justice: Racism and the Political Economy of the Music* (Monthly Review Press, 2019)

Hughes, Langston, *Selected Poems* (Serpent's Tail, 2020)

Hurston, Zora Neale, *Their Eyes Were Watching God* (Virago, 2020)

Iqbal, Haseeb, *Noting Voices: Contemplating London's Culture* (Rough Trade Editions, 2020)

James, C. L. R, *The Black Jacobins: Toussaint L'Overture and the San Domingo Revolution* (Penguin, 2001)

———, *Letters from London* (Signal, 2003)

Jay, Norman (with Lloyd Bradley), *Mister Good Times* (Dialogue, 2019)

bibliography

Johnson, Phil, *Massive Attack, Portishead, Tricky and the Roots of Trip-Hop* (Hodder and Stoughton, 1996)

Jones, LeRoi (Amiri Baraka), *Black Music* (Akashic Books, 2010)

————, *Blues People* (Harper Perennial, 2002)

Joseph, Peniel E., *Waiting 'Til the Midnight Hour: A Narrative History of Black Power in America* (Holt, 2006)

Kahn, Ashley, *The House that Trane Built: The Story of Impulse Records* (W.W Norton, 2006)

Kelley, William Melvin, *A Different Drummer* (Riverrun, 2018)

Kerouac, Jack, *On the Road* (Penguin, 2000)

————, *The Subterraneans* (Penguin, 2001)

Kofsky, Frank, *John Coltrane and the Jazz Revolution of the 1960s* (Pathfinder, 1998)

Lammy, David, *Tribes: A Search for Belonging in a Divided Society* (Constable, 2021)

Le Gendre, Kevin, *Don't Stop the Carnival: Black Music in Britain* (Peepal Tree, 2018)

Lipsitz, George, *Dangerous Crossroads: Popular Music, Postmodernism and the Poetics of Place* (Verso, 1994)

MacAdams, Lewis, *Birth of the Cool: Beat, Bebop and the American Avant-Garde* (Scribner, 2002)

Marsalis, Wynton (with Geoffrey C. Ward), *Moving to Higher Ground: How Jazz Can Change Your Life* (Random House, 2009)

McKay, George, *Circular Breathing: The Cultural Politics of Jazz in Britain* (Duke University Press, 2005)

Melville, Caspar, *It's a London Thing: How Rare Groove, Acid House and Jungle Remapped the City* (Manchester University Press, 2020)

Mezzrow, Mezz (with Bernard Wolfe), *Really the Blues* (New York Review Books, 2016)

Millar, Martin, *Lux the Poet* (Soft Skull Press, 2009)

Mingus, Charles, *Beneath the Underdog* (Canongate, 2011)

Morrison, Toni, *Beloved* (Vintage, 2007)

————, *Jazz* (Vintage, 2016)

Muggs, Joe and Brian David Stevens, *Bass, Mids, Tops: An Oral History of Soundsystem Culture* (Strange Attractor, 2019)

Murphy, Ben and Carl Loben, *Renegade Snares: The Resistance and Resilience of Drum and Bass* (Jawbone, 2021)

bibliography

Myers, Marc, *Why Jazz Happened* (University of California Press, 2013)

Newton, Francis, *The Jazz Scene* (Penguin, 1961)

Nicholson, Stuart, *Jazz and Culture in a Global Age* (Northeastern University Press, 2014)

Noah, Trevor, *Born a Crime: Stories From a South African Childhood* (John Murray, 2017)

Nowell, David, *The Story of Northern Soul: A Definitive History of the Dance Scene that Refuses to Die* (Portico, 2015)

Okorafor, Nnedi, *Who Fears Death* (DAW, 2010)

Olusoga, David, *Black and British: A Forgotten History* (Pan Books, 2017)

Ondaatje, Michael, *Coming through Slaughter* (Bloomsbury, 2004)

Pang, Alex Soojung-Kim, *Rest* (Penguin, 2018)

Parekh, Bhikhu, *Rethinking Multiculturalism: Cultural Diversity and Political Theory* (Palgrave, 2000)

Parkes, Simon (with J. S. Rafaeli), *Live at the Brixton Academy: A Riotous Life in the Music Business* (Serpent's Tail, 2014)

Patel, Ian Sanjay, *We're Here Because You Were There: Immigration and the End of Empire* (Verso, 2021)

Phillips, Caryl, *The European Tribe* (Vintage, 2000)

Pitts, Johnny, *Afropean: Notes from Black Europe* (Penguin, 2020)

Quinn, Eithne, *Nothin' But a 'G' Thang: The Culture and Commerce of Gangsta Rap* (Columbia University Press, 1995)

Randall, Dave, *Sound System: The Political Power of Music* (Pluto, 2017)

Reynolds, Simon, *Retromania: Pop Culture's Addiction to Its Own Past* (Faber & Faber, 2011)

Robertson, Alan, *Joe Harriott: Fire in his Soul* (Northway, 2003)

Scott-Heron, Gil, *The Last Holiday: A Memoir* (Canongate, 2013)

Said, Edward, *Culture and Imperialism* (Vintage, 1994)

———, *Orientalism* (Pantheon, 1978)

Searle, Chris, *Forward Groove: Jazz and the Real World from Louis Armstrong to Gilad Atzmon* (Northway, 2008)

Selvon, Sam, *The Lonely Londoners* (Penguin, 2006)

Shapiro, Nat and Hentoff, Nat, *Hear Me Talkin' to Ya: The Story of Jazz as Told by the Men Who Made It* (Dover, 1966)

Sidran, Ben, *There Was a Fire: Jews, Music and the American Dream* (Nardis, 2021)

Silver, Horace, *Let's Get to the Nitty Gritty: The Autobiography of Horace Silver* (University of California Press, 2007)

bibliography

Sivanandan, A., *Communities of Resistance: Writings on Black Struggles for Socialism* (Verso, 1990)

Slim, Iceberg, *Pimp: The Story of My Life* (Canongate, 2019)

Srnicek, Nick, *Platform Capitalism* (Polity, 2017)

Stearns, Marshall W., *The Story of Jazz* (Oxford University Press, 1970)

Strausbaugh, John, *Black Like You: Blackface, Whiteface, Insult and Imitation in American Popular Culture* (Tarcher/Penguin, 2007)

Taylor, Arthur, *Notes and Tones: Musician-to-Musician Interviews* (Da Capo, 1993)

Tenaille, Frank, *Music Is the Weapon of the Future: Fifty Years of African Popular Music*, trans. Stephen Toussaint and Hope Sandrine (Lawrence Hill Books, 2002)

Terkel, Studs, *Giants of Jazz* (The New Press, 2002)

Toffler, Alvin, *Future Shock* (Bantam Books, 1971)

Tolentino, Jia, *Trick Mirror* (4th Estate, 2019)

Tricky (with Andrew Perry), *Hell Is Round the Corner* (Blink, 2020)

Ward, Brian, *Just My Soul Responding: Rhythm and Blues, Black Consciousness and Race Relations* (UCL Press, 1998)

Warren, Emma, *Steam Down or How Things Begin* (Rough Trade Editions, 2020)

——, *Make Some Space: Tuning into Total Refreshment Centre* (Sweet Machine, 2019)

West, Cornel, *Race Matters* (Beacon, 2017)

Wilmer, Val, *As Serious as Your Life: Black Music and the Free Jazz Revolution, 1957–1977* (Serpent's Tail, 2018)

Wright, Richard, *The Outsider* (Vintage, 2021)

Žižek, Slavoj, *Pandemic! Covid-19 Shakes the World* (Polity, 2020)

FILMS

Absolute Beginners, dir. Julien Temple (Palace Pictures/Goldcrest Films International/Virgin, 1986)

Birth of the Blues, dir. Victor Schertzinger (Paramount Pictures, 1941)

Born To Be Blue, dir. Robert Budreau (New Real Films/Lumanity, 2015)

Elevator to the Gallows, dir. Louis Malle (Nouvelles Éditions de Films, 1958)

Gimme Shelter, dir. Albert and David Maysies/Charlotte Zwerin (Maysies Films/Penforta, 1970)

I Called him Morgan, dir. Kasper Collin (Kasper Collin Produktion/Sveriges Television, 2016)

bibliography

Mo Better Blues, dir. Spike Lee (Universal Pictures, 1990)

Small Axe, dir. Steve McQueen (BBC, 2020)

Some Like it Hot, dir. Billy Wilder (United Artists, 1970)

Song of the South, dir. Wilfred Jackson/Harve Foster (RKO Pictures, 1946)

Sonny Rolllins: Saxophone Colossus, dir. Robert Mugge (1986)

Soul, dir. Pete Docter/Kemp Powers (Disney/Pixar, 2020)

Space Is The Place, dir. John Coney (North American Star System, 1974)

Sun Ra: A Joyful Noise, dir. Robert Mugge (1980)

The Boat That Rocked, dir. Richard Curtis (Universal, 2009)

The Jazz Singer, dir. Alan Crosland (Warner Bros, 1927)

The Jungle Book, dir. Wolfgang Reitherman (Walt Disney Animation Studios, 1967)

Whiplash, dir. Damien Chazelle (Bold Films, 2014)

SERIES

Colin in Black and White, dir. Ava DuVernay (ARRAY Filmworks, 2021)

The Defiant Ones, dir. Allen Hughes (Alcon Entertainment, 2017)

DOCUMENTARIES

Art Blakey: The Jazz Messenger, dir. Dick Fontaine/Pat Hartley (Rhapsody Films, 1988)

Blue Note Records: Beyond the Notes, dir. Sophie Huber (BBC, 2018)

Jazz, dir. Ken Burns (BBC, 2001) *Jazz Britannia*, dir. Mike Connolly/Chris Rodley (BBC, 2005)

Radical Radio: The Story of Kiss Fm (Mentorn Films, 1990)

The Last Angel of History, dir. John Akomfrah (Black Studio Film Collective, 1996)

The Last Pirates: Britain's Rebel DJs, dir. Jaimie D'Cruz (ACME Films/BBC, 2017)

White Riot, dir. Rubika Shah (Smoking Bear, 2019)

Selected Discography

I've created Spotify playlists to accompany each chapter and I invite you to seek those out whilst listening: search 'Unapologetic Expression' within the app and they should all appear. However, if you like to own albums on vinyl, are ethically opposed to Spotify, or can't listen because it's 2298 and Spotify no longer exits, I've put together a list of relevant and recommended albums. This should of course be considered a starting point and not an exhaustive list, and I apologise to anyone not included.

CURRENT WAVE

Alfa Mist, *Antiphon* (Sekito, 2017); *Bring Backs* (Anti, 2021)

Binker and Moses, *Dem Ones* (Gearbox, 2015)

Blue Lab Beats, *Xover* (Blue Adventure, 2018); *Voyage* (Blue Adventure, All Points, 2019)

Camilla George, *The People Could Fly* (Ubuntu, 2018)

Chelsea Carmichael, *The River Doesn't Like Strangers* (Native Rebel, 2021)

Emanative, *The Light Years of the Darkness* (Brownswood Recordings, 2015)

Emma-Jean Thackray, *Ley Lines EP* (The Vinyl Factory, 2018); Rain *Dance EP* (Movementt, 2020); *Yellow* (Movementt, 2021)

Ezra Collective, *You Can't Steal My Joy* (Enter the Jungle, 2019); *Where I'm Meant to Be* (Partisan Records, 2022)

Floating Points, Pharoah Sanders, *Promises* (Luaka Bop, 2020)

Henry Wu, *Good Morning Peckham* (Rhythm Section International, 2015)

Joe Armon-Jones, *Starting Today* (Brownswood Recordings, 2018)

Joe Armon-Jones & Maxwell Owin, *Idiom* (YAM Recordings, 2017)

Kamaal Williams, *The Return* (Black Focus, 2018); *Wu-Hen* (Black Focus, 2020)

Kokoroko, *Kokoroko* (Brownswood Recordings, 2019); *Could We Be More* (Brownswood Recordings, 2022)

selected discography

Maisha, *Welcome to a New Welcome* (Jazz Re:freshed, 2016); *There Is a Place* (Brownswood Recordings, 2018)

Matthew Halsall, *Salute to the Sun* (Gondwana, 2020);

Matthew Halsall and the Gondwana Orchestra, *Into Forever* (Gondwana Records, 2015)

Moses Boyd, *Displaced Diaspora* (Exodus Records, 2018); *Dark Matter* (Exodus Records, 2020)

Nubya Garcia, *Nubya's 5ive* (Jazz Re:freshed, 2018); *Source* (Concord Jazz, 2020)

Nubiyan Twist, *Nubiyan Twist* (Wormfood, 2015); *Jungle Run* (Strut Records, 2019); *Freedom Fables* (Strut Records, 2021)

SEED Ensemble, *Driftglass* (Jazz Re:freshed, 2019)

Sons of Kemet, *Lest We Forget What We Came Here to Do* (Sons of Kemet, 2015); *Your Queen Is a Reptile* (Verve, 2018); *Black to the Future* (Impulse, 2021)

Tenderlonious, *On Flute* (22a, 2016)

The Comet is Coming, *Channel the Spirits* (The Leaf Label, 2016); *Trust In the Lifeforce of the Deep Mystery* (Impulse, 2019)

Theon Cross, *Fyah* (Gearbox, 2019); *Intra-I* (New Soil, 2021)

United Vibrations, *Galaxies Not Ghettos* (12tone C.I.C, 2011); *The Myth of the Golden Ratio* (Ubiquity, 2016)

Various Artists, *We Out Here* (Brownswood Recordings, 2018)

Various Artists, *Blue Note Re:Imagined* (Blue Note, 2020)

Yazz Ahmed, *La Saboteuse* (Naim, 2017); *Polyhymnia* (Ropeadope, 2019)

Yussef Dayes, Tom Misch, *What Kinda Music* (Blue Note, 2020)

Yussef Kamaal, *Black Focus* (Brownswood Recordings, 2016)

Zara McFarlane, *Arise* (Brownswood Recordings, 2017); *Songs of an Unknown Tongue* (Brownswood Recordings, 2020)

FOREBEARS

I've primarily focused on the decades immediately preceding the generation whose work is this book's main focus i.e. 1980s, 1990s and 2000s, but have thrown in a few important UK jazz albums from earlier periods and a small handful of classic albums that were my own bridge into jazz as a teenager or carry special relevance for this story.

4 Hero, *Two Pages* (Talkin' Loud, 1998)
Alice Coltrane ft Pharoah Sanders, *Journey In Satchidananda* (Impulse, 1971)

selected discography

A Tribe Called Quest, *The Low End Theory*, (Jive, 1991)

BadBadNotGood, *III* (Innovative Leisure, 2014); *IV* (Innovative Leisure, 2016)

Basquiat Strings, *Basquiat Strings With Seb Rochford* (F-IRE, 2007)

Bugz In The Attic, *Back in the Doghouse* (V2, 2006)

Charles Mingus, *Mingus Ah Um* (Columbia, 1959)

Cleveland Watkiss, *Green Chimneys* (Urban, 1989)

Common, *Like Water For Chocolate* (MCA, 2000)

Courtney Pine, *Journey to the Urge Within* (Antilles New Directions, 1986); *Modern Day Jazz Stories* (Antilles, 1995); *Another Story* (Talkin' Loud, 1998)

Dizzee Rascal, *Boy In Da Corner* (XL, 2003)

Dur-Dur Band, *Volume 5* (Awesome Tapes From Africa, 2013)

Erykah Badu, *Baduizm* (Universal, 1996)

Eska, *Eska* (Naim Edge, 2015)

Fela Kuti and Africa 70, *Gentleman* (EMI, 1973); *Expensive Shit* (Soundworkshop Records, 1975)

Fela Kuti And His Africa 70, *Fela's London Scene* (His Master's Voice, 1971)

Flying Lotus, *You're Dead* (Warp Records, 2014)

Guru, *Jazzmatazz Volume 1* (Chrysalis, 1993)

Hello Skinny, *Hello Skinny* (Slowfoot, 2012)

Idris Muhammad, *Power of Soul* (Kudu, 1974)

J Dilla, *Donuts* (Stones Throw Records, 2006)

Jay Dee aka J Dilla, *Welcome 2 Detroit* (BBE, 2001)

Jazzanova, *In Between* (Jazzanova Compost Records, 2002)

Jazz Jamaica, *The Jamaican Beat Vol.2: Jazz Jamaica Plays Blue Note Blue Beats* (Eau Records, 1994)

Jazz Warriors, *Out of Many, One People* (Antilles New Directions, 1987)

Joe Harriott, John Mayer, *Indo Jazz Suite* (EMI, 1966)

Joe Harriott & Amancio D'Silva Quartet, *Hum Dono* (Columbia, 1969)

John Coltrane, *Blue Train* (Blue Note, 1957); Giant *Steps* (Atlantic, 1960)

Kamasi Washington, *The Epic* (Brainfeeder, 2015)

Kendrick Lamar, *To Pimp a Butterfly* (Top Dawg/Aftermath/Interscope, 2015)

Loose Tubes, *Delightful Precipice* (Loose Tubes Limited, 1986)

Madlib, *Shades of Blue* (Blue Note, 2003)

Max Roach, *Members, Don't Git Weary* (Atlantic, 1968)

Michael Garrick Quintet ft Joe Harriott and Shake Keane, *October Woman* (Argo, 1965)

selected discography

Miles Davis, *Kind of Blue* (Columbia, 1959)

Mulatu Astatke, *Mulatu of Ethiopia* (Worthy Records, 1972)

New Sector Movements, *Download This* (Virgin, Main Squeeze, 2001)

Nikki Yeoh, *Solo Gemini* (Infinitum, 2016)

Orphy Robinson + Annavas, *When Tomorrow Comes* (Blue Note International, 1992)

Polar Bear, *Held On the Tips of Fingers* (Babel, 2005)

Project 23, *23* (Dorado, 1996)

Quite Sane, *Child of Troubled Times* (CoolHunter Music, 2002)

Robert Glasper Experiment, *Black Radio* (Blue Note, 2011); *Black Radio 2* (Blue Note, 2013)

Robert Mitchell and Omar Puente, *Bridges* (F-IRE, 2006)

Roni Size and Reprazent, *New Forms* (Talkin' Loud, 2017)

Roots Manuva, *Brand New Second Hand* (Big Dada, 1999)

Stan Getz, Joao Gilberto, *Getz/Gilberto* (Verve, 1964)

Steve Williamson, *Rhyme Time (That Fuss Was Us!)* (Verve Records, 1991)

Sun Ra, *The Futuristic Sounds of Sun Ra* (Savoy Records, 1962); Space *Is the Place* (Blue Thumb Records, 1973)

The Invisible, *The Invisible* (Accidental, 2009)

The Pharcyde, *Bizarre Ride II The Pharcyde* (Delicious, 1992)

The Stan Tracey Quartet, *Jazz Suite (Inspired by Dylan Thomas' Under Milk Wood)*

Thundercat, *Drunk* (Brainfeeder, 2017)

Tony Allen, *Black Voices* (Comet Records, 1999)

Tony Allen and Hugh Masekela, *We've Landed* (World Circuit, 2020)

Tubby Hayes, *Tubbs* (Fontana, 1961)

Various Artists, *Blue Note Revisited* (Blue Note, 2004)

Various Artists, *Ghana Special: Modern Highlife, Afro-Sounds & Ghanaian Blues 1968-81* (Soundway, 2009)

Various Artists, *London Is the Place For Me 2: Calypso & Kwela, Highlife & Jazz From Young Black London* (Honest Jon's, 2005)

Various Artists, *Nigeria 70: The Definitive Story of 1970's Funky Lagos* (Strut Records, 2008)

Various Artists, *The Blue Note Club Culture* (All Seeing Eye, 1996)

Various Artists, *Acid Jazz And Other Illicit Grooves* (Urban, 1988)

Various Artists, *Talkin Loud* (Talkin' Loud, 1990)

Wynton Marsalis, *Black Codes (From the Underground)* (Columbia, 1985)

Bonus Playlist

Janine Irons: Best of Tomorrow's Warriors

Gary Crosby's Nu Troop, 'Gorée Island'
Nubya Garcia, 'Source'
Jazz Jamaica All Stars, 'Vitamin A'
Julie Dexter, 'Wave'
Yazz Ahmed, 'One Girl Among Many'
Kokoroko, 'Abusey Junction'
Denys Baptiste, 'Parallax'
Rhythmica, 'Time Machine'
Andrew McCormack, 'Better than People'
Binker and Moses, 'No Long T'ings'
Cassie Kinoshi, SEED Ensemble, 'Mirrors'
Peter Edwards Trio, 'Meet You at El Malecon'
Jason Yarde, 'Skip, Dash, Flow'
Ezra Collective, 'People in Trouble'
Soweto Kinch, 'Suspended Adolescence'
Alex Wilson, 'Currulao Cool'
Shabaka, 'Ital Is Vital'
ESKA, 'To Be Remembered'
Zara McFarlane, 'Pride'
Camilla George, 'Ukpong'
Empirical, 'The Prophet'
Tomorrow's Warriors ft Mark Crown, 'The Fighter (Live at the Jazz Cafe)'

Index

References to albums are in *italics*.

411

index

index

index

415

index

index

index

index

index

index

index

index

index